T0340043

Making a Living in Ottoman Anatolia

Making a Living
in Ottoman Anatolia

Edited by

Ebru Boyar
Kate Fleet

BRILL

LEIDEN | BOSTON

Cover illustration: *View of Ankara*, anonymous painter, Turkey, 1700–1799. Rijksmuseum object number SK-A-2055. On loan to the Rahmi M. Koç-Ulus Museum in Ankara / Turkey until 2023.

Library of Congress Cataloging-in-Publication Data

Names: Boyar, Ebru, editor. | Fleet, Kate, editor.
Title: Making a living in Ottoman Anatolia / edited by Ebru Boyar, Kate
    Fleet.
Description: Leiden ; Boston : Brill, 2021. | Includes bibliographical
    references and index.
Identifiers: LCCN 2021024370 (print) | LCCN 2021024371 (ebook) | ISBN
    9789004466975 (hardback) | ISBN 9789004466982 (ebook)
Subjects: LCSH: Turkey—Economic conditions—1288–1918. | Turkey—Social
    conditions—1288–1918. | Turkey—Commerce—History. |
    Turkey—History—Ottoman Empire, 1288–1918.
Classification: LCC HC492 .M35 2021 (print) | LCC HC492 (ebook) | DDC
    330.9561—dc23
LC record available at https://lccn.loc.gov/2021024370
LC ebook record available at https://lccn.loc.gov/2021024371

Typeface for the Latin, Greek, and Cyrillic scripts: "Brill". See and download: brill.com/brill-typeface.

ISBN 978-90-04-46697-5 (hardback)
ISBN 978-90-04-46698-2 (e-book)

Contents

Acknowledgements

The chapters in this book are based on papers given at a conference, *Trade and Production in Ottoman Anatolia*, held in September 2017 at Vehbi Koç ve Ankara Araştırmaları Merkezi, Koç University (VEKAM) in Ankara and organised jointly by VEKAM and the Skilliter Centre for Ottoman Studies, Newnham College, Cambridge. We should like to thank all those at VEKAM and in particular the Director Professor Filiz Yenişehirlioğlu as well as all those who took part in the conference and those who contributed to this volume. As always, we would like to express our thanks to Nicolette van der Hoek, Acquisitions Editor Middle East and Islamic Studies, and Nienke Brienen-Moolenaar at Brill.

Diagrams and Maps

Tables

Contributors

Marc Aymes

is a Senior Research Fellow (Directeur de Recherche) at the French National Centre for Scientific Research (CNRS) and a Research Professor (Directeur d'Etudes) at the School for Advanced Studies in the Social Sciences (EHESS) in Paris. He currently chairs the Centre for Turkish, Ottoman, Balkan and Central Asian Studies (CETOBaC), a joint research unit of CNRS, the Collège de France, and EHESS. His research interests include philological and sociological encounters in the Ottoman empire, eighteenth to twentieth centuries, Ottoman translators at work and law as technique and as utterance. His publications include *Les Faux-Monnayeurs d'Istanbul* (Toulouse: Anacharsis, 2019), *A Provincial History of the Ottoman Empire. Cyprus and the Eastern Mediterranean in the Nineteenth Century* (London and New York: Routledge, 2014), and *"Un Grand Progrès – sur le papier". Histoire provinciale des réformes ottomanes à Chypre au XIXe siècle* (Paris, Louvain and Walpole, M.A.: Peeters, 2010).

Ebru Boyar

is Professor in the Department of International Relations, Middle East Technical University, Ankara, where she teaches Ottoman, Turkish and modern Middle Eastern history. She is also Academic Advisor at the Skilliter Centre for Ottoman Studies, Newnham College, University of Cambridge. Her current research interests include informal diplomacy in the late Ottoman empire and early Turkish republic and public health in the same period. Her publications include *Ottomans, Turks, and the Balkans: Empire Lost, Relations Altered* (London: I.B. Tauris, 2007), *A Social History of Ottoman Istanbul* (Cambridge: Cambridge University Press, 2010), co-authored with Kate Fleet, *Ottoman Women in Public Space* (Leiden: Brill, 2016), *Middle Eastern and North African Societies in the Interwar Period* (Leiden: Brill, 2018) and *Entertainment Among the Ottomans* (Leiden: Brill, 2019), co-edited with Kate Fleet.

Metin Coşgel

is Professor of economics at the University of Connecticut, U.S.A. He is the author of *The Economics of Ottoman Justice: Settlement and Trial in the Sharia Courts* (Cambridge: Cambridge University Press, 2016), with Boğaç Ergene. He has published widely on the economic history of the Ottoman empire, political economy of religion, and economics of social institutions. His current research interests include the economics of the system of judicial appointment in Ottoman courts, the effect of gender, religion, and location (center vs. province) on legal capabilities and performance, and the historical roots of comparative development in the Middle East and Eastern Europe. He maintains a website on The Economic History of the Ottoman Empire (ottoman.uconn.edu).

Suraiya Faroqhi

is a Professor of history at İbn Haldun University (Istanbul). Her focus is on Ottoman social history of the early modern period, especially women, artisan production, the use of objects as historical sources, as well as urban life and cross-cultural linkages, her most recent books being: *A Cultural History of the Ottomans: The Imperial Elite and its Artefacts* (London: I.B. Tauris, 2016), and *The Ottoman and Mughal Empires: Social History in the Early Modern World* (London: I.B. Tauris/Bloomsbury, 2019).

Kate Fleet

is the Director of the Skilliter Centre for Ottoman Studies, Newnham College, University of Cambridge. Her current research interests include various aspects of Ottoman commercial history and relations between the early Turkish republic and the Great Powers. Her books include *European and Islamic Trade in the Early Ottoman State: the Merchants of Genoa and Turkey* (Cambridge: Cambridge University Press, 1999), *A Social History of Ottoman Istanbul* (Cambridge: Cambridge University Press, 2010), together with Ebru Boyar and *Ottoman Economic Practices in Periods of Transformation: the Cases of Crete and Bulgaria* (Ankara: Türk Tarih Kurumu Basımevi, 2014), together with Svetla Ianeva. She has recently edited three volumes together with Ebru Boyar: *Ottoman Women in Public Space* (Leiden: Brill, 2016), *Middle Eastern and North African Societies in the Interwar Period* (Leiden: Brill, 2018) and *Entertainment Among the Ottomans* (Leiden: Brill, 2019).

Elena Frangakis-Syrett

is a Professor of Ottoman history at Queens College and the Graduate Center of the City University of New York. She specializes in Ottoman commercial, monetary and banking history and particularly in the economic relations between the Ottoman empire and the West from the late seventeenth to the early twentieth centuries. Her recent publications include: *Au coeur des mutations du négoce en Méditerranée*, co-edited with T. Allain and S. Lupo, *Rives Méditerranéennes*, 59 (2019) and *The Port-City in the Ottoman Middle East at the Age of Imperialism* (Istanbul: The Isis Press, 2017). She is currently working on an economic history of the Mediterranean in the early modern period.

Yonca Köksal

is Associate Professor of history at Koç University, Istanbul. Her research is on the late Ottoman state and society with a focus on provincial reforms in the Tanzimat era, animal trade from Anatolia to Istanbul and Muslim minorities in the Balkans. She has published many articles, book chapters and three books. Her most recent book is entitled *The Ottoman Empire in the Tanzimat Era: Provincial Perspectives from Ankara to Edirne* (London: Routledge, 2019).

Mehmet Öz

is a Professor in history at Hacettepe University, Ankara. His works focus on various aspects of Ottoman history from the fourteenth to the eighteenth centuries. His publications include *XV–XVI. Yüzyıllarda Canik Sancağı* (Ankara: Türk Tarih Kurumu Basımevi, 1999), *Kanun-ı Kadimin Peşinde-Osmanlı'da "Çözülme" ve Gelenekçi Yorumcuları* (Istanbul: Dergah Yayınları, first published in 1997, 8th edition in 2019), *Canik Sancağı Avarız Defterleri-1642* (Ankara: Türk Tarih Kurumu Basımevi, 2008), and *Söğüt'ten İstanbul'a-Osmanlı Devleti'nin Kuruluşu Üzerine Tartışmalar*, edited with Oktay Özel (Istanbul: İmge Kitabevi, first published in 2000, 4th edition in 2019). A two-volume collection of his articles on Ottoman political, intellectual, social and economic history has recently been published: *Osmanlı Tarihi Üzerine I Kuruluş, Kimlik ve Siyasi Düşünce* (Ankara: Cedit Neşriyat, 2019) and *Osmanlı Tarihi Üzerine II İnsan Toplum Ekonomi* (Ankara: Cedit Neşriyat, 2020).

Mehmet Polatel

is a non-resident research affiliate at the USC Shoah Foundation Center for Advanced Genocide Research. He researches on property regimes, legal history and socio-economic history with a particular focus on land disputes in the late Ottoman empire. He has authored several articles and book chapters along with a book co-authored with Uğur Ü. Üngör: *Confiscation and Destruction: The Young Turk Seizure of Armenian Property* (London: Bloomsbury, 2011).

Sadullah Yıldırım

is an Assistant Professor of economic history at Marmara University. His current research interests include the deep roots of comparative economic development, economics of religion, and Ottoman economic history. His work has appeared in journals such as *Journal of Comparative Economics*, and *Journal of Economic Behavior & Organization*.

CHAPTER 1

An Overview of Economic Life in Ottoman Anatolia

Ebru Boyar and Kate Fleet

Ah, let there be a garden for us where we can gaze in an intoxicated haze
Let its climate not be cold, and its weather sound and balmy

Let us not be pestered by fleas, let there be no snow or rain
Let the fly not buzz or even let its presence be forbidden

Let our faces turn white from consuming great buttery *çörek*s [buns] from
the plain of Dobruja
And with the butter of Akkerman

Let them make fatty meat stew from the sheep of all the world
When we begin to eat let there be no interruption

Let the world be filled up with the *helva* of the *gazi*s
Let the rings of *zülbiye*s [cake made with honey and almonds] too be full
of milk

Let there be there a lake of almond *paluze*s [blancmange, starch pudding]
When we bite into one side, let its edges be of honey and butter
Let these flat, well-watered plains not remain uncultivated

Let there be there juicy peaches and vineyards with many thousands
of grapes.[1]

In this poem Kaygusuz Abdal, who died in the first years of the fifteenth
century,[2] creates a picture of "all the blessings of the world which he could not

---

1 Gölpınarlı, Abdülbaki (ed.), *Alevî-Bektâşî Nefesleri* (Istanbul: Remzi Kitabevi, 1963), pp. 251–2.
2 Gölpınarlı, *Alevî-Bektâşî Nefesleri*, p. 14. Karamustafa dates his death to the first half of the
fifteenth century, Karamustafa, Ahmet T., "Kaygusuz Abdal: a medieval Turkish saint and the
formation of vernacular Islam in Anatolia", in *Unity in Diversity. Mysticism, Messianism and
the Construction of Religious Authority in Islam*, ed. Orkhan Mir-Kasimov (Leiden: Brill, 2013),
p. 330.

© KONINKLIJKE BRILL NV, LEIDEN, 2021 | DOI:10.1163/9789004466982_002

reach or attain", in the words of Abdülbaki Gölpınarlı, "all the things he dreamed of and brooded about".[3] In another poem "Dilek" (The Wish), Kaygusuz Abdal begs God to bestow upon him a wish list of a variety of rich food in abundance. Before he starts his list, though, he makes sure that God will understand his sincerity: "My God! This is my wish that I entreat from you/ It comes from my heart, it's not simple words or frivolity".[4] In these poems Kaygusuz Abdal presents both an imagined land of plenty, the unattainable desires of his heart, and in so doing opens up a glimpse of the often bitter realities of rural life in Anatolia in this period.

Kaygusuz Abdal lived in a rural provincial context, wrote in vernacular Turkish and, like *abdal*s in general, "sided with the Turkish-speaking rural masses", according to Ahmet Karamustafa, choosing to "blend in" with the ordinary people and hostile to the urbanite Sufis, whom he regarded as "idolaters of haughtiness".[5] Anatolia in this period, and indeed for the centuries following, was largely rural and much of its population consisted of peasantry. Evliya Çelebi described Anatolia as "consist[ing] mostly of Turkish peasants".[6] Many of them would have been poor. The Armenian traveller, Polonyalı Simeon, in Anatolia in the early seventeenth century, regarded the Anatolian population as very poor, crushed by the heavy tax burden imposed on it.[7]

Quite apart from any heavy taxation, the population of Anatolia was subject to the depredations of unscrupulous officials, such as the governor of Çorum who at the end of the sixteenth century collected barley and cartloads of straw and firewood from surrounding villages without paying for them.[8] Diseases and other natural disasters struck both peasants and their crops and livestock. Flocks could be preyed on by wild animals. The explanation put forward by a shepherd in court in Konya in 1582 for his failure to produce a ram, the property

---

3   Gölpınarlı, *Alevî-Bektâşî Nefesleri*, p. 243.
4   Kocatürk, Vasfi Mahir (ed.), *Şiir Defteri. Yunus Emre'den Bugüne Kadar Türk Edebiyatının Her Çeşitten Güzel Şiirleri* (Ankara: Edebiyat Yayınevi, 1965), p. 7.
5   Karamustafa, "Kaygusuz Abdal: a medieval Turkish saint and the formation of vernacular Islam in Anatolia", pp. 333, 336 and 337.
6   Dankoff, Robert and Sooyong Kim (trans. and commentary), *An Ottoman Traveller. Selections from* The Book of Travels *of Evliya Çelebi* (London: Eland, 2011), p. 76.
7   Andreasyan, Hrand D. (trans.), *Polonyalı Bir Seyyahın Gözünden 16. Asır Türkiyesi Polonyalı Simeon* (Istanbul: Köprü Kitapları, 2016), p. 130.
8   Faroqhi, Suraiya, "Town officials, *timar*-holders, and taxation: the late sixteenth-century crisis as seen from Çorum", *Turcica*, 18 (1986), pp. 61–2. The inhabitants of Çorum took their case to Istanbul and were issued with a *ferman* against the governor.

of orphans who were represented by a guardian, was that it had been eaten by a wolf. In this case, however, the *kadı* was unconvinced.[9]

The military put further burdens on the population. Overwintering of the army was costly for those in the areas where it encamped. In some cases, the burden could be crushing. Said Bey in a letter to the sultan probably in the autumn of 1514, argued that were the army to overwinter in the region of Bayburt, the "weak and frail" people of the area would disperse.[10] In 1595–1596, 200 camels wintered in Çorum. Although the inhabitants were paid for the fodder they provided, the sum paid was probably below that of the normal market price, Suraiya Faroqhi calculating that the local population was out of pocket by a couple of thousand *akçe*, at the very least.[11] Apart from the payment of extraordinary taxes (*avariz*) and forced provisions for the army, military campaigns left areas devastated. Mehmed II's campaign against Karaman in 1468, for example, involved considerable destruction and the forced expulsion of much of the population.[12] Scorched earth tactics resulted in devastation for any agricultural production. The French traveller Tavernier, who died in 1689, reported that the Safavid ruler had "ruined all the country" in the region of Kars, and in many other areas of the frontier, "for nine or ten days journey together".[13]

Revolts, such as those which broke out in southern and central Anatolia in the later 1520s, including that led by Kalender which erupted in 1528 in the area around Ankara and Kırşehir,[14] were considerably disruptive of economic life. The Celali revolts, which lasted from the later sixteenth into the seventeenth century and to whose impact Polonyalı Simeon made frequent reference,[15] caused "unprecedented levels of damage, depredation, and

9   Yörük, Doğan (ed.), *3 Numaralı Konya Şer'iye Sicili (987–1330 / 1579–1912) (Transkripsiyon ve Dizin)* (Konya: Palet Yayınları, 2013), no. 7–5, p. 35.

10   Beldiceanu-Steinherr, Irène and Jean-Louis Bacqué-Grammont, "A propose de quelques causes de malaises sociaux en Anatolie centrale aux XVIe et XVIIe siècles", *Archivum Ottomanicum*, 7 (1982), p. 81. Beldiceanu-Steinherr and Bacqué-Grammont date the document to the autumn of 1514, p. 72.

11   Faroqhi, "Town officials, *timar*-holders, and taxation", p. 76.

12   Boyar, Ebru, "Ottoman expansion in the East", in *The Cambridge History of Turkey. Volume 2 The Ottoman Empire as a World Power, 1453–1603*, ed. Suraiya Faroqhi and Kate Fleet (Cambridge: Cambridge University Press, 2013), pp. 79–83.

13   Tavernier, Jean-Baptiste, *The Six Voyages of John Baptista Tavernier* (London, 1678), p. 9.

14   On these revolts see, for example, Bacqué-Grammont, Jean-Louis, "Un rapport inédit sur la révolte anatolienne de 1527", *Studia Islamica*, 62 (1985), 155–71.

15   Andreasyan, *Polonyalı Bir Seyyahın Gözünden*, pp. 34, 124, 126, 132, 215, 216, 220, 221–2.

devastation throughout Anatolia".[16] The people of Tosya complained that "the Celali have occupied the *vilayet* of Anatolia and they go round marauding and they pillage and plunder our goods and provisions and burn the houses". No one remained in most of the villages and even those who did, did not have the strength to survive there.[17] Rebels and officials alike seized money and goods from the population. Karayazıcı, a major Celali leader whom the state sought to win over by appointing him *sancakbeyi* of Çorum at the end of the sixteenth century, announced that he would have "a hair from every beard" in his drive to extract *akçes* from the towns and villages of the district.[18] Crops were not harvested, as was the case around Sivas at the beginning of the seventeenth century.[19] It was probably the impact of the Celali revolts, according to Kayhan Orbay, that prevented the *vakıf* of Murad II from collecting part of its income from, among other things, water mills in the early seventeenth century,[20] and what lay in part behind the deterioration of the agricultural economy around Konya in the first half of the same century.[21]

Banditry and brigandage were a normal part of life in Anatolia, resulting in constant complaints to provincial authorities and to Istanbul. In the mid-eighteenth century, villagers from Mahmudlar and Korkmaz near Ankara,

---

16 Özel, Oktay, *The Collapse of Rural Order in Ottoman Anatolia. Amasya 1576–1643* (Leiden: Brill, 2016), p. 150. For the economic impact on the Celali revolts see Polat, Süleyman, "The economic consequences of the Celali revolts: the destruction and re-establishment of the state's taxation organisation", *Turkish Historical Review*, 4/1 (2013), 57–82. For two major works on the Celali revolts, see Akdağ, Mustafa, *Celâlî İsyanları 1550–1603* (Ankara: Ankara Üniversitesi Basımevi, 1963); Griswold, William J., *The Great Anatolian Rebellion, 1000–1020/1591–1611* (Berlin: Klaus Schwarz Verlag, 1983).

17 Beldiceanu-Steinherr and Bacqué-Grammont, "A propose de quelques causes de malaises sociaux en Anatolie centrale aux XVIᵉ et XVIIᵉ siècles", pp. 91, 92 (quote from p. 92). Beldiceanu-Steinherr and Bacqué-Grammont date the document to around the middle of the sixteenth century or later, p. 82.

18 Baykal, Bekir Sıtkı (ed.), *Peçevi İbrahim Efendi Peçevi Tarihi*, vol. II (Istanbul: Kültür ve Turizm Bakanlığı Yayınları, 1982), p. 237.

19 Orhonlu, Cengiz (ed.), *Osmanlı Tarihine Âid Belgeler Telhîsler (1597–1607)* (Istanbul: Edebiyat Fakültesi Basımevi, 1970), no. 22, p. 22. Quoted by Özel, *The Collapse of Rural Order in Ottoman Anatolia*, p. 155, footnote 71.

20 Orbay, Kayhan, "Bursa'da II. Murad Vakfı'nın Mali Tarihi (1608–1641)", *İstanbul Üniversitesi İktisat Fakültesi Mecmuası*, 61/2 (2011), p. 297.

21 Orbay, Kayhan, "Financial development of the waqfs in Konya and the agricultural economy in the Central Anatolia (late sixteenth–early seventeenth centuries)", *Journal of the Economic and Social History of the Orient*, 55 (2012), pp. 76, 108, 111. See also Faroqhi, Suraiya, "Vakıf administration in sixteenth century Konya: the zaviye of Sadreddin-i Konevi", *Journal of the Economic and Social History of the Orient*, 17/2 (1974), pp. 156–7, 162; Orbay, Kayhan, "Celâlîs recorded in the account books", *Rivista degli studi orientali*, 78/1–2 (2004), 71–83.

complained about the seditious actions of the inhabitants of Şeyhlü, a village near Beypazarı, where the well-known seditious rebel (*kapusuz levent*) Deli Veli and his brother Deli Ali had found refuge in Şeyhlü, assisted by two inhabitants of the village. According to complaints, these people had "destroyed the houses and barns of the people, seized all their goods and terrorized them".[22]

Against this backdrop of minor disruption to major destruction, agricultural production in Anatolia in the sixteenth century was conducted largely by the peasant family, the basic unit of labour, working on state-owned land (*miri*). For many the level of existence was one of subsistence, as Mehmet Öz discusses in his chapter on central Anatolia in the sixteenth century in this volume. Peasant families cultivated landholdings that could be worked by a man and a pair of oxen.[23] The centrality of the ox in an Anatolia peasant's life was celebrated by the famous sixteenth-century folk poet from Sivas, Pir Sultan Abdal, one of whose poems championed this animal explaining why the ox deserved the true appreciation of the peasant and should be treated with utmost kindness:

> The ox brings logs, clattering and clunking, down from the mountain
> He brings them down and they feed the fires
> The ox does the work of every house
> Peasants, look well upon the ox.

> Make the outhouse of the ox a little low
> Make sure that the ground under him is not damp but dry
> Each time you harness him caress and kiss him
> Peasants, look well upon the ox.[24]

The vast majority of the rural population working in arable farming were involved in the cultivation of grain, the staple produce for both human and animal consumption. Suraiya Faroqhi and Huri İslamoğlu calculated that in Anatolia overall in the sixteenth century grain cultivation represented the vast majority of arable crops ranging from between 60 and 95 per cent of total production.[25] In many areas of Anatolia wheat, followed by barley, was the major component of production. Huri İslamoğlu, in her study of north-central

---

22   Hezarfen, Ahmet (ed.), *Rumeli ve Anadolu Âyan ve Eşkiyası. Osmanlı Arşiv Belgeleri* (Istanbul: Kaynak Yayınları, 2002), pp. 208–9.

23   For a discussion of landholding see Mehmet Öz's chapter in this volume.

24   Gölpınarlı, *Alevî-Bektâşî Nefesleri*, p. 257.

25   İslamoğlu, Huri and Suraiya Faroqhi, "Crop patterns and agricultural production trends in sixteenth-century Anatolia", *Review (Fernand Braudel Center)*, 2/3 (1979), p. 408.

Anatolia, found that cereals, mostly wheat and barley, constituted a virtual monoculture.[26] Analysing data from the central Anatolian *sancak*s of Aksaray, Ankara, Bozok and Çankırı in his chapter in this volume, Mehmet Öz calculates that agricultural arable taxes in the *sancak* of Aksaray according to the *tahrir* registers for the year 1500 and again in 1584 show that around 95 per cent of the tax levied was collected on grain. Öz makes similar findings for the *sancak* of Ankara where in 1523 grain accounted for 93 per cent of the tax levied on agricultural crops and 90 per cent in 1572. The figure was even higher for Bozok where, according to data from the *tahrir* register of 1566, almost the entire tax income from crop production came from grain (99 per cent), a figure that drops only slightly for the share of grain in arable taxes in 1576 when it was 94 per cent.

Although grain production did dominate arable cultivation in many parts of Anatolia, and was central to much peasant livelihood, animal husbandry was also a significant factor in the livelihood of a large segment of the population, for in the sixteenth century nomads made up a significant percentage of the rural population. Öz argues that when animal husbandry is taken into account, it becomes clear that one cannot in fact speak of a quasi-total monoculture of grain, as is sometimes assumed.[27] Taking the taxes on animal husbandry into account in the four central Anatolian *sancak*s he examined, Öz calculates that the tax total for grain drops in the *sancak* of Aksaray in 1500 from 95 per cent to 73 per cent when the taxes on sheep and goats and for beehives are included. In 1584 the figure drops from 95 per cent to 84 per cent when animal husbandry is included in the calculation. In the *sancak* of Ankara, while grain represented 93 per cent of the total tax on arable crops in 1523, this figure drops to 85 per cent when the tax on sheep and goats is included; and the 1572 figure of 90 per cent drops to 84 per cent with the inclusion of animal husbandry taxes. In Bozok the total dominance of grain among arable crops, with 99 per cent of tax collected being levied on grain, drops to a considerably less dominant 76.5 per cent when the tax on sheep and goats is included, and the 94 per cent figure for 1576 becomes 80 per cent with the inclusion of taxes on animal

---

26   İslamoğlu-İnan, Huri, "State and peasants in the Ottoman empire: a study of a peasant
      economy in north-central Anatolia during the sixteenth century", in *The Ottoman Empire
      and the World Economy*, ed. Huri İslamoğlu-İnan (Cambridge: Cambridge University
      Press, 1987), p. 111.

27   İslamoğlu and Faroqhi, for example, suggested that for the Anatolian plateau "one might
      tentatively assume the existence of a central zone in which grain was almost a monocul-
      ture, possible complemented by a certain amount of animal husbandry", İslamoğlu and
      Faroqhi, "Crop patterns and agricultural production trends in sixteenth-century Anatolia",
      p. 420. For them, the central Anatolian core area represented a grain monoculture, p. 421.

husbandry, a figure indicating an increase in grain production and a decrease in sheep and goat husbandry over this period.

Öz thus argues that while the role of wheat and barley in crop production in central Anatolia in the sixteenth century was certainly highly dominant, this did not necessarily amount to a monoculture. By adding in taxes on animal husbandry, including taxes on flocks moving from winter to summer pastures, and on apiculture, one arrives at a more balanced view of overall agriculture production.

Arable production in general, as Öz argues, was much more diversified than appears to be the case when thinking only in terms of grain, and peasants cultivated a wide range of fruit and vegetables, as well as pulses (such as beans and chickpeas), olives and vines. Polonyalı Simeon referred to the orchards round Tosya, Merzifon and Amasya, where two types of quinces were grown,[28] the great number of orchards and vineyards round Kayseri, which produced many different types of grapes,[29] and at Beypazarı, from where very sweet melons and watermelons were sent to the sultan. The region between Beypazarı and Sarılar was covered in vineyards and orchards which produced "huge quinces, apples, oleasters, grapes, melons and watermelons". Here travellers could simply reach out and pick them and eat them as they went along.[30] The watermelons of İzmir were "one of the miracles created by God", according to Lüdeke who was there in the mid-eighteenth century,[31] while both Polonyalı Simeon and Evliya Çelebi waxed lyrical about the melons of Diyarbakır. "Huge, very juicy and sweet, with a delicious aroma as of musk and ambergris", a *zerde* [a yellow-rice dish] made with these Diyarbakır melons could not be surpassed even by the addition of Athens honey.[32] As fruit and vegetables were not taxed if they were not sold on the market, the level at which peasants cultivated fruit and vegetables for their own consumption is very hard to trace. But it is clear that their diet would have been diversified.

Such cultivation was also practiced by a more urban element who could vacate their towns in the summer season in order to cultivate their gardens and vines. In Malatya, for example, the city became empty in the summer and the population left for the villages to harvest the grapes.[33] A similar exodus

---

28 Andreasyan, *Polonyalı Bir Seyyahın Gözünden*, p. 123.

29 Andreasyan, *Polonyalı Bir Seyyahın Gözünden*, pp. 217–18.

30 Andreasyan, *Polonyalı Bir Seyyahın Gözünden*, p. 222.

31 Lüdeke, Christoph Wilhelm, *Türklerde Din ve Devlet Yönetimi. İzmir ve İstanbul 1759–1768*, trans. Türkis Noyan (Istanbul: Kitap Yayınevi, 2013), p. 29.

32 Dankoff and Kim, *An Ottoman Traveller*, p. 115 (for quote), Andreasyan, *Polonyalı Bir Seyyahın Gözünden*, p. 140.

33 Andreasyan, *Polonyalı Bir Seyyahın Gözünden*, p. 127.

occurred at Diyarbakır where, when the Tigris floods subsided, "all Diyarbakır's inhabitants, rich and poor alike, move with their entire families to the bank of the Tigris. They set up camp with their tents and pavilions along this wide water ... and cultivate their gardens with melons, watermelons, various vegetables and flowers".[34] But artisans returned each day to the city "to pursue their occupations" and returned in the late afternoon.[35]

Apart from crop cultivation, peasants were also able to supplement their diet through apiculture and, in areas where this was possible, fishing. Bee keeping was widespread, appearing, for example, in the provinces of Bursa, Aydın, Kütahya, Bolu, İç İl, Erzurum, Gelibolu and Malatya.[36] Fishing was practiced in coastal locations, such as in the villages along the sea of Marmara in the *sancak* of Bursa,[37] and in lakes, such as that at İznik, where the fish were apparently plentiful and cheap in the later sixteenth century.[38]

Thus although much peasant livelihood rotated round grain, what they grew and consumed was more diversified even in areas where grain cultivation was dominant. In areas which specialised in other crops, such as rice, which was grown in the regions of Tosya, Boyabad, in Bigadiç and in the provinces of Aydın, Bolu and Malatya,[39] then the diversification was greater.

Surplus and Consumption

After consumption and putting aside seed for the following year, many peasants would have had very little, if any, surplus available. However, what agricultural surplus there was, together with payment of taxes in kind in the case

---

34   Dankoff and Kim, *An Ottoman Traveller*, p. 114.

35   Dankoff and Kim, *An Ottoman Traveller*, pp. 114–15.

36   Barkan, Ömer Lütfi, *XV ve XVI inci Asırlarda Osmanlı İmpartorluğunda Zirai Ekonominin Hukuki ve Mali Esasları I. Kanunlar* (Istanbul: İstanbul Burhaneddin Matbaası, 1943), "Hüdavendigâr Livası Kanunnâmesi", 1487, p. 4; "Kanunu Livâ-i Aydın", 1528, p. 11; "Kütahya Livası Kanunu", 1538, pp. 25–6; "Bolu Livası Kanunu", 1528, p. 31; "İç İl Livâsı Kanunu", 1584, p. 51; "Erzurum Vilâyeti Kanunu", 1540, p. 68; "Kanun-ı Reayây-ı Livâ-i Gelibolu", 1519, p. 235; "Malatya Livası Kanunu", 1528, pp. 112–13; "Malatya Livası Kanunu", 1559, p. 116.

37   İnalcık, Halil, "A case study of the village microeconomy: villages in the Bursa *sancak*, 1520–1593", in İnalcık, Halil, *The Middle East and the Balkans under the Ottoman Empire. Essays on Economy and Society* (Indiana: Indiana University Turkish Studies, 1993), p. 161.

38   Lubenau, Reinhold, *Reinhold Lubenau Seyahatnamesi. Osmanlı Ülkesinde 1587–1589*, two vols., trans. Türkis Noyan (Istanbul: Kitap Yayınevi, 2012), vol. II, p. 515.

39   Barkan, *Kanunlar*, "Kanunu Livâ-i Aydın", 1528, p. 17; "Bolu Livası Kanunu", 1528, p. 31; "Malatya Livası Kanunu", 1528, p. 111–12. For rice cultivation in the empire see İnalcık, Halil, "Rice cultivation and the *Celtükçi-reʿāyā* system in the Ottoman empire", *Turcica*, 14 (1982), 69–141.

of grain, was sold on local markets. Peasants with very little to spare would still have needed to sell in order to enable them to pay taxes in cash. In this context, the significance of small denomination coinage should not be overlooked, as Şevket Pamuk has argued.[40] It was this agricultural surplus which allowed the development of urban centres which needed the produce of their hinterlands to survive and develop.

Much agricultural surplus would have been directed to local markets only. If markets were too distant or transportation too expensive to make marketing economically viable, then crops were left to rot in the fields. For many areas of Anatolia this remained the case into the nineteenth century. The introduction and extension of the railways into the western Anatolian interior from the 1860s had a major impact, creating "a real revolution in the economic conditions of the country", according to the French consul general in İzmir, and transforming lands which had been left uncultivated, due to lack of transportation, into productive centres of agriculture.[41] Similarly, the arrival of the railway in central Anatolia at the end of the century had a direct effect on agricultural production and in consequence on the income from agricultural taxes.[42] This did not, however, apply to all agricultural production, Yonca Köksal and Mehmet Polatel noting in their chapter in this volume that its effect on sheep production and trade was more restricted. The impact of limited and expensive transportation on productivity was thus still evident even in the late nineteenth century when price and distance meant that in some areas, goods such as grain, fruit or timber were only produced for local needs, not for export out of the region.[43]

Apart from the major staple, grain, weekly markets, occasional fairs, markets which grew up around caravanserais and everyday urban markets sold other agricultural produce, such as the plums, figs, apples, cherries, apricots, lemons, grapes, melons and watermelons which were sold in the markets of the provinces of Aydın, Kengiri, Malatya, Urfa, Ergani, Balıkesir, Karaman and

40   Pamuk, Şevket, *Monetary History of the Ottoman Empire* (Cambridge: Cambridge University Press, 2000), p. 39.

41   Rougon, R., *Smyrne. Situation commerciale et économique des pays compris dans la circonscription du consulat général de France (Vilayeti d'Aidin, de Konieh et des Iles)* (Paris-Nancy: Berger-Levrault et Cie, 1892), p. 148.

42   Biren, Tevfik, *Bürokrat Tevfik Biren'in II. Abdülhamid, Meşrutiyet, ve Mütareke Hatıraları*, two vols., ed. Fatma Rezan Hürmen (Istanbul: Pınar Yayınları, 2006), vol. 1, pp. 259–60.

43   Dincer, Celal, "Osmanlı Vezirlerinden Hasan Fehmi Paşa'nın Anadolu'nun Bayındırlık İşlerine Dair Hazırladığı Lâyiha", *Belgeler* 5–8/9–12 (1968–71), p. 165, 26 Cemaziülahir 1297/24 Mayıs 1296 (5 June 1880).

Mardin;[44] or the walnuts, almonds, hazelnuts and chestnuts sold in Aydın, Balıkesir, Diyarbakır, Mardin and Urfa;[45] or the dairy products (butter, cheese and yoghurt), honey and olive oil sold, for example, in the regions of Malatya, Mardin, Urfa, Diyarbakır, Balıkesir and Aydın.[46] Produce on the market was dependent on locality and on season. Fish, for example, was an important element in coastal towns. Anchovy (*hamsi*) season caused great excitement in Trabzon where, according to Evliya Çelebi, they were the favourite fish of the population, "the one they sacrifice themselves for one thousand times over and have bloody battles over when it is bought and sold".[47] The arrival of anchovies on the market even resulted in people interrupting prayers in the mosque, for "prayer is for ever" while anchovies were not.[48] The "Trabzon sophisticates" poked fun at the more simple townsfolk with little ditties like "Trabzon is our home / Our hand can't keep a penny / Because of hamsi fish / We have no cares, not any".[49]

Apart from absorbing surplus, markets also stimulated production. The production of the region round Adana, for example, shifted from a predominance of wheat production in the early sixteenth century to a predominance of cotton production in the second half of the century in order to meet Istanbul's demand for cotton.[50] It was the requirements of the imperial dockyards which stimulated the production of hemp, the raw material for sails and rope, in the *sancak* of Canik.[51]

44   Barkan, *Kanunlar*, "Kanunu Livâ-i Aydın", 1528, pp. 14–15; "Kanunnâme-i Livâs-ı Kengırı", 1578, p. 38; "Malatya Livası Kanunu", 1528, pp. 112, 113; "Ergani Livâsı Kanunu", time of Sultan Süleyman I, p. 154; "Defter-i Yasahâ-i Liva-i Ruha", 1518, p. 156; Kütükoğlu, Mübahat, "1624 Sikke Tashihinin Ardından Hazırlanan Narh Defterleri", *Tarih Dergisi*, 34 (1983–84), p. 132; Akgöz, Alaaddin, *Kanunî Devrine Ait 939–941 / 1532–1535 Tarihli Lârende [Karaman] Şer'iye Sicili Özet-Dizin-Tıpkıbasım* (Konya: Tablet Kitabevi, 2006), pp. 179–82.

45   Barkan, *Kanunlar*, "Kanunu Livâ-i Aydın", 1528, pp. 14–15; "Diyarbakır Vilayeti Kanunu", 1540, p. 138; "Defter-i Yasahâ-i Liva-i Ruha", 1518, p. 156; Kütükoğlu, "1624 Sikke Tashihinin Ardından Hazırlanan Narh Defterleri", p. 132.

46   Barkan, *Kanunlar*, "Kanunu Livâ-i Aydın", 1528, pp. 14–15; "Malatya Livası Kanunu", 1528, pp. 112, 113; "Diyarbakır Vilayeti Kanunu", 1540, p. 138; "Defter-i Yasahâ-i Liva-i Ruha", 1518, p. 156; Kütükoğlu, "1624 Sikke Tashihinin Ardından Hazırlanan Narh Defterleri", p. 132; Akgöz, *Kanunî Devrine Ait 939–941 / 1532–1535 Tarihli Lârende [Karaman] Şer'iye Sicili*, pp. 179–82.

47   Dankoff and Kim, *An Ottoman Traveller*, p. 44.

48   Dankoff and Kim, *An Ottoman Traveller*, p. 45.

49   Dankoff and Kim, *An Ottoman Traveller*, p. 46.

50   İslamoğlu and Faroqhi, "Crop patterns and agricultural production trends in sixteenth-century Anatolia", pp. 405, 413.

51   Bostan, İdris, *Osmanlı Bahriye Teşkilatı: XVII.Yüzyılda Tersâne-i Âmire* (Ankara: Türk Tarih Kurumu Basımevi, 1992), pp. 137–41.

Markets coated Anatolia, as did caravanserais, whose presence often encouraged the constructions of markets in their vicinities. In their chapter in this volume on the economic geography of Anatolia around 1530, Metin Coşgel and Sadullah Yıldırım use spatial analysis to map the presence of caravanserais. Caravanserais were a central feature of commerce in the empire. They provided security for merchants and their goods and were a major plank in the state's policy of stimulating and protecting trade, as shown by the stipulations concerning the security and measures to be taken to protect merchants and merchandise in such places in the law code of Selim I.[52] The map produced by Coşgel and Yıldırım shows the extent to which caravanserais were widespread, for they are dotted about all over Anatolia. They appear to be particularly densely spread in western Anatolia. Coşgel and Yıldırım found a high density of caravanserais at Tire, which was described by Polonyalı Simeon at the beginning of the seventeenth century as a large city where goods were loaded and from where caravans set out every day.[53] Their map also shows a large number of caravanserais in northern Anatolia. In central Anatolia the highest numbers of caravanserais were in the regions of Ankara, Aksaray, Karahisar, Konya and Kütahya. Another centre for caravanserais was Tokat, "one of the most remarkable Thoroughfares in the East", according to the French merchant Jean-Baptiste Tavernier (d. 1689), with caravans continuously arriving from Persia, Diyarbakır, Baghdad, Istanbul, İzmir, Sinop and other places. "This continuous concourse of the caravans trolls the money about at Tocat, and makes it one of the most considerable cities of Turkie".[54]

Markets were a major feature of the economic landscape of Anatolia, where the urban economy had been important from the early days of the Ottoman state, and indeed before.[55] Coşgel and Yıldırım also construct a map of markets across Anatolia around 1530. This shows broad similarities to that for caravanserais, as would be expected as both were related to main trade routes, but major conglomerations of markets are here to be found in urban centres. While large numbers of caravanserais are evident in eastern Anatolia, stopping and customs points before crossing the border into Iran, Coşgel and Yıldırım found no major conglomerations of markets in this region. In northern Anatolia, Coşgel and Yıldırım found many markets at Merzifon, Taşköprü and Sinop and, in the

---

52 Yaşar, Yücel and Selami Pulaha (eds.), *I. Selim Kanunnameleri (1512–1520)* (Ankara: Türk Tarih Kurumu Basımevi, 1995), pp. 35, 90–1, 154–5.

53 Andreasyan, *Polonyalı Bir Seyyahın Gözünden*, p. 36.

54 Tavernier, *Voyages*, p. 5.

55 Fleet, Kate, "The Turkish economy, 1071–1453", in *The Cambridge History of Turkey. Volume 1. Byzantium to Turkey 1071–1453*, ed. Kate Fleet (Cambridge: Cambridge University Press, 2009), pp. 227–65.

south, at Ulaş, Kara İsalu, Kars and Sis. In the west the major market conglomerations they map include those at Çeşme, İzmir, Ayasluğ, Yenişehir, Lazkiye
and Gölhisar and, to the north, Balıkesir and İvrindi. In central Anatolia, large
numbers of markets were found at, among other places, Konya and Beyşehir.

Some markets were major centres of international trade, such as Bursa,
always an important centre for, in particular, imported cloth, both from east
and west, or Ankara for mohair (sof), a commodity whose importance was
such that "most of the populace are merchants on land and sea, trading in
mohair wherever it is esteemed – İzmir, Frengistan, Arabia, Egypt, and the
seven climes".[56] There were apparently so many Poles there in the early seventeenth century that Polonyalı Simeon, who noted that mohair was exported
from there to all parts of the world and merchants "from every country" came
there to trade in it,[57] forgot the "pain of exile" and "finding consolation" stayed
there for one month.[58] The ports of Amasra, Sinop, described by Kritoboulos as
a major emporium and one of the richest cities on the Black Sea,[59] and Samsun
were important ports for import-export trade both with the west and with the
northern Black Sea region, as Kate Fleet discusses in her chapter in this volume
on Turkish-Genoese trade in northern Anatolia in the fourteenth and fifteenth
centuries. Apart from trade in copper, which was mined in northern Anatolia,
slaves and grain, these markets also sold imported European cloth, sugar
from Cyprus, grapes from western Anatolia, soap from Italy, salted fish and
furs from the northern Black Sea, leather and tanned ox hides and hemp. The
importance of these ports in international trade is evidenced by the presence
there of Genoese colonies. Although the Genoese colony of Samsun had been
established by the beginning of the fourteenth century, the exact dating of the
establishment of those at Amasra and Sinop is unclear, that of Sinop probably
dating, Fleet argues, to the third quarter of the fourteenth century, a similar
date being probable also for Amasra. The exact nature of these Genoese colonies is not entirely clear, as Fleet discusses, but their existence gives an idea of
the international nature of markets in this part of Anatolia in the early centuries of Ottoman rule.

Throughout the Ottoman period Anatolia was an export zone for agricultural produce, such as grain, to the west. From the early days of the Ottoman
state, such produce constituted a major export item in its trade. One major

---

56   Dankoff and Kim, An Ottoman Traveller, p. 78.
57   Andreasyan, Polonyalı Bir Seyyahın Gözünden, p. 220.
58   Andreasyan, Polonyalı Bir Seyyahın Gözünden, p. 221.
59   Kritoboulos, History of Mehmed the Conqueror. By Kritovoulos, trans. Charles T. Riggs
      (Princeton: Princeton University Press, 1954), p. 166.

commodity which became a significant export item from western Anatolia in the eighteenth and nineteenth centuries was cotton, which came to play "a pivotal role" in the economy of the region (and indeed in the world economy)[60] from the eighteenth century onwards. It was the cotton sector, Elena Frangakis-Syrett argues in her chapter in this volume on the production and trade of cotton in western Anatolia in the eighteenth and nineteenth centuries, that demonstrates how the Ottoman economy competed and participated effectively in the world economy. Seeking to account for why western Anatolia was able to remain competitive in the nineteenth century and to cope with the wide up- and down-swings in the cotton trade, Frangakis-Syrett draws attention to the experience and skill of the region's economic actors in both production and trade, arguing that it was their knowledge of cotton combined with their understanding of the workings of the competitive and volatile markets both within the empire and abroad that enabled them to succeed.

The port for export of the cotton was İzmir, the "Queen of Cities of Anatolia".[61] İzmir was in the nineteenth century, and even in the eighteenth, an export port par excellence. "Universally admitted to be one of the most opulent cities in the Levant and the first commercial town in the Ottoman dominions", at the beginning of the nineteenth century, it was in İzmir that "vessels from all quarters of the world rendezvous in the harbour, and make the magazine of their merchandise".[62] For Adna Brown, there at the end of the century, İzmir was "remarkably neat" with good water and good sewage. "The bazaars are far above the average of those we have seen since entering the Turkish territory. Many fine stores with many French goods in them are to be found here".[63] In fact, as Frangakis-Syrett notes, cotton that exited İzmir for France often returned in the form of textiles bought by urban Ottoman consumers.

Export-import trade did not dominate the Ottoman market, however, where internal trade was always more significant than external. International trade was thus not a dominant factor in the Anatolian economic landscape. Grain was produced for sale on the local market, cotton was grown in western Anatolia to provide the local textile manufacturing sector. While copper was mined and exported, being exported in the fourteenth and fifteenth centuries, as discussed by Fleet in this volume, it was also very much a local product for

---

60   Panza, Laura, "Globalization and the Near East: a study of cotton market integration in Egypt and western Anatolia", *The Journal of Economic History*, 73/3 (2013), p. 848.

61   Sullivan, James, *Diary of a Tour in the Autumn of 1856* (Printed for Presentation to his Friends, April 1857), pp. 16–17.

62   Joliffe, Thomas Robert, *Narrative of an Excursion from Corfu to Smyrna* (London: Printed for Black, Young and Young, 1827), letter XXVI, p. 257, June 1817.

63   Brown, Adna, *From Vermont to Damascus* (Boston: Geo. H. Ellis, 1895), p. 132.

the local market. Apart from its use in minting copper coins or for military munitions, it was also used to make pots and pans for cooking, *hamam* bowls, bowls and ewers for washing and the copper jugs with handles, spouts and lids, such as those sold on the markets of Bursa in the early seventeenth century.[64] Such items were in demand both by the wealthy and less wealthy consumer, as discussed by Suraiya Faroqhi in her chapter in this volume on working, marketing and consuming Ottoman copper. Even the poor apparently bought copper utensils, for Faroqhi refers to the entry in the 1640 Istanbul *narh defteri* (price register) for "copper pots for poor people", here items made from waste copper.

Among the Anatolian towns producing copperware for the local markets, Tokat was particularly famous. At the beginning of the eighteenth century, the French botanist, Joseph Pitton Tournefort, noted that "the chief Trade of Tocat is in Copper Vessels, as Kettles, drinking Vessels, Lanthorns, Candlesticks, which are made here very handsome, and sent to *Constantinople*, and into *Egypt*".[65] From the middle of the eighteenth century copper work became a very significant industry there and by the end of the century the state ordered all copper from the Ergani mine to be worked only in Tokat.[66] The smelting houses for refining copper were commented on by William Ainsworth, in Anatolia in the mid-nineteenth century for the Royal Geographical Society, who noted the large number of copper vessels produced there.[67]

Faroqhi notes that, despite the competition for resources at various times on the world market, the manufacture of copperware retained considerable vitality in Tokat. Based on *kadı* registers for the town, Faroqhi argues that local consumption was significant since the monetary value of copper vessels and implements made up a notable percentage of the goods left by deceased persons. The percentage share of copperware in the estates of Muslims of Tokat in the mid 1800s thus amounted to at least 5.8 per cent, while that for non-Muslims was slightly lower at 4.7 per cent. Faroqhi suggests that the difference in the percentages for Muslims and non-Muslims may be due to a smaller number of non-Muslim coppersmiths, or to non-Muslims possessing more goods and chattels, among which copperware therefore represented a smaller percentage. Given that Tokat had smelting works, such percentages may not be representative of the Anatolian population as a whole. As Faroqhi discusses, it is also difficult to establish to what extent women in general may have owned

---

64   Kütükoğlu, Mübahat, "1624 Sikke Tashihinin Ardından Hazırlanan Narh Defterleri", p. 141.

65   Tournefort, Joseph Pitton de, *A Voyage into the Levant* (London, 1718), vol. II, p. 325.

66   Tızlak, Fahrettin, "Osmanlı Devlet'inde Ham Bakır İşleme Merkezleri Olarak Tokat ve Diyarbakır", *Belleten*, 59/226 (1995), p. 646.

67   Ainsworth, William Francis, *Travels and Researches in Asia Minor, Mesopotamia, Chaldea, and Armenia*, two vols. (London: John W. Parker, 1842), vol. II, p. 18.

copperware, as opposed to men. It may be that, as copperware was compara-tively expensive, it was in the possession of men rather than women.

The Role of the State

Although not necessarily ever present in the daily lives of the population of Anatolia, its presence being felt among the rural poor only in the form of the sol-dier or the tax collector, the state nevertheless was a major factor in the shaping of the Anatolian economic landscape. Quite apart from surveying land, collect-ing taxes and exerting administrative control through the officials it assigned to urban areas, the capital itself dominated production in its Anatolian hin-terland. Anatolia provided provisions and clothing for the empire's military, soldiers for its army and sailors for its navy. It supplied fodder for the animals and food for the soldiers as they passed through Anatolian territory. Anatolia and the islands of the Aegean and the eastern Mediterranean, which thus were enfolded economically-speaking within the Anatolian unit, provided Istanbul with a vast array of agricultural products including grain, fruit, cheese, olive oil, dairy products and sugar from Cyprus. Grapes went from western Anatolia to Istanbul, the entire grape crop of Mudanya, for example, being shipped there at the beginning of the seventeenth century.[68] Gelibolu sent lettuce, radish, onion, garlic, marrows, melons and watermelons to Istanbul in the later six-teenth century and İznik provided salted fish and timber, including willow tree wood which was used by Istanbul craftsmen to make wooden items such as boxes.[69] Plums from Amasya and apricots from Larende and Akşehir were sold on the markets in Istanbul in the mid-seventeenth century, as were chestnuts and radishes from Bursa and chestnuts from İzmir.[70] Anatolia also produced cloth and textiles, which formed a very important element of Anatolian trade both internally for provincial towns and for Istanbul.

One commodity that Anatolia is not usually associated with in the provi-sioning of the capital is meat. As Yonca Köksal and Mehmet Polatel note in their chapter in this volume on the Cihanbeyli and the sheep trade, this trade is usually associated with Rumeli and little attention has been paid to the Anatolian meat supply and animal trade to Istanbul. Focusing on the activities

---

68 Faroqhi, Suraiya, "Rural society in Anatolia and the Balkans during the sixteenth century, I", *Turcica*, 9/1 (1977), pp. 174–5.
69 Lubenau, *Reinhold Lubenau Seyahatnamesi*, II, pp. 515, 525, 556; Tavernier, *Voyages*, p. 3.
70 Kütükoğlu, Mübahat (ed.), *Osmanlılarda Narh Müessesesi ve 1640 Tarihli Narh Defteri* (Istanbul: Enderun Kitabevi, 1983), pp. 95, 96.

of the Cihanbeyli, a semi-nomadic tribe in the province of Ankara active in the provision of sheep to Istanbul from the late eighteenth century, Köksal and Polatel argue that the Anatolian trade in animals to the capital, which in fact existed from the fifteenth century, was significant in itself and was not merely a temporary solution in times of dearth in Rumeli, as it is usually regarded.

Köksal and Polatel contend that changes in the nineteenth century resulted in a more competitive and less organised meat market. In line with the argument put forward by Donald Quaetert that following the adoption of liberal economic policies in the wake of the Treaty of Baltalimanı in 1838 Ottoman manufacturing went from an organised system of guild control to a disorganised and more disparate system marked by non-guild shops and home production, Köksal and Polatel argue that the state sedentarisation policy, which resulted in the sedentarisation of the Cihanbeyli by the 1850s, meant that the power of the tribal chief over the tribe, now dispersed through different villages, declined and his ability to control the meat trade consequently decreased. At the same time, the meat market became more competitive due to the liberal economic policies gradually adopted by the state after 1838. The nineteenth century thus saw the transformation of meat provisioning from an organised trade under a head trader into a disorganised trade conducted by individual merchants.

Apart from any liberalising of economic conditions, the nineteenth century saw another shift in government thinking and that concerned the role of the state in the lives of its subjects. The state came to be perceived as a provider of welfare, and the concept of the public good came to be increasingly invoked.[71] In his report on the economic conditions in Anatolia written for Abdülhamid II in 1880 Hasan Fehmi Paşa, the minister of public works, noted the need for the government to take public benefit into consideration when awarding concessions.[72]

The importance of public benefit could even override religious prohibition in a situation in which the state, strapped for cash, was offered a lucrative, but religiously dubious, source of revenue. Such was the case with the lottery, as Ebru Boyar demonstrates in her chapter in this volume on the lottery in İzmir in the early twentieth century. For the consuming public the lottery had an irresistible attraction, opening up the vista of otherwise unobtainable wealth

---

71   Boyar, Ebru, "Public good and private exploitation: criticism of the tobacco Régie in 1909", in *The Ottomans and Trade*, ed. Ebru Boyar and Kate Fleet (*Oriente Moderno*, 25/1, 2006) (Rome, 2006), pp. 193–200.

72   Dincer, "Osmanlı Vezirlerinden Hasan Fehmi Paşa'nın Anadolu'nun Bayındırlık İşlerine Dair Hazırladığı Lâyiha", p. 164.

which would accrue from the possession of a winning ticket. From a religious, moral or even legal standpoint, however, it was a form of gambling and thus unacceptable. The state, caught between consumption and religious rectitude, and itself drawn to the highly popular and profitable nature of the lottery, found a way out of the quandary by declaring in 1883 that lotteries organised for the public benefit and the need of religious communities were permissible, while those merely for private interests were not.

The İzmir lotteries, in particular the İzmir Hamidiye Artisanal School Lottery (İzmir Hamidiye Sanayi Mektebi Piyangosu), were immensely popular far beyond the city itself. Boyar argues that it was this popularity and the considerable income generated that ultimately led to the lottery's demise as it became enmeshed in political infighting and fell foul of palace intrigue. The ultimate banning of the İzmir lotteries was, Boyar argues, the result of the grand vezir Avlonyalı Mehmed Ferid Paşa's personal animosity towards Kamil Paşa, the governor of Aydın, and his desire to transfer the income generated by the lotteries away from İzmir, where it represented an autonomous revenue stream for Kamil Paşa, and into the central treasury. In his drive to achieve these twin aims he overplayed his hand with the sultan who, rather than simply taking control of the revenue, banned all lotteries, a position from which he had to be talked down, according to Boyar, allowing the continuation of one lottery, the Istanbul-controlled Ziraat Bankası Piyangosu (the Agricultural Bank Lottery), but not those of İzmir.

Indeed, uncertainty and the opacity of governance can be said to have marked much of the style of control exhibited by the Ottoman government in the late nineteenth and early twentieth centuries, and was present in much decision making, both political and economic. Economic decisions often rested on an amalgam of factors, some of which were not economic at all. Ebru Boyar's chapter shows clearly the extent to which central rapacity over provincial revenues, machinations motivated by personal political rivalry and sultanic impetuosity in decision making all fused and entwined inextricably together, even down to the language of obfuscation used in official documents, such as that artfully put together by the *Meclis-i Mahsusa-i Vükela* praising Abdülhamid's sagacity in making the wrong decision and subtly enticing him back on to the economic straight and narrow.

In the realm of economics, Germano Maifreda has percipiently noted the dangers of modern perceptions recasting those of the past and has reminded us that we need "to resist the temptation to treat the past as a mere repository of 'premises', 'forerunners' and 'anticipations' of the present, taking for granted a homogenous and obligatory development and choosing from among the wide variety of data that the past offers those on which our present reality casts a false glow of inevitability".[73] The Tanzimat, or the Ottoman nineteenth century, is thus often couched in terms of linear progress to modernity, to systemisation and centralisation, all seen as markers of development and the movement out of backwardness and retrograde practices. In economic terms, however, this risks missing the point for, as Marc Aymes's chapter in this volume on the *nizam*, uncertainty and the activation of economic norms in nineteenth-century provincial contexts shows, the application of economic practice was not about imposing order on chaos, or replacing uncertainty with certainty, but of functioning within manifold economic realities and gradations of knowledge, from the very local to the epitome of central bureaucracy. Abdülhamid ɪɪ's *modus operandi* was marked by its ad hoc nature rather than by any systematic order, as highlighted by Ebru Boyar's chapter in this volume.

In his chapter Marc Aymes considers issues of regulation and knowledge. Economic dealings, he notes, "rely, in one way or another, on an ordering scheme of things", this being in essence what political economy is all about. However, as Aymes notes, economy is not simply about order but is equally shaped by the existence of uncertainty. It is "this conundrum of uncertainty and the activation of economic norms" that Marc Aymes sets out to examine in the context of the nineteenth century through a close reading of two documents, an *arzuhal* from Cyprus dated late 1845/early 1846, and a report dated 1894, sent by the Ottoman commissioner for duties and taxes (*rüsumat emini*) to the ministry of the interior (*Dahiliye Nezareti*). What emerges is less order, and centrality, and more uncertainty, and the importance of localised differences. This is a useful antidote to the tendency to lose touch with the on-the-ground reality in pursuit of the chimera of centralisation, the belief in the march to modernisation. What Marc Aymes's close reading highlights is that the supposed linear progress from chaos to order, from local variation to central control needs to be re-thought. In other words, the Sublime Porte did not become "the dream bureaucracy of some compact and unified rational-legal elite", as Aymes puts it. Instead, what existed both at the beginning of the Tanzimat and after it at the end of the nineteenth century was a quintessentially provincial procedure which operated, Aymes argues, within a context of uncertainty management marked by patterns both devolved and scattered.

For the population in Anatolia, therefore, survival at a basic level, or the attainment and maintenance of wealth was always subject to uncertainty. Government control could be dictated by factors unrelated to economic calculation, and driven, in the case of the lottery for example, by personal ambition

---

73   Maifreda, Germano, *From* Oikonomia *to Political Economy. Constructing Economic Knowledge from the Renaissance to the Scientific Revolution* (Farnham: Ashgate, 2012), p. 2.

and political intrigue. Dealing with the bureaucracy of Istanbul was, as Aymes argues, an exercise in uncertainty management. The state's ability to control the Anatolian economy was often undercut not just by machinations at the centre or political manoeuvrings in the provinces, but also by famine, plague, such as the devastating rinderpest which attacked cattle, buffalo and oxen in the nineteenth century,[74] and other natural disasters. The constant flooding caused by lakes, swamps and overflowing rivers in the regions of Samsun and İzmit forced peasants to abandon villages, left much fertile and productive agricultural land under water and reduced towns and villages in the area to ruins in the 1880s.[75]

The destitution and desperation of the population in the *vilayet* of Konya struck the new governor, Said Paşa, forcefully when he took up his post in 1881. The people from the villages round Ereğli petitioned him about their state of total destitution which had reduced them to eating grass. Despite this, they were still being crushed by demands for tax.[76] Said Paşa was faced with the same situation when he visited the town of Karapınar, a place largely in ruins and one which the governor heartedly disliked. Unable to sell their sheep, people were therefore unable to pay the sheep tax. Added to this was the plague of locusts which had reduced most people there that year to surviving on a diet of grass.[77] Indeed the whole of the *vilayet* of Konya had been stricken. Locusts had "stripped and swept away" the agricultural production of the region, leaving it facing a major famine. In Said Paşa's bleak assessment, the population had scattered and the *vilayet* lay in ruins.[78] This "curse of locusts" had seen these insects descend on the *vilayet* in terrifying numbers. The bleakness of the position of the population was summed up by Said Paşa: poverty and lack of money reduced the population to eating grass, the state incurred crippling expenses conscripting auxiliary soldiers (another crushing burden on the population Said Paşa had noted),[79] and the area was struck by "the truly terrible

74 Ak, Mehmet, "Osmanlı Devleti'nde Veba-i Bakarî (Sığır Vebası)", *Ankara Üniversitesi Osmanlı Tarihi Araştırma ve Uygulama Merkezi Dergisi*, 39 (2016), 215–40. Ainsworth refers to the severe epidemics among cattle near Ankara and one devastating flocks in the same region in 1840, Ainsworth, *Travels and Researches*, I, pp. 136–7, 142.

75 Dincer, "Osmanlı Vezirlerinden Hasan Fehmi Paşa'nın Anadolu'nun Bayındırlık İşlerine Dair Hazırladığı Lâyiha", p. 9, 26 Cemaziülahır 1297/24 Mayıs 1296 (5 June 1880).

76 Işık, Ali (ed.), *Vali İngiliz Sait Paşa'nın Konya Günleri* (Konya and Istanbul: Çizgi Kitabevi, 2018), p. 31.

77 Işık, *Vali İngiliz Sait Paşa'nın Konya Günleri*, p. 34.

78 Işık, *Vali İngiliz Sait Paşa'nın Konya Günleri*, p. 41.

79 Işık, *Vali İngiliz Sait Paşa'nın Konya Günleri*, p. 35.

and destructive scourge of locusts". "All this", he concluded, "happened to our province this year".[80]

The thin line for many in Anatolia between survival and destitution or, as Suraiya Faroqhi puts it referring to the sixteenth century, the "precariousness of peasant living",[81] was evident in the verses of the nineteenth-century poet from Erzurum, Noksani, who wrote of the uncertainty of fate and how everything could be overturned in an instant:

> Do not say God's land is my property
> Do not say I have a right in harvests and barns
> Do not say I am strong and sturdy and having backing
> There exists a force which will knock a man to the ground
> Even if you fall into penury do not say I am poor
> I know what is the end of wealth.[82]

---

80   Işık, *Vali İngiliz Sait Paşa'nın Konya Günleri*, pp. 47–8.

81   Faroqhi, "Vakıf administration in sixteenth century Konya", p. 168.

82   Güney, Eflatun Cem (ed.), *Halk Şiiri Antolojisi. Başlangıçtan Bugüne Türk Şiiri: 2* (Istanbul: Varlık Yayınları, 1959), p. 131.

CHAPTER 2

Agricultural Production in Central Anatolia in the Classical Ottoman Period: an Investigation into the *Sancak*s of Aksaray, Ankara, Bozok and Çankırı

Mehmet Öz

The basic means of production in the agricultural economy in the context of the *miri* land regime in the classical Ottoman period was, in the areas in which the *timar* system was in operation, the plough drawn by a pair of oxen. Apart from changes in the construction of the plough, made from wood or iron, there was, in a climatic environment which favoured dry farming and the sowing of wheat or barley, no major innovation in agricultural technology until the period of mechanisation. The basic unit of labour in this traditional agricultural setting was the peasant family, symbolised by its male head.[1] The Ottoman *miri-tapulu* land system, whose origins stretch back to ancient Iran and the late period of the Roman empire and which relied on peasant production based on the labour of a pair of oxen and a family, was described by Halil İnalcık as the "çift-hane system". In this system the unit of production was the combination of family labour, a pair of oxen and the land worked by both, which therefore constituted a financial unit.[2] In Anatolia and Rumeli, particularly in the classical period, agricultural activity was to a great extent carried out within the framework of this system. Peasants were divided into categories such as *çift*, *nim-çift*, *bennak*, *caba* or *mücerred* according to the size of the land they worked and/or their marital status, and they paid *çift resmi* and other taxes, which differed according to region, on the basis of these categories.[3]

---

1 İnalcık, Halil, "Köy, Köylü ve İmparatorluk", in *V. Milletlerarası Türkiye Sosyal ve İktisat Tarihi Kongresi-Tebliğler (İstanbul, 21–25 Ağustos 1989)* (Ankara: Türk Tarih Kurumu Basımevi, 1990), pp. 1–11. For an annotated version of this article see İnalcık, Halil, *Osmanlı İmparatorluğu Toplum ve Ekonomi* (Istanbul: Eren Yayıncılık, 1993), pp. 1–14, in particular p. 2.

2 İnalcık, "Köy, Köylü ve İmparatorluk", pp. 2–3.

3 For detailed information on this subject see İnalcık, Halil, "Osmanlılarda Raiyyet Rüsumu", *Belleten*, 23/92 (1959), 575–610. Those whose land was half the size of a *çift* (*nim-çift*) paid half the *çift resmi*, those whose land was less than half a *çift* paid the (*ekinlü*) *bennak resmi*. While *caba* usually meant a married, landless head of a household (*hane*), in some places such as Karaman and İç-il, it meant an unmarried male who was able to secure his own livelihood. Of those designated as bachelors (*mücerred*), some paid taxes, while others in some *sancak*s did not. Non-Muslim *reaya* paid a standard tax called *ispençe* in place of the *resm-i çift/çift resmi*.

According to Ömer Lütfi Barkan, one of the founding fathers of Ottoman economic history, much of the land of the empire, in accordance with the requirements of the *miri* land system, was divided into individual units, *reaya çiftlik*s or *baştine*s among the Slavs in the Balkan territories, which were calculated on the basis of a size sufficient for an independent peasant to work and the specific conditions of each location. These *çiftlik*s were rented out for a cash payment called *tapu bedeli* to peasant farmers (*çiftçiler*) who were able to work them and were handed over under a "continuous and hereditary kind of rent" agreement. Various different methods were used to measure the *çiftlik*s. In some places the *çift* was the entire agricultural unit "of a size which could be ploughed and sown using a pair of oxen", half of which was called *öküzlük*. There are also examples of a *çiftlik* of a *reaya* being described as "a piece of land which is suitable for planting wheat in determined quantities". According to the official classification, which changed according to locality and soil quality, land was defined as *ala* (60 to 80 *dönüm*s for very good land), *evsat* (80–100 *dönüm*s for middle-quality land) and *edna* or *kıraç* (100–150 *dönüm*s for the lowest quality land), a *dönüm* being a piece of land close to 1,000 m^2, approximately 40 paces in length and breadth. Drawing attention to the rule "the *çift resmi* is tied to land and not the ox", Barkan argued, on the basis of indications in the *defter*s and the use in the *defter*s of the phrase "çift resmi", not "çiftlik", that although there was a connection between the *çiftlik* as popularly understood (a place whose size could be worked by a pair of oxen) and the true *çiftlik* which was measured in *dönüm*s, on more careful examination it became clear that the *çift resmi* was not just a tax levied on places that were worked by a pair of oxen but was a tax levied on a variety of obligations.[4]

It is known that the Ottomans placed great importance on the continuation of un-divided *çiftlik*s of the *reaya* which they regarded as the most suitable unit for production and subsistence economy. However, practice does not always fit theory. Research based on the data of the *tahrir defter*s shows that the *çiftlik*s began to break up most probably as a result of population pressure, in particular in the sixteenth century, and/or the policies adopted by the state to counter the damage caused by the drop in the *akçe* value of the *çift resmi* in

---

But in some *eyalet*s in Anatolia, non-Muslims, like Muslims, were earlier subject to *çift resmi* and only in the second half of the sixteenth century were they registered, like those in other places, for the *ispençe*. On this subject see Yediyıldız, Bahaeddin, *Ordu Kazası Sosyal Tarihi* (Ankara: Kültür ve Turizm Bakanlığı Yayınları, 1985), p. 155.

4   Barkan, Ö. Lütfi, "Çiftlik", *İslam Ansiklopedisi, İslâm Âlemî Coğrafya, Etnoğrafya ve Biyografya Lügatî*, ed. Adnan Adıvar *et al.* (Istanbul: Milli Eğitim Basımevi, 1940–1988), vol. III, pp. 392–7 (republished in Barkan, Ö. Lütfi, *Türkiye'de Toprak Meselesi* (Istanbul: Gözlem Yayınları, 1980), pp. 789–97).

the *kanunname*s, which paralleled the loss of value of the *akçe*.[5] Further, close investigation of *tahrir defter*s shows that a parcel of land that was registered to one person was in some circumstances worked by more than one family (usually brothers). As is made clear in clauses of the *sancak kanunname*s which explain the transfer of the land of someone who had died to his sons, such lands were used by brothers "müşa ve müşterek", "undivided and in common". For example, it is stated in the Çankırı (Kengiri) Kanunnamesi that:

> When a tax-payer recorded as *çift* (i.e. holding a *çift*) in the previous (old) register had died and three or four of his sons had remained, those who were married were registered as *caba*[6] In such a case when the *çift*-tax was levied, the *caba resmi* and the *yer resmi* [land-tax] should be combined, they [brothers] should pay the value in proportion of their shares of the taxes and work the land in common. *Reaya* who are *caba bennak* [with no recorded land] cannot be denied the land of their father.[7]

In the system whose main lines are explained above, freehold possession of agricultural land was *miri*, that is it belonged to the state. Villagers used this land with the status, in Barkan's phrase, of "hereditary and continuous leasehold[ers]", and paid tithes and taxes (*öşür* and *resim*) to the *dirlik*[8] owners, or in some places to *vakıf* (pious endowment) and *mülk* (freehold ownership) owners. A fine, called *çiftbozan akçesi*, was taken from those who left land uncultivated for three years in a row. Although how much land was sown every year is not very clear, at least there are some *kanunname* registers related to what quantity it was necessary to plant.[9]

---

5 The findings concerning this in the research of M.A. Cook on Aydın, Hamid and Rum (Tokat and its surroundings) have generally been corroborated in later research. See Yediyıldız, *Ordu Kazası Sosyal Tarihi*, p. 71; Emecen, Feridun M., *XVI. Asırda Manisa Kazası* (Ankara: Türk Tarih Kurumu Basımevi, 1989), p. 231; Ünal, M. Ali, *XVI. Yüzyılda Harput Sancağı (1518–1566)* (Ankara: Türk Tarih Kurumu Basımevi, 1989), p. 93; Öz, Mehmet, *XV–XVI. Yüzyıllarda Canik Sancağı* (Ankara: Türk Tarih Kurumu Basımevi, 1999), pp. 48–52.

6 In these areas *caba* (*bennak*) meant a married man with no registered land. In practice when a man with a full or half *çift* or less than half a *çift* died, his sons took over his land together, while the land was registered in the name of only one of them (mostly the unmarried son), while other sons were recorded as *caba*.

7 Kankal, Ahmet, *XVI. Yüzyılda Çankırı* (Çankırı: Çankırı Belediyesi Kültür Yayınları, 2009), p. 221.

8 A *dirlik* was an assignment by the state of a salary or an income from land; the assignment of a landholding such as a *timar*; or income from a *has, timar* or *zeamet*.

9 Barkan, Ö. Lütfi, "Osmanlı İmparatorluğu'nda Çiftçi Sınıfların Hukukî Statüsü", *Ülkü Mecmuası*, 9/49, 50, 53; 10/56, 58, 59 (1937) (republished in Barkan, *Türkiye'de Toprak Meselesi*, pp. 725–88). As an example of registers on this subject see *Türkiye'de Toprak Meselesi*, p. 751:

I have chosen to begin with this introduction because the main focus of the chapter is agriculture produce and production in central Anatolia in the classical Ottoman period. In earlier work using data from research on the structure of production in the Ottoman empire in general and on rural Anatolia in particular based on the *tahrir defter*s, I have tried to demonstrate the tax burden, living conditions and the share of agricultural produce in general production. Here I would like to develop further my earlier findings, or rather to re-examine them in a more restricted environment. To do this I will try here to consider agricultural production, the rural economy and the living conditions of the peasants in various *sancak*s in central Anatolia.

The main question which my research will investigate is the extent to which, relying heavily on the data in the *tahrir*s, the view that agricultural production was based on wheat and barley production is accurate. It is the case that before industrialisation, a great deal of agricultural activity in agricultural societies was related to grain. However, when geography, climatic conditions and various social and state factors are taken into account, it becomes clear that there was a more diverse array of production. Taking into account previous research conducted on various regions of Anatolia, I will analyse in this chapter various *sancak*s in central Anatolia, which have similar geographical characteristics. Our basic hypothesis is that the structure of production in this region was more varied than expected and that regional differences further enriched this diversification of production. I shall also consider whether the areas of central Anatolia, which were unaffected by war, represented an environment of relative stability over a long period in the classical era. Such research clearly requires an analysis of a range of different factors including climatic conditions, natural disasters and insect infestation which existed in the period. By carefully considering the nature of the data, I suggest that it should be possible to produce a picture of the position in the region at least before the very well-known Celali revolts which affected Anatolia in the last years of the sixteenth century.

In this context, I shall give an analytical description of the taxes on agricultural production as well as on animal husbandry, and examine the connection between the capacity of agricultural production in the areas under

---

"Ve bir raiyyetin elinde çiftliği olsa Bursa müddü ile dört müd tohum ekmek her yıl borcudur. Hiç ekmediği yılda elli akçe, ekmediği için alına ve alâhâzâ amma dört tohum, tamam ekdikden sonra dayri san'at işler ise dahi taarruz olunmaya". It is expressed in another way in the Karaman Kanunnamesi thus (*Türkiye'de Toprak Meselesi*, pp. 751–2): "Bir çiftlik yer tasarruf eden raiyete Bursa müddü ile yılda dört müd tohum ekmek lazımdır. Ekmedüğü yılda elli akçe vere. Amma Karaman müddü ile bir müd ekse yirmi beş akçe vere ve alâhâzâ vesair umuruna dahlolunmaz ve eğer bir raiyyete âfet yetişüb bîmecâl olub çiftin bıraksa sipahisi ol yeri ahara verüb andan resm-i bennak alına resm-i çift taleb olunmaya".

consideration and the population, in other words between household (*hane*) and individual production. My hypothesis here is that there was agricultural production at a subsistence level in the areas examined and that there was no significant change in this structure over the century. While taking full account of the difficulties of using *tahrir* data for economic historical research and the problems that stem from the nature of this data, I shall also consider whether in this region, where a significant sector of the population was nomadic, the average production of village families, based largely on the cultivation of grain, allowed them to live above a subsistence level.

I shall not enter into a discussion of the nature of *tahrir* data and its reliability from a methodological point of view.[10] I shall confine myself to saying only this. Some studies, for example Erdoğan's unpublished thesis on Ankara, do not provide us with the quantitative data found in the tax-registers but convert tithe (*öşür*) figures into estimated production figures. Here, on the basis of tax rates, I have converted these kinds of figures into the original tithe figure in order to compare the figures from different districts on a standard basis. This therefore ensures that the data can be compared. Whether the data gathered during the process of producing a *tahrir* register did or did not reflect the actual position is another matter. However, it seems feasible that in this research, by establishing the place of each product within the overall tax taken on all production and by basing assessments on this, it will be possible to construct a picture the outlines of which will be close to reality. A second calculation made by adding the tax taken on the rearing of goats and sheep and on apiculture, important components of the rural economy, should allow for a more reliable assessment of the extent to which wheat and barley production constituted a monoculture in the rural economy. It is possible to argue that in relation to the actual value of the income from arable and animal husbandry production, the assessment made by Bruce McGowan 50 years ago using the coefficients developed according to the FAO (United Nations Food

---

10   There is an extensive literature on this subject. I shall confine myself to referring here to only a few works: Barkan, Ö. Lütfi, "Türkiye'de İmparatorluk Devirlerinin Büyük Nüfus ve Arazi Tahrirleri ve Hakana Mahsus İstatistik Defterleri I", *İstanbul Üniversitesi İktisat Fakültesi Mecmuası*, 2/1 (1940), 20–59; Barkan, Ö. Lütfi, "Türkiye'de İmparatorluk Devirlerinin Büyük Nüfus ve Arazi Tahrirleri ve Hakana Mahsus İstatistik Defterleri II", *İstanbul Üniversitesi İktisat Fakültesi Mecmuası*, 2/2 (1941), 214–47; İnalcık, Halil, "Giriş", *438 Numaralı Muhâsebe-i Vilâyet-i Anadolu Defteri, I* (Ankara: Devlet Arşivleri Genel Müdürlüğü Yayını, 1993), pp. 1–7; Öz, Mehmet, "Tahrir Defterlerinin Osmanlı Tarihi Araştırmalarında Kullanılması Hakkında Bazı Düşünceler", *Vakıflar Dergisi*, 22 (1991), 429–39. As an example of critical studies concerning the use of *tahrir* data see Heywood, Colin, "Between historical myth and 'mytho-history'. The limits of Ottoman history", *Byzantine and Modern Greek Studies*, 12 (1988), 315–45.

and Agriculture Organization) indexes[11] is more reliable. Historians, including Suraiya Faroqhi and myself, have used them in the past in this context, but my aim here is to be able to present a picture drawn up on the basis of tax values rather than such complicated calculations. What is important here is to be able to establish rough production patterns. For this I have converted the grain and other production in Ankara, Bozok and Çankırı, using the *akçe* values of the tithe (*öşür*) rates, as will be explained in more detail below, from the kilogramme weight into kilogrammes of economic wheat equivalent.[12] Of course such a calculation is of a very rough nature but as long as care is taken that the main production element is grain, this will not produce major errors in the results. Using the results of these calculations, I shall try to test whether or not the rise in population between the beginning of the sixteenth century and the third quarter of the century resulted in difficulties for the subsistence economy in three *sancak*s in particular (Ankara, Çankırı and Aksaray). There is detailed data for Bozok for the years 1556 and 1576.

Agricultural Production in Anatolia in the Sixteenth Century: Earlier Research

It can easily be argued that grains formed the majority of agricultural activity in the classical period. However, animal husbandry could represent a significant share in overall production in particular regions in which nomadic life dominated. In regions which specialised in cotton, rice, hemp, viticulture or other production or where such activities predominated, a clear diversification in production and, in some situations, a balanced structure of agricultural production could appear.[13] In the 2000s, I attempted to demonstrate by closer examination the place of crops cultivated in Ottoman territory within total agricultural production. Taking research undertaken earlier by Suraiya Faroqhi

---

11   McGowan, Bruce, "Food supply and taxation on the Middle Danube 1568–1579", *Archivum Ottomanicum*, 1, (1969), 139–96.

12   The *tahrir* value (as *akçe*) of wheat in the period of the *tahrir* was taken as the basis for converting the *akçe* values from kilogrammes into kilogrammes of economic wheat equivalent. For example, in Aksaray in 1500 the value of one *kile* (approximately 25 kg.) of wheat was four *akçe*. Thus, while one *müd* (the Istanbul *müd* was around 513 kg.) was 80 *akçe*, in 1584 this figure had risen to seven *akçe* per *kile*, that is 140 *akçe* for one *müd*. (Yörük, Doğan, *XVI. Yüzyılda Aksaray Sancağı (1500–1584)* (Konya: Tablet Kitabevi, 2005), pp. 154–5).

13   Öz, Mehmet, "XV–XVI. Yüzyıllar Anadolusu'nda Tarım ve Tarım Ürünleri", *Kebikeç-İnsan Bilimleri Dergisi*, 23 (2007), p. 122.

and Huri İslamoğlu-İnan in 1979 as an example[14] and using later research on various specific *sancak*s, I presented a more general assessment. I was careful that the *sancak*s I chose were from different regions of Anatolia.

In the research which Faroqhi and İslamoğlu did on agricultural production trends in Anatolia in the sixteenth century, they tried to establish the place of agricultural crops within total production by taking *nahiye*s (administrative sub-districts) which represented different agricultural areas in Anatolia. Putting to one side the difficulties of data in the *tahrir defter*s as the main source for such research, the results are worthy of note. It emerges that in the *nahiye*s on the Anatolian plateau, grain was a virtual monoculture accounting for 90 per cent or more of total production and that the remaining production probably came from animal husbandry. The appearance of considerable hemp production in the district of Ünye stemmed from its specialisation in this cultivation due to its position supplying the hemp needs of the dockyards.[15] Similarly, Bigadiç presented differences in production with rice cultivation, Adana with cotton, Tire with rice and cotton and Uluborlu with opium poppies. Fruit and vine production predominated in Kasaba, Uluborlu, Güre, Bigadiç, Ünye, Göl, Tire and especially Zeytun and İznik. There was clear diversification in agricultural production in Tire, Bigadiç and to a certain degree in Ünye, İznik, Zeytun and Uluborlu. We see the most obvious example of this in Tire and Bigadiç.

In my earlier research on this subject, I evaluated two data sets for the first and second half of the sixteenth century.[16] Here I have taken the table that was made using data mostly from the second half of the sixteenth century. For the purpose of comparison, I have constructed a table adding data from the *kaza*s (districts) of Maraş and Denizli in addition to the *sancak*s for which I gave data in another of my earlier works, and data from the *sancak* of Bozok in 1556 and 1576.[17] Using material from the doctoral thesis of Yılmaz Kurt,

---

14   İslamoğlu, Huri and Suraiya Faroqhi, "Crop patterns and agricultural production trends in sixteenth-century Anatolia", *Review (Fernand Braudel Center)*, 2/3 (1979), 401–36.

15   Bostan, İdris, *Osmanlı Bahriye Teşkilatı: XVII. Yüzyılda Tersâne-i Âmire* (Ankara: Türk Tarih Kurumu Basımevi, 1992), pp. 137–42; Öz, *XV–XVI. Yüzyıllarda Canik Sancağı*, pp. 96–7.

16   For my earlier work on agricultural production and productivity see Öz, Mehmet, "Osmanlı Klasik Döneminde Tarım", *Osmanlı*, vol. 3, ed. Güler Eren, Kemal Çiçek and Cem Oğuz (Ankara: Yeni Türkiye Yayınları, 1999), pp. 66–73; Öz, "XV–XVI. Yüzyıllar Anadolusu'nda", 111–28. For my articles on the subjects of tax load and productivity see Öz, Mehmet, "XVI. Yüzyıl Anadolu'sunda Köylülerin Vergi Yükü ve Geçim Durumu Hakkında Bir Araştırma", *Osmanlı Araştırmaları – The Journal of Ottoman Studies*, 17 (1997), 77–90; Öz, Mehmet, "XVI. Yüzyılda Anadolu'da Tarımda Verimlilik Problemi", *XIII. Türk Tarih Kongresi – Ankara, 4–8 Ekim 1999 – Kongreye Sunulan Bildiriler*, vol. 3/3 (Ankara: Türk Tarih Kurumu Basımevi, 2002), pp. 1643–51.

17   Öz, "XV–XVI. Yüzyıllar Anadolusu'nda", p. 120.

I have also added into this table data from 1572 related to Adana, which formed part of the Faroqhi and İslamoğlu study.[18] Even if there are some differences between the two sets of data, the picture which emerges is basically very similar. These tables were constructed by collecting the tax values (as *akçe*) which were taken from the *defter*s of agricultural produce. By taking the *tahrir* values as the base in places where it was possible, the quantities of tithe (*öşür*) which were given as a measurement of weight only were converted into *akçe*s. Thus, it was possible to compare all the regions. The ratio of an individual crop was calculated within the total production which was obtained. For grain, it is feasible to make a comparison on the basis not of *akçe* value but of quantity, but I consider the most suitable criteria for making a comparison for all production to be the *tahrir* values. Such a calculation automatically shows the ratio of wheat, which has the highest *tahrir* value, as being higher than it was, particularly within grain production. In order to compensate for this, it is possible to calculate using other amounts of value (*müd, kile*) for wheat, barley, millet and other grain.[19] I shall not pursue this here. Let it suffice to say that the ratio between the *tahrir* values of wheat and those of barley and millet was roughly ten to eight.[20]

One point that must be stressed is that since some crops were produced in small quantities and are subsumed into the "other" category and some are not given because, due to the quantity being too small, it is not possible to convert them into *akçe*, the variety of agricultural production becomes much more diversified than it appears here. Further, if one takes into account both that legumes (lentils, chickpeas, broad-beans, black-eyed beans), which appeared

---

18   Kurt, Yılmaz, "XVI. Yüzyıl Adana Tarihi", Ph.D. Dissertation, Hacettepe Üniversitesi, 2002.

19   As is known, one *müd* was 20 *kile* and the weight of a *kile* and in consequence its kilogramme equivalent varied from *sancak* to *sancak*. For example, one Istanbul *kile* was 25.656 kg. of wheat, 22.25 kg. of barley and 12.828 kg. of rice. Therefore one *müd* of wheat in places where the Istanbul *kile* was in use was 513.12 kg. and one *müd* of barley was 445 kg. See Hinz, Walter, *İslâm'da Ölçü Sistemleri*, trans. Acar Sevim (Istanbul: Marmara Üniversitesi Yayınları, 1990), pp. 51, 57–8. For a detailed study of Ottoman units of weight in different periods and different regions see İnalcık, Halil, "Introduction to Ottoman metrology", *Turcica*, 15 (1983), 311–42. For example, the *vukiye* equivalent of one *kile* was different in different *kaza*s in the same *eyalet* and as a result of complaints was fixed by a *ferman* at one *kile* to 30 *okka* (*vukiye*), İnalcık, "Introduction to Ottoman metrology", p. 330. See also Koç, Yunus, "Zirai Tarih Araştırmalarında Ölçü Tartı Birimleri Sorunu: Bursa Müddü Örneği", *Uluslararası Kuruluşunun 700. Yıl Dönümünde Bütün Yönleriyle Osmanlı Devleti Kongresi, Konya, 7–9 Nisan 1999* (Konya: Selçuk Üniversitesi Basımevi, 2000), pp. 541–6.

20   For example, in the *eyalet* of Rum in the 1570s while the value of one *müd* of wheat was 120 *akçe*, one *müd* of barley or millet was 100 *akçe*. In other words, one *kile* of wheat was six *akçe*, one *kile* of barley was five. See Öz, *XV–XVI. Yüzyıllarda Canik Sancağı*, p. 88.

under the category "other", and fruit and vegetables, which were included among vineyards, orchards and gardens (grapes, onions, garlic, vegetables, pears, pomegranates, walnuts and fruit in general), represented a very wide range of production, and that fruit and vegetable production which was not sold on the market was not taxed in the Ottoman system and thus not entered in the registers, it becomes evident that they were more significant in production and consumption than shown here. The figures which I give for the minimum subsistence level of peasants basically reflect the production which I estimate based on the taxes registered. Therefore, fruit and vegetables which peasant families grew for their own needs and which were not intended for the market and the production they obtained from their cattle do not appear here. It is necessary to keep this in mind when analysing the production figures per household (*hane*) and per capita which are given below.

TABLE 2.1 Percentages of agricultural production in certain *nahiye*s in the second half of the sixteenth century[a]

Nahiye	Date	Wheat	Barley	Other grain	Vineyard and orchard fruit	Cotton	Flax-hemp	Sesame	Rice
Çorum	1576	58	33	0.8	7		0.3		
Koçhisar	1584	56.5	39		4				
Melegübü	1584	53	40		7				
Kasaba	1559–60	56	18	3	13.5	9.5			
Mindaval	1569–70	63.5	33	0.16	2.5	1.2			
Kafirni	1576–7	59	33	1					
Uluborlu	c. 1566	54	26.5		11			9	
Güre	1570–1	60	19	12	9				
Bigadiç	1573–4	26.5	15.5	25	9	2.5		5	17
Ünye	1576–7	35.7	26	8.5	14.7		13.7		0.8
Adana	1572–3	27.5	30.5	1.5	2	36		2.5	
Zeytun	1563–4	54	15	1.5	29	1			
Tire	1575–6	26	26	12.5	11.5	15.5	3.5	0.05	3
İznik	Ahmed I	33.5	16.5	24	21	1			5

a The *nahiye* of Koçhisar was in Karaman, that of Melegübü was in Niğde, Mindaval in Şarki (Şebin) Karahisar, Kafirni in Tokat, Uluborlu in Hamid, Bigadiç in Karesi, Tire in Aydın, Göl in the *sancak* of Kastamonu, Kasaba in Manisa, Ünye in Canik, Zeytun in Maraş and Güre in Kütahya. See İslamoğlu and Faroqhi, "Crop patterns and agricultural production trends in sixteenth-century Anatolia", pp. 418–19.

TABLE 2.2   Percentages of agricultural production in various *sancak*s and *kaza*s in the sixteenth century

Sancak/Kaza	Date	Wheat	Barley	Millet and other grain	Vineyard and orchard fruit and vegetables	Rice	Cotton	Flax-hemp	Other	Total
Bolu	1519	50.3	18.7	20.9	7.6			1.7	0.8	100
	1568	39.1	23.7	23.8	9.9			1.4	2.1	100
Canik	1485	47.9	27.9		3	15		6	0.2	100
	1576	46	30	6	4	4		8	2	100
Harput	1518	56.1	18.1	5.7	9.8		9.1		1.2	100
	1566	55	22,6	0.2	6.9		13.9		1.4	100
Karahisar-ı Şarki	1547	60.7	32.6	0.1	5.9		0.2	0.5		100
	1569	59.3	34.3	0.2	4.2		1.3	0.7		100
Manisa	1531	49.5	25	1.7	7.9	8.8	5.7	0.4	1	100
	1575	52.1	26.5	4.4	4.9	6.7	3.6	0.3	1.5	100
Tokat	1520	61	29.8		8.6		0.2	0.4		100
	1574	56.5	31.4	0.1	9.4		1.4	0.8	0.4	100
Bozok	1576	60.78	30.07		0.96		0.27	0.1	7.82	100
Maraş Kazası	1563	53	24.5	0.3	9.7	7	5.1		0.4	100
Lazıkiye (Denizli)	1571	40.5	15.7	1.9	11.4	9.9	20.4		0.2	100
Adana	1572	30.5	27.6	0.2	4.3	1.1	34.3		2	100

Notes on the tables[a]

1. The rates have been worked out on *akçe* values. In the tables, when *kile* or other units were used, the *akçe* value was calculated by multiplying by the *tahrir* values.

---

a   Sources for the table are: Taş, Kenan Ziya, "Tapu Tahrir Defterlerine Göre 16. Yüzyılda Bolu Sancağı", Ph.D. Dissertation, Ankara Üniversitesi, 1993, pp. 142–52; Öz, *XV–XVI. Yüzyıllarda Canik Sancağı*, pp. 94–5; Ünal, *XVI. Yüzyılda Harput Sancağı (1518–1566)*, pp. 164–6; Acun, Fatma, *Karahisar-ı Şarkî ve Koyulhisar Kazaları Örneğinde Osmanlı Taşra İdaresi (1485–1569)* (Ankara: Türk Tarih Kurumu Basımevi, 2006), p. 124; Emecen, *XVI. Asırda Manisa Kazası*, pp. 242–61; Şimşirgil, Ahmet, "Osmanlı Taşra Teşkilâtında Tokat (1455–1574)", Ph.D. Dissertation, Marmara Üniversitesi, 1990, pp. 301–9; Gökçe, Turan, *XVI. ve XVII. Yüzyıllarda Lâzıkıyye (Denizli) Kazâsı* (Ankara: Türk Tarih Kurumu Basımevi, 2000), pp. 354–76; Solak, İbrahim, *XVI. Asırda Maraş Kazâsı (1526–1563)* (Ankara: Akçağ Yayınları, 2004), pp. 142–54; Kurt, "XVI. Yüzyıl Adana Tarihi", pp. 213–15; Özdeğer, Mehtap, *15–16. Yüzyıl Arşiv Kaynaklarına Göre Uşak Kazasının Sosyal ve Ekonomik Tarihi* (Istanbul: Filiz Kitabevi, 2001), pp. 299–311. For Bozok, I used the detailed registers of TD 315 in the Tapu-Tahrir section of BOA (State Archives of Turkey, Istanbul)) and TD 31 in the General Directorate of the Land Registry in Ankara. I thank my colleague Dr. Yunus Koç (Hacettepe University) with whom I deciphered and classified the data from these registers.

2. The "other" category in Canik in 1576 was made up to a large extent of *lazot* (corn), vegetables, legumes, and small quantities of olives and cotton. The "other" category in Tokat was legumes. In Manisa and Denizli, because the value of the *akçe* was not given, the percentage of cotton is not provided. In Manisa the "other" category consisted of legumes and there were raw materials for industrial use included among flax and hemp. In Bozok 4.4 per cent of the "other" category was made up of fodder, hay, common vetch and vetch with a very small amount of legumes. The remaining part is in general made up of vineyard and orchard products, hemp, hay and other produce. In Maraş the ratio of sesame was 0.1 per cent and the majority of the vineyard and orchard category was made up of vineyard produce (a total of seven per cent). In Adana the "other" category was sesame, and in Denizli it was legumes. In Lazikiye 3,115 *kıye* of sesame income, the *akçe* value of which was not given, was not included in the calculation. In Uşak the "other" category included legumes, flax, cotton, acorns, sumac and black cumin (the largest part being legumes).

3. It was established that there was 82,779 *kıye* of cotton in Lazikiye. I based the calculation of its value in *akçe* on the fact that one *men* of cotton was 7.2 *akçe*[b] and that one *men* equalled six *okka/kıye*. This produced the result that one *okka* of cotton was 1.2 *akçe*. The tax value of cotton was calculated according to this measure.

---

b   Solak, *XVI. Asırda Maraş Kazâsı (1526–1563)*, p. 149.

Table 2.2 is in line with the analysis done partly on a smaller amount of data by Faroqhi and İslamoğlu. It establishes that in *sancak*s or *kaza*s where crops such as cotton or rice were not dominant, 80 to 90 per cent of the agricultural crops were wheat, barley, millet and other grain. It shows that in places like Çorum, Karahisar-ı Şarki, including Mindaval, and Bozok, grain, in particular wheat and barley, formed a monoculture. It must of course always be kept in mind that animal husbandry is not included in this table. In areas such as Bozok, where a semi-nomadic life style was still significant, this is particularly important. It is important to remember that in Karahisar-ı Şarki alum production was an important economic activity. On the other hand, it is also necessary to note that in the regions of Bolu, Harput, Manisa, Denizli, Tokat and Maraş, vineyard and orchard, vegetable, garden and fruit production reached considerable levels. Karahisar-ı Şarki was significant for viticulture, and Adana for summer fruit. The agricultural picture is affected to a certain extent both by production of cotton and of vineyard and orchard fruit in Adana, Manisa and Denizli, while the production of hemp for the docks in the eastern area of Canik is noteworthy.

It is possible to add Uşak as a new example from western Anatolia to the *sancak*s and *kaza*s which I examined in earlier work. When the taxes for sheep and goats and beehives are added into the calculation, the tax on produce other than wheat and barley in the reign of Bayezid II was around 30 per cent. This figure had fallen in the 1570s to 16 per cent. In other words, the increase in the percentage of wheat and barley taxes shows that a monoculture had been established. This is, of course, a finding that can been questioned.

TABLE 2.3   Distribution of agricultural taxes in the kaza of Uşak[a]

Period	Wheat	Barley	Oats, millet and other grain	Vineyards, gardens, fruit, market gardens	Cotton, flax, acorns, sumac	Legumes	Total
Bayezid II- akçe	63135	28227	6523	7146	1378	1760	108169
Percentage	58.4	26.1	6	6.6	1.3	1.6	100
1570-akçe	244933	97740	2747	19781	1367	31690	398258
Percentage	61.5	24.5	0.7	5	0.3	8	100

a   Sources: Özdeğer, *15–16. Yüzyıl Arşiv Kaynaklarına Göre Uşak Kazasının Sosyal ve Ekonomik Tarihi*, pp. 298–310. In the reign of Bayezid II the *ağnam resmi* was 19,721 *akçe* and in 1570 it was 10,678; the *kovan* tax was 380 *akçe* and 1,402 *akçe* respectively (p. 312).

Keeping in mind the importance of animal husbandry in the economy of various regions where animal husbandry and nomadic life were dominant, the tables and figures given above show clearly that in many *sancak*s in Anatolia in the sixteenth century wheat production made up half and sometimes even more than half of the total agricultural production. In areas where there was a specialisation in a particular activity such as rice sowing, cotton production and viticulture, this figure fell to 25 to 30 per cent. However, it shows that wheat production, together with barley, millet and other grains, was the most important element. When we look at Anatolia, we can see that rice in particular especially in the regions of Tosya-Boyabat,[21] cotton in the regions of Adana, Manisa, Harput and other areas, hemp around Ünye-Terme and viticulture in very many areas had a significant importance in the local economy.[22]

Wheat and other grain provided both the basic foodstuff for people and fodder (barley, straw, etc.) for animals which were very important given the needs of transportation and the military. It is clear that in the Ottoman period wheat production dominated agricultural activity. On the other hand, the increase in population or various developments which opened the way for wheat being unable to meet demand, resulted in the fall in production of wheat and the rise

21   İnalcık, Halil, "Rice cultivation and the *çeltükçi reaya* system in the Ottoman empire", *Turcica*, 14 (1982), 69–141.

22   For this subject see Kurt's research on Adana, Emecen on Manisa and Ünal on Harput.

in importance of the planting of millet and other grain which were of lower quality but more productive per *dönüm*.[23]

In some areas millet, which earlier appeared rarely in the *tahrir defter*s, was produced in significant quantities in the second half of the sixteenth century.[24] As the research of Tevfik Güran in his book *19. Yüzyılda Osmanlı Tarımı Üzerine Araştırmalar* (Research on Ottoman Agriculture in the Nineteenth Century) clearly shows, from the point of view of production per unit of seed, millet is at least three times more productive than wheat.[25] Thus, in the conditions created by population pressure in the second half of the sixteenth century, the increase in land given over to millet production appears reasonable. In this context, whether the word *gavers* which appears in the *tahrir defter*s of the sixteenth century means millet or maize is a subject of dispute. Noting that in many places in Turkey the word millet (*darı*) is used for maize (*mısır*), it is possible to suggest that they were synonymous. Even if what is meant here is a type of maize, the possibility of it being maize coming from America seems to me slight.[26] In any case, the fundamental point here is that this increase in production in the second half of the sixteenth century did not result by chance or from the method used for registration, but stemmed from the choice of a very highly productive crop as a result of population pressure.[27]

In Güran's work, agricultural policy in the nineteenth century and the beginning of the twentieth, the conditions of agriculture activity, agricultural productivity and other issues were examined in detail.[28] According to the findings for this period, when agricultural technology and productivity were not

---

23 For a classic work on wheat and the taxes levied on wheat in the classical Ottoman period see Güçer, Lütfi, *XVI ve XVII. Asırlarda Osmanlı İmparatorluğu'nda Hububat Meselesi ve Hububattan Alınan Vergiler* (Istanbul: İstanbul Üniversitesi Yayınları, 1964).

24 Öz, *XV–XVI. Yüzyıllarda Canik Sancağı*, pp. 94–5, 121.

25 Güran, Tevfik, *19. Yüzyılda Osmanlı Tarımı Üzerine Araştırmalar* (Istanbul: Eren Yayıncılık, 1998), p. 99. For an important and comprehensive study of agricultural productivity on the basis of the *tahrir defter*s see Venzke, Margaret L., "The Ottoman *tahrir defterleri* and agricultural productivity", *Osmanlı Araştırmaları – The Journal of Ottoman Studies*, 17 (1997), 1–61.

26 Emecen has given detailed information and, in my estimation, shed a great deal of light on this subject: Emecen, Feridun M., *Doğu Karadeniz'de İki Kıyı Kasabasının Tarihi Bulancak-Piraziz* (Istanbul: Kitabevi, 2005), pp. 148–9.

27 The issue of productivity in agricultural production and the seed to yield ratio has been discussed in the literature. See McGowan, "Food supply and taxation on the Middle Danube 1568–1579", pp. 167–8; Öz, *XV–XVI. Yüzyıllarda Canik Sancağı*, pp. 112–15; Güran, *19. Yüzyılda Osmanlı Tarımı Üzerine Araştırmalar*, p. 99. See also Nagata, Yuzo, *Tarihte Âyânlar-Karaosmanoğulları Üzerinde Bir İnceleme* (Ankara: Türk Tarih Kurumu Basımevi, 1997), pp. 122–4.

28 Güran, *19. Yüzyılda Osmanlı Tarımı Üzerine Araştırmalar*.

much changed from the sixteenth century, around 85 per cent of sown land in Anatolia was given over to grain, 2.7 per cent to legumes, five per cent to raw materials for industrial use and 7.6 per cent to vines. The share in total production of grain was 60 per cent, vineyards and gardens, ten per cent and animal products, 23 per cent.[29] In comparison with my findings, leaving aside animal products, grain had a 72 per cent share of total production and vineyards and orchards 14 to 15 per cent. In the period 1907 to 1909, the production per unit of seed was 4.8 per cent for wheat in Rumeli, 5.5 per cent in Anatolia, while millet was around 18 per cent.[30]

One of the researchers who has recently drawn attention to Ottoman agricultural history is Kayhan Orbay. In his article, Orbay, who has examined productivity in agriculture in the Ottoman period and analytically assessed existing research, notes the limits and weaknesses of our data on this subject, stating that the FAO multipliers used by McGowan – and indicated here in my calculations – do not produce consistent results in investigations made at a micro level when converting agricultural crops into wheat equivalents, and demonstrates that the *vakıf* account books and in particular the *müfredat defter*s include important data for this subject.[31]

Before moving on to the *sancak*s of central Anatolia which I have examined in the context of this research, one last point must be made. For comparative purposes, I have included a table showing the situation in the *sancak* of Bolu, which was bordered by Ankara and Çankırı. When taking only agricultural crops, it shows that in the *sancak* of Bolu grain represented 90 per cent of the total tax income in 1519, and 86 per cent in 1568. It is also striking that the percentage in 1569 for vineyard, orchard, fruit and vegetable production for the market was around ten per cent.

Agricultural Production in Central Anatolia

In this section I shall try to analyse the composition of the agricultural production of four *sancak*s on the central Anatolian plateau using *tahrir* data. First I shall briefly describe the geographical locations and characteristics of these *sancak*s.

Aksaray, which was one of the *sancak*s of the Karaman *beylerbeyliği* and corresponds approximately to the province which today carries the same name,

---

29   Güran, *19. Yüzyılda Osmanlı Tarımı Üzerine Araştırmalar*, pp. 77–8.
30   Güran, *19. Yüzyılda Osmanlı Tarımı Üzerine Araştırmalar*, p. 99.
31   Orbay, Kayhan, "Osmanlı İmparatorluğu'nda Tarımsal Üretkenlik Üzerine Tetkikat ve Notlar", *Belleten*, 81/292 (2017), 787–856.

is a plateau in the form of a flat plain at around 1,000 metres above sea level. In the west the borders of the *sancak* are bounded by a lake, Tuz Gölü, in the north by the Kızılırmak river, in the south by the Obruk plateau and in the southeast by two mountains, Hasan Dağı and Melendiz Dağı. Grain cultivation is practiced today in this region, which is deficient in natural plant cover and water sources. For long the home of nomadic groups, there is also widespread animal husbandry.[32]

The *sancak* of Ankara, which was part of the Anadolu *beylerbeyliği*, corresponds partly to today's Ankara province. In 1523 the *sancak* consisted of the *nahiye*s of Çubuk, Murtazaabad, Yabanabad, Ayaş and Bacı, with Ankara as its centre, and in 1571 consisted of the *nahiye*s of Kasaba, Çubuk, Murtazaabad, Yabanabad, Ayaş and Bacı, and covered approximately what is today central Ankara, Elmadağ, Çubuk, Mürted, Ayaş, Kızılcahamam and Haymana.[33] The region extending as far as Beypazarı and Sivrihisar was part of the Ankara *sancak*, while areas such as Beypazarı and Nallıhan formed part of the *sancak* of Hüdavendigar. When we look at the physical geography of this *sancak*, it is important to note its location on the central Anatolian plateau and that, apart from the areas between the Kızılırmak and Sakarya rivers and along streams and rivers, it was deficient in natural plant cover. The area, which has an average height above sea level of 1,000 metres, is a transit zone between mountainous and wooded north Anatolia and the dry Konya plain. The plains of Haymana, Ankara, Çubuk and Mürted are located in today's Ankara province, of which around 27 per cent is mountainous.[34]

The *sancak* of Bozok, part of which fell under the Zülkadriye (Dulkadir) *beylerbeyliği* and part under the Rum *beylerbeyliği* at the beginning of the sixteenth century and which in the second half of the century was definitively attached to the Rum (later known as the Sivas) *beylerbeyliği*, covered approximately half of the northern part of Akdağmadeni and, apart from Çekerek, today's Yozgat, Şarkışla and Gemerek. Looking at the geographical structure of this area, in the region of Bozok (today's Yozgat), which is inside the arc of the Kızılırmak, there are mountains reaching a height of 2,235 metres and roughly 38 per cent of its surface area is covered by mountains, 11 per cent by plains and 51 per cent by plateaus. Bozok, which has plant cover consisting of sparsely vegetated plain and forests, has a continental climate with harsh winters.[35]

---

32   Yörük, *XVI. Yüzyılda Aksaray Sancağı (1500–1584)*, pp. 21–2.
33   Erdoğan [Özünlü], Emine, "Ankara'nın Bütüncül Tarihi Çerçevesinde Ankara Tahrir Defterleri'nin Analizi", Ph.D. Dissertation, Gazi Üniversitesi, 2004, pp. 26–8.
34   "Ankara", *Yurt Ansiklopedisi*, vol. I (Istanbul: Anadolu Yayıncılık, 1981), pp. 511–13.
35   For the *sancak* of Bozok see Koç, Yunus, *XVI. Yüzyılda Bir Osmanlı Sancağı'nın İskân ve Nüfus Yapısı* (Ankara: Kültür Bakanlığı Yayınları, 1988).

Of the *sancak*s of the Anadolu *beylerbeyliği*, the *sancak* of Kengiri (Çankırı) covers approximately today's Çankırı, Keskin (administratively part of Kırıkkale), Kalecik (administratively part of Ankara), Kargı (administratively part of Çorum), Tosya and Ilgaz (administratively part of Kastamonu). Rice production and viticulture along the Kızılırmak and a group of streams and creeks in the region, which has rugged terrain rising between 500 and 1,350 metres above sea level, is widespread. There are flat areas which can be counted as plains in the *nahiye*s of Çerkeş and Keskin.[36]

A brief comparison between arable agriculture and animal husbandry based on the data in the sixteenth-century *tahrir defter*s for these four *sancak*s (Aksaray, Ankara, Bozok and Çankırı) shows that:

TABLE 2.4A Distribution of agricultural taxes in the *sancak* of Aksaray (1500)[a]

	Grain	Vineyards	Orchards, vegetables, gardens, fruit	Flax	Total
Akçe	522905	20836	7513	430	551684
Percentage	94.8	3.8	1.3	0.1	100

a Source: Yörük, *XVI. Yüzyılda Aksaray Sancağı (1500–1584)*, pp. 155–70.

TABLE 2.4B Distribution of agricultural taxes in the *sancak* of Aksaray (1584)[a]

	Grain	Wheat	Barley	Vineyards	Orchards, vegetables, gardens, fruit	Flax	Total
Akçe	1688	546798	390861	37432	19681	600	997060
Percentage	0.17	54.8	39.2	3.7	2	0.13	100

a Note that the sheep tax collected from the *yüzdeciyan* [a nomadic group paying one sheep per 100 sheep] in 1584 is unclear. There are also entries for significant amounts of salt tax in the region (12,000 *akçe* in 1500 and 30,000 in 1584).

---

36   Kankal, *XVI. Yüzyılda Çankırı*, pp. 3–4.

TABLE 2.4C Distribution of arable and animal husbandry taxes in the *sancak* of Aksaray (1500)

	Grain	Vineyards	Orchards, vegetables, gardens, fruit	Flax	Beehives	Sheep-goats (*ganem*)	Total
Akçe	522905	20836	7513	430	7203	153077	711964
Percentage	73.4	2.9	1	0.2	1	21.5	

TABLE 2.4D Distribution of arable and animal husbandry taxes in the *sancak* of Aksaray (1584)

	Grain	Wheat	Barley	Vineyards	Orchards, vegetables, gardens, fruit	Flax	Bee-hives	Sheep-goats (*ganem*)	Total
Akçe	1688	546798	390861	37432	19681	600	22502	91745	1111307
Percentage	0.15	49.2	35.2	3.4	1.8	0.05	2	8.2	100

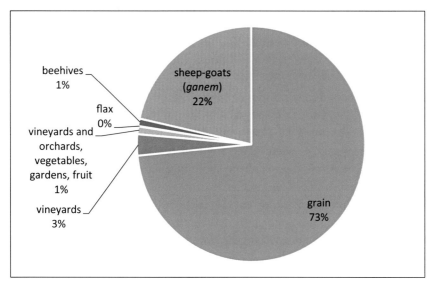

DIAGRAM 2.1A Distribution of arable and animal husbandry taxes in the *sancak* of Aksaray (1500)

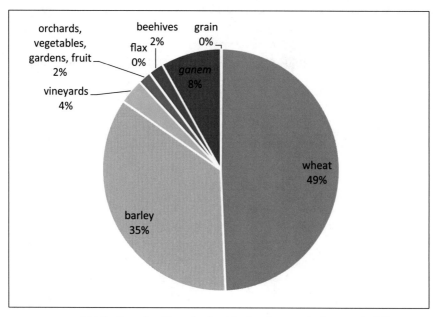

DIAGRAM 2.1B Distribution of arable and animal husbandry taxes in the *sancak* of Aksaray
(1584)

In the *sancak* of Aksaray of the total agricultural taxes in the 1500 *tahrir*,
around 95 per cent was made up of those levied on grain; there were also taxes
on vineyards, orchards, fruit, vegetables and flax. When, however, the taxes for
sheep and goats (*ağnam*) and beehives are included in the table, the share of
grain drops to 73 per cent. This shows that animal husbandry was a significant
activity in this region. When we come to 1584, we see that the share of grain in
agricultural production continues at 95 per cent but when animal husbandry
production is added, the share of grain falls to 84 per cent.

In 1584 in the *sancak* of Aksaray, of the 995,372 *akçe* total income from
agricultural crops, 55 per cent came from wheat, 39.3 per cent from barley,
3.76 per cent from tithes (*öşür*) on vineyards and about two per cent on orchard
produce, gardens, fruit and vegetables.[37] However, it is important to note that
salt production played an important role in the economy, to which sheep husbandry also contributed significantly.[38] When the fact that there was an important percentage of nomads within the population of the region is taken into
account, the table becomes more comprehensible. Around 1500 nomads made

37   Yörük, *XVI. Yüzyılda Aksaray Sancağı*, pp. 158–67.
38   Yörük, *XVI. Yüzyılda Aksaray Sancağı*, pp. 168–72.

up approximately 30 per centre of the total adult male tax-paying population, both urban and rural. Later this percentage gradually declined.[39]

TABLE 2.5A   Distribution of agricultural taxes of the *sancak* of Ankara

Date	Wheat	Barley	Total of vines, gardens and fruit	Total
1523-*akçe*	294399	163084	31240	488723
1523-Percentage	60	33	7	100
1571-*akçe*	723943	354116	121142	1199201
1571-Percentage	60.4	29.5	10.1	100

TABLE 2.5B   Distribution of arable and animal husbandry taxes of the *sancak* of Ankara (including summer pastures)[a]

Date	Wheat	Barley	Vines, gardens and fruit	Sheep-goats (*ağnam*) and beehives	Summer pastures	Total
1523-*akçe*	294399	163084	31240	42403	4311	535437
1523-Percentage	55	30.5	5.8	7.9	0.8	100
1571-*akçe*	723943	354116	121142	81694	20358	1301253
1571-Percentage	55.6	27.2	9.3	6.3	1.6	100

a   Source for tables 2.5a and 2.5b: Erdoğan [Özünlü], 'Ankara'nın Bütüncül Tarihi Çerçevesinde Ankara Tahrir Defterleri'nin Analizi', pp. 151–63. The beehive tax was 9,666 *akçe* and the *ağnam* tax was 32,737 in 1523 and the beehive tax was 9,495 and the *ağnam* tax was 72,199 in 1571. Emine Erdoğan converted the grain data into kilogrammes. In her work she calculated one *müd* of wheat as 513.12 kg. and one *müd* of barley as 445 kg. (p. 153). The *akçe* values for these figures were calculated according to the *tahrir* values in the relevant *tahrir* registers (one *müd* of wheat was 60 *akçe* in 1523 and 80 in 1571; one *müd* of barley was 50 in 1523 and 60 in 1571) (the tables between pp. 155 and 161). There is no figure for cotton production but, with the exception of Çubuk, there was cotton production in the other *kaza*s, the largest production being in Ayaş. It is striking that the tax on summer pastures, which was 4,311 *akçe* in 1523, had risen to 20,358 in 1571.

---

39   Yörük, *XVI. Yüzyılda Aksaray Sancağı*, p. 90, Tablo XXII. According to the table here, the percentage of nomads in 1584 had declined to nine per cent.

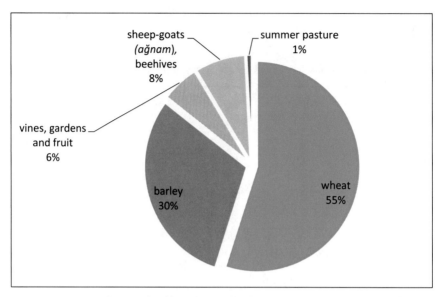

DIAGRAM 2.2A Distribution of arable and animal husbandry taxes in the *sancak* of Ankara (1523)

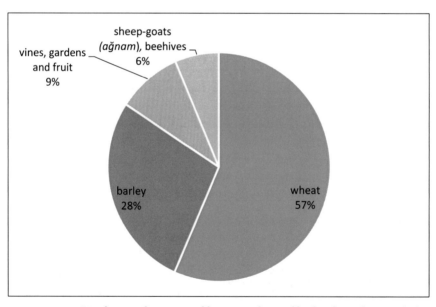

DIAGRAM 2.2B Distribution of taxes on arable crops and animal husbandry in the *sancak* of Ankara (1571)

The percentage of tax levied on grain in 1523 in the *sancak* of Ankara was 93 per cent when the *ağnam* tax is extracted and 85 per cent when it is included. When we look at the tax of the *sancak* of Ankara for 1572, the percentage of taxes levied on grain within the total agricultural taxes is 90 per cent, and when the taxes on animal husbandry are included, it is 84 per cent. When we look only at the tax on wheat, we see that it is 60 per cent of agricultural production. If the taxes on animal husbandry are included, this percentage then falls to 55. Thus, taxes which were levied on the grain production of the *sancak* of Ankara in both periods represented about 90 per cent of the total agricultural production. When the taxes on sheep and goats and on summer pastures are included, the percentage is still very high.

Research done on the *kaza* of Çubuk shows that of the tax registered (as *akçe*) on agricultural production on *miri* land in 1523, 95 per cent was from grain, three per cent from vegetables and fruit, one per cent from vineyards, and one per cent from legumes. The position for *miri* land in 1571 was more or less the same, with a small increase in vineyards and fruit and subsequent decrease in the grain ratio: 91 per cent for grain, five for fruit and vegetables, three for vineyards and one for legumes. Data exists for *vakıf* lands in the same period and here grain appears less dominant: 74 per cent for grain, 13 for fruit and vegetables, nine for legumes and four for vineyards. In the *kaza* in general, in 1571, 92 per cent of the tithe (*öşür*) came from grain on *miri* land and eight on *vakıf* land, 82.5 per cent was from vineyard and garden produce on *miri* land, and 17.5 on *vakıf* land.[40]

When all these figures are considered, on the basis of the registered taxes wheat and barley appear as a total monoculture in agricultural production but when animal husbandry is added, the picture changes, even if only by a very small amount.

In the *sancak* of Ankara one of the indicators of trade is without doubt the markets and the taxes levied there. Outside the city of Ankara, a total of 28,269 *akçe* in market taxes was collected in 1523 from five places made up of one market in Murtazaabad (Zir/İstanos), two in Çubuk (Çubukpazarı and Şorba), one in Bacı (Şabanözü) and one in Yabanabad (Güneysaray). A large part of the tax (21,969 *akçe*, including income from villages) was from the market of Zir. In 1571 this figure came to 35,600 but this time from 11 places. The market tax of

40   See Çınar, Hüseyin and Osman Gümüşçü, *Osmanlıdan Cumhuriyete Çubuk Kazası* (Ankara: Bilge Yayınevi, 2002), pp. 168, 174, 176.

Zir registered at 1,000 *akçe* is striking.[41] Thus it is clear that the figures here are far from reflecting the true value of the markets.

It would be difficult to accept that these figures reflected the commercial capacity of the arable agriculture and animal husbandry of Ankara in the sixteenth century, because, as is well-known, this region was very important for the production and export of mohair, as has been demonstrated by many researchers, in particular Özer Ergenç and Suraiya Faroqhi.[42]

It should be noted that apart from the entries in the table, there were other taxes including those for meadows, hay, wintering herds (*yatak*) and pasturage.

TABLE 2.6A Distribution of agricultural taxes in the *sancak* of Bozok (1556)[a]

	Grain	Wheat (*gendüm*)	Barley (*şair*)	Legumes	Beehives (*küvvare*)	Sheep-goats (*ağnam*)	Fruit-vines-orchards-gardens	Total
Total-*akçe*	718448	13616	5294	1177	3739	344155	5749	1092178
Percentage	65.8	1.2	0.5	0.2	0.3	31.5	0.5	100

a The data for the *sancak* of Bozok was collected from the *tahrir defter*s of Bozok and formulated into tables by Mehmet Öz and Yunus Koç.

TABLE 2.6B Distribution of agricultural taxes in the *sancak* of Bozok (1576)

	Wheat	Barley	Legumes	Vines, orchards, fruit, gardens	Cotton	Flax	Other	Total
Total-*akçe*	741238	374718	27698	11763	3372	1264	23115	1183168
Percentage	62.6	31.7	2.3	1	0.3	0.1	2	100

41   Erdoğan [Özünlü], "Ankara'nın Bütüncül Tarihi Çerçevesinde Ankara Tahrir Defterleri'nin Analizi", pp. 164–9.

42   Ergenç, Özer, *XVI. Yüzyılda Ankara ve Konya* (Ankara: Ankara Enstitüsü Vakfı Yayınları, 1995), in particular pp. 99–101, 113–16; Faroqhi, Suraiya, "Onyedinci Yüzyıl Ankara'sında Sof İmalatı ve Sof Atölyeleri", *İstanbul Üniversitesi İktisat Fakültesi Mecmuası*, 41/1–4 (1985), 237–59.

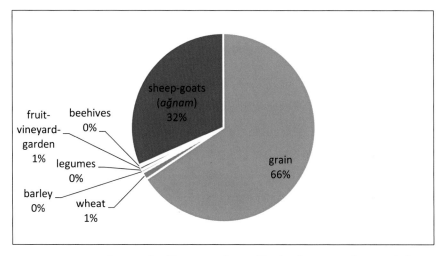

DIAGRAM 2.3A Distribution of arable crops and animal husbandry taxes in the *sancak* of
Bozok (1556)

TABLE 2.6C Distribution of arable and animal husbandry taxes in the *sancak* of Bozok (1576)

	Wheat	Barley	Legumes	Vineyards-orchards-fruit-gardens	Cotton	Flax	Other	Sheep-goats (*ağnam*)	Bee-hives	Total
Total-*akçe*	741238	374718	27698	11763	3372	1264	23115	219193	4221	1406582
Percentage	62.6	31.7	2.3	1	0.3	0.1	2			100

When we look at the *tahrir* registers for 1556 for the *sancak* of Bozok we see
that the majority of the population is registered as groups occupied with agriculture in arable fields (*mezraa*) but that in the register for 20 years later most
of the arable land is registered as villages. It is possible that this change in ter-
minology expresses the process of settlement.[43] When we look at the figures in
this context, the taxes on agricultural crops in 1556 come almost entirely from
grain (99 per cent). A great part of this is entered as "galle" (grain) without distinguishing what type of grain and a very small portion is registered as either

---

43   See Öz, Mehmet, "Bozok Sancağında İskân ve Nüfus, 1539–1642", *XII. Türk Tarih Kongresi,
      Bildiriler (Eylül 1994),* vol. 3 (Ankara: Türk Tarih Kurumu Basımevi, 2000), pp. 787–94; Koç,
      XVI. Yüzyılda Bir Osmanlı Sancağının İskân ve Nüfus Yapısı.

wheat or barley. When the taxes on animal husbandry for the same period are included, the percentage for grain becomes 67.5, and that for sheep and goats (*ağnam*) 31.5 per cent. According to the *tahrir* data for 1576, the share of grain in arable taxes had fallen very slightly to 94 per cent, and was close to 80 per cent of all taxes; a clearer fall is observable in the percentage of sheep and goat (*ağnam*) tax, which was now reduced to 16 per cent of total taxes.

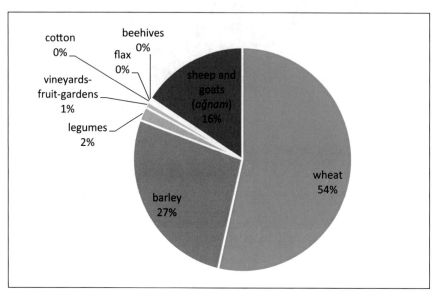

DIAGRAM 2.3B   Distribution of arable crops and animal husbandry taxes in the *sancak* of Bozok (1576)

TABLE 2.7A   Distribution of agricultural taxes in the *sancak* of Çankırı (1521)[a]

	Wheat	Barley	Legumes	Fruit, etc.	Garden vegetables	Vineyards	Other	Total
Akçe	285853	139478	6629	17911	7029	31449	22760	511109
Percentage	56	27.3	1.3	3.5	1.4	6.1	4.4	100

Note: the "other" category included rice, reeds, fresh fodder, cotton, flax and millet.

a   For data on Çankırı see Kankal, *XVI. Yüzyılda Çankırı*.

TABLE 2.7B   Distribution of agricultural taxes in the *sancak* of Çankırı (1579)

	Wheat	Barley	Legumes	Fruit, etc.	Garden vegetables	Vineyards	Other	Total
Akçe	734575	435933	32927	41365	20147	162558	45692	1473197
Percentage	49.9	29.6	2.2	2.8	1.4	11	3.1	100

TABLE 2.7C   Distribution of arable and animal husbandry taxes in the *sancak* of Çankırı (1521)

	Wheat	Barley	Legumes	Fruit etc.	Garden vegetables	Vineyards	Sheepgoats (*ağnam*)/ beehives	Pasturage	Other	Total
Akçe	285853	139478	6629	17911	7029	31449	(35731+ 23063) 88000	27854	22760	626963
Percentage	45.6	22.25	1.06	2.86	1.12	5.01	14.03	4.44	3.63	100

Note: By adding here animal husbandry taxes such as *ağnam* and *yaylak* (the tax on flocks moving to summer pasturage) and those on beekeeping, a more balanced view of the rural sector of the economy emerges.

TABLE 2.7D   Distribution of arable and animal husbandry taxes in the *sancak* of Çankırı (1579)

	Wheat	Barley	Legumes	Fruit etc.	Gardens, vegetables	Vineyards	Sheepgoats (*ağnam*), beehives	*Yaylak*	Other	Total
Akçe	734575	435933	32927	41365	20147	162558	(18190+ 63444) 83861	41295	45692	1598353
Percentage	46	27.3	2	2.6	1.3	10.1	5.2	2.6	2.9	100

Note: 80 per cent of the sheep and goats and beehive taxes were for beehives. The others included flax, cotton, *göl* (tax on fisheries), reeds and *isperek* (tax on a kind of yellow tree used for dyeing). There was no rice or millet.

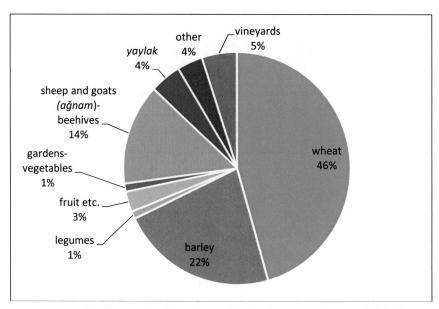

DIAGRAM 2.6A Distribution of arable and animal husbandry taxes in the *sancak* of Çankırı
(1521)

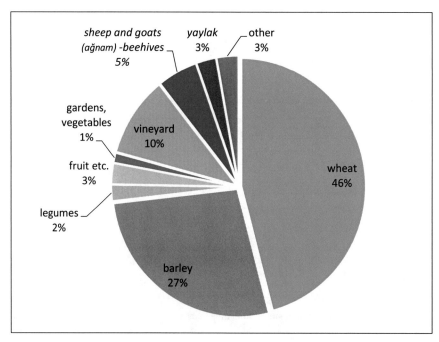

DIAGRAM 2.6B Distribution of arable and animal husbandry taxes in the *sancak* of Çankırı
(1579)

In the *sancak* of Çankırı the ratio of grain was slightly less than in Ankara, but the considerable percentage of the tax coming from grain is still striking. In 1523 the tax on grain represented 83 per cent of total arable taxes while, when the taxes on animal husbandry are included, grain had a 68 per cent share. When we look only at wheat, among agricultural crops the percentage was 56, and when animal husbandry is included, the share is 50 per cent. In the same *sancak* the percentage of tax levied in 1579 on grain within the total of agricultural taxes is 80, and when animal husbandry taxes are included it is 73. The percentage of wheat alone among all agricultural crops is 50, and when animal husbandry is included it is 46 per cent.

As in other *sancak*s, there are various differences among the *nahiye*s in the *sancak* of Çankırı. Here I shall confine myself to comparing two *nahiye*s. For example, while in the *nahiye* of Çankırı in 1579 the share of wheat among total tax income for all arable and animal husbandry was 40 per cent with 25.5 per cent for barley, in the *nahiye* of Çerkeş the share was 53.1 and 36.1 per cent respectively. In the *nahiye* of Çankırı there were taxes on items such as clover (8.5 per cent), beehives (5.3 per cent), *yaylak* (4.1 per cent), sheep and goats (*ağnam*) (2.5 per cent) and fruit (3.8 per cent), as well as on items such as legumes and a variety of fruits and vegetables (including walnuts), cotton and fresh fodder. In Çerkeş, however, apart from the taxes on grain, there was a very low level of taxes on flax (three per cent), beehives (3.7 per cent), fruit, *göl* (fishery), and fresh fodder.

When looked at as a whole, 56 per cent of the taxes on agricultural produce in Çankırı in 1523 was made up by wheat and 27 per cent by barley. The six per cent share of viticulture is noteworthy. When the sheep and goats (*ağnam*) and beehive (*kovan*) taxes are included, their 14 per cent share shows their importance in the rural economy. There is no significant change in the general picture in 1579, but the doubling of the taxes on the production of legumes shows a similarity to other places (with a general rise from one to two per cent). There is also a similar rise in the income on vineyards. There is, however, a fall which must be explained in the income of the sheep and goats tax (*ağnam*). The income from sheep and goats (*ağnam*) and beehives was 5.2 per cent, but of this 80 per cent was the income from beehives. Thus in total, the income from the *ağnam* tax was approximately one per cent. The income from the tax on flocks moving to summer pastures (*yaylak*) fell from 4.4 per cent to 2.6 per cent. Whether there was an actual fall in *ağnam* income or whether an important part of this income in this period was tied to a tax farm is impossible to say on the basis of the sources that we have.

In order to understand the actual agricultural potential of a *sancak*, it is useful to look at its *kanunname* (regulations), as well as the conjectural data in the *tahrir defter*s. Thus, in the section of the *kanunname* of Çankırı on taxes levied on goods taken to market and sold, these goods and products appear: grain, male and female slaves, horses, mules, oxen, sheep; and, sold by the horse-, mule- and donkey-load, fresh grapes, apples, pears, cherries and other fruit, wool and mohair, cloth and linen and linen cloth.[44] The grain, legumes, fruit, vineyard and market garden produce which appear in the *defter*s are wheat, barley and millet; chickpeas, lentils, broad beans, common vetch and clover; vineyard and market garden produce, fruit, walnuts, pears, almonds, onion, garlic, flax, hemp, cotton and acorns. Apart from these, we also find the *kovan, ağnam, kışlak* and *yaylak* taxes related to apiculture and sheep and goat husbandry. Among other taxes we come across dues on fisheries, meadows, meadows of *dirlik* holders, reeds and canes and plain butter. Even if this evidence does not bring into the question the dominance of grain, it does support the idea that, apart from the produce whose taxes are registered in the *tahrir defter*s, other produce and goods had a place in the livelihood of the *reaya* and therefore the variety of production was more diversified.

Subsistence Economy and Per Household and Per Capita Production in Rural Areas

Fifty years ago Bruce McGowan, using data from the Ottoman *tahrir defter*s in relation to peasant livelihood and especially average per capita production, converted grain and animal production into economic wheat equivalent on the basis of the factors proposed by the FAO for modern Middle Eastern countries, incorporating into his calculation such elements as seed and harvest loss, predation affecting farm animals and disease, and calculated the average per household (*hane*) and per capita income. He compared the figures which resulted with the minimum subsistence level in pre-industrial agricultural societies.[45] While de Vries stated that the minimum subsistence level was a little below the economic wheat equivalent of 300 kg., Clark and Haswell argued that the lowest level was between 230 and 275 kg. of unmilled grain per head, depending on factors such as an individual's size, the climate and

---

44   Kankal, *XVI. Yüzyılda Çankırı*, pp. 221–4.

45   McGowan, "Food supply and taxation on the Middle Danube, 1568–1579", 139–96. Relying heavily on Clark and Haswell, McGowan explains the usefulness of this, despite various disadvantages, thus "According to Clark and Haswell the kilogram of wheat equivalent is 'the natural unit for measuring real product in communities in which the greater part of the output is grain, grown for subsistence consumption with only a small and unrepresentative part of it traded for money'" (p. 154).

relative youth of the population.[46] Here I have taken 250 kg. of economic wheat equivalent as an average figure.

In my book on the *sancak* of Canik[47] I too used the method adopted by McGowan, but in some of my later works, while still to a large extent using this method, I simplified it. In this research I have calculated the total population based on the taxed population in the rural section of the *sancak* under consideration (on a calculation of household × 5). Thus, I have calculated the per capita production by dividing the per household production by five. I have calculated total production on the basis of the taxes. Here the tithe (*öşür*) figure levied on grain and other produce according to the *kanunname*s, was taken as the base. For the income from *ağnam* and *kovan*, however, instead of making detailed calculations,[48] I counted the taxes as being roughly ten per cent of the total tax income. I extracted the total tax (the figures for production) as *akçe* from the quantity of total estimated production. McGowan calculated grain on the basis of one third but, on the basis of research on agricultural history and on the findings of Güran, I have assumed that the yield per seed was on average approximately between one fourth and one fifth. Therefore, loss of seed, in milling, and in harvesting and other losses are calculated as representing a quarter of gross production. I have converted the remaining figure, taking as the base the *tahrir* value registered in the *tahrir defter* for wheat (the *akçe* equivalent of one *kile* of wheat), first into *kile*s and then into kilogrammes, taking one *kile* as being approximately 25 kg. (one Istanbul *kile* = 25.656 kg.). Thus the total production of a *sancak* (minus taxes, seeds etc.), is arrived at. When we divide this by the number of households, we reach the figure for per household production, and when we estimate five people per household and divide the figure by five, we arrive at the per capita production figure. My basic aim here is to understand, however crudely, whether or not there was an appreciable change in the subsistence of peasants between the beginning and the third quarter of the sixteenth century.

---

46 McGowan, "Food supply and taxation on the Middle Danube, 1568–1579", p. 155.

47 Öz, *XV–XVI. Yüzyıllarda Canik Sancağı*, pp. 91, 112–15.

48 For example, in converting sheep production into kilogrammes of economic wheat equivalent McGowan assumes that five per cent of the sheep in a settlement was lost per year due to diseases and predators. Forty per cent of the average flock would be available for slaughter annually. "Of this 40 %, four tenths are lambs averaging 6 kg. liveweight, while six tenths are mature sheep averaging 12 kg. liveweight". The FAO factor for the economic wheat equivalent of the lamb and mutton liveweight is 3.6. He also made a calculation for milk production (McGowan, "Food supply and taxation on the Middle Danube 1568–1579", p. 168).

TABLE 2.8   The tax population (as households) of villagers and nomads in the *sancak*s of
central Anatolia

Sancak	The First *Tahrir*	The Second *Tahrir*
Aksaray	4868	10852
Ankara	22166	47614
Bozok	14673	18933
Çankırı	17605	29868

Note: The dates of the *tahrir*s for the *sancak*s vary. See the tables above.

When the total tax figures are converted using the *akçe* value, as was indicated above, the rate of the tithe (*öşür*) and the *tahrir* value of wheat for every
sancak is taken into account. For example, in Aksaray in 1500 the tithe (*öşür*)
was taken at a ratio of one fifth (*hums*). Apart from the tithe, sharecroppers
also paid half of the produce as tax. In 1500 the *tahrir* value of grain was
3.5 *akçe* per *kile* while it was four *akçe* per *kile* for wheat. In 1584 the *tahrir*
value of wheat was seven *akçe*. At this time, because it formed part of the *salariye* (the tax collectors' share of the crop), the ratio of the tithe could rise to
one quarter in some places. Taking these characteristics into consideration,
I took Doğan Yörük's figures in relation to grain production. In converting production that was not grain into wheat equivalent, I took the *tahrir* value of
wheat as the base.[49] According to Yörük, in 1500 the total grain production was
22,049,247 kg. and the per capita production was 2,706 kg. In 1584 the total production was 23,116,933 kg. with a per capita figure of 939 kg. (Here it is important to keep in mind that there are different views on the kilogramme weight
of the *kile* used in different areas).[50] When these figures are converted into per
capita production, in accordance with the estimate of population, they should
of course correspond to a figure between at least one third and one fourth of
the population, because, in order to convert the figures given by Yörük for individuals (adult males) into total population, it is necessary to take into account
the fact that in pre-industrial societies the ratio of adult male population to
total population is estimated to have been around one third to one quarter.[51]

---

49   Yörük, *XVI. Yüzyılda Aksaray Sancağı*, pp. 154–72.
50   Yörük, *XVI. Yüzyılda Aksaray Sancağı*, p. 160.
51   Erder, Leila, "The measurement of preindustrial population changes. The Ottoman
empire from the 15th to the 17th century", *Middle Eastern Studies*, 11 (1975), pp. 284–301.

In my own calculations, I took into consideration the number of households (*hane*). Because the numbers of households are not given in Yörük's table, I calculated the total households as the total of the categories of *çift*, *nim* and *bennak* for the Muslims, non-Muslims and nomads subject to tax registered in the villages on the basis of the *kanunname* for 1584.

Although there is no sure information related to the proportion of the tithe (*öşür*) in the *sancak* of Ankara, it is known that in the *sancak*s of the Anadolu *beylerbeyliği* of which it formed a part, the ratio of *öşür* was one tenth and that for grain, together with *salariye*, was one eighth. The *tahrir* value of wheat in 1523 was 60 *akçe* for one *müd*, that is three *akçe* for one *kile*, and in 1571 one *müd* was 80 *akçe*, that is four *akçe* for one *kile*.[52] The *tahrir* value of grain in the *sancak* of Bozok in 1566 was five *akçe* for one *kile* of wheat and four for one *kile* of barley, and in 1576 it was six *akçe* for one *kile* of wheat and five for one *kile* of barley. The ratio of *öşür* was one fifth.[53]

The *tahrir defter*s registered four *akçe* for one *kile* of wheat in 1521 and five in 1579 in Çankırı where the ratio of the *öşür* for grain was one eighth.[54] According to Ahmet Kankal's calculations, the estimated population in 1521 was 97,110, the per capita production was 223.3 kg. of wheat production and 205.9 kg. of barley production. In 1579 the estimated population was around 170,000, the per capita wheat production was 200 and that of barley was 184 kg.[55]

Using the techniques and method explained above, I shall translate the total production in the four *sancak*s into total production on the basis of the *akçe* tax values. According to this, the picture of subsistence economy in the four *sancak*s appears thus:

---

52   Erdoğan [Özünlü], "Ankara'nın Bütüncül Tarihi Çerçevesinde Ankara Tahrir Defterleri'nin Analizi", p. 154.

53   In the Bozok *kanunname* it is stated that previously a tax called *hezir akçesi* (a due on transporting the harvest) had been levied in this district before threshing, but that thereafter it was forbidden to levy *hezir akçesi* after one-fifth (*hums*) had been taken following the measurement of the total harvest. "Ve mukaddema her raiyyetün ekini harmana gelmeden artuğa kesdüğünden gayrı hezir akçesi deyü bir mikdar akçesin alduktan sonra humüs üzere behresin alurlar imiş (...) [bundan böyle] hemen humüs hasıl alınub hezir akçesi alınmaya", Ö. Lütfi Barkan, *XV ve XVI ıncı Asırlarda Osmanlı İmparatorluğunda Ziraî Ekonominin Hukukî ve Malî Esasları I. Kanunlar* (İstanbul: Bürhaneddin Matbaası, 1943), p. 128.

54   Kankal, *XVI. Yüzyılda Çankırı*, pp. 117–88.

55   Kankal, *XVI. Yüzyılda Çankırı*, p. 121.

TABLE 2.9   Household and per capita production in the *sancaks* (as kilogrammes of
             economic wheat equivalent)

Sancak	Date	Per Household Production (in kg. of e.w.e.)	Per Capita Production (in kg. of e.w.e.)
Aksaray	1500	2618	520
	1584	1013	202
Ankara	1523	1260	252
	1571	1160	232
Bozok	1556	898	180
	1576	742	148
Çankırı	1521	1258	252
	1579	1717	343

According to Yörük, the total grain production in the *sancak* of Aksaray in 1500
was 22,049,247 kg. and the per capita production was 2,706 kg. In 1584 the total
production was 23,226,933 kg. with a per capita figure of 939 kg.[56] According
to my calculations, which took the ratio of *öşür* of total production as one fifth
(*hums*) and did not take *salariye* into account, in the rural sector, the per household production for 4,868 households was 2,618 kg. economic wheat equivalent, making a per capita figure of 520 kg. of economic wheat equivalent on
the basis of per capita production. The fact that this figure is noticeably higher
when compared with the other *sancaks* and the figures for Aksaray for 1584,
leads one to think that the *kile* here was not the Istanbul *kile* which was around
25 kg. If one accepts that here it was the Konya *müd* of 118 kg., as Yunus Koç has
claimed,[57] and that therefore a *kile* was 5.9 kg., the figure per household comes
out at 352 kg. of economic wheat equivalent. This, however, is very low. Here
the issue is complicated by the calculation of the actual kilogramme value of
the Konya *müd*. If one takes into account the fact that in various *sancaks* in this
period the *tahrir* value of wheat was around five to six *akçe* and in Aksaray it
was four *akçe* in 1500 and six *akçe* in 1522, one arrives at the result that the kilogramme value of the *kile* was not much different from other areas. It is possible

---

56   Yörük, *XVI. Yüzyılda Aksaray Sancağı*, p. 160. In this calculation the Konya *kile* is taken
      as being 32.07 kg. Here I also made a calculation taking the Istanbul *kile*. For this reason,
      the figure that I have reached for household and per capita production in Aksaray could
      be higher.

57   Koç, "Zirai Tarih Araştırmalarında Ölçü Tartı Birimleri Sorunu: Bursa Müddü Örneği",
      pp. 544–5.

to explain the high average income in the *sancak* of Aksaray as being due to the productivity of the soil in this *kaza* and the comparatively high income from sheep and goats or to the fact that the *tahrir* figure was closer to the actual position. The picture for 1584 in the same *sancak* shows a production of 1,013 kg. of economic wheat equivalent per household and of 202 kg. of economic wheat equivalent per head. Even if it appears as if there is a large drop here, it is possible to argue that the true situation was different. It is generally the case that in the last *tahrir*s in particular the incomes from *mukataa*s are registered not according to their actual values but by transferring the figures from earlier *tahrir defter*s. It is thus possible to conjecture that the same could be true for the *ağnam* income.

Moving to the *sancak* of Ankara, I have calculated using estimated figures because the sources that I used contain information for taxes such as the *öşür* and *bad-ı heva* but no *resm-i çift* figures. By multiplying the income from arable and animal husbandry by ten, I obtained an estimate for production. After extracting taxes from this figure, a quarter of total production was subtracted for seed and other losses and the remaining figure was multiplied by 25 (one *kile* being 25 kg.). I calculated *raiyyet rüsumu* (from *bad-ı heva* and other taxes at around 60,000 *akçe*, but *raiyyet rüsumu* overall is unclear) and incidental taxes at approximately 350,000 *akçe*. This produced the finding that the subsistence level of the rural population was close to the minimum subsistence level. The production per household was 1,260 kg. of economic wheat equivalent, and 252 kg. of economic wheat equivalent per head. In 1571, however, there was approximately 72,000 *akçe* of casual, unpredicted tax income from *bad-ı heva*, *arusiye* and *deştbani*. I calculated the total *raiyyet rüsumu* as being roughly 500,000 *akçe*. Thus, the income per household was 1,160 kg. of economic wheat equivalent and per capita 232 kg of economic wheat equivalent. If I had made the detailed calculations, particularly concerning *ağnam*, that McGowan did (adding milk and meat to the calculation), I would probably have produced slightly higher figures, but in any case, after having paid their taxes, people living in the rural area of the *sancak* of Ankara were only able to survive at a subsistence level.

In the *sancak* of Bozok in 1556 the number of households was 14,673 and the total production was 1,944,208 *akçe*. The taxes on production were 1,092,128 *akçe* and, as the level of tax was one fifth (*hums*), the estimated value of the total produce was approximately 5,460,590 *akçe*. Although it would normally be necessary to multiply the taxes, other than *ağnam* and grain, with a greater multiplier, I adopted a simpler calculation. Instead, I took out the total tax income (1,944,208) including *raiyyet rüsumu* etc., and seed and other losses, and converted the remaining figure to *kile* (5,237,502) on the basis of the *tahrir* value of wheat (five *akçe*) and then into kilogrammes. As a result, a net production figure of 13,187,560 kg. of economic wheat equivalent was arrived at. Dividing this according to the number of households, the resulting figure is 898 kg. of economic wheat equivalent. If the number of people per household is calculated at five, then the net production per head falls to approximately 180 kg. of economic wheat equivalent. This is below the minimum subsistence level.

When the same calculations are made for the 1576 tahrir, the result is an average income per household of 742 kg. and 148 kg. per head of economic wheat equivalent, which is considerably below the minimum subsistence level. At this date the total production was 2,537,308 akçe, the tax on production was 1,406,582 akçe and the number of households was 18,933. However, it is reasonable to assume that the actual value of nomadism and sheep and goat production is higher than our calculation. In this sancak, almost the entire population was recorded and registered as having the use of arable fields (mezraa). By 1576 the great majority of these arable fields (mezraa) were recorded as villages. This shows us that the process of sedentarisation was still new. It is probably for this reason that the ağnam appears as much reduced.

Following the same calculation, while in Çankırı in 1521 the income per household was 1,258 kg. of economic wheat equivalent and that per head was 252 kg. of economic wheat equivalent, in 1579 the income per household was 1,717 kg. of economic wheat equivalent and 343 kg. of economic wheat equivalent per head. Here the rate of öşür was ten per cent. I used this figure for grain in my calculations but in fact the true figure for grain, on the basis of its share of salariye, was one eighth. The total tax of the villages of Çankırı in 1579 was 2,312,040 akçe.[58] The total tax on production in 1579 was 1,598,353 akçe. After calculating the total gross production as 15,983,530 akçe, the total tax figure is subtracted, and from the remaining figure (13,671,490) a quarter (3,417,872) is subtracted for seed and other losses. The remaining figure (10,253,618), after being divided by the tahrir value of wheat in the tahrir defter (one kile at five akçe), is converted into kilogrammes. From the total net production figure (51,268,090 kg. of economic wheat equivalent) which is obtained in this way, the approximate production is calculated according to the number of households and people. As a result, in the rural areas of Çankırı the figures arrived at are 1,717 kg. of economic wheat equivalent for the production per household

---

58   Further, there are some small incomes from arable land (mezraa) (see the tables in Kankal, XVI. Yüzyılda Çankırı, between pp. 225 and 246). However, I did not include these in the calculation because there is inconsistency over nahiyes and the tahrir entries in different tahrir defters. In any case these figures are not sufficiently large to affect the general picture.

and 343 kg. economic wheat equivalent for the production per head. This result for Çankırı could stem partly from my calculations being made on the basis of the ratio of *öşür* being 1/10th instead of 1/8th. It is possible to suggest that the regional registers indicate a proportional increase in economic well-being in the rural areas.

In Place of a Conclusion

In order to be able to analyse the results of this research within the general context of Anatolia, I have combined the data from the central Anatolian *sancak*s which I have examined in detail with data from the second half of the sixteenth century (see Table 2.2) which I used in my earlier work in Table 2.10. One can of course question whether it is possible to compare data from different periods. However, a rough comparison of data from these *kaza*s and *sancak*s which were surveyed within a nine to ten-year period, with the exception of Harput, Maraş and Bolu, can give us some sort of picture of agricultural production in Ottoman Anatolia around 1570.

On the basis of *tahrir* data for Canik and Tokat in the north, Adana and Maraş in the south, Denizli (Lazikiye), Manisa and Uşak in the west, Karahisar-ı Şarki in the north-east and Harput in the east, and the *sancak*s of Bolu, Bozok, Ankara and Çankırı in central Anatolia, Table 2.10 shows the approximate figures for tax income on agricultural production in these regions between roughly 1570 and 1580. When we look at this table we see that within the estimated total agricultural tax income, the figure from wheat varies *sancak* to *sancak* from 20 per cent to 62 per cent; that in Adana and Denizli, where the figure for wheat was low, the income from cotton (varying between 34 and 20 per cent) was high; and that in Bolu, apart from wheat and barley, the income from millet and other grain formed an importance percentage (roughly 24 per cent). Concerning agricultural production in the four *sancak*s which I examined in more detail, wheat and barley formed a monoculture in Bozok and Aksaray, while in comparison in Ankara and Çankırı the income from viticulture, orchards and fruit attained an important percentage.

Geography and the continental climate certainly played an important role in the economic life of these four *sancak*s, located on the central Anatolian plateau, an area that was for the most part not rich in plant cover. Fruit and vegetable production along rivers and streams and animal husbandry on the high plateaus without doubt contributed to a more diversified structure of production and to an extent balanced grain production which appears to have formed a monoculture.

TABLE 2.10 The percentages of agricultural taxes in various *sancak*s and *kaza*s in the second half of the sixteenth century (at dates between 1563 and 1584)

Sancak/ Kaza	Date	Wheat	Barley	Millet and other grain	Vineyards-orchards, fruit, gardens	Rice	Cotton	Flax, hemp	Legumes	Other	Total
Canik	1576	46	30	6	4	4		8		2	100
Harput	1566	55	22.6	0.2	6.9		13.9			1.4	100
Karahisar-ı Şarki	1569	59.3	34.3	0.2	4.2		1.3	0.7			100
Manisa	1575	52.1	26.5	4.4	4.9	6.7	3.6	0.3		1.5	100
Tokat	1574	56.5	31.4	0.1	9.4		1.4	0.8		0.4	100
Maraş Kazası	1563	53	24.5	0.3	9.7	7	5.1			0.4	100
Lazikiye (Denizli)	1571	40.5	15.7	1.9	11.4	9.9	20.4			0.2	100
Adana	1572	30.5	27.6	0.2	4.3	1.1	34.3			2	100
Uşak	1570	61.5	24.5	0.7	5		0.3		8		100
Bolu	1568	39.1	23.7	23.8	9.9		1.4			2.1	100
Bozok	1576	62.6	31.7		1		0.3	0.1	2.3	2	100
Ankara	1571	60.4	29.5		10.1						100
Çankırı	1579	49.9	29.6		15.2				2.2	3.1	100
Aksaray	1584	54.8	39.2	0.17	5.7			0.13			100

While, on the basis of research using *tahrir defter*s, the proportional distribution of agricultural production in this or that *sancak* or *kaza* is established, it is necessary to note that the assessments made for some *sancak*s underestimate internal differences and variations within the *sancak*. As mentioned above, this can clearly be seen when looking more closely at the *nahiye*s of Çankırı, one of the *sancak*s which I have considered in my own work. The calculations which I made, simplifying the method that McGowan used 50 years ago and partly modifying it, produced figures that, when I estimated the economic position of the population at subsistence level in central Anatolia in *sancak*s where nomadism was important, appear reasonable but which in some cases need further explanation. It is necessary to stress again the need to be cautious in using *tahrir* data for calculations of production. This said, however, this data can be used for economic history research, provided that the individual attributes of each *sancak* and the various inconsistencies which appear in the tax office registers resulting from changes occurring over time in the practice of registration which are reflected in the figures, are taken into account.

As it is highly likely that the *ağnam* tax load for the *sancak* of Bozok, which had still not moved from nomadism to settlement, is not sufficiently represented in the *defter*s, it is necessary to approach with caution the production figures per household and per head calculated for this *sancak*. For the other three *sancak*s, average production figures have been obtained which are around the level of economic subsistence, with some under, some over, and even in Aksaray in 1500 considerably above that level.

In conclusion, even though our knowledge of Ottoman agricultural history in the classical era has increased, it is possible to say that our understanding of it empire-wide is still not at a satisfactory level. The lack of a sufficient standard to date for research data as well as various methodological problems hampering any general assessment play a role in this. There is a clear need to construct a comprehensive inventory using *kanunname*s (it must be taken into account that the entries for produce sold in the markets in the *sancak kanunname*s do not appear by chance but must have reflected economic activities in that particular district), *mühimme defter*s and other sources together with the *tahrir* data in order to considerably strengthen the analysis made here within a much more modest framework. Incorporating the production from animal husbandry and activities such as mining alongside arable production can produce a more detailed picture of the rural economy. In such research it is necessary to create lists of every type of product which is taxed according to location and the period in which it is registered. Grain, fruit and vegetables, which are registered under different names, and industrial plant-based raw material need to be assessed individually. In this way, a detailed picture of Anatolian agricultural history can be obtained. One important point that must be noted is the need for an inter-disciplinary approach which benefits effectively from the disciplines of geography and agriculture.

CHAPTER 3

The Economic Geography of Ottoman Anatolia: People, Places, and Political Economy around 1530

Metin Coşgel and Sadullah Yıldırım

The early decades of the sixteenth century witnessed a vast expansion of Ottoman rule in Anatolia and lands farther east and south. With the conquests of sultans Selim I and Süleyman I, the empire became a dominant world power and experienced an enormous transformation of its population and economy. In addition to growing in size, the population changed significantly in ethnic and religious composition. Whereas the Ottomans ruled over a largely non-Muslim population in the fifteenth century, by the 1530s the subjects included numerous peoples from the central Islamic lands. The sources of revenue and methods of taxation were also different in the newly conquered lands in the east and south that were previously controlled by the Safavids and the Mamluks.

This chapter will examine the economic geography of Ottoman Anatolia soon after the vast expansion of the empire in Asian territories. For a consistent and systematic account of resources and activities, we use data from the official accounting registers (*muhasebe defteri*) of the empire recorded around the year 1530, available at the district (*kaza*) level from the State Archives in Turkey.[1] Based on the detailed tax records known as the *defter-i hakani*,

---

1 The accounting registers used in this study are (1) *166 Numaralı Muhâsebe-i Vilâyet-i Anadolu Defteri (937/1530) Hüdâvendigâr, Biga, Karesi, Saruhân, Aydın, Menteşe, Teke, Alâiye Livâları* (Ankara: Osmanlı Arşivi Daire Başkanlığı, 1995); (2) *387 Numaralı Muhâsebe-i Vilâyet-i Karaman ve Rûm Defteri (937/1530) I: Konya, Bey-Şehri, Ak-Şehir, Larende, Ak-Saray, Niğde, Kayseriyye ve İç-İl Livâları* (Ankara: Osmanlı Arşivi Daire Başkanlığı, 1996); (3) *387 Numaralı Muhâsebe-i Vilâyet-i Karaman ve Rûm Defteri (937/1530) II: Amasya, Çorumlu, Sivas-Tokat, Sonisa-Niksar, Karahisar-ı Şarkî, Canik, Trabzon, Kemah, Bayburd, Malatya, Gerger-Kahta ve Divriği-Darende Livâları* (Ankara: Osmanlı Arşivi Daire Başkanlığı, 1997); (4) *438 Numaralı Muhâsebe-i Vilâyet-i Anadolu Defteri (937/1530) I: Kütahya, Karahisâr-ı Sâhip, Sultanönü, Hamîd ve Ankara Livâları* (Ankara: Osmanlı Arşivi Daire Başkanlığı, 1993); (5) *998 Numaralı Muhâsebe-i Vilâyet-i Diyar-i Bekr ve Arab ve Zü'l-Kadriyye Defteri (937/1530) I: Âmid, Mardin, Sincar, Musul, Arapkir, Ergani, Çirmük, Siverek, Kiği, Çemişkezek, Harput, Ruha, Ana-Hit ve Deyr-Rahbe Livâları ile Hısn-ı Keyf ve Siürd Kazaları* (Ankara: Osmanlı Arşivi Daire Başkanlığı, 1998); (6) *998 Numaralı Muhâsebe-i Vilâyet-i Diyar-i Bekr ve Arab ve Zü'l-Kadriyye Defteri (937/1530) II: Âmid, Mardin, Sincar, Musul, Arapkir, Ergani, Çirmük, Siverek, Kiği, Çemişkezek,*

accounting registers for this period provide the first comprehensive inventory of taxable resources and activities for the whole empire.

We use the tools of spatial analysis to process the information from official accounting registers for a geographic representation of the people, places, and political economy in Anatolia during this period. Ottoman historiography has made significant progress in recent decades in studying the evolution of society and institutions, mainly through microanalysis of specific regions and segments of society over time. We wish to promote a spatial dimension in the analysis by highlighting the regional diversity of the Ottoman economy, even within the limited geographic span of the Anatolian plateau, in a macroeconomic framework.

The archival data recorded in the accounting registers include detailed information regarding the amounts and essential features of the inhabitants and resources of the empire, especially in relation to the fiscal and administrative capacity of the state. Since the data are given at the level of the district, we use the name of the district to georeference its location, calculate district-level values of several representative indicators, and use GIS software to display the geographic dispersion of these indicators on maps. Regarding people, we determine the total number of taxpaying inhabitants in a district and the fractions of inhabitants who were non-Muslims and those exempt from taxation. In the same vein, we use the information regarding productive resources to calculate the numbers of mills, caravanserais, and markets in each district. Finally, as an indicator of political economy constraints that the Ottomans faced in newly conquered territories, we provide information regarding the spatial implementation of the *malikane-divani* system, an unusual method of dividing tax revenues between the state and local private recipients (*mülk, vakıf*).

People

The Ottoman empire expanded rapidly and substantially in Asia during the century following the conquest of Istanbul in 1453. Soon after conquering Istanbul, Mehmed II extended Ottoman control in Anatolia, first along the Black Sea coast in the north and later towards the southeast with victories against the Akkoyunlu and Karaman states. Rapid expansion continued during the reign of his grandson, Selim I, who nearly doubled Ottoman lands through encounters with the Safavids and by conquering the lands previously controlled by the

---

Harput, Ruha, Ana-Hit ve Deyr-Rahbe Livâları İle Hısn-ı Keyf ve Siird Kazaları (Ankara: Osmanlı Arşivi Daire Başkanlığı, 1999).

Mamluks, including the holy cities of Mecca, Medina, and Jerusalem. The next campaign against the Safavids under Süleyman I resulted in the conquest of Iraq and the extension of Ottoman rule onto the Persian Gulf.[2]

As the Ottomans took control of new lands, they surveyed taxable resources and activities in the region and recorded the information in tax registers called *defter-i hakani*, also known as the *tapu tahrir*.[3] The registers were used for a variety of purposes, including serving as official records to establish legal claims to land, assessing the expected tax revenues, and appropriating some of the revenues to the military and administrative officials as remuneration for local services. Although some historians have unfortunately criticized the tax registers as being sources with "pitfalls and limitations",[4] the concern can obviously be raised for any historical or current source of information and must not be the basis for preventing useful lines of inquiry or to generate a list of investigation types to avoid. The information contained in tax registers must have been sufficiently high in quality that the empire's officials evidently relied on them extensively in administering the fiscal and military affairs of the state. By the same token, they must surely be informative enough for the capable historian to rely on them in making reasonable inferences regarding the history of this empire by carefully considering the concerns that might potentially bias the analysis. Despite their natural imperfections under contemporary circumstances, tax registers contain invaluable information to facilitate the spatial analysis of the people, the buildings and places of production and trade, and the political economy of taxation in Ottoman Anatolia.

The tax registers for the years around 1530 are particularly important for our analysis because of their rather comprehensive coverage for the whole empire,

---

2   For a detailed account of the Ottoman expansion in Asia, see Boyar, Ebru, "Ottoman expansion in the East", in *The Cambridge History of Turkey, Volume 2. The Ottoman Empire as a World Power, 1453–1603*, ed. Suraiya Faroqhi and Kate Fleet (Cambridge: Cambridge University Press, 2013), pp. 74–140.

3   Barkan, Ömer Lütfi, "Türkiye'de İmparatorluk Devirlerinin Büyük Nüfus ve Arazi Tahrirleri ve Hakana Mahsus İstatistik Defterleri I", *İstanbul Üniversitesi İktisat Fakültesi Mecmuası*, 1 (1940–1941), 20–59; Barkan, Ömer Lütfi, "Türkiye'de İmparatorluk Devirlerinin Büyük Nüfus ve Arazi Tahrirleri ve Hakana Mahsus İstatistik Defterleri II", *İstanbul Üniversitesi İktisat Fakültesi Mecmuası*, 2 (1940–1941), 214–47; Coşgel, Metin M., "Ottoman tax registers (tahrir defterleri)", *Historical Methods*, 37/2 (2004), 87–100; Faroqhi, Suraiya, "Ottoman Population", in Faroqhi and Fleet, *The Cambridge History of Turkey, Volume 2. The Ottoman Empire as a World Power, 1453–1603*, pp. 356–403.

4   Lowry, Heath W., "The Ottoman *tahrîr defterleri* as a source for social and economic history: pitfalls and limitations", in Lowry, Heath W., *Studies in Defterology: Ottoman Society in the Fifteenth and Sixteenth Centuries* (Istanbul: Isis Press, 1992), pp. 3–18.

including Anatolia. Conducted during the reign of Süleyman I, the tax records for this period were the only collection that covered all provinces in (circa) the same year. Moreover, they were the only collection for which the officials aggregated the information at the district (*kaza*) level in accounting registers called *muhasebe-i vilayet* to facilitate book-keeping and decision-making.[5] In aggregating from detailed tax records to accounting registers, they omitted certain information, such as the names of the heads of households and recipients of tax revenues. But for each district they listed in aggregate the total numbers of towns, villages, bachelor and married inhabitants (broken down by religion and taxpayer-status), and the total amount of expected tax revenue from all sources, all itemized by types of recipient (e.g., *timar, zeamet, mirmiran, padişah, vakıf*). In addition, the accounting registers listed the types and numbers of individuals exempted from taxation and the numbers of various other things (e.g., shops, mosques, mills, rivers and other geographic features) that were deemed important for official accounts and planning.

Map 3.1 shows the locations of districts recorded in the accounting registers of the Ottoman empire for the years around 1530. For reference, the map includes the frontier of the empire in 1535 as well as the borders of today's countries. As seen in the map, tax registers are not available for some of the districts in the east near the Ottoman border with the Safavid state and in the west near the borders with Austria and Poland-Lithuania. In total, the registers include information regarding 454 districts of the empire for this period.

In the analysis that follows, we focus on the districts in Anatolia, rather than the whole empire, for consistency with the geographic coverage of this book. We exclude from the dataset all of the districts in Europe, listed under the provinces (*vilayet*) of Rumeli. In addition, we drop some of the districts of the province of Arab, such as those in the sub-provinces of Şam, Gazze, Safed, and Salt, which lie to the south of Anatolia proper. The latter exclusion is also necessary because the information was less detailed and complete for these districts than others, as they had been recently conquered at the time of our registers. With the more focused coverage, our dataset consists of 269 districts in Ottoman Anatolia that belonged to the provinces of Anadolu, Arab, Diyarbakır, Karaman, Rum, and Zülkadir during this period.

---

5 İnalcık, Halil, "Giriş", in *438 Numaralı Muhâsebe-i Vilâyet-i Anadolu Defteri (937/1530) I: Kütahya, Karahisâr-i Sâhip, Sultanönü, Hamîd ve Ankara Livâları*. See also Barkan, Ömer Lütfi, "Tarihî Demografi Araştırmaları ve Osmanlı Tarihi", *Türkiyat Mecmuası*, 10 (1953), 1–26, for an analysis of Ottoman population based on these accounting registers.

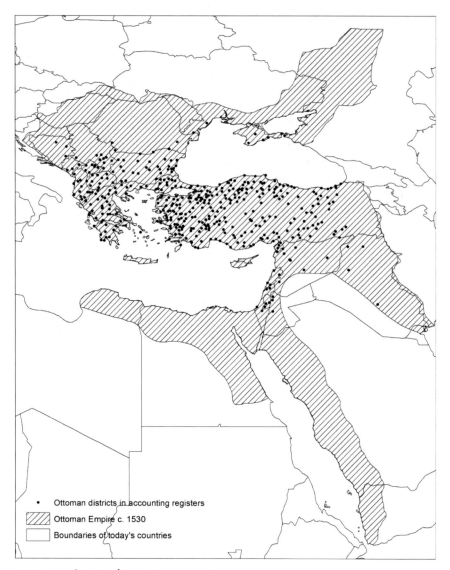

MAP 3.1   Ottoman districts in accounting registers, c. 1530

Focusing on inhabitants first, in this section we use the data to calculate representative indicators of population at the district level. Ottoman tax records enumerated the adults, including bachelors (*mücerred*) and heads of household (*hane*), but not children. Moreover, they did not systematically record women. Although they registered the widowed women (*bive*) among the Christian population as a taxpayer category enduring from pre-Ottoman systems of taxation, they did not enter the same category for Muslims. For a standard indicator that was recorded consistently across registers, we thus exclude

the widows from our calculations, and use the number of adult males to ana-
lyze the spatial variation of the size and composition of people across districts.
Unless the age and gender ratios varied systematically across districts, indicators based on the numbers of adult males should serve as rough guides for
comparative spatial analyses of broad characteristics of the population.

We use the information from accounting registers to calculate three indicators of people, namely the total number of taxpaying adult male inhabitants,
the fraction of those who were non-Muslims, and the fraction of enumerated
adult males who were exempt from the *avarız* tax. Maps 3.2–3.4 show the geographic distribution of these indicators across the districts in the dataset.

The first indicator is simply the number of male taxpayers enumerated in a
district (*nefer*), which is the sum of all taxpaying bachelors and heads of households, regardless of their landholding status (e.g., *bennak, caba, çift*).[6] Although
the land size of districts likely varied considerably across regions, we can use
the numbers of taxpayers as a rough measure of the dispersion of population
for a comparative spatial analysis across districts.

As seen in Map 3.2, several of the highly populated districts, such as Kütahya,
Manisa, Lazkiye, and Bursa, were located in western Anatolia. Although the
districts in southeastern Anatolia generally had low numbers of taxpaying
households, Maraş and Mardin clearly stood out as significant exceptions to
this trend. Similarly, Trabzon had exceptionally high numbers of taxpaying
inhabitants in the northeast. The highest numbers of taxpaying inhabitants in
central Anatolia were in the districts of Ankara, Bozok, and Kırşehri.

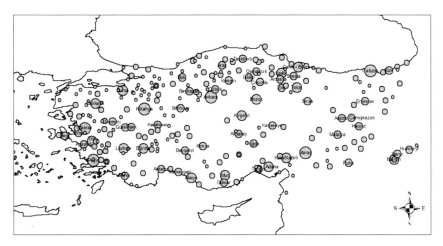

MAP 3.2   The number of male taxpayers

---

6   İnalcık, Halil, "Osmanlılarda Raiyyet Rüsumu", *Belleten*, 23 (1959), 575–610.

Historians of the Ottoman empire have long used the information from accounting registers regarding the number of male taxpayers to estimate the changing size of population over time in specific regions or for the empire as a whole. In a seminal contribution to the literature on the topic, Barkan introduced the procedure of using a household multiplier to transform the numbers of households recorded in the registers of Anadolu, Karaman, Zülkadir, Diyarbakır, Rum, Arab, and Rumeli in estimating the size of the population in these provinces and in various cities throughout the empire.[7] Since no comparable accounting register was available for the inhabitants of Istanbul, he approximated the population of the capital city from other sources to generate an estimate of the total population of the empire as a whole.

Although Barkan was keenly aware of the limitations of his sources and proposed methodology, he also knew that scholars of European and Mediterranean historical demography faced similar difficulties. With the objective of engaging this literature, he was interested in contributing estimates of how the Ottoman population changed over time for a comparative analysis. Recognizing the infancy of scholarship on Ottoman population despite rich archival sources, he understood that other researchers would soon advance his methodology and supplement other sources to improve on his estimates regarding the changes in Ottoman population over time.

Subsequent developments proved Barkan right in the way his estimates opened the door for future scholarship. A huge literature soon developed to debate with greater precision how the rural and urban population of the Ottoman empire changed over time. In addition, using the information from tax registers, court records, and various other sources, historians have investigated the causes and consequences of these demographic changes. Mustafa Akdağ and Michael Cook, for example, developed the argument that the population grew at such high rates in the second half of the sixteenth century that it caused significant social and economic problems in the countryside.[8] With the help of other sources and analytical methods, researchers have continued to debate whether the Ottoman population experienced a significant expansion in the sixteenth century, followed by a demographic crisis in the next century, and how these changes affected social, economic, and political behavior and institutions.[9]

---

7   Barkan, "Tarihi Demografi Araştırmaları", p. 11.
8   Akdağ, Mustafa, *Türkiye'nin İktisadi ve İçtimai Tarihi* (Ankara: Türk Tarih Kurumu Basımevi, 1959); Cook, M.A., *Population Pressure in Rural Anatolia, 1450–1600* (London and New York: Oxford University Press, 1972).
9   For a review of this literature, see Özel, Oktay, "Population changes in Ottoman Anatolia during the 16th and 17th centuries: the 'demographic crisis' reconsidered", *International Journal of Middle East Studies*, 36/2 (2004), 183–205.

Our approach shifts the emphasis from temporal changes to regional differences in promoting the use of *tahrirs* and derivative accounting registers as sources for useful inquiry into spatial analysis. In this respect, we build on the work of Suraiya Faroqhi, who in a series of books and articles used the information regarding the numbers of taxpayers contained in tax registers in conjunction with the maps of Anatolia in the nineteenth and twentieth centuries to identify the locations of districts that were enumerated in these sources and to determine significant changes in the spatial distribution of Ottoman population during the sixteenth century. Using this approach, she studied, for example, whether the administrative importance of towns (e.g., as district center) led to faster population growth over time through greater economic and political prosperity.[10] Recently developed tools of geographic information systems allow us to identify the locations of districts with greater precision and expand the scope of inquiry to various other indicators of interest.

The next indicator of central interest in our analysis is the religious composition of inhabitants. If the inhabitants of a district all shared the same religion, the accounting registers did not always specify religious affiliation. When two or more religious groups lived in a district, however, the numbers in each category were explicitly recorded, in addition to the marital and taxpayer status of inhabitants, provided that they were "People of the Book" (Jews and Christians). Sometimes the non-Muslims were denoted under a single category, such as *kafir* or *zimmi*. In most cases, the enumerators further specified the categories of non-Muslims, for example by indicating the numbers of Armenians (*Ermeni*), Orthodox Christians (*Gebran*), and Jews (*Yahudiyan*) separately. Regardless of specific affiliation, we group all non-Muslims in a single category and use the fraction of non-Muslims in districts as a broad and consistent measure of religious composition for spatial analysis.

Map 3.3 shows the distribution of non-Muslim peoples in districts comprising our dataset in Ottoman Anatolia around the year 1530. Clearly, non-Muslims constituted a greater proportion of taxpaying population in eastern Anatolia. The greatest concentration of non-Muslims during this period was in the northeastern regions of Anatolia, such as in the districts of İspir, Torul, Of, Kemah, Trabzon, and Rize.

The legal and tax status of non-Muslims have been topics of great interest among historians of the Ottoman empire. Consistent with the tradition of previous Islamic states, the Ottomans considered Jews and Christians as protected peoples (*zimmi*) with distinct rights and obligations. Their legal rights included the ability to resolve disputes in their own courts, which ruled based on their

---

10 Faroqhi, Suraiya, *Towns and Townsmen of Ottoman Anatolia: Trade, Crafts, and Food Production in an Urban Setting, 1520–1650* (Cambridge: Cambridge University Press, 1984).

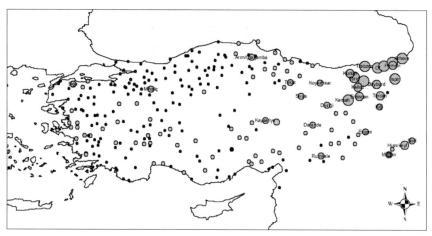

MAP 3.3   The fraction of non-Muslim inhabitants

own laws, traditions, and procedures. Their leaders had a certain degree of autonomy from the state in administering their community's social, religious, and economic affairs. In a well-known example of this autonomy, while the Ottoman rulers heavily regulated the printing press and waited almost three centuries to sanction printing in Ottoman Turkish (in Arabic characters), various Jewish and Christian communities were allowed during this period to use the press for publications in their own scripts and languages.[11] In another well-known example, they could borrow and lend at interest, transactions banned for Muslims. On the other hand, they were excluded from military service and certain government occupations. Given such differential rights and constraints between Muslims and non-Muslims, an important question that arises for the economic historian is how these differences shaped the occupational choices and behavior of the people, not just non-Muslims but the whole population. A related question concerns the impact of differential rights and constraints on the long-term development of Ottoman society and economy.

Tax obligations of the protected peoples were also different. Part of this difference originated from the conquest of lands populated by specific non-Muslim communities, as the Ottomans adopted from previous states the local tax code that included items that were distinct from the code that applied to Muslims in Anatolia. For example, the tax registers recorded the widowed women (*bíve*) distinctly among the Christian communities but not in mainly

---

11   For a political economy approach to the Ottoman ban on the printing press, see Coşgel,
        Metin M., Thomas J. Miceli and Jared Rubin, "The political economy of mass printing:
        legitimacy and technological change in the Ottoman empire", *Journal of Comparative
        Economics*, 40/3 (2012), 357–71.

Muslim districts, as noted above. The more systematic differential tax obligation was the poll tax called *cizye*, collected only from non-Muslim subjects throughout the empire. The Ottomans regularly recorded information regarding the number of individuals liable for the poll tax and the expected revenue in each district in special registers.

The special poll-tax registers have the advantage of providing information about non-Muslim subjects of the empire at greater frequency than the tax registers. Although they are therefore very useful for the historian studying population movements among non-Muslims, they are of limited use for comparative studies with the Muslims because they do not contain information regarding them. Despite the limited yearly frequency of accounting registers, we have relied on them for our analysis because of their comprehensive spatial coverage of the religious affiliation of all taxpayers. Comprehensive data is essential for researchers interested in investigating, for example, the long-term economic effects of the differential rights or tax obligations of non-Muslims. Such an investigation would require a comparative analysis of not just the numbers of non-Muslims across Ottoman districts but their fraction in the total population. Map 3.3 illustrates this information visually.

For our next indicator of interest related to people, we turn to information regarding individuals who were exempt from taxation. Broadly speaking, the Ottoman system of taxation included two levels of exemptions. In the first level, a subject could be exempt from all or specific categories of *regular* taxes. More specifically, this included exemption from some or all of the three major categories of Ottoman taxation, namely personal taxes levied on people or households that resulted from the dependent status of the subjects, trade taxes on the goods and services brought to market for sale, and production taxes on various farming and manufacturing activities.[12] This type of exemption was rare and granted either generically to a whole class of individuals, such as the clergy (*imam*), or specifically to certain individuals or communities for exceptional considerations.

The second and more common level of exemption applied to an *extraordinary* tax called the *avarız*, collected to finance expenditures of wars.[13] Although this extraordinary tax eventually became a more regular form of taxation with restricted exemptions in the seventeenth century, it was still an occasional

---

12   For a description and systematic analysis of the categories of the Ottoman system of taxation, see Coşgel, Metin M., "Efficiency and continuity in public finance: the Ottoman system of taxation", *International Journal of Middle East Studies*, 37/4 (2005), 567–86.

13   For different types of tax exemptions in the Ottoman empire, see İnalcık, "Osmanlılarda Raiyyet Rüsumu", pp. 594–601 and Acun, Fatma, "The other side of the coin: tax exemptions within the context of Ottoman taxation history", *Bulgarian Historical Review*, 1–2 (2002), 125–39.

tax with widespread exemptions during our period. All individuals who were exempt from the first level of regular taxes were also granted an exemption from the extraordinary tax. In addition, exemptions were given to local agents and functionaries of the state who provided a variety of religious, official, and professional services to the state or the local population. This included the judiciary (*kadı*), scholars (*ulema*), rice growers, and various professionals in charge of such things as mail delivery, medical services, and maintenance of roads and bridges. The type and amount of exemption varied over time and across services, presumably based on the importance of the service to the state and various other local economic and political considerations.

Our spatial analysis is based on the exemptions from extraordinary taxes because they involve greater numbers of people and broader categories of services. The accounting registers show the numbers of individuals benefiting from this exemption as agents and functionaries of the state in each district, itemized by the specific service that they provided. We lack detailed information regarding the remuneration scheme for these services, presumably a function of qualifications and job characteristics. Tax registers nevertheless provide useful information regarding the number and types of local personnel involved in the provision of various public goods and services.

Using this information, we show in Map 3.4 the spatial distribution of populations exempt from extraordinary taxes. For this illustration, we simply calculated the total number of all such individuals who received exemptions without making a distinction regarding the specific service that warranted the exemption. Clearly, the districts with the highest fractions of inhabitants exempt from taxation were concentrated in the southcentral regions of Anatolia extending into the northwest. Although this is clearly an interesting

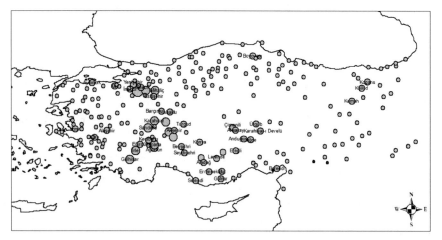

MAP 3.4   The fraction of tax-exempt inhabitants

broad pattern, we need additional information to probe deeper into the reasons for such a regional concentration.

Space limitations prevent us from producing a separate map for each type of service that was granted an exemption from extraordinary taxes and from analyzing it in detail to identify spatial patterns in allocation. Map 3.4 nevertheless illustrates the possibilities for the interested reader. For example, one could use the information regarding the exemptions granted to religious personnel (*imam, rahib, müezzin*) to examine regional differences in the provision of religious services. Likewise, the records show the numbers of military and administrative personnel in each district by specific categories, useful information that can be used for a spatial analysis of how the Ottoman military and bureaucracy functioned in the provinces.

Buildings and Places of Trade and Production

The accounting registers of the Ottoman empire include information regarding various structures that were essential for the state's fiscal, religious, military, and administrative functions. For example, the records show the numbers of mills, mines, markets, irrigation dikes (for rice growing), and various types of shops in towns that were sources of tax revenue. Likewise, the enumerators recorded the numbers of mosques, churches, monasteries, schools, and other religious buildings; as well as the numbers of castles, towers, and other structures for military defense. In addition, for each district the registers entered not just the numbers of uninhabited productive grain fields or the types of tribes and town neighborhoods, but information regarding structures that served various administrative functions, such as border crossings, soup kitchens serving the poor, and bridges that needed maintenance.

We use the numbers of watermills, caravanserais, and markets as representative indicators of structures involved in trade and production in Ottoman districts. In Anatolia, mills were mostly powered by water. The registers typically recorded the watermills (*asiyab*) in each district, sometimes distinguishing among them by type and function. Since the watermill taxes depended on the amount of stones (*bab*) available to grind flour, the accounting registers typically listed the number of millstones in each district. Although the size and functions of watermills likely varied across districts, we can use the total number of millstones as a rough indicator of grain production and the associated economic activity.[14]

---

14   Özcan, Ruhi, "Arşiv Belgeleri Diliyle Su Değirmenleri (Âsiyâb)", *Ankara Üniversitesi Osmanlı Tarihi Araştırma ve Uygulama Merkezi Dergisi*, 40 (2016), 195–203.

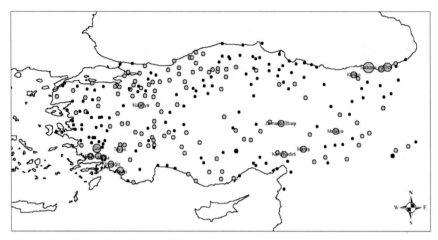

MAP 3.5   The number of watermill stones

As seen in Map 3.5, it was a common practice throughout Anatolia to use water-mills as sources of power for various economic activities during this period. Although the tax registers do not provide the exact locations of watermills, presumably they were built in places of easy access to streams. In addition, we would expect them to be concentrated more heavily in areas of high demand for the products that require the service, likely correlated with population density. The spatial distribution of millstones observed in Map 3.5 is consistent with these expectations. The map indicates that there were more watermills in western regions than in eastern Anatolia, consistent with the distribution of taxpaying inhabitants we observed on Map 3.2. The highest number of water-mill stones was in Trabzon. In the same vein, Maraş and Mardin were notable exceptions in eastern Anatolia as districts with significantly high numbers of watermill stones.

Another set of buildings typically recorded in accounting registers are the caravanserais, which provide information regarding trade routes and commercial activities in Ottoman Anatolia during our period.[15] Typically located in towns or along trade routes, caravanserais fulfilled several functions related to the needs of traders and others who used the roads for long-distance travel (e.g., pilgrims, emissaries). Most important, they provided security from raids and robbers, shelter against weather conditions, and food and water to animals and travelers.

---

15   For an analysis of caravanserais and trade routes based on a rich variety of sources, see Faroqhi, *Towns and Townsmen*, Chapter 2.

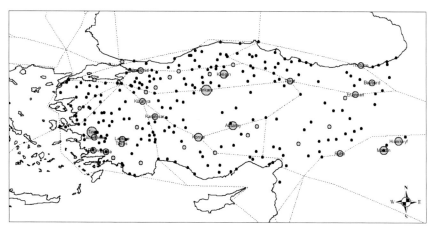

MAP 3.6   The number of caravanserais

Map 3.6 shows the total numbers of caravanserais in Ottoman districts identified in our records during this period. In addition to the spatial locations of
districts, the map includes main trade routes in the Ottoman empire, as identified by Matthew Ciolek to have existed during the period between 1300–1600.[16]
As one would expect, most of the caravanserais were in districts that were
located along the main trade routes. In central Anatolia, for example, the highest numbers of caravanserais were in the districts of Ankara, Konya, Aksaray,
Karahisar, and Kütahya, all along the main trade routes. The map also shows
high numbers of caravanserais in certain districts, such as Tire, that were not
on the main trade routes identified by Ciolek but obviously along other routes
heavily travelled by traders and others.

Finally, we calculate the number of markets in each district as a rough indicator of commercial exchange. The Ottoman empire taxed trade through various channels, such as the market tax levied on the goods brought to periodic
markets for sale and the dues payable to the market supervisor. The detailed
tax registers typically itemized the amounts of market taxes for towns and
villages, which can be used as an indicator of the volume of trade in specific
regions.[17] Although the accounting registers lack the same level of detail
regarding market taxes because of aggregation, they nevertheless include the

---

16   Ciolek, T. Matthew, *Georeferenced Data Set (Series 1 – Routes): Trade Routes in the Ottoman
      Empire 1300–1600 CE*. OWTRAD Dromographic Digital Data Archives (ODDDA). Old World
      Trade Routes (OWTRAD) Project (Canberra: Asia Pacific Research Online, www.ciolek
      .com/OWTRAD/DATA/tmcTRm1300.html, 2005).
17   For an economic analysis of the Ottoman tax system and the difference between trade
      taxes and other types of tax categories see Coşgel, "Efficiency and continuity in public

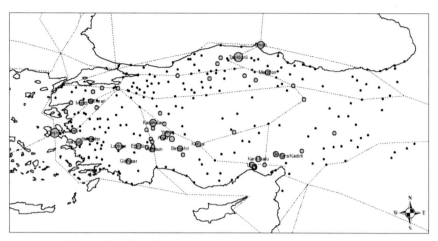

MAP 3.7   The number of markets

number of markets in each district. Notwithstanding the variation in the volume of trade across markets, the number of markets in each district provides useful information regarding opportunities available for trade.

As seen in Map 3.7, just as most of the caravanserais were located along the main trade routes, so too most of the markets were held in districts along or near these routes. This was clearly the case, for example, for Sinop and Taşköprü in northcentral Anatolia, for İzmir and Çeşme in the west, and for Kusun, Konya, and Karahisar in central Anatolia. In southwestern Anatolia, there were districts, such as Lazkiye and Ayasluğ, that were not along the main trade routes identified by Ciolek but were nevertheless important centers for trade through the periodic markets that they hosted in their regions.

The Political Economy of the Dual-Recipient (*Malikane-Divani*) System of Taxation

A peculiar system of taxation observed in certain districts of Ottoman Anatolia was the formal division of tax revenue between the state and private recipients. Under the standard arrangement prevalent in other districts, the tax revenue of a unit of taxation (e.g., a village, watermill, town market) was typically allocated exclusively to a single recipient. The recipient could be an agent of the state (e.g., central government, provincial governor, local soldier

---

finance: the Ottoman system of taxation". See also, for a study of Anatolian markets based on *tahrirs*, Faroqhi, Suraiya, "Sixteenth century periodic markets in various Anatolian sancaks", *Journal of the Economic and Social History of the Orient*, 22/1 (1979), 32–80.

or administrator) or a private recipient such as a landholder (*mülk*) or a pious foundation (*vakıf*).[18] Under the dual-recipient system called the *malikane-divani* system, by contrast, a private recipient (*malikane*) and an agent of the state (*divani*) shared the tax revenue between them. The shares of the state and private recipients were not at a uniform ratio throughout the empire. Although the distinct characteristic of this system was the division of revenue, the relative shares of recipients could vary significantly across districts.

Scholars have proposed various arguments regarding the historical origins of the dual-recipient system of taxation.[19] Although the arrangement is clearly not unique to the Ottomans, neither does it seem to have a unique precedent. Barkan considered the system to be based on the Islamic law of land and believed that it could be widely observed not just in parts of Anatolia but also in Syria and possibly other lands previously ruled by Turkish-Islamic states. Focusing more specifically on Anatolia, Beldiceanu-Steinherr found the origin in the Anatolian Selçuk state, based on the overlap that she observed between the geographic coverage of this state and the Ottoman districts that practiced dual-recipient system of taxation. Likewise, Venzke found evidence to indicate that the system observed in Aleppo was based on the Mamluk legacy.[20]

Regardless of its historical origins, the system must have served essential useful functions to be able to pass the test of time and survive into the period of Ottoman rule. We can group the functions noted by historians into two categories depending on the presumed power asymmetry between the state and local private powerholders. The first is the argument that the dual-recipient system helped the state to ensure the loyalty of local elements, such as powerful families who owned land prior to Ottomans and could form resistance unless included in the allocation of tax revenue. İnalcık, for example, notes that the reason the system was observed in the Turcoman regions was because it facilitated the Ottoman rule through revenue concessions that secured support from the hereditary tribal lords.[21]

---

18   Coşgel, Metin M. and Thomas J. Miceli, "Risk, transaction costs, and tax assignment: government finance in the Ottoman empire", *Journal of Economic History*, 65/3 (2005), 806–21.

19   For a discussion of the historical origins of the system see Venzke, Margaret L., "Aleppo's mālikāne-dīvānī system", *Journal of the American Oriental Society*, 106/3 (1986), pp. 461–9.

20   Barkan, Ömer Lütfi, "Türk-İslam Toprak Hukuku Tatbikatının Osmanlı İmparatorluğunda Aldığı Şekiller: Malikâne-Divânî Sistemi", *Türk-Hukuk ve İktisat Tarihi Mecmuası*, 2 (1939), pp. 119–84; Beldiceanu-Steinherr, Irène, "Fiscalité et formes de possession de la terre arable dans l'Anatolie préottomane", *Journal of the Economic and Social History of the Orient*, 19/3 (1976), 233–312; Venzke, "Aleppo's mālikāne-dīvānī system".

21   İnalcık, Halil and Donald Quataert (eds.), *An Economic and Social History of the Ottoman Empire, 1300–1914* (Cambridge: Cambridge University Press, 1994), p. 129.

Scholars have noted a second category of reasons for the system's existence, based on different presumptions regarding the relative powers of state and private elements. In this view, the essential function of the dual-recipient system is for the government to penetrate into previously feudal relationships by claiming some of the revenue that previously belonged to private agents as state's share. Venzke, for example, argues that the system allowed "the state to maintain a palpable political presence in *vaqf* and *mülk* villages and other fiscal units from which it would otherwise have been shut out".[22]

It is easy to see that the two approaches are in fact consistent with each other and that we can put them in a coherent whole by clarifying how the dual-recipient system allowed the government to maximize revenue subject to the risk of revolt while balancing the interests of the state and local powerholders. The key indicator of the balance is the relative share of the state's revenue relative to private recipients. Of course, the state would have preferred to appropriate all of the tax revenue for its own agents, possible if there were no constraints to its power of allocation. At the other extreme, the state could be so weak in its power in a district that it might have no choice but to yield most or all of the revenue to local elements. In the more usual cases between these extremes, we would expect the division of revenue to depend on the strength of the state relative to local powerholders and the associated risk of revolt faced by the state in raising revenue. If the power of the state over local elements was greater in a district relative to another, it could lower the fraction of revenue assigned to private recipients, sufficient to maintain an appropriate alignment of interests while controlling the risk of revolt.

For a spatial analysis of the way the dual-recipient system functioned around the year 1530, we thus need to identify the districts in which the system was implemented and calculate the relative shares of the state and private recipients in those districts. The system was observed in only 31 of the 292 districts covered in our dataset, though of course it may have existed elsewhere prior to the 1530s or in districts that were outside of the coverage of accounting registers recorded around 1530. For the 31 districts that practiced the dual-recipient system, the registers show the allocation of tax revenue among the recipients. In addition to listing the total amount of the tax revenue expected from the villages, towns, and other units paying their taxes to a certain state agent (e.g., *timar, zeamet, mirmiran, padişah*), the registers show the division of revenue

---

22   Venzke, "Aleppo's Mālikāne-Dīvānī System", p. 455.

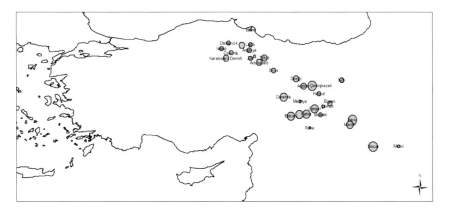

MAP 3.8   The state's share of the revenue in dual recipient (*malikane-divani*) system of
             tax-collection

between the state agent and private recipients (*vakıf* and/or *mülk*). We use this
information to aggregate the total amount received by the state's agents and
private recipients in each district and calculate the fraction received by the
state's agent as an indicator of the balance of power between them.

Map 3.8 shows the spatial distribution of the share of state among the districts practicing the dual-recipient system of allocation. The result is surprising
because it shows that the state's share of the tax revenue increased in many
districts going from the northcentral districts towards southeastern Anatolia.
Based on the foregoing reasoning, we would have expected the state's power
to decline as we moved away from the center because of the presumption that
the state's capacity to rule in a region was directly proportional to its physical ability to reach the region given the means of transportation. Given the
Ottoman seat of power in Istanbul, this would have implied a declining state's
share as we moved away from Istanbul.

We need additional information regarding the reasons for the increase in
the state's share of the tax revenue in the spatial pattern observed in Map 3.8.
It is possible that the fractions that we observe in 1530 show more the pre-
Ottoman balance of power between the predecessor states and local powerholders than the established relative strength of the Ottoman state. It is also
possible that the rise in the state's power represented more the state's desire
to assert control in the farther districts during this period than the actual balance of power. A systematic analysis of the data is necessary to investigate the
likelihood of these and other possibilities as an explanation for the observed
pattern.

Conclusion

This chapter has analyzed the economic geography of Anatolia around the year 1530. We used information from the official accounting registers of the empire, which are unique sources for their comprehensive coverage of most Ottoman districts during this period. Examining this information with new tools of spatial analysis, we explored patterns in the geographic distribution of various representative indicators of Anatolian people, places, and political economy. The ultimate objective has been to illustrate how these tools would complement the traditional approach of Ottoman historians by shifting the main focus of investigation from important developments over time to puzzling patterns and variations across districts. Our analysis uncovered various preliminary results regarding the size, religious composition, and tax-status of the people in Ottoman districts; the numbers of watermills, caravanserais, and markets as representative indicators of buildings and places of production; and the geographic variation in the power of the state as seen through its share of the revenue in the dual-recipient system of taxation.

Regarding people, our results showed that certain regions of Anatolia were more densely populated by taxpaying inhabitants than others, though no dominant patterns emerged from a preliminary analysis. Although many of the densely populated districts lay along coasts, numerous others were inland, which raises questions about the interactions between historical, economic, and political factors in determining the numbers of taxpaying inhabitants observed around the year 1530. The patterns were more visible for the religious composition of the population. Non-Muslims clearly constituted a greater proportion of taxpaying inhabitants in eastern Anatolia, the greatest concentration being in the northeast. Likewise, the fractions of individuals exempt from the extraordinary taxes collected to finance war expenditures were notably higher in the southcentral regions of Anatolia.

Our analysis identified similarly interesting patterns and puzzles regarding the spatial distribution of the numbers of mills, caravanserais, and markets in Anatolian districts. For example, there was a greater concentration of watermills in western and northeastern Anatolia, presumably determined by the availability of suitable streams and the high demand for generated power. Caravanserais were built mostly along the main transportation networks and important secondary routes. Districts in southwestern Anatolia had some of the largest numbers of regional markets, though notable concentrations of markets could be observed in other areas along the main trade routes.

Finally, we examined the state's share of the revenue under the dual recipient system of tax collection, an unusual system of allocation that was observed during this period in certain districts located between northcentral and south-eastern Anatolia. Contrary to hypothesized expectation based on the balance of power between the state and local private powerholders, our results show that the state's share of the tax revenue mostly increased in districts located far-ther from the capital, specifically from northcentral to southeastern Anatolia.

It is beyond the scope of this chapter to examine the nature, reasons, and consequences of the patterns and puzzles depicted in our spatial analysis. Our modest objective was simply to show the richness of the information contained in the accounting registers of the empire, the benefits of using new tools of spatial analysis, and the potential questions of research for fur-ther exploration. We leave it to future research to investigate these questions systematically.

CHAPTER 4

Turkish-Genoese Trade in Northern Anatolia c. 1300–1461

Kate Fleet

Ottoman-Genoese commercial relations date from the early days of the Ottoman state's existence. The Genoese also had trade relations with other Turkish *beylik*s, such as the İsfendiyaroğulları established in northern Anatolia, a region which was closely connected to Crimea where the Genoese had a major trading colony at Caffa. The level of Genoese activity in this area of Anatolia is confirmed by the establishment of three Genoese settlements along the coast at Amasra, Sinop and Samsun.

In the fourteenth and fifteenth centuries political control of northern Anatolia was divided up between various petty Turkish rulers, including the Taceddinoğulları based in Niksar and the coastal region round Terme, Çarşamba, Ünye, Ordu and Giresun, the İsfendiyaroğulları *beylik*, the Byzantine state of Trebizond and the Ottomans, who came to dominate the region through the fifteenth century until Mehmed II conquered it entirely in 1461.

Throughout most of the fourteenth century, much of northern Anatolia was under the control of the İsfendiyaroğulları (or Candaroğulları), a small Turkish *beylik* which emerged "under murky circumstances"[1] at the end of the thirteenth century. Under its second ruler, Süleyman I (c. 1308–c. 1341), the *beylik* expanded, taking Kastamonu by 1314 and Sinop after 1322, possibly around 1326. Ottoman expansion into the region under the İsfendiyaroğulları began under Murad I, who, in 1384, established Ottoman suzerainty over Kastamonu, governed by Süleyman II (1385–1392), son of the İsfendiyaroğulları ruler Kötürüm Bayezid (1361–1385) who then withdrew to Sinop where he ruled together with another son İsfendiyar. In 1392 Bayezid I removed Süleyman and established direct Ottoman control over Kastamonu.[2] İsfendiyar, who had succeeded his

---

1 Lindner, Rudi Paul, "Anatolia, 1300–1451", in *The Cambridge History of Turkey. Volume 1 Byzantium to Turkey 1071–1453*, ed. Kate Fleet (Cambridge: Cambridge University Press, 2009), pp. 115–16.

2 Yücel, Yaşar, *Anadolu Beylikleri Hakkında Araştırmalar. XIII–XV. Yüzyıllarda Kuzey-Batı Anadolu Tarihi. Çoban-oğulları Beyliği. Candar-oğulları Beyliği. I* (Ankara: Türk Tarih Kurumu Basımevi, 1988), p. 83 gives the date as 1392; Imber, Colin, *The Ottoman Empire 1300–1481*

father in 1385, continued to rule in Sinop having come to some sort of under-standing with the Ottomans.[3] Sometime in the 1390s Bayezid also took Samsun from the İsfendiyaroğulları.[4]

After Bayezid's defeat by Timur in 1402, İsfendiyar regained the *beylik*. Under Mehmed I, however, probably in 1417, the Ottomans seized Samsun, Bafra, Çankırı and Kastamonu from the İsfendiyaroğulları, leaving İsfendiyar with Sinop. Briefly regaining independence at the beginning of the reign of Murad II, the *beylik* was soon brought back into a vassal relationship with the Ottomans, Kastamonu falling to Murad in 1423. This position continued until the conquest of the *beylik* by Mehmed II in 1461, the same year in which he conquered Trebizond.

The dominant Latin trading state in the Black Sea region in the fourteenth and fifteenth centuries was Genoa which established a major trading base in Caffa, "the great emporium of the pontic regions",[5] around 1268.[6] Genoese merchants were active on the Anatolian Black Sea coast certainly from the later thirteenth century. According to Shukurov, the Genoese had probably established a settlement in Trebizond by 1281, and the Venetians, the other major western traders in the region, not long before 1291.[7] There were Genoese

(Istanbul: The Isis Press, 1990), states that by the end of 1391 "Bayezid had presumably forced the lords of northern Anatolia, as far east as the Kızılırmak, to accept his suzerainty", p. 39.

3 Yücel, Yaşar, "Candar-oğlu Çelebi İsfendiyar Bey 1392–1439", *Tarih Araştırmaları Dergisi*, 2/2–3 (1964), pp. 159–61.

4 Kastritsis, Dimitri K. (trans.), *An Early Ottoman History. The Oxford Anonymous Chronicle (Bodleian Library, Ms Marsh 313)* (Liverpool: Liverpool University Press, 2017), p. 89; Aşıkpaşazade, *Die Altosmanische Chronik des Ašıkpašazāde*, ed. Fredrich Giese (Leipzig, 1929, reprinted Osnabrük: Otto Zeller Verlag, 1972), bab 65, p. 65; Neşri, *Kitâb-ı Cihan-nümâ. Neşri Tarihi*, vol. I, ed. Faik Reşit Unat and Mehmed A. Köymen (Ankara: Türk Tarih Kurumu Basımevi, 1987), p. 322; Schiltberger, Johann, *The Bondage and Travels of Johann Schiltberger, A Native of Bavaria, in Europe, Asia and Africa, 1396–1427*, trans. J. Buchan Telfer (London: The Hakluyt Society, 1879), ch. 7, p. 12; Silay, Kemal, "Ahmedī's history of the Ottoman dynasty", *Journal of Turkish Studies. Türklük Bilgisi Araştırmaları*, 16 (1992), *Richard Nelson Frye Festschrift I*, ed. Şinasi Tekin and Gönül Alp Tekin, p. 142; Imber, *Ottoman Empire*, p. 41.

5 Balard, Michel, "Notes sur la fiscalité génoise à Caffa au XVe siècle", *Bulletin de la Société nationale des antiquaires de France* (1993), p. 224.

6 For the origins of Genoese Caffa, see Khvalkov, Evgeny, *The Colonies of Genoa in the Black Sea Region. Evolution and Transformation* (New York and Abingdon, Oxon: Routledge, 2018), pp. 65–6.

7 Shukurov, Rustam, "Foreigners in the empire of Trebizond (the case of Orientals and Latins)", in *At the Crossroads of Empires: 14th–15th Century Eastern Anatolia. Proceedings of the International Symposium Held in Istanbul, 4th–6th May 2007* (Istanbul: Institut français d'études anatoliennes-Georges Dumézil, 2012), p. 78.

consuls in Trebizond, Galvano di Negro in around 1285[8] and Paolino Doria in 1290,[9] while a notary deed was enacted in Trebizond in 1302 in the *loggia* where the Genoese authorities conducted affairs.[10] The Venetians were established there from the last the quarter of the thirteenth century, later than the Genoese, whom Bratianu, quoting Pachymeres, states had been there for a long time.[11] Genoese merchants were active at Fatsa (Vatiza), for in 1274 the Genoese notary Federico di Pizzalunga, enacted several deeds there in the house of the Genoese merchant, Guilielmo Mastraccio de Sampierdarena.[12] The fact that the deeds were enacted in a merchant's house shows that there was no consul or *loggia* there, Genoese merchant interests being perhaps handled by the Genoese consul in Trebizond,[13] but also indicates that the Genoese presence was sufficiently important for a merchant to be based there at this point, while the deeds themselves demonstrate a certain level of commercial activity. The Genoese were certainly trading in Sinop and Samsun from the late thirteenth century. Merchants enacted a contract in 1280 in Sivas, "in the *fondaco* of Kemaleddin where the Genoese live in a chapel", for the hire of a ship to load their goods at either Sinop or Samsun from where the ship was to sail to Genoa,[14] and merchants in Pera[15] and Caffa made trade partnerships for trade in Sinop.[16]

From their base in Caffa, the Genoese dominated the trade of the Black Sea region in the fourteenth and the first half of the fifteenth centuries. They established three trading settlements on the northern Anatolian coast at Amasra, Sinop and Samsun, trading with the Turkish hinterland, with Caffa and along the Anatolian coast, importing goods from the west and exporting goods out into the Mediterranean and to the Mamluk sultanate.

---

8   Bratianu, G.I., *Recherches sur le commerce génois dans la mer noire au xiiie siècle* (Paris: Libraire Orientaliste Paul Geuthner, 1929), p. 175.

9   Bratianu, *Recherches*, p. 174. He is referred to in Bratianu, G.I., *Actes des notaires génois de Péra et de Caffa de la fin du treizième siècle 1281–1290* (Bucharest: Cultura Nationala, 1927), doc. CCCI, p. 274.

10   Bratianu, *Recherches*, p. 175.

11   Bratianu, *Recherches*, p. 175.

12   Bratianu, *Recherches*, doc. III, p. 303; doc. IV, pp. 303–4; doc. V, pp. 304–5; doc. VI, pp. 306–7 and Balletto, Laura, *Notai genovese in oltremare. Atti rogati a Laiazzo da Federico di Pizzalunga (1274) e Pietro di Bargone (1277, 1279)* (Genoa: Università di Genova, 1989), docs. 111, 112, 113 and 114, pp. 152–6.

13   Bratianu, *Recherches*, pp. 172–3.

14   Bratianu, *Recherches*, doc. XII, pp. 312–14.

15   Bratianu, *Actes*, doc. XXXV, pp. 94–5.

16   Bratianu, *Actes*, doc. XXXV, pp. 94–5; doc. CLXXIV, pp. 187–8; doc. CCLXXIII, p. 253.

The Commodities of Trade

Throughout this period, the northern Anatolian coastal region was part of a Black Sea trading zone with trade oriented to and from Crimea. This orientation is evident in the late thirteenth century with trade being conducted between Fatsa and Soldaia[17] and between Caffa and Sinop,[18] Samsun[19] and Trebizond.[20] Goods traded into Anatolia from the northern Black Sea included cheese,[21] fish,[22] salt,[23] and leather.[24] Transit goods, such as spices and silk, were shipped from the Anatolian coast to the north. William of Rubruck refers to merchants from Turchia (that is the land under Turkish control) trading "cloths of cotton or bombax, silk stuffs and sweet-smelling spices" to "the northern countries", while merchants from "Roscia and the northern countries" traded furs into Turchia.[25] There was also trade east-west between the coastal ports and with Constantinople in the west and Trebizond in the east,[26] and with the Anatolian hinterland. In the late thirteenth century goods were transported overland from Lajazzo (Ayas, modern Yumurtalık in the province of Adana) on the southern coast across Anatolia to Sivas and from there to the Black Sea coast.[27]

Throughout the fourteenth and the first half of the fifteenth centuries, Genoese-Turkish trade revolved largely round the export of natural products from Anatolia, the import of goods from the west, and trade in natural

---

17   Bratianu, *Recherches*, doc. VI, pp. 306–7; Balletto, *Notai genovese*, doc. 114, pp. 156–7.

18   Bratianu, *Actes*, doc. CLXXIV, pp. 187–8; doc. CCLXXIII, p. 253.

19   Bratianu, *Actes*, doc. CXCV, pp. 201–2; doc. CCXVI, p. 215; doc. CCXVIII, p. 216.

20   Bratianu, *Actes*, doc. CCXIX, pp. 216–17; doc. CCXX, p. 217; doc. CLXXV, p. 188; doc. CLXXXII, p. 194; doc. CLXXXVI, p. 196; doc. CXCV, pp. 201–2; doc. CCIII, p. 207; doc. CCXVII, pp. 215–16; doc. CCXIX, pp. 216–17; doc. CCXX, p. 217; doc. CCXXIII, p. 219; doc. CCXXVI, p. 221; doc. CCXXXVI, p. 228; doc. CCXXXVII, p. 229; doc. CCXLII, p. 232; doc. CCXLIV, p. 233; doc. CCLXXIII, p. 253; doc. CCLXXVIII, pp. 256–7.

21   Bratianu, *Actes*, doc. CCIII, p. 207.

22   Bratianu, *Actes*, doc. CCLXXXVI, pp. 262–3; doc. CCCVI, pp. 279–80, doc. CCCXII, pp. 283–4; Balard, Michel, *Gênes et l'Outre-Mer I. Les actes de Caffa du notaire Lamberto di Sambuceto 1289–1290* (Paris and the Hague: Mouton and Co., 1973), doc. 740, p. 291; doc. 903, pp. 378–9.

23   Bratianu, *Actes*, doc. CCXXIII, p. 219; doc. CCCV, pp. 278–9; Balard, *Gênes et l'Outre-Mer*, doc. 629, p. 235; doc. 843, p. 345.

24   Balard, *Gênes et l'Outre-Mer*, doc. 740, p. 291.

25   Rubruck, William, *The Journal of William of Rubruck to the Eastern Parts of the World 1253–55*, ed. and trans. William Woodville Rockhill (London: The Hakluyt Society, 1900), p. 44.

26   Bratianu, *Recherches*, doc. V, pp. 304–5; Balletto, *Notai genovese*, doc. 113, pp. 154–5; Bratianu, *Actes*, doc. XXXV, pp. 94–5.

27   Bratianu, *Recherches*, pp. 157–9.

products of the region back and forth across the Black Sea, Heyd noting the "incessant movement of navigation of the southern [Genoese] colonies of the Black Sea to Caffa ... and Tana".[28] Items traded from Anatolia included grain, alum, produced in Şebinkarahisar and exported through Giresun (Kerasunt),[29] and wine, also exported from Giresun and sold in Pera and Caffa.[30] Goods traded into Anatolia from the northern Black Sea included fish, leather and hides, leather being exported from Tana to Trebizond and Samsun,[31] as well as a substantial trade in slaves. Imported goods from the west, some of which came via Caffa, included cloth in considerable quantities,[32] soap,[33] and wine.[34] Much trade ran along the northern Anatolian coast between Constantinople and Trebizond, stopping at ports on the way, or from Constantinople to ports such as Samsun and then across the Black Sea to Caffa. The vessel on which the Spanish traveller Pero Tafur sailed in 1437, for example, called at Sinop, spending two days "discharging merchandise, and loading other goods" before sailing on to Trebizond.[35] The year before, goods loaded in Constantinople for Sinop, the "best and richest" of the towns on the Black Sea, according to Kritoboulos and "a common emporium for the whole region as well as for no small part of lower Asia",[36] included one bale of six pieces of *pane loesti* (a course cloth) of which four were scarlet, one green and one deep blue.[37]

28 Heyd, Wilhelm, *Histoire du commerce du Levant au moyen-âge*, vol. II (Leipzig: Otto Harrassowitz, 1886), p. 360.

29 Pegolotti, *Fr Balducci Pegolotti, La Pratica della Mercature*, ed. A. Evans (Cambridge, Mass.: The Medieval Academy of America, 1936), pp. 43 and 369.

30 Balard, Michel, *La Romanie génoise (XIIe–début du XVe siècle)*, 2 vols. (Genoa: Società Ligure di Storia Patria, and Paris: École Française de Rome, 1978), vol. II, p. 844; Balard, *Gênes et l'Outre-Mer*, doc. 768, p. 307.

31 Balard, *Romanie génoise*, II, p. 737.

32 Bratianu, *Actes*, doc. CLXXXVI, p. 196; doc. CCXXVI, p. 221; doc. CCCXXX, p. 297; Badoer, Giacomo, *Il Libro dei Conti di Giacomo Badoer (Costantinopoli 1436–1440)*, ed. Umberto Dorini and Tommaso Bertelè (Rome: Istituto Poligrafico dello Stato, Libreria dello Stato, 1956), c. 44, p. 88, c. 13, p. 27; Archivio di Stato di Genova [hereafter ASG], Notaio Giovanni Labaino Sc. 40 filze 1, doc. 15; Basso, Enrico, "Gli atti di Giovanni de Labaino (1410–1412): note su una fonte inedita per la storia di Caffe e del Mar Nero", in Море и берега К 60-летию Сергея Павловича Карпова от коллег и учеников ["Mare et Litora". Essays Presented to Sergei Pavlovich Karpov for his 60th Birthday], ed. Rustam Shukurov (Moscow: INDRIK, 2009), p. 510; Khvalkov, *Colonies*, p. 354.

33 Basso, "Gli atti di Giovanni de Labaino", p. 510.

34 Balard, *Romanie Génoise*, I, pp. 131–2.

35 Tafur, Pero, *Travels and Adventures, 1435–1439*, trans. and ed. Malcolm Letts (London: George Routledge and Sons, 1926), pp. 129–30.

36 Kritoboulos, *History of Mehmed the Conqueror. By Kritovoulos*, trans. C.T. Riggs (Westport, Connecticut: Greenwood Press, 1954), p. 166.

37 Badoer, *Libro*, c. 13, p. 27; c. 7, p. 14.

A clear idea of the type of trade conducted along the route Constantinople-Samsun-Trebizond is given by entries in the account book of the Venetian merchant Giacomo Badoer who was active in Constantinople in the late 1430s. Goods loaded in Constantinople in 1436 for Samsun and Trebizond included one box containing 92 cones of refined sugar from Cyprus, seven butts of dried grapes from Lichomedia (? İzmit), bartered by Ahmet Turcho for two pieces of cloth, one green and one deep blue,[38] seven cases of soap of Ancona, two butts of salted fish (*sconbri saladi*), four pieces of *pani loesti*, of which three were scarlet and one green, and ten small pieces of white cotton cloth (*fostagni*).[39] Many goods were sold in Samsun[40] by Antonio da Negroponte, who was acting in partnership with Giacomo Badoer and who was himself an inhabitant of Trebizond.[41]

In Samsun Antonio da Negroponte sold seven butts of dried grapes, seven cases of soap, one butt of dried fish, four pieces of *pani loesti* and ten pieces of cotton cloth (*fostagni*). All the prices at which he sold the commodities were given in *akçe* apart from the cloth which was given in Turkish ducats with an exchange rate of 36 *akçe* for one Turkish ducat. The weight of the seven cases of soap was given in the weight at which it was weighed in Samsun. The costs incurred in connection with these sales in Samsun were for renting a warehouse, porters to unload the goods, drink for the sailors, brokerage at one per cent and import customs at two per cent.[42] Antonio left one *butt* of dried fish (*sconbri saladi*) with Todaro Xingi, a Greek and an inhabitant of Samsun who was to sell it and to hand the money over to the Genoese Polo Morson, presumably an inhabitant of Samsun acting as Badoer's agent.[43]

Antonio bought in Samsun 90 pieces of leather (*cordoani*), 304 *dexena* (an amount of ten) of hair,[44] 11 *chapizi de rexi*[45] at 50 *akçe* per Ottoman *batman*,

---

38   Badoer, *Libro*, c. 13, p. 27; Fleet, Kate, *European and Islamic Trade in the Early Ottoman State: The Merchants of Genoa and Turkey* (Cambridge: Cambridge University Press, 1999), p. 75.

39   Badoer, *Libro*, c. 43, p. 86 and p. 87; c. 44, p. 88; c. 13, p. 27; c. 14, p. 29; c. 51, p. 102. In the entry c. 44, p. 88 the number of pieces of sugar is given as 90.

40   Badoer, *Libro*, c. 152, p. 306.

41   Badoer, *Libro*, c. 44, p. 88.

42   Badoer, *Libro*, c. 44, p. 89.

43   Badoer, *Libro*, c. 166, p. 334; c. 44, p. 89. The Genoese appears as Marzion in the entry c. 166, p. 334 and as Morson in c. 44, p. 89.

44   For hair see Fleet, *Trade*, pp. 30, 33–4.

45   I have not been able to identify the meaning of this phrase. However, *chapizi* is probably a measurement of weight, given that the second reference in Badoer to this refers to 11 *batimani* of *rexi*. The *batimano* or *batman*, was a measurement of weight used in western Anatolia, North Africa and the Black Sea in this period (Fleet, *Trade*, p. 185). *Chapizi* may

33 pieces of tanned oxhide, 13 *cantars* and 73 *rotoli* of hemp, 26 Samsun *moza* of grain (*formenti*), 60 pieces of bocasin (a cloth of very fine linen) in various colours (blue, green and white), two pieces of camlet, one blue and one black, taffetas (*zendadi*)[46] and seven *cantars* and nine *rotoli* of flour (*farina*). All the prices for the goods bought were given in Samsun *akçes* or, in the case of the hemp, in Turkish ducats, and converted in the account book of Giacomo Badoer into *perpera* at the rate of 19 *akçe* per *perpera*.[47] Antonio also bought 26 marten furs and four tanned beech martens (*fuine*).[48]

Antonio then sailed on to Trebizond where he sold the goods that he had bought in Samsun: 57 pieces of leather (*cordoani*), 304 of hair, *rexi* (11 *batimani*), 33 pieces of tanned oxhide, 11 *cantars* and 60 *rotoli* of hemp, 26 *moza* of grain (*formenti*) and 60 pieces of bocasin.[49] He also sold 43 cones of refined sugar.[50] The two pieces of camlet, the taffeta and the flour he kept for his own account.[51] He handed over 47 cones of refined sugar to ser Griguol Chontarini in Trebizond.[52] There also remained 26 pieces of leather (*cordoani*) which he left in Trebizond.[53]

While cloth predominated among the goods imported by the Genoese and other Latin merchants into the region, exports either from Anatolia or into Anatolia from the northern Black Sea were dominated by three important commodities: grain, copper and slaves. Apart from providing information on merchandise traded, an examination of these commodities also sheds light on the politics of the period and on regional production.

Grain

A major item of trade was grain. Both the northern Black Sea region and northern Anatolia were grain producing areas.[54] The northern Black Sea was a major exporter of grain to the west. Pegolotti referred to grain being loaded there for

---

be a variant of the word *capide*, defined in Florio as "a kind of measure in Persia" (Florio, John, *Queen Anna's New World of Words or Dictionarie of the Italian and English Tongues* (London: Melch, Bradwood, 1611)).

46   The number of pieces is missing in the text.
47   Badoer, *Libro*, c. 152, p. 306.
48   Badoer, *Libro*, c. 152, p. 307; c. 102, p. 206.
49   Badoer, *Libro*, c. 152, p. 307.
50   Badoer, *Libro*, c. 44, p. 89; c. 166, p. 334.
51   Badoer, *Libro*, c. 44, p. 88; c. 152, p. 307.
52   Badoer, *Libro*, c. 44, p. 89; c. 51, p. 102; c. 173, p. 348.
53   Badoer, *Libro*, c. 166, pp. 334 and 335.
54   Ibn Battuta, *Voyages d'Ibn Batoutah*, vol. 11, ed. and trans. C. Defrémery and R. Sanguinetti (Paris: L'Imprimerie Impériale, 1854), p. 344.

export to Constantinople and Pera and "other parts of the world".[55] Turchia was an important supplier for Genoa and Venice.[56] There was also a trade in grain between northern Anatolia and the northern Black Sea. In the earlier part of the period, the orientation of the trade was north-south, grain coming into Anatolia from Crimea, but from around the mid-1380s this shifted to a south-north orientation with grain moving in the opposite direction. This raises the question of why the orientation changed in the late fourteenth century.

Karpov has argued that the shift in orientation was due to crop failures and the political situation in Caffa.[57] While the conditions in the northern Black Sea region undoubtedly affected the Black Sea grain trade, it is also possible to argue that a further significant factor at this point was Ottoman political power and economic policy.

Up to the late fourteenth century grain was being traded into Anatolia. In the late thirteenth century there are references to millet, wheat and barley being exported from Caffa to Trebizond, Giresun and Samsun,[58] and in the fourteenth century Samsun was importing grain from Caffa.[59] Given that northern Anatolia was grain producing, to the extent that it was exporting the commodity to Caffa from the late fourteenth century, the grain imported at this point was presumably not for the Turkish market, although lack of sources makes any comment on the local Anatolian grain market necessarily speculative. It was therefore presumably imported, at least in part, to supply the Genoese trading colonies at Amasra, Sinop and Samsun, as well as Trebizond, which was shut off from the grain-producing hinterland. This is supported by the fact that in 1382 the expenses for several hundred *mud*s of grain shipped there from Caffa were debited against the treasurer of the Genoese trading settlement at Samsun.[60] If this was the case, it would indicate that the Genoese colonies were supplied at this point by Caffa, rather than buying from the Anatolian market. This could be the result of a deliberate Genoese policy of avoiding dependence for a basic foodstuff on a foreign power, or it could perhaps be related to the cost of supply of grain to the Anatolian coast from the hinterland which would have depended on potentially costly overland transportation, making provision cheaper by sea from Caffa.

---

55   Pegolotti, *Pratica*, p. 54.

56   Fleet, *Trade*, pp. 63–73.

57   Karpov, S.P., "The grain trade in the southern Black Sea region: the thirteenth to the fifteenth century", *Mediterranean Historical Review*, 8/1 (1993), pp. 65–6.

58   Bratianu, *Actes*, doc. CXCV, pp. 201–2; doc. CCXXIII, p. 219; doc. CCCXIII, p. 285; doc. CCCXI, p. 283; Balard, *Gênes et l'Outre-Mer*, doc. 404, p. 159; doc. 409, p. 162.

59   Balard, *Romanie génoise*, I, pp. 133, 337.

60   Balard, *Romanie génoise*, I, p. 400.

From around the mid-1380s the direction of the grain trade changed. In 1385 the consul in Samsun was instructed by the consul in Caffa to buy grain, barley, millet, chickpeas and beans there to be sent to Caffa.[61] The following year grain was being bought in Samsun both for Caffa and for the Genoese trading settlement in Samsun,[62] the treasurers of Caffa bought grain in Amasra,[63] and grain and millet were exported from Samsun to Caffa.[64] Following the argument that the direction changed due in part to political conditions in the northern Black Sea region, one might have expected such a shift to have occurred in the 1340s when the Tatar khan banned the export of grain as a result of a dispute with Venice, but this was apparently not the case. In 1386, the war with the Tatars of Solgat did, according to Balard, result in Caffa turning to Turchia for grain.[65] There is, however, another factor here at this point and that is the rise of the Ottomans in the northern Anatolian region, a region from which they had been absent in the 1340s.

Ottoman policy appears to have involved both controlling the quantity of grain exported from Ottoman territory, a policy possibly introduced by Murad I,[66] and imposing a trade ban on the commodity. In 1390 Bayezid I banned the export of grain from his territories.[67] The ban was still in operation in 1400.[68] By this time, Bayezid's territories included much of northern Anatolia. Given that the Ottoman ban on grain exports hit Genoa's grain supplies from western Anatolia, it is possible to suggest that grain from northern

61 Khvalkov, *Colonies*, p. 341.

62 Karpov, "Grain trade", p. 65.

63 Balard, *Romanie génoise*, I, p. 130.

64 Balard, *Romanie génoise*, I, p. 338.

65 Balard, *Romanie génoise*, II, p. 761.

66 Fleet, Kate, "Ottoman grain exports from western Anatolia at the end of the fourteenth century", *Journal of the Economic and Social History of the Orient*, 40/3 (1997), p. 292.

67 Chrysostomides, Julian (ed.), *Monumenta Peloponnesiaca. Documents for the History of the Peloponnese in the 14th and 15th Centuries* (Camberely: Porphyrogenitus, 1995), doc. 68, p. 138, note 2; Doukas, *Historia Byzantina*, ed. Immanuel Bekker (Bonn: E. Weber, 1834), p. 47; Doukas, *Decline and Fall of Byzantium to the Ottoman Turks*, trans. H.J. Magoulias (Detroit: Wayne State University Press, 1975), p. 81; Luttrell, Anthony and Elizabeth A. Zachariadou (eds.), *Sources for Turkish History in the Hospitallers' Rhodian Archive 1389–1422* (Athens: National Hellenic Research Foundation Institute for Byzantine Research, 2008), no. 5, p. 95; no. 8, p. 97; Zachariadou, Elizabeth A., *Trade and Crusade: Venetian Crete and the Emirates of Menteshe and Aydin (1300–1415)* (Venice: Istituto Ellenico di Studi Bizantini e Postbizantini di Venezia, 1983), p. 78.

68 Noiret, H., *Documents inédits pour servir à l'histoire de la domination vénitienne en Crète de 1380 à 1485* (Paris: E. Thorin, 1892), pp. 110–11; Thiriet, F., *Régestes des délibérations du Sénat de Venise concernant la Romanie*, 3 vols. (Paris: Mouton, 1958–1961), vol. II, doc. 988, pp. 12–13; Iorga, N., *Notes et extraits pour servir à l'histoire de croisades au XVᵉ siecle*, 3 vols. (Paris: Ernest Leroux, 1899–1902), vol. I, p. 102.

Anatolia could have been exported northwards to Caffa and from there to Genoa. Grain could have been exported more easily from this region in part because the Ottoman conquest was recent and the İsfendiyaroğulları did apparently retain some independence, and because Bayezid's target for the ban seems largely to have been Constantinople, which he put under siege in 1394. Grain going to Caffa and from there to Genoa would not, therefore, have been his prime concern. Why grain would not have been exported from Caffa to Anatolia can thus be explained by Genoa's own needs for grain in the new environment where western Anatolia was not the reliable grain market it had been.

With the collapse of Ottoman power in the wake of the battle of Ankara in 1402, the position changed. Under the 1403 treaty between Süleyman Çelebi and Byzantium, Genoa, Venice and the Hospitallers, any restriction on grain export was removed, a clause in the agreement stating that all ports (*scale*) under his control were open and any quantity of grain could be exported without hindrance from the Ottoman customs officials (*comerchieri*).[69] It would appear that this treaty covered at least the western part of northern Anatolia. Ruy González de Clavijo, when on an embassy to Timur, described Bender Ereğli (Pontoraquia, Heraclea Pontica), where he stayed one night on his second voyage into the Black Sea in March 1404, as "a city belonging to Süleyman Çelebi, who is the eldest son of the late Sultan".[70] Further to the east, İsfendiyaroğulları control was briefly re-established, but by the beginning of the reign of Murad II, the Ottomans were once more dominant in the region. From the 1420s more and more grain was going from northern Anatolia to Crimea. In the late 1420s and 1430s Caffa was buying grain from northern Anatolia, including from Samsun, Bafra and Amasra.[71] Grain was also shipped from Constantinople to Trebizond in the 1430s,[72] and grain was bought in Samsun and shipped to Trebizond where it was sold in the same period.[73]

By the 1450s it would appear that the Ottomans were once more using the control of the grain supply as a political lever, this time to apply pressure to Caffa. In this period, Caffa suffered increasingly from a dearth of grain. In 1455 the region was hit by drought and in August Caffan officials reported that Caffa

---

69   Dennis, G.T., "The Byzantine-Turkish Treaty of 1403", *Orientalia Christiana Periodica*, 33 (1967), cl. 13, p. 79.

70   de Clavijo, Ruy González, *Narrative of the Embassy of Ruy González de Clavijo to the Court of Samarcand, A.D. 1403–6* (London: Hakluyt Society, 1859), p. 104.

71   Karpov, "Grain trade", pp. 66, 67.

72   Badoer, *Libro*, c. 65, p. 131; c. 51, p. 103; c. 65, p. 130; c. 153, p. 308.

73   Badoer, *Libro*, c. 152, p. 306 and c. 152, p. 307.

was very short of grain.[74] In September the Caffan consul despatched ships to "Leona" near Samsun to buy grain,[75] although apparently hope of obtaining supplies from Turchia was very low.[76] This indicates that there may have been some sort of prevention of the export of grain to Caffa at this point. This would have been reasonable as Mehmed II was certainly contemplating the capture of Caffa from which he demanded tribute in 1454, according to Demetrio Vivaldi, the Genoese consul there.[77] A tribute of 3,000 ducats was duly paid under an agreement made by the Genoese officials of Caffa in 1455, according to the report of the Genoese authorities on Chios.[78] Applying a stranglehold on the supply of grain to Caffa would have served Ottoman purposes well.

Copper

From a commodity point of view, grain was, however, probably not the main reason for Ottoman interest in the region, for northern Anatolia was a producer of another valuable commodity: copper. Copper was mined in Kastamonu, Sinop, Samsun and Osmancık. Of high quality according to Chalkokondyles,[79] it was the most important product of the region of Sinop, Kritoboulos describing it as being exported "everywhere in Asia and Europe", and being a major source of revenue.[80] The mines and quarries of Kastamonu were highly productive.[81]

There was extensive trade in copper from northern Anatolia. Caffa's main supply of copper came from Anatolia, according to Khvalkov,[82] and supplies of copper leaf were shipped from Sinop to Caffa.[83] In 1402 a ship owner of Pera undertook to go and load copper at Sinop.[84] The Genoese traded in large quantities of copper with the İsfendiyaroğulları. In 1390 two Genoese merchants from Pera established a partnership (società) to purchase copper from

---

74   Vigna, P. Amadeo (ed.), "Codice diplomatico delle colonie Tauro-Ligure durante la signoria dell'Ufficio di S. Giorgio (MCCCCLIII–MCCCLXXV)", Atti della Società Ligure di Storia Patria, 6/1 (1868), doc. CL, p. 359.
75   Vigna, "Codice", doc. CLI, pp. 367–8.
76   Vigna, "Codice", doc. CLII, p. 368.
77   Vigna, "Codice", doc. XXXIII, p. 106.
78   Vigna, "Codice", doc. CXVII, p. 299.
79   Chalkokondyles, Historiarum Libri Decem, ed. Immanuel Bekker (Bonn: E. Weber, 1843), p. 498; Chalkokondyles, The Histories, 2 vols., trans. Anthony Kaldellis (Cambridge, Mass.: Harvard University Press, 2014), vol. II, pp. 350/351.
80   Kritoboulos, History, p. 166.
81   Promontorio, Iacopo de, Die Aufzeichnungen des Genuesen Iacopo de Promontorio-de Campis über den Osmanenstaat um 1475, ed. Franz Babinger (Munich: Verlag der Bayerischen Akademie der Wissenschaften, 1957), p. 67.
82   Khvalkov, Colonies, p. 351.
83   Balard, Romanie génoise, II, p. 784.
84   Balard, Romanie génoise, II, p. 784.

the İsfendiyaroğulları ruler Süleyman for the substantial sum of 476,000 silver *akçe* of Kastamonu.[85] Venetian merchants, too, were purchasing copper from Kastamonu in the same period[86] and the Senate set out freight charges for copper from Kastamonu on Venetian vessels in 1434.[87] Copper appears very frequently in the account books of the Venetian merchant Giacomo Badoer, who was in Constantinople in the late 1430s and who traded extensively with the Black Sea and Anatolia. Any copper appearing is his accounts is highly likely to have been from the copper mines of northern Anatolia. The copper loaded in 1448 onto a ship from Ancona in Constantinople was also most probably from the same source.[88]

One of the reasons for Ottoman advance in the region was to seize control of the copper resources from the İsfendiyaroğulları. Bayezid I, Mehmed I and Murad II all focused on obtaining copper rather than outright conquest, leaving the İsfendiyaroğulları in place but paying tribute in copper.[89] Mehmed II also received tribute from the İsfendiyaroğulları in copper for, according to a Genoese document from 1453, a ship (a *griparia*) seized by a Genoese captain was carrying, among other goods, 500 *cantar*s of copper which the "lord of Sinop" was to give as part of his tribute to the sultan.[90]

Copper was used for two main purposes: minting coins and casting cannon. Copper coins (*mangır*) were struck by various *beylik*s, including Karesi, Saruhan and the İsfendiyaroğulları.[91] The Ottomans first minted them probably in the reign of Murad I,[92] though it is also argued that they were struck

---

85   ASG, Notai C.476, Donato de Clavaro, doc. 26. A summary and transcription of this document is in Fleet, *Trade*, Appendix, doc. 3, pp. 158–61. A summary has also been published by Balard, Michel, Angeliki L. Laiou and Catherine Otten-Froux, *Les Italiens à Byzance et présentation de documents* (Paris: Publications de la Sorbonne, 1987), no. 82, p. 37.

86   Thiriet, *Régestes*, I, no. 863, p. 204.

87   Thiriet, *Régestes*, II, no. 2349, p. 38.

88   Thiriet, *Régestes*, II, no. 2777, p. 145.

89   Chalkokondyles, *Historiarum Libri Decem*, p. 185; Chalkokondyles, *Histories*, I, pp. 406/407; Aşıkpaşazade, *Chronik*, pp. 92–3; Neşri, *Kitâb-ı Cihan-nümâ*, II, pp. 574–7; Imber, *Ottoman Empire*, pp. 88, 95–6.

90   Vigna, "Codice", doc. CXXXVI, p. 333.

91   Artuk, İbrahim, "Karesi-oğulları Adına Basılmış Olan İki Sikke", *İstanbul Üniversitesi Edebiyat Fakültesi Tarih Dergisi*, 33 (1980–1981), p. 284; Schindel, Nikolaus, "The earliest Ottoman copper coin?", *Numismatic Circular*, 120/4 (2014), p. 138; Ender, Celil, Üstün Erek and Gültekin Teoman, *Candaroğulları Beyliği (İsfendiyaroğulları Beyliği) Paraları Kataloğu* (Istanbul: Ender Nümismatik Yayınları, 2003), pp. 141,142, 242–7.

92   Artuk, İbrahim, "I. Murad'ın Sikkelerine Genel Bir Bakış 761–792 (1359–1389)", *Belleten*, 46/184 (1982), p. 789; Pamuk, Şevket, *A Monetary History of the Ottoman Empire* (Cambridge: Cambridge University Press, 2000), p. 38; Bölükbaşı, Ömerül Faruk, "Mangır", in *Encyclopaedia of Islam, Three*, ed. Kate Fleet, Gudrun Krämer, Denis

under Orhan I.[93] İsfendiyaroğulları copper coins were in circulation in Ankara before Murad I conquered it and replaced them with *mangırs* struck in Bursa.[94] Often regarded as primarily a source of taxation through the levying of seigniorage, these coins were important in small market transactions, an "indispensable role", according to Pamuk, which should not be underestimated.[95]

However significant copper coins may or may not have been for local market exchange in this period, it would seem unlikely that the Ottoman drive to control the copper resources of the region was motivated entirely by the need for copper coinage. It should be noted, however, that the Genoese merchant Jacopo de Promontorio, who lived in the courts of both Murad II and Mehmed II and wrote an account of the Ottoman state in 1476, stated that the copper from the mines and quarries in the province of Kastamonu was used to manufacture money.[96] A more likely explanation for Ottoman conquest policy here is the making of weapons.

The date at which the Ottomans first cast cannons is not clearly established. Àgoston is sceptical about Danişmend's claim that the first Ottoman cannon was cast in 1364 (though Danişmend says elsewhere that it was cast in Bursa four years before this so in 1361),[97] or that cannons were used in 1354 in the taking of Gelibolu and at the battle of Kosovo in 1389, as these claims are based on much later Ottoman sources.[98] According to Àgoston the Ottomans were "acquainted with gunpowder weapons" from the 1380s, and used cannon at the first siege of Constantinople from 1394 to 1402. They are also known to have used cannon at subsequent sieges, including those of Constantinople in 1422, Thessaloniki in 1422 and 1430, Antalya in 1424 and Smenderevo in 1439.[99] They were certainly casting cannon in the early years of Mehmed II's

Matringe, John Nawas and Everett Rowson (Leiden: Brill, 2007–), online http://dx.doi .org/10.1163/1573-3912_ei3_COM_36161.

93   Schindel, "Earliest Ottoman copper coin?", p. 138.

94   Artuk, "I. Murad'ın Sikkelerine Genel Bir Bakış", pp. 790–1.

95   Pamuk, *Monetary History*, p. 39.

96   de Promontorio, *Die Aufzeichnungen*, p. 67.

97   Danişmend, İsmail Hakkı, "Eski Türk Ordusunun Silah ve Teknik Üstünlüğü", in Danişmend, İsmail Hakkı, *Tarihi Hakikatler* (Istanbul: Bilgeoğuz, 2016), p. 254.

98   Àgoston, Gàbor, "Early modern Ottoman and European gunpowder technology", in *Multicultural Science in the Ottoman Empire*, ed. Ekmeleddin İhsanoğlu, Efthymios Nicolaïdis and Konstantinos Chatzis (Turnhout: Brepols, 2003), pp. 16–17.

99   Àgoston, Gàbor, "Firearms and military adaptation: the Ottomans and the European military revolution, 1450–1800", *Journal of World History*, 25/1 (2014), p. 88; Àgoston, Gàbor, *Guns for the Sultan. Military Power and the Weapons Industry in the Ottoman Empire* (Cambridge: Cambridge University Press, 2005), pp. 16–21; Heywood, Colin, "Notes on production of fifteenth-century Ottoman cannon", in Heywood, Colin, *Writing Ottoman History: Documents and Interpretations* (Aldershot: Ashgate, 2002), XVI, pp. 3–9.

reign. Canon were placed in the fortress of Rumeli Hisarı[100] and the capture of Constantinople involved cannons including a very large one cast by a
Hungarian renegade to whom, Doukas specifies, bronze was supplied.[101] The
imperial cannon foundry (Tophane-i Amire), the centre for Ottoman cannon
casting, was set up by Mehmed II in Istanbul after the conquest.[102] According
to the Genoese captain who seized the ship transporting the İsfendiyaroğulları
copper to Istanbul in 1453, the copper (in the captain's statement about
400 *cantars* not 500 as stated by the consul) was not tribute but belonged to
the Ottoman ruler, "who had sent one of his slaves to buy it in Sinop in order to
have cannons made from it to be used to attack the Christians and especially
our ships".[103] The captain's version of the origin of the copper was probably
related to his dispute with the consul of Caffa who, furious at the seizure of the
ship and fearful of Ottoman reprisals,[104] had sequestered all the goods seized
by the captain. Either way, the use to which the Ottomans put the copper
is clear.

The Ottoman drive to capture the copper resources of northern Anatolia
in the late fourteenth century is thus most probably related to the production
of weapons. This has implications for the dating at which the Ottomans first
struck cannon and reinforces the argument that the Ottomans did not need
to import weapons, the arms trade thus being hard to track in the sources not
because it was concealed but because it did not exist to the extent that has
sometimes been assumed.[105]

Slaves

Another major commodity was slaves. The northern Black Sea region was
a major exporter of slaves, a trade largely in the hands of the Genoese who
exported slaves to Italy and to the Mamluk sultanate. Genoa sought to monop-
olise the trade as much as possible, probably encouraged in this direction,
Balard suggests, by the impact of the Black Death which increased the need

---

100   Doukas, *Historia Byzantina*, p. 26; Doukas, *Decline and Fall*, p. 199; Tursun Bey, *Târîh-i
       Ebü'l-Feth*, ed. Mertol Tulum (Istanbul: Baha Matbaası, 1977), p. 45; Kritoboulos, *History*,
       50, p. 21, Barbaro, Nicolò, "Giornale dell'assedio di Costantinopoli", in *La caduta di
       Costantinopoli. Le testimonianze dei contemporanei*, vol. I, ed. Agostino Pertusi (Milan:
       Mondadori, 1999), pp. 9–11.

101   Doukas, *Historia Byzantina*, pp. 247–8, 258, 272; Doukas, *Decline and Fall*, pp. 200, 207, 215;
       Kritoboulos, *History*, pp. 41–47, 51–3, 58, 59; Barbaro, "Giornale", pp. 10, 14–15, 17, 23–4, 27.

102   Ágoston, "Firearms", p. 101.

103   Vigna, "Codice", doc. CXXXIV, p. 324.

104   Vigna, "Codice", p. 182.

105   Fleet, *Trade*, p. 119.

for labour in the west.[106] All trade in the northern Black Sea was required to transit through Caffa where it was taxed.[107] Genoese control of the trade was a considerable source of irritation to the Venetians. In 1384 Venice complained that the Genoese had forbidden the Venetians from transporting Tatar subjects to Turchia. A Venetian ship had been arrested in the Black Sea, an act which Venice deemed totally unacceptable.[108] The slave trade was controlled by the *officium capitum Sancti Antonii*[109] whose job it was, according to Khvalkov, "to secure the Genoese slave trade monopoly, especially against the Venetians and the Turks".[110] Turks trading slaves who attempted to evade Caffa and paying tax there subjected to financial penalties. In 1384 a person from Sinop transported slaves from Tana to Leffecti without going through Caffa. He was denounced by "Bachi" of Sinop and the ambassador of the *emir* of Sinop, "Coiha Toghan", had to pay 21 *sommi* for the settlement of the tax (*commercium*) on "Saracin heads". One third of this sum went to the person who had denounced him and to his sailors.[111] Stello, however, has argued that this control was aimed at Tana and thus did not affect the trade to the southern Black Sea, also noting that it was in any case difficult to enforce and that it was largely ignored from the 1420s onwards.[112]

The fact that there was the imposition of a charge on Turkish merchants trading in the Black Sea gives an indication of the importance of such traders, and serves to call into question Balard's assertion that local trade was carried on by "Oriental businessmen", referring here to Greeks, Armenians and Jews, but not to Turks, and that the Genoese probably used Greeks "in order to bring the local resources of the Pontic shores to the great *emporium* of Caffa".[113]

---

106   Balard, *Romanie génoise*, I, p. 299.

107   Khvalkov, *Colonies*, p. 155; Stello, Annika, "La traite d'esclaves en mer Noire (première moitié du XVᵉ siècle)", in *Les esclavages en Méditerranée: espaces et dynamiques économiques*, ed. Fabienne Guillén and Salah Trabelsi (Madrid: Casa de Velázquez, 2012), pp. 177–8; Belgrano, L.T., "Cinque documenti genovesi-orientali", *Atti della Società Ligure di Storia Patria*, 17 (1885–1886), doc. 5, pp. 149–50.

108   Thiriet, *Régestes*, I, no. 683, p. 166.

109   Khvalkov, *Colonies*, p. 155; Balard, *Romanie génoise*, II, pp. 299–300; Barker, Hannah, *That Most Precious Merchandise. The Mediterranean Trade in Black Sea Slaves, 1260–1500* (Philadelphia: University of Pennsylvania Press, 2019), pp. 137–40; Stello, "La traite d'esclaves", p. 173.

110   Khvalkov, *Colonies*, p. 360; Balard, *Romanie génoise*, I, p. 299.

111   Balard, *Romanie génoise*, I, pp. 132 and 301.

112   Stello, "La traite des esclaves ", p. 178.

113   Balard, Michel, "The Greeks of Crimea under Genoese rule in the XIVth and XVth centuries", *Dumbarton Oaks Papers*, 49 (1995), p. 29.

Turkish ships were certainly involved in trading.[114] Chalkokondyles noted that there were many ships in the harbour of Sinop "including a merchant ship built by İsmail [the İsfendiyaroğulları ruler] with a capacity of nine hundred *pithoi*" when Mehmed II took the port.[115] That Turks were trading in slaves in the Black Sea is made clear by their presence in the *massarie* of Caffa (the account books of the Genoese *comune*). Stello has calculated that while 74 of the 170 slave merchants who are named in the *massarie* from the first half of the fifteenth century, were Italians, 27 were "sarraceni", that is Muslim or Turkish, of whom nine were from the coast of Anatolia, and 38 were Greek, some of whom could potentially also have been from the same region.[116] According to Khvalkov, the Turks gained a dominant position in the slave trade in the 1450s to 1460s.[117]

There was a substantial slave trade from the northern Black Sea into Anatolia.[118] In the early fifteenth century, large numbers of slaves were being imported into Samsun and Sinop,[119] Balard describing Sinop as a "plaque tournante" of the slave trade into Anatolia in this period.[120] Slaves were being traded into the Samsun region from Crimea in the early 1430s. In around 1430 the *officium sancti Antonii* imposed a ban on the importation of slaves from Sevastopolis, in Crimea, to "the places of the Turks" or to "any other places named in the decree", perhaps as a result of the drop in numbers of slaves reaching Genoa in this period from the Black Sea.[121] The existence of the ban further demonstrates a significant amount of slave trading into Anatolia, which appears to have continued despite this prohibition for a merchant who shipped 20 slaves from Sevastopolis to the region of Samsun in around 1431 was pardoned for this contravention of the ban.[122] According to Khvalkov, just

---

114 Vigna, "Codice", doc. CXXXVI, pp. 332–3; doc. CLI, pp. 366–7; Balard, "The Greeks of Crimea", p. 29.

115 Chalkokondyles, *Historiarum Libri Decem*, p. 489; Chalkokondyles, *Histories*, II, pp. 350/351. A *pithos* was a unit of storage capacity, *Histories*, II, note 112, p. 515.

116 Stello, "La traite des esclaves", pp. 176–7. See also Khvalkov, *Colonies*, pp. 369–70.

117 Khvalkov, *Colonies*, p. 370.

118 For a discussion of the direction of the trade in slaves see Barker, *That Most Precious Merchandise*, p. 140.

119 Balard, *Romanie génoise*, II, p. 828 and note 100; Balard, "The Greeks of Crimea", p. 29.

120 Balard, "The Greeks of Crimea", p. 29.

121 ASG, San Giorgio, Sala 39, busta 88, doc. 440; Fleet, Kate, "Caffa, Turkey and the slave trade: the case of Battista Macio", in *Europa e Islam tra i Secoli XIV e XVI. Europe and Islam between 14th and 16th Centuries*, ed. Michele Bernardini, Clara Borrelli, Anna Cerbo and Encarnación Sánchez Garcia (Naples: Istituto Universitario Orientale. Collana "Matteo Ripa" XVIII, 2002), pp. 382–4. The document is given in the appendix to this article, pp. 385–7.

122 ASG, San Giorgio, Sala 39, busta 88, doc. 440.

over 23 per cent of slaves reported in the Caffa *massarie* between 1410 and 1441 were shipped to Sinop, the figure being 25.5 per cent in 1410/11 and 40 per cent in 1441/42.[123] In 1410 to 1411, 1,080 slaves were taken from Caffa to the southern shores of the Black Sea. This is in contrast to only 310 slaves shipped to Pera.[124] Slaves were imported presumably in part for sale on the Bursa market, Khvalkov giving a figure of 15.6 per cent of the slaves reported in the Caffa *massarie* as being sent to Bursa in the period 1410 to 1441.[125]

The question that this trade raises is why were so many slaves being imported into Anatolia. Given Genoese dominance and Genoa's trade in slaves to the west and to the Mamluk sultanate, one would have expected the vast bulk of slaves to be shipped out via the Straits. Stello has argued that the annual number of slaves shipped from Caffa and the figure given by Piloti, a Venetian merchant from Crete, for the annual arrival of slaves in the Mamluk sultanate do not add up, leading one to question if the sultanate was in fact entirely provided by the route Caffa-Constantinople-Alexandria.[126] While many ships were transporting slaves to Anatolia, there were not so many going via Constantinople or Pera, as should have been the case if that route was supplying the Mamluks. Stello proposes two explanations for this: that slaves shipped to Anatolia were sold there and remained in the region, or that the slaves crossed Anatolia in order to avoid the route through the Straits in times of political unrest and problems with the Ottomans. Stello opts for the second explanation, arguing that the slaves were transported across Anatolia to the southern coast or to the Mediterranean coast of Syria and shipped from there to Egypt.[127] However, if this were the case one might have expected the slaves to have been shipped not to Sinop, Balard's "plaque tournante" of the trade, but to Samsun, "a much more obvious port for importing goods from across the Black Sea to Anatolia and beyond", according to Peacock who argues that the mountains directly south of Sinop and the apparent lack of caravanserais close to the city "may have made routes south from Sinop a rather unattractive option".[128]

In support of her argument that the slaves shipped into Anatolia were en-route for Egypt, Stello states that "there could not have been sufficient demand [in northern Anatolia] to make this commerce profitable".[129] However, it seems

---

123   Khvalkov, *Colonies*, p. 366.

124   Balard, *Romanie génoise*, II, p. 828, note 100.

125   Khvalkov, *Colonies*, p. 366.

126   Stello, "La traite des esclaves", p. 177.

127   Stello, "La traite des esclaves", pp. 178–9.

128   Peacock, Andrew C.S., "Sinop: a frontier city in Seljuq and Mongol Anatolia", *Ancient Civilizations from Scythia to Siberia*, 16 (2010), p. 116.

129   Stello, "La traite des esclaves", p. 178.

possible to argue that the northern Anatolian market was in fact lucrative and extensive. Bursa was a major slave market, and, from Khvalkov's figures, around 16 per cent of slaves reported in the *massarie* were destined for the market there in the first half of the fifteenth century.[130] Some slaves could have been intended for local domestic use. In 1344, for example, a slave sale was enacted in Caffa of a female slave called Cotuliha, a Tatar, 22 years old, to the agent of Pietro di Simisso (i.e. Samsun), a butcher, for 731 *aspers*.[131] Barker notes that Trebizond was a "second-tier slave market" with slaves sold there being "mainly for local use".[132] Female slaves were, however, according to Stello, mostly sent to western Europe.[133] The bulk of the slaves on the Anatolian market would therefore have been male. If one argues that the Anatolian market was sufficient to soak up the imported slaves, or at least a percentage of them, rather than the region being a conduit for the slave trade to the Mamluk sultanate, one would need to demonstrate the existence of a labour-intensive activity in the region. The presence of a large number of copper mines and quarries in northern Anatolia would seem potentially to account for this.[134] As these mines were highly productive and lucrative, Chalkokondyles referring to the annual tax income from the mines of Sinop when Mehmed II conquered them being 50,000 gold pieces,[135] they would presumably have required a sizable workforce. There were also silver mines in the region, which were working at least in the earlier fourteenth century.[136] There appears to be no extant information on the mines or the labour force involved to work them in this period. It is therefore impossible to assess with any certainty the number of people who would have been employed in the mines, but, given that they were both numerous and productive, the workforce required might well have been substantial. Comparisons are difficult due to the lack of sources, but as some sort of guide, there were 170 miners working in mines, including copper mines, in the Hron region of Hungary in 1543, and in the nearby region of Hodruš in

---

130   Khvalkov, *Colonies*, p. 366.

131   Balbi, Giovanna and Silvana Raiteri, *Notai genovesi in oltremare. Atti rogati a Caffa e a Licostomo (sec. XIV)* (Bordighera: Istituto Internazionale di Studi Liguri, 1973), doc. 46, pp. 91–2.

132   Barker, *That Most Precious Merchandise*, p. 145.

133   Stello, "La traite des esclaves", p. 175.

134   Fleet, "Caffa, Turkey and the slave trade", pp. 373–81.

135   Chalkokondyles, *Historiarum Libri Decem*, p. 489; Chalkokondyles, *Histories*, II, pp. 350/351.

136   Ibn Battuta, *Voyages d'ibn Batoutah*, vol. II, trans. C. Defremery and B.R. Sanguinetti (Paris, 1854), p 293; al-'Umari, "Notice de l'ouvrage qui a pour titre Masalek alabsar fi memalek alamsar, Voyages des yeux dans les royaumes des différentes contrées (ms. arabe 583)", ed. E. Quatremère, in *Notices et Extraits des mss. de la Bibliothèque du Roi*, vol. XIII (Paris, 1838), pp. 337, 350, 355.

1535, 4,000 people were employed in mining and processing.[137] Yakupoğlu has calculated that in 1487 there were in Küre around 150 to 200 people, excluding slaves, involved in working the mine there, and suggests that at the end of the fifteenth century, there were around 1,370 households in the villages of the region involved in working at the Küre mine. In the fifteenth century slaves worked the Küre mine and were employed in the hard labour and in extracting the metal from greater depths.[138] Slave labour was employed in later periods in extracting the copper in region of Kastamonu.[139] Katip Çelebi refers to slaves working the mines there, noting that they were in a weak condition and produced an unpleasant odour.[140] In this period there were insufficient numbers of slaves to work the Küre mine.[141] Slaves were also working the Küre copper mine in the early eighteenth century.[142]

Genoese Trading Settlements

One important aspect of the trade of northern Anatolia in the fourteenth and first half of the fifteenth centuries was the existence of Genoese trading settlements established along the Anatolian Black Sea coast at Amasra, Sinop and Samsun, described by Heyd as well-known to western merchants as "stopping points" on the Trebizond, Caffa and Tana routes.[143] All three had consuls, underlining their importance for not all trading settlements had consular protection, Maurocastro (Akkerman, Cetatea Albă, modern Bilhorod-Dnistrovskyi)

---

137 Batizi, Zoltán, "Mining in medieval Hungary", in *The Economy of Medieval Hungary*, ed. József Laszlovszky, Balázs Nagy, Péter Szabó and András Vadas (Leiden: Brill, 2018), p. 179.

138 Yakupoğlu, Cevdet, "Kastamonu'nun Doğal Zenginliklerinden Küre Madenlerinin Tarihî Arka Planı", *Kastamonu'nun Doğal Zenginlikleri Sempozyumu, 16–17 Ekim 2012* (n.p.p.: n.p., n.d.) p. 39.

139 Coşgel, Metin and Boğaç Ergene, *The Economics of Ottoman Justice. Settlement and Trial in the Sharia Courts* (Cambridge: Cambridge University Press, 2016), p. 40.

140 Maden, Fahri, "XVIII. Yüzyıl Sonu XIX. Yüzyıl Başlarında Kastamonu'da Esnaf Grupları, Zanaatkârlar ve Ticari Faliyetler", *Karadeniz Araştırmaları*, 15 (2007), p. 153, note 14; Faroqhi, Suraiya, "Working, Marketing and Consuming Ottoman Copper – with a Special Emphasis on Female Involvement", ch. 6 in this volume; Yakupoğlu, "Kastamonu'nun Doğal Zenginliklerinden Küre Madenlerinin Tarihî Arka Planı", p. 43.

141 Yakupoğlu, "Kastamonu'nun Doğal Zenginliklerinden Küre Madenlerinin Tarihî Arka Planı", p. 43.

142 Yaman, Talat Mümtaz, "Küre Bakır Madenine Dair Vesikalar", *Tarih Vesikaları*, 1/4 (1941), doc. 7, pp. 272–3. Maden, "XVIII. Yüzyıl Sonu XIX. Yüzyıl Başlarında Kastamonu'da", p. 153, note 4, notes that the number of slaves employed in the mines declined in the eighteenth and nineteenth centuries.

143 Heyd, *Histoire*, I, p. 551.

for example, never had a consul.[144] As Basso has noted, the nature of Genoese trading settlements depended on the purpose they were intended to serve: as bases for trade routes into the hinterland, as support for navigation and provisioning, or to protect commercial routes.[145] Heyd regarded the Genoese colony of Sinop as not large, but prosperous,[146] and Amasra, Sinop and Samsun as "more than simple stations on the commercial route of Trebizond" for they were "independent markets",[147] indicating their importance in the coastal trade of the northern Anatolian region.

According to Bratianu, the Genoese colonies along the Anatolian Black Sea coast must have been established immediately after the treaty of Nymphaeum, concluded between the Genoese and Michael VIII Palaeologos in 1261, when the Black Sea was opened up to the Genoese.[148] This view is echoed by Pistarino, who has argued that the Genoese established themselves in Anatolia (regardless of whether the territory was Turkish or Byzantine) and on the shores of the Black Sea within 20 to 30 years after the treaty of Nymphaeum and that within a generation Genoese settlements, including those at Amasra and Sinop, were flourishing.[149] According to Karpov, the Genoese colony of Samsun was established around 1289.[150] There was certainly a settlement there at the beginning of the fourteenth century for a Genoese consul and notary were there from 1302.[151] At this point Samsun was under the control of the empire of Trebizond. Laiou notes that the 1319 treaty between Venice and Trebizond opened up the

144   Deletant, Dennis, "Genoese, Tatars and Rumanians at the mouth of the Danube in the fourteenth century", *The Slavonic and East European Review*, 62/4 (1984), p. 524.

145   Basso, Enrico, "El systema de puertos genoveses entre el mediterráneo y el mar negro", in *Navegación y puertos en época medieval y moderna*, ed. Adela Fábregas García (Granada: Grupo de Investigación Toponimia, Historia y Arqueología del Reino de Granada, 2012), p. 105.

146   Heyd, *Histoire*, II, p. 359.

147   Heyd, *Histoire*, II, pp. 359–60.

148   Bratianu, *Recherches*, p. 157.

149   Pistarino, Geo, *Genovesi d'oriente* (Genoa: Civico Istituto Colombiano, 1990), pp. 123, 124.

150   Karpov, Sergej Pavlovič, *L'impero di Trapezunda, Venezia Genova e Roma 1204–1461. Raporti politici, diplomatici e commerciali* (Rome: Il Veltro Editrice, 1986), p. 142. Karpov, S.P., Итальянские морские республики и Южное Причерноморье в XIII–XV вв.: проблемы торговли [Italian Maritime Republics and the Southern Black Sea Region in the Thirteenth–Fifteenth Centuries: Trade Relations] (Moscow: Izd-vo MGU, 1990), p. 86, states that the presence of the Genoese there can be traced back to the 1280s. I should like to thank Dr. Sheila Watts for translating this passage for me.

151   Balard, *Romanie génoise*, I, pp. 132–3. Balard notes that the date was not 1317, as Heyd thought (*Histoire*, I, p. 53), p. 132, note 22; Karpov, Итальянские морские республики, p. 86. I should like to thank Dr. Sheila Watts again for translating this passage for me.

ports of the empire, including Samsun, to the Venetians.[152] The size of the Genoese community increased in the years after 1314, the Doge of Genoa noting in 1351 that "there are many Genoese there".[153]

While the Genoese settlement of Samsun was thus in place within 20 to 30 years after the treaty of Nymphaeum, as Pistarino has argued for the Genoese settlements, this does not seem to be the case for either Sinop or Amasra. Establishing the dates at which these settlements were set up would give an indication of the development of Genoese trade in northern Anatolia.

Citing the "Anonymi descriptio Europae Orientalis", Zachariadou has suggested that the Genoese were established in Sinop by 1308.[154] What this source actually says is "in the region of that port [Constantinople], with the agreement of the emperor, the Genoese have two states/settlements [*civitates*] of which one is called Trapason [Trebizond] and the other Senopi [Sinop]".[155] This is clearly odd as neither Trebizond nor Sinop can be described as near Constantinople, leading the editor of the text to suggest that the anonymous author had received this information from someone else and had not remembered it well.[156] While it seems highly unlikely that there was a Genoese settlement at Sinop at this point, there was one at Samsun by the early fourteenth century. It therefore seems possible that the place referred to here was not in fact Sinop but Samsun. Although Zachariadou states that the Genoese were expelled by Gazi Çelebi, the ruler of Sinop, a few years after 1308, she gives no source for this.[157] If this had been the case, then one might have expected to find some reference to this event in Genoese sources. The more likely explanation is that it did not exist in the first place.

That this was the case is supported by Gazi Çelebi's hostility towards the Genoese. In 1313 Gazi Çelebi, according to the continuation of the chronicle of Jacopo da Varagine, sailed with nine galleys to Caffa where he killed "many good men" and captured many Genoese ships (*ligna*). The following year he again set sail for Caffa but was unsuccessful and withdrew with "damage,

152   Liaou, Angeliki E., *Constantinople and the Latins. The Foreign Policy of Andronicus II, 1282–1328* (Cambridge, Mass.: Harvard University Press, 1972), p. 270.

153   Belgrano, "Cinque documenti genovesi-orientali", doc. 5, p. 250.

154   Zachariadou, Elizabeth A., "Gazi Çelebi of Sinope", in *Oriente e occidente tra medioevo ed età moderna. Studi in onore di Geo Pistarino*, ed. Laura Balletto (Genoa: Glauco Brigati, 1997), vol. II, p. 1273, note 7.

155   *Anonymi descriptio Europae Orientalis imperium Constantinopolitanum, Albania, Serbia, Bulgaria, Ruthenia, Ungaria, Polonia, Bohemia. Anno MCCCVIII exarata*, ed. Dr. Olgierd Górka (Kraków: Gebethner et Socii, 1916, reprinted by Pranava Books, India), pp. 9–10.

156   *Anonymi Descriptio*, pp. xxvi and xxxv.

157   Zachariadou, "Gazi Çelebi", p. 1273.

shame and sadness".[158] According to Balard, the raid of 1313 was made by Alexios II of Trebizond in alliance with the *emir* of Sinop, Gazi Çelebi, in retaliation for the Genoese attack on Trebizond in 1311,[159] Shukurov, too, regarding this as an anti-Genoese alliance.[160] Karpov states that there was an alliance between Alexios II of Trebizond and Gazi Çelebi, probably in response to the Genoese attacks on Trebizond,[161] and that in 1313 there was a joint campaign between Sinop and Trebizond against Caffa involving eight galleys of Sinop and some Trebizuntine ships.[162] Balard notes that the raid was responded to by the Genoese who sank Turkish and Trebizond ships, so making it seem more likely that the raid referred to here was that in 1314.[163] Zachariadou, while noting that the 1314 raid was less successful than that in the previous year, states that Gazi Çelebi "continued to harass the commercial activity of the Genoese who were obliged to reconstruct Caffa".[164] Karpov also suggests that the alliance between Alexios II of Trebizond and Gazi Çelebi was reinforced by a marriage between the daughter of Alexios of Trebizond, Eudochia, and Gazi Çelebi,[165] a suggestion, however, dismissed by Bryer who notes that while we do not know who Gazi Çelebi was, the one thing we do know is that he was "not the husband of Eudokia, despoina of Sinope and daughter of Alexios II".[166] Presumably any alliance with Alexios was short-lived for, according to Paneretos, "in 1318/19, a great fire was started by men from Sinope and the fire destroyed all of the city's splendours both within and without".[167] Apart from demonstrating that Gazi Çelebi had a fleet and was quite capable of using it, these raids against Caffa and the alliance with Trebizond would seem to demonstrate that there was no Genoese trading settlement in Sinop in this period.

---

158   Promis, Vincenzo (ed.), "Continuazione della cronaca de Jacopo da Varagine dal MCCXCVII al MCCCXXXII", *Atti della Società Ligure di Storia Patria*, 10 (1874), p. 502.

159   Balard, *Romanie génoise*, I, pp. 135–6.

160   Shukurov, Rustam, "Trebizond and the Seljuks (1204–1299)", *Méogeios*, 25–26 (2005), p. 135.

161   Karpov, *L'impero*, p. 146.

162   Karpov, *L'impero*, p. 146.

163   Balard, *Romanie génoise*, I, pp. 135–6.

164   Zachariadou, "Gazi Çelebi", p. 1273.

165   Karpov, *L'impero*, p. 181, note 38.

166   Bryer, Anthony, "Greeks and Türkmen: the Pontic exception", *Dumbarton Oaks Papers*, 29 (1975), p. 128. For further discussion of her identity, see Bryer, Anthony and David Winfield, *The Byzantine Monuments and Topography of the Pontos*, vol. 1 (Washington D.C.: Dumbarton Oaks, 1985), p. 73.

167   Panaretos, Michael, "On the emperors of Trebizond", in *Two Works on Trebizond. Michael Panaretos, Bessarion*, ed. and trans. Scott Kennedy (Cambridge, Mass.: Harvard University Press, 2019), pp. 8/9.

Several years later, in 1324 (or 1323 according to the Genoese chronicler
Stella and the Florentine chronicler Villani) the ruler of Sinop was again
involved in a clash with Genoese forces, this time a force sent from Genoa,
now in the hands of the Guelfs, against the Ghibelline-supporting Genoese
colonies of Pera and the Black Sea.[168] In April a fleet under Carlo Grimaldi
sailed into the Black Sea, doing much damage. According to Villani, Grimaldi
was accompanied in his raiding by the *emir* of Sinop, described as "a great *emir*
of Turchia".[169] On its return, the fleet found its way through the Straits blocked
by 16 galleys of the Genoese of Pera. Unable to pass, Grimaldi took the fleet to
Sinop where he made an agreement with the ruler of Sinop, called Zarabi in
Stella, Zalapi in "Continuazione" and Cerabi in Villani (i.e. Çelebi), described
by Stella as being "from the people who are called Sarracena".[170] Zalapi
promised the Guelfs to protect them against their enemies, presumably the
Ghibellenes.[171] Once the agreement had been reached (which was done in a
very few days, according to "Continuazione"),[172] the Genoese landed "joyfully"
and occupied themselves with games.[173] Zalapi invited them to the baths and
to a feast, showing them great honour and tricking them by his behaviour into
trusting him more.[174] Zalapi had in fact concealed armed men who, on the
sound of a drum (or a trumpet in "Continuazione"), attacked the Genoese, cap-
turing 15,000 good men of whom 700 were killed. He took 11 galleys, according
to "Continuazione", and the captains of almost all the galleys were imprisoned
and ransomed eight years later.[175]

The ruler of Sinop at this point cannot have been Gazi Çelebi who, according to the date on his tombstone, died in 1322.[176] At some time after 1322, the

---

168   Petti Balbi, Giovanna (ed.), *Georgii et Iohannis Stellae, Annales genovenses* (Bologna:
      Zanicelli, 1975), p. 106, note 1, notes that "almost all the Genoese colonies of the Black
      Sea were in the possession of Ghibelline families like the Doria, Spinola, Della Volta and
      Grillo".
169   Villani, Giovanni, *Nuova Cronaca* (Parma: Guanda, 1991), ch. CCXVII, p. 371.
170   Petti Balbi, *Georgii et Iohannis Stellae, Annales genovenses*, p. 106.
171   Petti Balbi, *Georgii et Iohannis Stellae, Annales genovenses*, p. 106.
172   Promis, "Continuazione", p. 506.
173   Petti Balbi, *Georgii et Iohannis Stellae, Annales genovenses*, p. 106.
174   Petti Balbi, *Georgii et Iohannis Stellae, Annales genovenses*, p. 106. Villani, *Cronica*,
      ch. CCXVII, p. 371, described the ruler as receiving them very well with feasts and banquets.
175   Promis, "Continuazione", pp. 505–6; Petti Balbi, *Georgii et Iohannis Stellae, Annales geno-
      venses*, pp. 105–6.
176   Ülkütaşır, M.Ş., "Sinop'ta Selçukiler Zamanına Ait Tarihi Eserler", *Türk Tarih, Arkeologya
      ve Etnografya Dergisi*, 5 (1949), p. 147; Yücel, *Çoban-oğulları Beyliği Candar-oğulları Beyliği*,
      p. 59; Peacock, "Sinop", p. 110. Zachariadou, however, places his death date at after 1324,
      regarding the 1322 date as "not accurate", and takes the ruler of Sinop here as Gazi Çelebi,
      Zacharioudou "Gazi Çelebi", p. 1275, and note 15.

İsfendiyaroğulları ruler Süleyman took Sinop, though the date of this is not clear. The reason for Sinop's hostility to the Genoese may lie in Heyd's description of Sinop as a "nest of corsairs".[177] If the rulers of Sinop pursued a policy of piracy, preying on Latin merchant shipping in the Black Sea, which, given the constant trade activity, would presumably have been lucrative, then hostility would not have been aimed at the Genoese in particular but at merchant shipping in general. It would also explain Sinop's apparently extensive naval resources.

The account of Grimaldi's activities in the Black Sea raises interesting questions. Why did Grimaldi go to Sinop? How did he know to try and negotiate with the ruler there, presumably thinking that this was a good idea and likely to be successful? Is it significant that, according to Stella, Zalapi offered to help the Guelf forces against their presumably Ghibelline enemies, here presumably meaning Caffa, or, more likely, Pera,[178] implying naval and military support from Sinop? If Pera was meant here, then that would imply that the ruler of Sinop would provide military and naval assistance to break the blockade of the Straits. In fact the account in Stella refers to Zalapi offering to arm three ships (two galleys and one *navigio*).[179] The agreement between Grimaldi and Zalapi would seem to indicate some political knowledge about Genoese affairs on the part of the ruler of Sinop, and by Grimaldi about the likely stance of Zalapi. That Grimaldi was sent by Guelf Genoa to attack Ghibelline-supporting Genoese settlements in Pera and the Black Sea, gives a clear indication of Sinop's relations with the Genoese in the Black Sea and seems fairly conclusive evidence that there was no Genoese settlement in Sinop at this time. Further, if the ruler of Sinop was in a position to offer substantial naval help to Grimaldi, then he would surely have been capable of removing any Genoese settlement in Sinop (given the location and fact that this would have required an attack by sea).

In the early 1330s, ibn Battuta described Sinop (by this time under İbrahim, son of the İsfendiyaroğulları ruler Süleyman), where he stayed for some time, as "a very populous town which combines strength and beauty", surrounded on all sides by the sea except for one point in the east where there was a gate, though which one could only enter with the permission of the *emir*. He refers to 11 Greek Orthodox villages, under Muslim protection, and a hermitage of Hızır

177   Heyd, *Histoire*, I, p. 551.
178   Laiou, Angeliki E., *Constantinople and the Latins. The Foreign Policy of Andronicus II, 1282–1328* (Cambridge, Mass.: Harvard University Press, 1972), p. 301, says that the ruler of Sinop promised to help Grimaldi against Pera.
179   Petti Balbi, *Georgii et Iohannis Stellae, Annales genovenses*, p. 106.

and İlyas, on the mountain which stretches into the sea (i.e modern Boztepe Burnu).[180] What he does not mention is any Genoese trading settlement. Given that his description of his stay in Sinop is fairly detailed, this omission seems to indicate that there was no such settlement at that time. Al-'Umari, who also describes Sinop, makes no mention of a Genoese settlement, and it is perhaps significant here that one of his informants was the Genoese Domenico Doria.[181]

One can therefore argue that it seems unlikely that there was a Genoese trading settlement in Sinop in the early 1330s. This seems to have been the case also in the following decade, when hostility between the Genoese and Sinop continued. When, in 1340, Simon de Quarto, who had sailed into Pera with nine merchant galleys, heard that Çelebi "the lord of the Turks" had armed 12 galleys and *ligna subtilia* and had captured many Genoese and Venetian men and ships, he had sailed to Sinop "to the presence of this Çelebi" to investigate. In response, the ruler of Sinop had replied that his galleys were not armed against the Genoese, but against the Byzantines.[182] The hostility of Sinop towards the Genoese of Caffa seems to have continued, for on 5 April 1345 the Genoese of Caffa decided to despatch a ship to Sinop to investigate whether the ruler there intended to send an armed naval force against Caffa. If this was indeed the case, then the Genoese would mount an attack.[183] The Genoese were clearly enraged by the actions of the ruler of Sinop for in 1346, according to Villani, 11 galleys were sent from Genoa to punish the ruler of Sinop, described as "Çelebi lord of the Turks of the Black Sea", for his actions against the Genoese. They "took the land of Sinop and they pillaged and destroyed it and raided the region and seized much goods and merchandise of the Turks".[184] Given these various activities in the mid-1340s, the existence of a Genoese trading settlement at Sinop is unlikely. There is, however, an argument to be made for the existence of one by 1351.

The Laurentian portolan, traditionally dated to 1351,[185] has Genoese flags flying over Amasra, Sinop and Samsun, apparently demonstrating the presence of Genoese settlements there at that date.[186] This, however, depends

180   Ibn Battuta, *Voyages d'ibn Batoutah*, pp. 348–54.
181   Al-'Umari, "Voyages", pp. 347, 361–2.
182   Petti Balbi, *Georgii et Iohannis Stellae, Annales genovenses*, p. 134.
183   Morozzo della Rocca, Raimondo, "Notizie da Caffa", in *Studi in onore di Amintore Fanfani III. Medioevo* (Milan: A. Giuffrè, 1962), doc. 9, p. 289.
184   Villani, *Cronica*, ch. LXX, p. 672.
185   Serristori, Luigi, *Illustrazione di una carta del Mar Nero del 1351 e ricordi sul Caucaso, sulla Spagna, sul Marocco ... Con tavole* (Florence: Società Editrice Fiorentine, 1856, reprinted by British Library, Historical Prints Editions, 2011).
186   Desimoni, C. and L.T. Belgrano, "Atlante idrografico del medio evo posseduto dal Prof. Tammar Luxuro", *Atti della Società Ligure di Storia Patria*, v (1867), pp. 133, 134.

on the accuracy of the dating of the portolan. Philips, who describes it as usually dated to 1351,[187] notes the problem of the representation of Africa, leading to a possible explanation that the map was in fact modified in the fifteenth century.[188] While Kimble argued that 1351 should be retained as "the approximate date" of the original map and the African part regarded as the work of later editors,[189] Suárez states that the map is now thought to date as late as the early fifteenth century.[190]

If one does accept 1351 as the date for the portolan, or at least for the Black Sea part, then one can suggest that the Genoese trading settlement in Sinop was established sometime after 1346. If so, then the ruler with whom the Genoese must have negotiated the settlement would have been Adil, who ruled from 1346 to 1361. Yücel states that establishment of the Genoese and Venetian trading settlements at Sinop date from Adil's reign, though he gives no reference for this.[191] Balard, who notes that the Laurentian portolan of 1351 has the cross of St George flying over Sinop, so by implication accepting that there was a settlement there at that date, however states that the Genoese community was not properly organised there until the end of the fourteenth century,[192] making the establishment of a trading settlement at this point perhaps less convincing.

There was certainly a Genoese trading settlement in Sinop by the 1380s, for a consul was nominated for Sinop between 1380 and 1390 and nine consuls were appointed between 1390 and 1403.[193] Certainly relations between Sinop and the Genoese in Caffa appear to have improved by this time. In 1387 the Genoese consul in Caffa received an ambassador from Sinop, described as the Sarasin Coiha Toghan, who presented the Genoese consul with a horse and received a gift of Florentine cloth.[194] At the end of the century only the consul of Sinop was still dependant on the administration of Pera, which paid him, Amasra and Samsun by then being under the authority of the consul of Caffa.[195] Given that there were apparently friendly relations between Sinop and the

---

187   Philips, J.R.S., *The Medieval Expansion of Europe* (Oxford: Oxford University Press, 1998), pp. 149, 151, 207.

188   Philips, *Medieval Expansion*, pp. 151–2.

189   Kimble, George H.T., "The Laurentian world map with special reference to its portrayal of Africa", *Imago Mundi*, 1 (1935), p. 33.

190   Suárez, Thomas, *Early Mapping of Southeast Asia* (Hong Kong: Periplus, 1999), p. 267, note 122.

191   Yücel, Yaşar, "Candaroğulları", in *Türkiye Diyanet Vakfı İslâm Ansiklopedisi*, vol. 7 (1993), p. 147.

192   Balard, *Romanie génoise*, I, p. 131.

193   Balard, *Romanie génoise*, I, p. 131, II, p. 903.

194   Balard, *Romanie génoise*, I, p. 132; Khvalkov, *Colonies*, p. 354.

195   Balard, *La Romanie génoise*, I, p. 360.

Genoese of Caffa in the 1380s, and that a trading settlement was in place some-time in that decade, it seems possible (if one takes the Laurentian portolan to date from later than 1351) to suggest that the establishment of the trading settlement dates to the third quarter of the fourteenth century.

The Genoese colony of Amasra may date to the same period, Eyice suggest-ing that the Genoese control was established there in the second half of the fourteenth century.[196] According to Hasluk, the construction by the Genoese of the citadel at Amasra can be dated to 1363 from an inscription, showing that there was a settlement there by that date.[197] The existence of the arms of the *doge* of Genoa Simon Boccanegra on a wall of the keep of the castle date it to either 1339 to 1344, the years of his first period as *doge*, or to 1361 to 1363, those of his second, the latter dating being the more likely.[198] The first mention of a consul in Amasra dates to 1386, according to Balard, who notes that Heyd's dat-ing of 1398 is incorrect.[199]

It therefore seems possible to argue that the two Genoese trading settle-ments of Sinop and Amasra were established at some time between 1360 and 1380. If this is the case, this would then indicate that Genoese-Turkish trade in northern Anatolia had developed to an extent that warranted the establish-ment of two further trading stations in the region in the second half of the fourteenth century.

The Nature of the Trading Settlements

By the end of the fourteenth century all three Genoese settlements were thus established and functioning. But what exactly was the nature of these settle-ments? For Khvalkov the Genoese settlements of Amasra, Sinop and Samsun "can hardly be considered colonies in a proper sense, and are more like 'trading stations', because they were established in the already large and prosperous trading cities and enjoyed a small degree of autonomy, being allowed to exist on the territory of the hosting state rather than becoming masters on their own".[200] Basso defines the Genoese settlements in the southern part of the western Black Sea as being similar to those in Syria: "commercial *scali* in which the Genoese limited themselves to controlling a quarter provided with extra-territoriality around urban nuclei tied to a centralised state power". More to the

196   Eyice, Semavi, "Amasra'da Cenova Hâkimiyeti Devrine Ait Bir Armalı Levha", *Belleten*, 65 (1953), p. 31.
197   Hasluk, F.W., "Genoese heraldry and inscriptions at Amasra", *Annual of the British School at Athens*, 17 (1910–1911), p. 139.
198   Eyice, "Amasra'da", p. 31, note 14.
199   Balard, *Romanie génoise*, I, p. 130; Heyd, *Histoire*, II, p. 358.
200   Khvalkov, *Colonies*, p. 116.

north, however, between the Danube delta and the Dniester, where there was less organised state power, the Genoese had "urban settlements completely under the authority of colonial Genoese magistrates and removed from the control of the local rulers".[201]

The Genoese colonies along the northern coast of Anatolia seem thus to fit into the pattern of the settlements in Syria and the southern part of the western Black Sea and were, in Khvalkov's phrase, trading stations. That they did exercise an element of autonomy is indicated by references in contemporary sources. Kritoboulos described Sinop at the time of Mehmed II's conquest as being "in the midst of the territory of the Sultan" but not under Ottoman control.[202] According to Tursun Bey, Amasra was a strong castle "connected to the Franks ... whose ruler was unclear" and who paid a certain amount of *haraç* and controlled a few tucked-away streets.[203]

That such autonomy was provisional is indicated by the relationship with the *subaşı* in Samsun. In 1425 the right of compensation and sequestration of the goods (*represalia*) of the *subaşı* was granted in Caffa to Antonio Adorno and Ansaldo Doria, in response to the theft by the *subaşı* of goods and merchandise of the late Barnabe Doria, Ansaldo's brother.[204] How such a right against an Ottoman official was obtained is not known but it can hardly have been granted without Ottoman involvement. However, only two years earlier, in a case in 1423 involving the confiscation by the *subaşı* of Samsun of the goods of a deceased Genoese merchant there, the Genoese authorities did not grant the merchant's family the right of reprisal, the explanation given being that "granting reprisal could be dangerous for the people of Caffa".[205]

The Genoese trading settlements were clearly important both to the Genoese and to the Turkish rulers. After the fall of their settlement at Samsun to Mehmed I in 1420,[206] the Genoese opened negotiations with the Ottomans to re-establish it. In 1421 Gerolamo di Negro was instructed to procure 100 ducats worth of gifts to be given to the ambassadors of Samsun with whom the Genoese authorities had been negotiating after the loss of their settlement

201   Basso, Enrico, *Genova: un impero sul mare* (Cagliari: Consiglio Nazionale delle Ricerche, Istituto sui Rapporti Italo-Iberici, 1994), pp. 120–1.
202   Kritoboulos, *History*, p. 168.
203   Tursun Bey, *Târîh-i Ebü'l-Feth*, pp. 104–5.
204   ASG, San Giorgio, Sala 34, 590 1308/2, f. 36r–v.
205   Karpov, S.P., "New documents on the relations between the Latins and the local populations in the Black Sea area (1392–1462)", *Dumbarton Oaks Papers*, 49 (1995), p. 39.
206   Imber, *Ottoman Empire*, p. 88. Aşıkpaşazade, *Chronik*, bab 76, pp. 79–80; Neşri, *Kitâb-ı Cihan-nümâ*, II, pp. 540–2.

the year before.[207] Negotiations apparently took some time for in early 1424 the Genoese authorities wrote to Imperiale Lomelino, the *podestà* in Pera, stating that Iacopo Adorno had been given the task of securing the right to rebuild the settlement at Samsun from Murad II. Genoa seemed somewhat anxious over the issue for it wished the *podestà* to remain vigilant and to see if he could arrange something through some other friend of the Genoese.[208] In February 1424 the government of Genoa wrote to the Genoese colony of Caffa with instructions that Battista Vairolo, appointed Genoese consul in Samsun in the same month,[209] obtain permission from the Ottoman sultan Murad II for the refortification of the Genoese castle of Samsun.[210] If these negotiations were successful, as the *doge* very much hoped they would be, then Battista would be appointed consul in Samsun for two years. A few weeks later another letter was sent from Genoa to Caffa appointing Battista Vairolo to the post of consul of Samsun for two years.[211] Caffa was responsible for the costs of repairs to the consulate in Samsun carried out by the consul Andrea Ususmaris in 1424.[212] In this year, various people, including stone masons, were sent from Caffa for the rebuilding work in Samsun.[213]

Given that Mehmed I had just destroyed the Genoese settlement, one has to ask why Murad II would have given permission for its re-establishment. This must in part reflect good relations between Murad II and the Genoese. Basso claims that the Genoese had succeeded in obtaining permission for the restoration of their settlement at Samsun thanks to the influence they had gained at the Ottoman court.[214] At this time Iacopo Adorno, the *podestà* of Phokaea (Foça), was brokering a peace between Murad II and the Byzantine emperor and instructions about this were sent from Genoa to the *podestà* of Pera at the end of February 1424.[215] According to the letter sent by the *doge* to Iacopo

---

207   Karpov, Serghej Pavlović, "Una famiglia nobile del mondo coloniale genovese: i Di Negro, mercanti e "baroni" dei Grandi Comneni dei Trebisonda", in *Oriente e occidente tra medio-evo ed età moderna. Studi in onore di Geo Pistarino* (Genoa: Glauco Brigati, 1997), vol. II, p. 595.

208   ASG, San Giorgio, Sala 34, 590 1308/2, ff. 28ᵛ–30r (1425.i.30).

209   ASG, San Giorgio, Sala 34, 590 1308/2, f. 11ᵣ (1424.ii.1).

210   ASG, San Giorgio, Sala 34, 590 1308/2, ff. 1ʳ–3ᵛ (1424.ii.1).

211   ASG, San Giorgio, Sala 34, 590 1308/2, f. 11ʳ (1424.ii.24).

212   ASG, San Giorgio, Sala 34, 590 1308/2, f. 6ʳ (1424.ii.1); see also f.1ʳ.

213   Khalkov, *Colonies*, pp. 163 and 303.

214   Basso, Enrico, "Genova e gli Ottomani nel XV secolo: gli "itali Teucri" e il Gran Sultano", in *L'Europa dopo la Caduta di Costantinopoli: 29 maggio 1453. Atti del XLIV Convegno Storico Internazionale* (Spoleto: Fondazione Centro Italiano di Studi sull'Alto Medioevo, 2008), p. 388 and note 34.

215   ASG, San Giorgio, Sala 34, 590 1308/2, f. 10ʳ (1424.ii.28).

Adorno, Iacopo was to "persuade and induce" Murad to make peace with the Byzantine emperor, pointing out to him that peace would be very useful to him and would bring him much security. If, however, no peace was arranged, then the emperor could wage a damaging war against him at a time when the Venetians had strengthened their fleet, a point that the Genoese felt would not be wasted on the Ottomans. The *doge* noted in his letter to Adorno that the Byzantine emperor was at present in Venice where the desperation of his situation was plain to see. If Adorno considered that Murad was inclined to peace, then he was immediately to inform the *podestà*.[216]

Murad's relations with the Genoese of Pera were certainly very close, in fact rather too close for the government back in Genoa. In April 1424 the Genoese government reported its considerable displeasure and "grave perturbation of mind" on hearing that Murad had given materials and money to the Genoese *comune* of Pera for the building of a strong, high tower on condition that the *comune* place his "insignia" on the tower, something regarded by the government in Genoa as totally unacceptable.[217]

Apart from any close relations, it is possible that permission was granted for financial reasons. Genoa's determination to re-establish its settlement in Samsun is a clear indication of its commercial value. Its commercial importance for the Ottomans is indicated by Aşıkpaşazade's account of Mehmed I's conquest of Samsun. Having conquered "infidel Samsun", that is the Genoese settlement, the Ottomans then attacked "Muslim Samsun". When asked by the Rumeli Beylerbeyi Hamza why he had surrendered without a fight, İsfendiyaroğlu Hızır replied: "the livelihood of our city was tied to the infidel city. The infidel city is in ruins and has passed into your hands. From now on there will be no peace for us here and our being neighbours with you is like a duck being the neighbour of a hawk".[218] This sheds interesting light on the strong commercial inter-connection between the Genoese and the İsfendiyaroğulları rulers.

The attraction of a Genoese settlement for Murad II may also have been to do with tax revenue. Although very little is known about tax in northern Anatolia in this period, it is clear that the Ottomans did collect customs or some form of transit tax. After being shipwrecked off Kefken Adası in November 1403 de Clavijo and his companions transported their goods overland to Carpi

216   ASG, San Giorgio, Sala 34, 590 1308/2, f. 72ʳ⁻ᵛ (1424.ii.28).
217   Belgrano, L.T., "Prima serie di documenti riguardanti la colonia di Pera", *Atti della Società Ligure di Storia Patria*, XIII (1877), doc. LIX, pp. 187–8; Manfroni, C., "Le relazioni fra Genova, l'impero Bizantino e i Turchi", *Atti della Società Ligure di Storia Patria*, XXVIII (1896), pp. 727–8.
218   Aşıkpaşazade, *Chronik*, bab 76, p. 80.

(Kerpe Limanı) where "a Turk who was chief of a village" approached the ambassadors demanding payment of tax which was due as they had taken cloth and other goods "through the territory of his master".[219] De Clavijo and his companions had claimed to be Genoese and he notes that the Turk demanded payment "because the Turks had found out that they were not Genoese, nor of the city of Pera".[220] Given the location and period, this region was then under the control of Süleyman Çelebi, de Clavijo describing Bender Ereğli in 1404 as belonging to him.[221]

The import customs tax in Samsun in the late 1430s was two per cent. This rate comes from the entries in the account book of Giacomo Badoer which do not specify to whom the customs was paid.[222] In entries for Trebizond, customs was paid to both the emperor, at one and a quarter per cent, and to the Genoese or the Venetians at one per cent,[223] or at three quarters of a percent to the emperor and half a per cent to the Venetian *bailo*.[224] One entry has the rate at two and a quarter per cent for the emperor and one for the Venetian *bailo*.[225] Is it possible that in Samsun there was a similar arrangement with customs being paid both to the Genoese consul and to Ottoman customs officials, or was the financial arrangement one of tribute, as seems from Tursun Bey's account, to have been the case in Amasra?[226] Without further data, this has to remain a matter of speculation.

The Importance of the Trading Settlements

The role of the Genoese settlements in trade in northern Anatolia was clearly significant. Their importance was even reflected in internal Genoese politics during the rule of Filippo Maria, the duke of Milan, who took over control of Genoa between 1421 and 1435. Visconti, wanting to reward his political allies, clashed with the Genoese administration, whose job it was to make colonial appointments. It was this situation which, Basso argues, resulted in the appointing in 1425 of two different consuls for Amasra at the same time, Manfredo Ghisolfi, appointed by the *Officium Provisionis Romanie* and

219   de Clavijo, *Narrative*, p. 54.
220   de Clavijo, *Narrative*, p. 54.
221   de Clavijo, *Narrative*, p. 54.
222   Badoer, *Libro*, c. 44, p. 89.
223   Badoer, *Libro*, c. 152, p. 307; c. 51, p. 103; c. 173, p. 348.
224   Badoer, *Libro*, c. 153, p. 308; c. 7, p. 15.
225   Badoer, *Libro*, c. 7, p. 15.
226   Discussion of tribute for Amasra appears in the instructions to the Genoese ambassadors to Mehmed II in March 1454, Belgrano, "Prime serie", doc. CLIV, p. 269.

Pietro Re, appointed by Visconti.[227] Basso argues that in his attempts to control appointments of colonial officials, Visconti focused on certain colonies, not because of any coherent administrative policy in the Levant but due to their lucrative nature and their use as sinecures with which to recompense his supporters.[228]

The trading settlements acted as centres for Genoese-Turkish trade, linking the Anatolian hinterland with Caffa and with the west. For Heyd it was from Amasra, Sinop and Samsun that the industrial products of Europe were distributed and from where local products such as timber, alum, copper, silver, goat's hair and morocco leather from Kastamonu were exported.[229] They also connected trade along the coast of Anatolia, and linked trade between Constantinople and Trebizond. The mere fact that the Genoese established three settlements along this coastline highlights the importance to them of trade in this region.

For both the İsfendiyaroğulları and the Ottomans the settlements brought them a significant foreign merchant presence. Quite what that presence meant in terms of financial contribution to the coffers of the state is very difficult to establish with any certainty. However, commercial activity did involve customs and dues, as indicated by de Clavijo's account of the demand for payment for the goods they transported overland after their shipwreck off Kefken Adası[230] and Badoer's entry for import customs for Samsun.[231] It also, possibly, involved tribute, as implied in Tursun Bey's depiction of Amasra[232] and perhaps hinted at in the accounts of the Genoese negotiations with Murad II over the re-establishment of the settlement at Samsun.[233] That Murad would have allowed the re-establishment without some form of financial arrangement seems unlikely. Apart from any such arrangements, the settlements brought into Anatolia exports from the west, as well as from the northern Black Sea region, and provided a market for the sale for the Turks of local products, in particular grain and copper.

The value of the settlements to the Genoese is reflected in their determination to keep them in the post-1453 world when the Ottoman conquest of Constantinople and control of the entrance to the Black Sea considerably

227   Basso, *Genova: un impero sul mare*, p. 153.
228   Basso, *Genova: un impero sul mare*, p. 160.
229   Heyd, *Histoire*, II, p. 360.
230   de Clavijo, *Narrative*, p. 54.
231   Badoer, *Libro*, c. 44, p. 89.
232   Tursun Bey, *Târîh-i Ebü'l-Feth*, pp. 104–5.
233   ASG, San Giorgio, Sala 34, 590 1308/2, ff. 28ᵛ–30r (1425.i.30); Karpov, "Una famiglia nobile", p. 595.

complicated the Genoese position in the region. Now defending "Caffa, Soldaia, Samastra [Amasra], Symbolum [Cembalo, Balaklava] and other towns and lands which the excellent *comune* of Genoa holds in various regions of the Black Sea"[234] was increasingly difficult, and it was at this point that Genoa handed over the colonies to the control of the Banco di San Giorgio. In 1455 Pope Niccolò v issued a bull calling for all Genoese to help in the defence of Caffa and of other Genoese settlements on the Black Sea threatened by the Turks and Tatars,[235] followed by another bull in the same year.[236]

Defending, however, was not so easy, particularly the trading settlements on the Anatolian coastline. Of these the Genoese seem to have been most preoccupied with Amasra in the immediate aftermath of the conquest of Constantinople, presumably because it was the first in line in any Ottoman advance eastward along the Black Sea coast. In September 1454, Demetrio Vivaldi, consul in Caffa, wrote to the Banco di San Giorgio reporting that Mehmed was planning to take Amasra (which he in fact did shortly afterwards), and that he was demanding tribute for Caffa. According to the information he had received, Demetrio Vivaldi stated that an annual tribute of 2,000 ducats would probably satisfy the sultan. In Vivaldi's opinion, it would be better to pay than to end up in a ruinous war with the Ottomans. The problem, however, was what to do about Amasra, when things were exceptional and negotiation difficult. Vivaldi stated bluntly that they did not know. Clearly wishing to retain "this town and this place", he noted that there were two ways to do this: peace or war. Peace required tribute, which, though not explicitly stated, did not appear to be an option for Amasra.[237] War was also clearly off the table, the best that Genoa could offer being supplies of food and soldiers. That things were not going well in Amasra is indicated by the fact that Vivaldi reported that they had decided to send a new consul because the current consul was unable to continue "in a good way". They had therefore elected Giovanni Cavalo, an expert in military matters, as consul with full powers and advised that he be confirmed for one year.[238]

Bitterly disappointed by the failure of the ambassadors Luciano Spinola and Baldassare Maruffo, whose mission to Mehmed II, "a triumph of wishful thinking over common sense", according Setton,[239] was in part to try and secure

---

234   Vigna, "Codice", doc. IV, p. 33.
235   Vigna, "Codice", doc. LXIV, pp. 255–6.
236   Vigna, "Codice", doc.CXVIII, p. 302.
237   Vigna, "Codice", doc. XXXIII, p. 106.
238   Vigna, "Codice", doc. XXXIII, p. 111.
239   Setton, Kenneth M., *The Papacy and the Levant (1204–1571). Volume II. The Fifteenth Century* (Philadelphia: The American Philosophical Society, 1978), p. 143.

freedom of Genoese access to the Black Sea,[240] Genoese officials in Caffa made a treaty with Mehmed, paying 3,000 rather than 2,000 ducats, according to reports reaching the Genoese authorities on Chios.[241] Amasra was excluded from the peace treaty, an omission that the authorities on Chios regarded with great displeasure, a view they were sure the authorities in Genoa would share. It had never been their view that Amasra or any other Genoese settlement in the Black Sea should be excluded from the peace treaty, they assured Genoa, stating explicitly that they were writing to make this clear in order to ensure that the authorities in Genoa would not think that they had any part in excluding Amasra from the agreement.[242]

Regardless of this omission, Genoa did attempt to support Amasra. In March 1455 the officials of the Banco di San Giorgio informed the consul and officials of Amasra that two ships had been sent from Chios carrying men, arms and munition "for the protection of Caffa and you and all our other territories in the Black Sea". There had been no economising on these provisions for "we and all the citizens have such concern for the wealth and protection of Caffa and you". The captain of the two ships had been commissioned to leave sufficient arms and soldiers in Amasra. If he was unable to approach the coast, then he was to send the men and provisions to Amasra as soon as possible after his arrival in Caffa. The officials of the Banco di San Giorgio declared themselves confidant that the omnipowerful God would free the people of Amasra "from these cares and dangers".[243] Such provisioning, however, was not always possible, due to contrary winds, bad weather conditions, or lack of provisions.[244]

What ultimately doomed the settlements was Ottoman desire to conquer them, something about which Genoa could do very little. By this time, with Ottoman control established over the entrance to the Black Sea and with Caffa under threat, Genoa was in no position to protect either Amasra or Sinop, both of which had fallen to Mehmed by 1461. Although this was undoubtedly a blow to Genoa, though of nowhere near the significance that the loss of Caffa was to be 14 years later, its commercial impact was minimal, for trade continued but with different partners as the Black Sea was drawn into the orbit of Istanbul and became increasingly a major source of provisioning for the new capital of the Ottoman empire.

---

240   Vigna, "Codice", doc. XXXVIII, p. 118; doc. XXXIX, p. 121; Belgrano, "Prima serie", doc. CLIV, pp. 267–8.
241   Vigna, "Codice", doc. CXVII, p. 299.
242   Vigna, "Codice", doc. CXVII, pp. 299–300.
243   Vigna, "Codice", doc. CXVI, pp. 296–7.
244   Vigna, "Codice", doc. CXXXV, p. 327; doc. CL, p. 355; doc. CXXXVI, p. 333.

CHAPTER 5

Production and Trade of Cotton in Ottoman Western Anatolia c. 1700–1914

Elena Frangakis-Syrett

This study examines the role of cotton in the western Anatolian economy in the late Ottoman period, a formative time for the Ottoman economy when its transition from the early modern to the modern era took place. Within that time period cotton played a pivotal role: in the course of the eighteenth century Anatolian cotton emerged as an important produce used in the local manufacturing sector and competitively traded both within the domestic market and international markets, as its brand status of top quality cotton, became increasingly better known. By the mid-eighteenth century, it started to play a pivotal role in Ottoman-European trade, a role it maintained and re-enforced through to the early nineteenth century. Cotton's role in the regional economy remained important in the nineteenth and early twentieth centuries, as a result of changes that were taking place in the global economy as well as in the regional western Anatolian economy.[1] In the second quarter of the nineteenth century the fortunes of cotton together with cotton yarn, the two primary commodities amongst Anatolia's exports took quite a dramatic dip.[2] There were certainly years of market corrections, allowing cotton growers and exporters to prove that western Anatolian cotton could still command the European markets. This would again change in the 50 years or so before the First World War, allowing western Anatolia's cotton to re-enter the markets, this time on a global scale and in a new economic environment that was increasingly shaped by a modern world economy. In that period cotton became important in the local economy, too, as the Ottoman manufacturing sector catering for the domestic market entered a new phase of growth. In the process, cotton remained not only relevant but one of the main products that underpinned the prosperity of the region.

---

1   Archives Nationales, Paris [hereafter ANF], AE Biii vol. 415, Trade Statistics for İzmir, 1858; Archives du Ministère des Affaires Étrangères, Paris [hereafter AMAE], ADC, vol. 654, Trade Statistics for İzmir, 1863.
2   Archives de la Chambre de Commerce de Marseille, Marseilles [hereafter ACCM], M.Q 5.1 Series, Trade Statistics for İzmir, 1825–1830.

The fact that cotton remained highly visible in the regional (Anatolian) and in the national (imperial) economy for over two centuries was to a large extent due to the fact that it could answer the needs of multiple and interconnected economic sectors: namely agriculture, trade and manufacture. Being at the interface of these three sectors, cotton entered the distributive markets at different times in the process of production and consumption either as raw material or as finished product. As the world economy grew and became better inter-connected, investment possibilities for the production and distribution of cotton were further developed. This underpinned its profitability and indispensability, giving cotton its name of 'white gold'. Following the American Civil War (1861–65) cotton was considered in the commentary of the time, and in subsequent historiography as well, as having contributed to the globalization of the world economy.[3] Anatolia's businessmen were able to benefit from such propitious circumstances by for example, positioning themselves, in terms of variety, quality and accessibility to markets, between the United States and India in the global cotton supply markets.[4] Certainly, it was the US that was the most important force in the global cotton supply markets. However, western Anatolia was able to take advantage of opportunities offered by changing conditions in the US. As a result, Anatolia's cotton production and trade sector would again successfully grow in the latter nineteenth and early twentieth centuries. A commodity that had in essence propelled İzmir to the top amongst the empire's export ports from the mid-eighteenth century onward had made a successful comeback. Yet, as we will argue below, western Anatolia was never a one-commodity regional economy, neither in its agricultural nor in its commercial profile. As for İzmir, it remained until the end of Ottoman rule, the premier city-port of the empire for exports.[5]

The Eighteenth Century

Cotton, a fibre that in the mid-18th century accounted for a tiny percentage of Europe's textile production, by the early decades of the following century had become the most important textile in the West characterized

---

3   Beckert, Sven, "Emancipation and empire: reconstructing the world wide web of cotton production in the age of the American Civil War", *American Historical Review*, 109/5 (2004), p. 1405.

4   AMAE, CCC, vol. 52, Memorandum on Cotton, French Consul General H. Pellissier, İzmir, 2 April 1879; see also, AMAE, NS, vol. 480, Trade Report for İzmir, 1903.

5   Issawi, Charles, *The Economic History of Turkey, 1800–1914* (Chicago: University of Chicago Press, 1980), pp. 108–13; see also Frangakis-Syrett, Elena, *The Port-City in the Ottoman Middle East at the Age of Imperialism* (Istanbul: The Isis Press, 2017), pp. 89–109.

by new mechanized and urbanized structures of production. Historically, no other area of the world had ever so radically changed its manufacturing economy, transforming a previously minor sector into the largest of these industries.[6]

This is how Riello summarized the discovery by both producers and consumers of the potential of cotton as a well-liked fiber to wear as well as a profitable one to produce. This was becoming apparent since the late seventeenth century and industries in Europe, which were producing woolens or linens or textiles using a mixture of linen and cotton, were not slow to react to the growing appreciation of their consumers for Indian cotton goods and the adverse effects it had on their own sectors. In an effort to save their industries, woolen or linen manufacturers sought to have such imports banned in Europe. Indeed all across Europe from 1686–1774 total prohibitions of imports of Indian cotton goods were put in place, but to no avail. Consumers continued to buy these goods.[7] In the Ottoman empire, as the example of western Anatolia shows us, local producers of cotton textiles were equally interested in maintaining their markets, in this case for cotton as a raw material. As a result, Europeans buying cotton for their commercial houses in Europe often could not find any cotton in Anatolia. It was because the well-established networks of buyers of the raw material for local cotton manufacturers were forcing the Europeans to either increase their prices or to improve their access to cotton cultivators' or merchants' networks to compete with other purchasers. This was noticeable by the middle of the eighteenth century just as interest for cotton textiles was growing in Europe. Since exports of the raw material from İzmir continued to increase, the Europeans were able to improve their access to such networks.[8]

---

6 Riello, Giorgio, "Cotton: the making of a modern commodity", *East Asian Journal of British History*, 5 (2016), p. 146; see also Riello, Giorgio, *Cotton: the Fabric that Made the Modern World* (Cambridge: Cambridge University Press, 2013), *passim*.

7 Lemire, Beverly, *Fashion's Favourite: The Cotton Trade and the Consumer in Britain, 1600–1800* (Oxford: Oxford University Press, 1991) cited in Riello, "Cotton: the making of a modern commodity", p. 138. See also Lee, Young-Suk, "Why did they admire the machinery? Rethinking intellectuals' view from the perspective of the competition between English cotton goods and Indian handicraft ones in the early Industrial Revolution", *The East Asian Journal of British History*, 5 (2016), 151–60. For a later period see Micklewright, Nancy, "London, Paris, Istanbul and Cairo: fashion and international trade in the 19th century", *New Perspectives on Turkey*, 7 (1992), 125–36.

8 This indeed was already observed by Charles-Claude de Peyssonnel, the French Consul in İzmir, in a detailed report he authored in 1751. An intellectual with a keen interest in Ottoman society and culture, Peyssonnel was usually very well informed about the state of affairs in the city-port and in the region at large. ANF, AE Bi 1053, Consul Charles de Peyssonnel, Mémoire, İzmir, 22 November 1751.

Interestingly, imports of Indian cottons in İzmir, as in other Ottoman markets in the eighteenth century, remained popular resulting in deficits in the empire's trade with India.[9]

What further helped the success of cotton was the fact that it coincided with a clear pace of expansionism of the world economy, which continued unabated, despite downward fluctuations, until the Industrial Revolution. This allowed two dynamics to come into play at the same time: continuous supplies that could largely match demand and vice-versa. The ability of the economies of western Europe to find suppliers of the raw material from India and the Americas to the Ottoman empire (even though the latter were in markets outside Europe) as well as find consumers of the finished product, both at home and abroad, – for cotton textiles produced in Europe were not necessarily all consumed locally –, were equally crucial in allowing the sector to keep growing at a strong and solid pace. Europe, even though it was not the only market, was a very important one nevertheless, capable of impacting the emergent world economy. In turn, elasticity in the supply markets due to the ability of Europe to maintain continuous access to supply markets and the capabilities of these markets to answer European demand had a direct impact on prices, at both stages of production, in cultivation and in manufacture, internationally. Leading economies in western Europe where textile manufacturers were increasing production output such as Britain, France, Austria or the Netherlands were able to imitate each other successfully in terms of company organization, sources of supply, costs of production and entry to markets to remain competitive. As a result, in the course of the second half of the eighteenth century, prices for the raw material were kept from rising too much despite continuous increase in demand; prices for the finished product showing equally similar trends.

Steady but not spectacular increases in the price of cotton despite growing demand and a growing volume of cotton exports in the second half of the eighteenth century is extremely well manifested in the case of İzmir. From 1700 to 1751 exports in value and volume increased steadily with an upward trend evident in prices, too, which reached their highest levels in 1749–50.[10] One would venture three explanations for this: increase in demand for cotton as raw material in Europe and Anatolia, coupled with the on-going expansion of the world economy which was noticeable by mid-eighteenth century as well as the end

---

9   ANF, AE Biii 243, Félix de Beaujour, Inspection générale du Levant, 1817. See also Tuchscherer, Michel, "Activités des Turcs dans le commerce de la mer Rouge au XVIIIe siècle", in *Les villes dans l'empire ottoman: activités et sociétés*, two vols., ed. Daniel Panzac (Paris: Editions du Centre national de la recherche scientifique, 1991), vol. I, pp. 322–4.

10   ACCM, Statistics Series I, vol. 26, Exports of cotton from İzmir to Marseilles, for 1748–59.

of the War of the Austrian Succession (1744–48). The trend started to change in the following decade, 1751–58, when prices started to drop. However, it reversed itself in 1758–64, due to the Seven Years' War (1756–63), a bitterly fought Anglo-French maritime conflict, which had once again created factors exogenous to the market, in particular inaccessibility of Marseilles to İzmir's exporters due to the British navy's blockading activities.[11] As a result, there were no imports from İzmir to Marseilles at all in 1757 and very few imports in 1759. Not surprisingly, cotton prices in the years 1759–60 rose by 30 percent.[12] Increases in insurance premium rates due to growing risks in maritime transportation and the general level of economic and political uncertainty kept prices going up right until 1764. Once war had ended and the markets had acquired new confidence, prices started to drop once more; they continued to do so until 1775 reflecting the overall downward trend in cotton prices internationally as well as western Anatolia's cotton sector's integration into these markets. The price decrease was again reversed in 1776 as the world economy entered a new period of commercial disruptions and political uncertainty highly evident in the credit and currency markets, too. This was the time of protracted wars that went from the American War of Independence (1776–82) to the end of the Napoleonic Wars (1803–15), as far as the Mediterranean maritime routes were concerned, with only short intervals of peace.[13] From 1776 to 1789 prices fluctuated but remained overall in an upward trend. Yet the downward price trend, which had started in the second half of the eighteenth century, wartime years apart, was not entirely broken. Indeed, the highest price levels reached in those years were still *not* higher than the level reached in 1749.[14] This was also the case internationally.

Cotton textiles' prices continued to be increasingly more affordable to consumers of different socio-economic levels, allowing cotton to become an internationally-produced and, in terms of the eighteenth century, a mass-consumed commodity. Some of the raw cotton and cotton yarn exported

---

11   Williams, Judith, *British Commercial Policy and Trade Expansion, 1750–1850* (Oxford: Clarendon Press, 1972), pp. 364–5.

12   Indeed, the British navy's superiority in the Mediterranean at the time meant that it was able to enforce neutral powers to abide by the blockade. Pares, Richard, *Colonial Blockades and Neutral Rights, 1739–1763* (Oxford: Clarendon Press, 1938), *passim*.

13   ANF, AE Bi 1087, French Consul M. Fraunnery, Trieste, 27 January 1789 to Minister, Paris; see also ANF, AE Bi 1069, French Consul Amoureux, İzmir, 9 April 1790 to Minister, Paris; and The National Archives, London [hereafter TNA], SP 105/132, Consul Francis Werry, İzmir, 9 July 1809 to Levant Company, London.

14   For annual cotton export trade data, 1700–89 see Frangakis-Syrett, Elena, *The Commerce of Smyrna in the Eighteenth Century, 1700–1820* (Athens: Centre for Asia Minor Studies, 1992), pp. 314–19.

from Anatolia to Marseilles, for the use of manufacturers located in southern France, was in turn, exported back to İzmir as a finished product. Ottoman purchasers of different qualities of such textiles were usually urban dwellers in the empire's biggest cities with a certain disposable income. Nevertheless they did not represent the elites by any means nor a single ethno-confessional community.[15] Of course, top luxury qualities of European fabrics were imported mostly for the elites. Naturally, Istanbul got the lion share of such imports; yet they figured, though in lesser quantities, amongst İzmir's cloth imports, too.[16] Consumption of cotton was revolutionizing tastes in apparel and had the potential of overturning long-held sartorial traditions. The fact that the Ottoman state issued sartorial codes several times in the latter eighteenth and early nineteenth centuries forbidding the new fashions can be seen as a reflection of such an anxiety.[17] That cultural changes in terms of apparel were taking place becomes more understandable when we note that the circulation at market-friendly prices of cotton, both as raw material and as finished product, shows that the chain of production, going from agriculture to trade, manufacture and consumption, was already completing the cycle, with success, even before technological inventions in manufacture and production in the West had fully revolutionized the sector. It was indeed within such rapidly evolving dynamics, with cotton becoming a global commodity that Anatolia's cotton was able to participate in and benefit from. In many respects hence the story of western Anatolia's cotton sector is part of the way the Ottoman economy was active, competitive and an efficient participant in the global markets, as the world economy evolved, from early eighteenth to early twentieth centuries.

Cotton for Cloth: a Commercially Symbiotic Relationship

Agriculture, which was highly diversified as a sector, formed a crucial part of the Ottoman economy for the entire period under study here; within it cotton constituted one of its most important staple crops. Since cotton was grown for the market – whether local, regional or international – it was also in some respects a bell weather of the state of the western Anatolian market in the way

15   Zilfi, Madeline, "Women and society in the Tulip Era, 1718–1730", in *Women, the Family, and Divorce Laws in Islamic History*, ed. Amira El Azhary Sonbol (New York: Syracuse University Press, 1996), pp. 290–303.

16   ANF, AE Biii 283, États des draps expediés de Marseille pour chaque échelle du Levant, 1756–1788.

17   Quataert, Donald, "Clothing laws, state and society in the Ottoman empire, 1720–1829", *International Journal of Middle East Studies*, 29/3 (1997), pp. 403–25.

the latter functioned and reacted to political events as well as to economic conjunctures whether they were local, national or international. One can gage the region's response mechanisms to changes in the economic environment through the ups and downs of the cotton sector, the way the regional economy sought to gain from opportunities, and/or contain adverse ones, and the degree of success in any of these strategies. For instance, the region's producers as well as the merchants displayed a considerable degree of adaptability as well as flexibility in modifying their economic activities – the crops they were cultivating, for instance – so as to remain solvent and return to the sector later if propitious conditions made it desirable, as it turned out to be the case for cotton. In the course of the nineteenth century, this was a process that encompassed multiple economic actors' participation and often went across the class divide: from small-scale producers to journeymen and middlemen of all sorts, to medium and large scale producers and exporters. As such, cotton became integral in the process of incorporation of the Anatolian economy, itself one of the heartlands of the Ottoman empire, into the world economy. Regionally, cotton became a vehicle for the better inter-connectivity of different sectors of the economy. This was an active process where Anatolia (as elsewhere in the empire) had agency and choices most, if not at all times. This was so to a large extent because trade was (and is) ultimately an open economic sector and cotton was (and is) a highly recognizable and sought-after product whether locally or internationally. Even more than Ankara mohair yarn or Bursa silk, which were transported to İzmir from their place of production (for export) cotton was cultivated in its immediate vicinity in the plains of Bakır, Gediz, Kırkağaç, Akhisar, Bergama, Kasaba, and Manisa as well as along the valleys of the Küçük and Büyük Menderes rivers in the neighborhood of the cities of Bayındır, Tire, Ödemiş, Aydın, and Denizli. Cotton from these areas was considered to be amongst the best in the Near East, and even better than that of Syria or Adana, with the top quality being produced in Aydın and Subaşı (near Alaşehir, in Manisa).[18] Indeed, in the latter nineteenth and early twentieth centuries, cotton from Aydın and Subaşı fetched higher prices in the global markets, even compared to that produced in the same areas but with American cotton seed.[19]

---

18   It was sold both as raw cotton and as cotton yarn, either white or dyed red, the last one being the most sought-after form of the commodity in all markets, domestic and European. ANF, AE Bi 1053, Peyssonnel, Mémoire, İzmir, 22 November 1751; ANF, AE Biii 242, Fourcade, Mémoire, İzmir, c. 1812. On yarn dyeing process, see Katsiardi-Hering, Olga, Τεχνίτες και τεχνικές βαφής νημάτων (Athens: Herodotos, 2003), pp. 99–125.

19   *Hellenic Chamber of Commerce Bulletin* [hereafter *HC of C Bulletin*], Year 11, Istanbul, 29 January 1911.

Of course trade with Europe was not by itself a large sector in terms of the empire's internal trade or its overall economy, especially in the eighteenth century. Indeed, the empire had an active trade with Iran and India, too.[20] However, the commercial sector tied to the external markets, both to the West and to the East and Far East, was already of crucial importance for the economy of İzmir since the eighteenth century. And İzmir was one of the most important city-ports in the Ottoman empire not only in its external but also in its internal trade. Furthermore, İzmir was active not only in trade but also in the currency and credit markets. The city's merchants and small-scale bankers – of all denominations and ethno-linguistic groups – supplied the funds, expertise as well as networks needed to undertake clearance operations for commercial transactions carried out in the interior of Anatolia. In addition, İzmir often furnished credit to stimulate trade by alleviating liquidity stress not only in Anatolia's economy but often beyond it, to service other markets in the empire, too.[21] Cotton certainly played an important part in İzmir's prominence within the empire as an important merchant banking center not only a commercial one.[22] In the eighteenth century, in particular, lack of an adequate circulating medium affected multiple countries, although in different ways and degrees. Within this context, it can be said that specie scarcity in Ottoman major active markets was relative to other markets, such as the Italian ones, more endemic and often more acute too. The fact that cotton was sold primarily through barter in exchange for cloth – that is, raw material for the finished product – was paramount in facilitating the sector's growth. Of course whilst not presupposing that cash – either in commercial paper, or specie – as well as credit were not at times also part of a cotton sale transaction, it did not necessitate it either.[23] At all times Europeans buying cotton in İzmir had to compete with Ottomans buying for the local sector; as the Mediterranean economy grew and likewise the Ottoman economy,[24] buying western Anatolian cotton became highly

---

20   Fukasawa, Katsumi, *Toilerie et commerce du Levant, d'Alep à Marseille* (Paris: Editions du Centre national de la recherche scientifique, 1987), pp. 39–45.

21   Frangakis-Syrett, Elena, *Trade and Money: The Ottoman Economy in the Eighteenth and Early Nineteenth Centuries* (Istanbul: The Isis Press, 2007), pp. 75–96.

22   TNA, SP 105/117, Levant Company, London, 13 January 1735 to British Consul Williams, İzmir. See also ANF, AE Bi 1057, French Consul Charles-Claude de Peyssonnel (son of Charles de Peyssonnel), Mémoire, İzmir, 29 April 1769 to the Chamber of Commerce of Marseilles.

23   ANF, AE Bi 1052, Peyssonnel, İzmir, 19 December 1749 to French Minister, Paris.

24   From the 1770s, onwards, there was an increasing number of factories in İzmir dyeing cotton yarn and printing cloth and muslins for export to Switzerland, Germany and Great Britain; they also catered to an internal market. ANF, AE Biii 242, M. Fourcade, Mémoire, İzmir, 1812. For a parallel situation in Ottoman Aleppo, see Banat, Rabih and Amézianne

competitive, often leading to a level of pricing in İzmir that could not be met in Marseilles or in the Italian markets, whose trading networks were closely connected to those of the French port. What made such competition even stronger was the growing demand for the supply of cotton as well as for an outlet for textiles. This made the protectionist regimes of Britain and France, by the end of the eighteenth century, start allowing growing amounts of cotton imports to reach their markets, indirectly if need be, for instance, by allowing French merchants to deal in cotton through the Italian ports or by allowing Ottoman ships to reach British ports.[25] Indeed, for most of the eighteenth century Ottoman cotton – with western Anatolian varieties playing a prominent role – was a far more important supplier to north western Europe's textile sector, than cotton from British America.[26] By the end of the century, new markets were developing a taste for Anatolian cotton, for instance in central Europe, led by Austria, which would play an important role in the external trade of Ottoman Anatolia from the 1770s to the 1920s.[27]

It was not only cotton prices that were rising in the city's markets. The predominance of cotton amongst its exports coincided almost to the year (1747) with the predominance of İzmir as the biggest western-bound exporting port of the empire. The following figures may place the importance of İzmir as an outlet for Anatolian cotton in the eighteenth century in a better context. In the third quarter of the eighteenth century, the share of cotton in the overall value of exports of İzmir to France – which accounted for almost half of the empire's trade to Europe –, ranged from 30 to 59 percent. The peak year for cotton exports was 1788 when it realized a share of 72 percent of İzmir's total exports! Earlier, in 1777 in fact, its share had reached 70 percent; in terms of bales exported, there were 23,570 bales in 1777 and 26,400 in 1788. In 1777, İzmir's share of the empire's total exports to France was 45 percent, and in 1788, 39 percent. In the 1780s, overall, cotton exports continued to grow in absolute terms, their share in relation to the exports of İzmir averaging

---

Ferguène, "La production et le commerce du textile à Alep sous l'empire ottoman: une forte contribution à l'essor économique de la ville", *Histoire, Économie et Sociétés*, 2 (2010), pp. 12–17.

25   TNA, SP 105/126, Werry, İzmir, 17 July 1797 to Levant Company, London; SP 105/122, Levant Company, London, 30 January 1798 to Werry, İzmir.

26   Quataert, Donald, *Ottoman Manufacturing in the Age of the Industrial Revolution* (Cambridge: Cambridge University Press, 1993), p. 27.

27   E.g., AMAE, CCC, vol. 36, Trade Report for İzmir, 1820; AMAE, CCC, vol. 43, Trade Report for İzmir, 1832; AMAE, CCC, vol. 54, Trade Report for İzmir, 1881; *Parliamentary Papers, Accounts & Papers* [hereafter *PP, A&P*], vol. LXV, Trade Report for İzmir, 1882–1885 (London, 1886); AMAE, NS, vol. 480, Trade Report for İzmir, 1901; AMAE, NS, vol. 480, Trade Report for İzmir, 1906; *PP, A&P*, vol. CIII, Trade Report for İzmir, 1909 (London, 1910).

49 percent annually. Yet, in 1782 İzmir's cotton exports represented 60 percent of all Ottoman cotton exported to France, or to *other* markets through French commercial networks as was increasingly the case by then; this share dropped in the next two years, but in 1785 it rose this time to 65 percent. At the time İzmir's greatest rival, Thessaloniki (Selanik), had an average share of 19 percent of the empire's cotton exports ostensibly to France, but most likely to Italian ports, and from there to central or northern Europe, with all the other Ottoman ports providing the rest.[28] Within Ottoman-European trade, overall, Marseilles and İzmir played pivotal roles, as did Ottoman cotton and European cloth. That this was so was largely due to a highly successful commercial exchange based on the export of Ottoman cotton and cotton yarn and import of French cloth. It was an operation involving a number of inter-related economic sectors located in southern France and western Anatolia respectively. In France, it included considerable long-term financing since it took up to two years for returns to be realized. Financing took the form of investment in textile enterprises to the building and/or chartering of a ship, to insuring it and its cargo, to funding a commercial transaction that covered the purchase of cotton in İzmir, or from its interior, to the making of cloth, in southern France and its sale in the Ottoman markets, the transaction going the opposite way, for the whole affair to be completed. Financing agricultural production, transportation of the produce from the interior to the harbor and its sale took place in İzmir too even when it might have been done through investors in Istanbul as may also have been the case with Lyons bankers investing in Marseilles.

In terms of cotton produced, as opposed to exported, data available at present does not allow us to quantify production levels and hence the share that was exported to the West. One can perhaps assess trends in production levels by calculating the exports of cotton to Marseilles, for the eighteenth century, which accounted consistently for a good 50 percent of İzmir's trade to Europe. Taking the average for every decade in the second half of the eighteenth century, we have the following figures: in the 1750s, 8,270 bales[29] were exported annually; in the 1760s this increased to 12,285 bales annually – an increase of 48.5 percent; in the 1770s, the annual average dropped slightly to 12,235 bales and in the 1780s it rose to 20,279 bales – an increase of 66 percent.[30] In 1750 alone exports amounted to 7,319 bales. In 1784, amounts exported to Europe were: 12,000–13,000 bales to France; 8,000 bales to the Netherlands; 5,000 to

---

28   ANF, AE Bi 1087, Fraunnery, Trieste, 27 January 1789 to Minister, Paris.
29   Each bale is calculated at 300 lbs. TNA, FO 78/1760, Consul C. Blunt, İzmir, 23 January 1863 to Foreign Office in London.
30   ACCM, Series I, Trade Statistics, vols. 26–28.

Italy (some of which was most likely destined for the British market) and 3,000 bales to Britain.[31] With the end of the American War of Independence (1776–82), the Eli Whitney cotton ginning invention just a few years away and the British Industrial Revolution in full swing, it was American cotton that was by then increasingly supplying Britain.

In 1788, a peak export year for cotton and İzmir's exports overall, they more than trebled reaching 26,402 bales. There was a substantial increase in the export of cotton in the closing decades of the eighteenth century which carried over into the nineteenth century. From 1788 to 1820, cotton exports trebled to almost 70,000 bales. In 1820, we have the following breakdown of the export figures: Güzelhisar (Aliağa in İzmir) and Subaşı sent for export to the market of İzmir 8,000 bales; Kırkağaç (in Manisa), a seat of the Karaosmanoğlu family, the biggest cotton producer and local administrator, sent 25,000 bales of second quality cotton to İzmir annually. Akhisar, Bergama, and Kınık furnished İzmir with another 25,000 bales of third quality cotton. Kasaba furnished the city with 10,000 bales annually and Manisa with 4,000 bales.[32] The considerable growth of cotton exports, at least until 1820, reflects not only the dimensions of commercial growth of İzmir but potentially point to growing production levels since there was growing demand for the raw material for local manufacture, at the turn of the century. Growing exports also reflect the fact that Europeans were extending the scope and volume of their trading activities, too. From the early 1800s onward, they started going regularly inland to trade. Before that date they did so only occasionally.[33]

Mustafa Ağa Karaosmanoğlu, whose family had amassed titles and wealth initially through service to the sultan, sent at least in certain years the biggest amount of cotton to the markets abroad; he was quite likely the biggest landowner, *de facto* if not *de jure*, and cotton producer in the region, already in mid-eighteenth century.[34] Having given favorable terms to cultivators from the Morea and the Aegean islands who settled in his lands from the 1770s onwards as sharecroppers, he maintained his primary position as cotton grower and exporter. Besides owning the means of production, he owned the largest number of camels in the caravan trade in the Anatolian interior used to bring the

---

31   État du Commerce du Levant, 1784 cited in Issawi, *The Economic History of Turkey*, p. 235.

32   ANF, Paris, AE Biii, Fourcade, Mémoire, İzmir, 1820.

33   Cunningham, A.B. (ed.), "The journal of Christophe Aubin: a report of the Levant trade in 1812", *Archivum Ottomanicum*, 8 (1983), p. 38. For further details see Frangakis-Syrett, Elena, "Commerce in the eastern Mediterranean from the eighteenth to the early twentieth centuries: the city-port of Izmir and its hinterland", *International Journal of Maritime History*, 10/2 (1998), 125–54.

34   ANF, AE Bi 1053, Peyssonnel, Mémoire, İzmir, 22 November 1751.

cotton to the coast. He was also active in the Isfahan-İzmir silk trade route.[35] Small-scale peasant proprietorship, which was more prevalent in nineteenth-century western Anatolia,[36] was in evidence in the eighteenth century too, although most of the peasants were sharecroppers, as well as some seasonal laborers, for large-scale landowners who held land under feudal terms of ownership; as late as 1792, the province of Aydın is recorded as having supported 110 *zaim* holders, 4,235 timariots, and one *beylerbeyi* whose annual revenue was 923,000 *akçes*.[37] Nevertheless commercialized agriculture was a very active and growing sector; from the 1750s to the 1820s large-scale landowners such as the Karaosmanoğlu and the Araboğlu – a major wheat grower and exporter in the region – were dominant in this sector.[38]

The growing ability of producers to answer market opportunities in the course of the nineteenth century was in part because of the way agricultural relations of production evolved.[39] Many of them became small-scale cultivators with the 1858 land code allowing private property, although many more remained indebted to merchants who as advance purchasers could at times and often did take a lion's share of the profits. Other types of rural investors, including money-lenders and tax farmers, could equally siphon off producers' surpluses in good years leading many of them to become sharecroppers, or worse wage laborers; nevertheless others did better and were able to establish themselves as owners of sustainable small-scale production units, especially in the closing decades of the nineteenth and even more so in the early twentieth centuries. As such they could choose what crops to cultivate, and even switch crops not only from one year to the next, but also within the same year's cultivating season if the desired crop needed same soil preparation as the other one but was likely to do better in the global market conditions of that year.[40] To be able to make such decisions, producers and their investors too had to be well informed, and coordinated – according to the relationship that they

35   ANF, Biii 242, Jumelin, Commerce du Levant en général, c. September 1812.

36   Kurmuş, Orhan, *Emperyalizmin Türkiye'ye Girişi* (Istanbul: Bilim Yayınları, 1974), pp. 148–50.

37   Habesci, Elias, *État actuel de l'empire ottoman*, two vols. (Paris: Lavillette, 1792), vol. I, p. 205; vol. II, pp. 21–2.

38   İnalcık, Halil, "The emergence of big farms, *çiftliks*: state, landlords and tenants", in *Landholding and Commercial Agriculture in the Middle East*, ed. Çağlar Keyder and Faruk Tabak (Albany, N.Y.: State University of New York Press, 1991), pp. 17–34. See also Veinstein, Gilles, "On the *çiftlik* debate", in Keyder and Tabak, *Landholding and Commercial Agriculture in the Middle East*, pp. 39–43, 47–53.

39   Centre des Archives Diplomatiques, Nantes, Ministère des Affaires Étrangères [hereafter CADN, MAE], Fonds Constantinople, Box No. 42, Economic Report, İzmir, 12 February 1845.

40   *HC of C Bulletin*, Istanbul, Year 11, 19 and 29 January 1911.

had to each other – as well as be up-to-date, with market conditions. They had to be well informed of the latest movement, however slight, in the prices and potential sales of one produce as opposed to another as well as to be able to tell genuine information as opposed to rumors, well-intentioned or otherwise. In the course of the second half of the nineteenth century and beyond, there developed a very active print media in İzmir, from dailies to weeklies, printed in different languages,[41] where business news of all kinds was regularly covered. The plethora of articles on economic issues especially the commodities markets that appeared in such outlets displayed an acute awareness of what was going on. By the early twentieth century, given the existence of railways and mass urban transportation[42] as well as the telegraph, newspapers and other print media must have connected the city-port with its surrounding towns very well and within the wider western Anatolian region relatively well creating a savvy business environment, knowledgeable and sophisticated. Any changes in prices in Washington D.C. or in the expected levels of the cotton harvest in the US were immediately registered in İzmir.[43]

The Nineteenth Century

When Eli Whitney invented the cotton gin machine in 1793, the latter became an international phenomenon in terms of its repercussions which vibrated from the American and British markets to the French and Ottoman ones, Anatolia's market included, and beyond. As a result, and despite the absolute increase in the production and exports of cotton, its *share* in the value of exports of the western Anatolian port dropped dramatically in the early nineteenth century. It was not particularly detrimental for the commercial sector of İzmir, or even its export sector, both of which continued to grow in relative and absolute terms. As for its producers, large and small-scale cultivators, although the latter must have been the least prepared, one should note that they were able to switch with agility and furnish İzmir with other commodities to maintain and

---

41   Mansel, Philip, *Splendor and Catastrophe on the Mediterranean* (New Haven, CT.: Yale University Press, 2011), pp. 164–5.

42   Frangakis-Syrett, Elena, "L'économie de l'Anatolie occidentale, 1908–1918", in *La Turquie entre trois mondes: actes du Colloque International de Montpellier, 5, 6 et 7 octobre 1995*, ed. Marcel Bazin, Salgur Kançal, Roland Perez and Jacques Thobie (Paris: L'Harmattan, 1998), pp. 239–48.

43   *HC of C Bulletin*, Year 6, Istanbul, 2 January 1906; see also *HC of C Bulletin*, Year 7, Istanbul, 16 June 1907; *HC of C Bulletin*, Year 9, Istanbul, 7 March and 11 July 1909; *HC of C Bulletin*, Year 11, Istanbul, 29 January 1911.

even enlarge its export sector. To the degree that the agricultural sector was tied to the external markets, which was in the first quarter of the nineteenth century still very relative – although it increased in scope and degree in the latter nineteenth century – Anatolia never only exported one or two crops but a variety of them. Diversified agriculture was indeed a strong feature of western Anatolia's economy throughout the period under study here. In the second half of the eighteenth century, large-scale producers and merchants turned increasingly to exporting cotton, as opposed to silk or mohair yarn, because it made economic sense to do so given that it was in its immediate vicinity. In addition, demand for cotton was growing not only from established markets such as France and Britain but from new ones, too, such as Austria and Germany for which there existed another advantage, that of a profitable route through Trieste. The latter combined both maritime and land transportation which ensured access to the continental European markets profitably even at times of war.[44] Although certain large-scale landowners were cotton producers, most notably Karaosmanoğlu, others were not; Araboğlu, for instance, was a primary producer and exporter of wheat in the region.[45] In addition, the region's commercial networks continued to export other products, even during the last quarter of the eighteenth century, when cotton exports reached their highest levels. For instance, wool exports remained strong competing with cotton in different years; exports of silk and mohair did not disappear either. When the highly competitive American cotton entered the European markets, at the turn of the century, affecting cotton exporters globally, İzmir's export sector did not seem to have suffered much. This was despite the fact that its premier trading partner, France, was at the same time experiencing, for different reasons, a temporary disarray of its commercial networks. İzmir already had other trading partners, besides France, and was venturing into new partnerships at exactly that period.[46] In this respect the region's cotton sector becomes a good manifestation, as shown below, of the agency western Anatolia exercised, the decisions its economic actors took and the strategies they adopted for the region's active participation in the world economy.

Certainly the Marseilles-İzmir trading relationship was affected by these changes. Already in the 1820s, Anatolian cotton's share of the French markets (or at least what went through French trading networks) started to fluctuate

---

44   ANF, B/7, 446, French Consul Bertrand, 19 October 1782 in Commerce des ports d' Europe, 1 February 1783.

45   ANF, AE Bi 1054, Peyssonnel, İzmir, 7 July 1754 to Minister, Paris.

46   For İzmir's trade figures and its trading partners, c. 1775–1820, see Frangakis-Syrett, *The Commerce of Smyrna*, pp. 274–9.

widely: it went from as little as five percent in value (1824) to as much as 50 percent (1825). It is interesting to note that even when cotton traders were able still to capture a good share of the trading activity, trade to France had greatly diminished. Given the increase in cotton availability for the external markets, noted in contemporary accounts, the decrease in bales exported to France, – under 9,000 in 1825 –, illustrates the decrease in İzmir's trade with France overall. To better meet the fluctuations in cotton demand, İzmir turned to wool (mohair and lamb's wool) and silk; the latter two commodities shared the gap left by cotton in the French market.[47] As far as Anatolian cotton exports to France were concerned the situation did not change in the following decade: in 1831–38 the average annual share of cotton among İzmir's exports to Marseilles was 14 percent; the list was topped by wool and, increasingly by dried fruit.[48] Overall the Marseilles-İzmir trading relationship survived. Ultimately, this may have been the best result for French imports from İzmir, because it meant that the industrial regions of north-western France would not be competitively enough linked to the western Anatolian market.[49] This was at least in part due to reluctance by the trading networks of Marseilles to open up and establish more competitive maritime routes to link other regions of France with İzmir. Instead, these networks appeared to have retained their privileged place within a trading relationship, which was *overall* of a lesser scope and scale, than previously.[50]

Of course the region's cotton producers and İzmir's cotton traders, too, had to adjust in order to fill the gap left by cotton for other of their markets, such as the British. To achieve this, they turned to other goods, which were increasingly popular in the western markets, such as valonea, gum adragante, or alizarin, used for dyeing or medicinal purposes, besides wool, silk and opium.[51] Even more than in the eighteenth century, in the nineteenth and early

---

47   AMAE, CCC, vol. 36, Exports and Imports of İzmir, 1820; see also ACCM, M.Q.5.1., Exports and Imports of İzmir, 1824–1825.

48   CADN, MAE, Fonds Constantinople, Box No. 40, Trade Reports for İzmir, 1831–1838.

49   There were exceptional circumstances such as the phylloxera attack of the 1870s that devastated French vineyards making it competitive and cost-effective, in terms of the transportation costs and intermediaries, to import quantities of raisins from western Anatolia. Premium prices for raisins were necessary to maintain the wine and alcohol industries of north-west France. For more details, see Frangakis-Syrett, Elena, "XVII. Yüzyıl Başından, XX. Yüzyıl Başlarına Kadar Krala Gemiyle İzmir'den Giden Sultaniye Kuru Üzüm İhracatı", in *Üzümün Akdeniz'deki Yolculuğu. Konferans Bildirileri*, ed. Ertekin Akpınar and Ekrem Tükenmez (İzmir: İzmir Akdeniz Akademisi, 2017), pp. 121–31.

50   AMAE, CCC, vol. 52, H. Pellissier, İzmir, 7 May 1879 to Foreign Minister, Paris.

51   *PP, A&P*, vol. LXVIII, Trade Report for İzmir, 1866 (London, 1867); *PP, A&P*, vol. LXXVII, Trade Report for İzmir, 1874 (London, 1875); see also AMAE, CCC, vol. 49, French Consul

twentieth century no export topped İzmir's list year after year; rather the contrary. There was great mobility amongst its half a dozen, or slightly more, major exports with any one of them likely to top the list in any given year.[52] Here a further qualification should be made: the share of the top produce was never of the magnitude of cotton in the previous century, rarely going over 30 percent, although this did occur, too. In terms of the export trends of its primary agricultural products, they were exported on a two to four years' cycle. The longer time span was more unusual and occurred only if there were special market circumstances favoring it. Following this two to four year cycle, the commodity in question would switch with another one which would take first position in the exports of Anatolia, most likely for one or two years. Sometimes two products would switch with one another for first ranking position, taking almost equal share each year. In part this was due to the overselling in a specific market, or in any number of markets at the same time, causing it to become over stocked; importers had to reduce their stock of the product in the subsequent year. Another reason had to do with climatic conditions which could potentially produce low harvests, for probably more than one year, leading to replenishment and then to overstocking in a given market(s) and hence to lesser sales to that market(s) subsequently. It also reflected a degree of inelasticity in the consuming markets, world-wide.

Events exogenous to the market could occur and change the commercial landscape of the cotton sector, potentially worldwide. During the French Revolutionary and Napoleonic Wars, (1792–1801, 1803–15), the Americans entered the Mediterranean, as neutrals, filling a gap left by the warring Europeans. As a result, an active trade developed through American and Ottoman trading networks, between the East Coast and western Anatolia, in imports of opium and dried fruit to the US and exports of sugar, coffee and cloth to İzmir.[53] By the time these wars had ended, Austria had already taken the place of Britain as the second most important trading partner of the region and Britain the place of France as its first trading partner.[54] Although Austria would be an important and on-going purchaser of Anatolian cotton, Britain would do so only incrementally and the US not at all. In fact, the global markets

---

Th. Pichon, İzmir, 17 July 1854 to Foreign Affairs Minister, Paris; *PP, A&P*, vol. 51, French Consul G. Auberely, İzmir, 28 October 1872 to Foreign Affairs Minister, Paris.

52   There were of course exceptions to this rule. For instance, leeches, in high demand in the middle decades of the nineteenth century, ceased to be so later on.

53   TNA, SP 105/127, Werry, İzmir, 2 August 1800 to Levant Company, London.

54   On the share of the British in İzmir's trade, see, Frangakis-Syrett, Elena, "The making of an Ottoman port: the quay of Izmir in the nineteenth century", *The Journal of Transport History*, 22/1 (2001), 23–46.

for cotton had already changed irrevocably and a restructuring of Anatolia's agricultural exporting profile had inevitably to take place. This occurred in the late 1820s and early 1830s with dried fruit starting to appear and raw materials for manufacture – especially cotton – receding to a share in single digits – four to eight percent.[55] Certainly this share could and did go up. For it was tied increasingly to the size of American and Indian production, both of which as any agricultural produce, including Anatolian cotton, were vulnerable to weather. Hence there were years when any decrease in the US production volume, in particular, was met by other exporters including Anatolia for markets in Europe. Anatolian growers and exporters had both a well-known product and the networks to channel it competitively to meet such markets' demand. Such a case occurred in 1832 when France and Austria imported almost equal amounts in value of cotton although this represented 38 percent of the French market and 24 percent of the Austrian one.[56] This was also the year that signaled the entry of other consumers for Anatolian cotton, Russia, and Italy – the latter for its own use rather than as a redistributive market, as had often been the case in the eighteenth century – to be followed in the second half of the nineteenth century, by Spain, Portugal and Greece.

In the 1840s,[57] and 1850s, and despite the robust growth of Anatolia's external trade overall, cotton was still not being exported on the scale it had been before. In 1858, with the value of agricultural produce passing through İzmir having grown two a half times since 1832 – and taking into account that 1858 was not a good year for the European economy – the share of cotton at eight percent tied with silk; it was surpassed by opium's share at ten percent, raisins' share at 12 percent with alizarin topping the list at 38 percent.[58] For the cotton export trade all this was to change in three short years. Within two years from the start of the American Civil War, in 1863, western Anatolian cotton exports, given rising prices too, reached in value 34 percent of İzmir's total trade; it became its first export for that year, too, with Britain taking the largest share.[59] In just two years after hostilities had ended, the US had come back as a cotton supplier: İzmir's cotton exports registered, not surprisingly, a precipitous drop,

---

55   AMAE, CCC, vol. 42, Trade Report for İzmir, for 1828.

56   AMAE, CCC, vol. 43, Trade Report for İzmir, for 1832.

57   CADN, MAE, Fonds Constantinople, Box no. 42, Report on the Trade of İzmir, 1842–1843 by French Consul, İzmir, 12 February 1845 to French Ambassador, Istanbul. See also CADN, MAE, Fonds Constantinople, Box No. 42, Trade Reports for İzmir, 1844–1847.

58   ANF, AE Biii 415, Global Trade of İzmir for 1858.

59   AMAE, ADC, vol. 654, Global Trade of İzmir for 1863; see also AMAE, CCC, vol.53, Pellissier, İzmir, 2 April 1879 to Foreign Minister, Paris.

both in value and volume, with prices falling by almost 70 percent.[60] The war and its aftermath did destabilize the supply markets for a number of years and led to the re-structuring of the global pattern of cotton production; however the dynamics of expansion of the global economy in the latter nineteenth and early twentieth centuries proved the most important directional force. In other words, the US cotton supplier market was one of the most influential global players, but not the only one. Given the rate of global economic expansion, southern Anatolia, the Adana region, became an important growing producer of cotton, using American seed, as did other regions in the world. Its annual production grew rapidly reaching 100,000 bales by the end of the nineteenth century,[61] and even more in the early twentieth century.[62] However, western Anatolia did not go that route: a harvest of 50,000 bales would be considered an excellent one, and more likely to be at the 40,000 bales mark. For instance, in 1877 cotton production would surpass the 50,000 bales mark and be the region's first export for that year with a share of 34 percent with raisins, another visible export of the region, that year taking a share of only two percent. Yet just two years later in 1879 raisins would be the first export with a share of 25 percent and cotton's share would drop to three percent.[63]

In the immediate aftermath of the war, as US cotton exports re-entered the supply markets and Italian and German Unification movements led to wars in continental Europe, the bottom fell out of the cotton supply markets which of course affected all, including western Anatolia, an impact exacerbated by the economic crises in the later 1860s which further negatively impacted the markets across the board. With the recovery of the world economy in the early 1870s, demand for cotton entered a new phase of sustainable increase from which western Anatolia benefited once again. Indeed, the 1870s would turn out to be good years in terms of climatic conditions too producing good harvests and strong exports for western Anatolia despite the growth in demand for the raw material domestically. Cotton would be the first export in 1874 and 1876,

---

60   AMAE, CCC, vol. 51, Trade Report for İzmir for 1867; see also, AMAE, CCC, vol. 51, French Consul Bentivoglio, İzmir, 30 January 1868 to Foreign Affairs Minister, Paris.

61   PP, A&P, Trade Report for Adana, 1894, cited in Toksöz, Meltem, Nomads, Migrants and Cotton in the Eastern Mediterranean (Leiden: Brill, 2011), p. 144 and see also pp. 141–3.

62   HC of C Bulletin, Istanbul, Year 7, 6 January and 16 June 1907; HC of C Bulletin, Year 10, Istanbul, 2 October 1910; HC of C Bulletin, Year 11, Istanbul, 1 January 1911; see also Toksöz, Nomads, Migrants and Cotton in the Eastern Mediterranean, p. 181; and Akder, A. Halis, "Yirminci Yüzyılın Başında Çukurova'ya Pamuk Ekmenin Maliyeti", in Osmanlı'nın Peşinde bir Yaşam. Suraiya Faroqhi'ye Armağan, ed. Onur Yıldırım (Ankara: İmge Kitabevi Yayınları, 2008), pp. 221–69.

63   PP, A&P, vol. LXXIII, Trade Report for İzmir, 1877–1881 (London, 1883). See also AMAE, CCC, vol. 53, Pellissier, İzmir, 7 May 1879 to Foreign Affairs Minister, Paris.

reaching in the latter year the highest ever production figure, of 75,073 bales.[64] However a series of years with bad climate and attacks by locusts in the late 1870s, followed by the Great Depression starting to make its mark on global trade in the course of the 1880s, cotton production fell once more as the region turned to other goods.[65] It would take to 1884 for it to surpass 50,000 bales,[66] dropping in the late 1880s and early 1890s to half this level.[67] In that period, however, there was for Anatolia and İzmir the bonanza of exports of raisins to meet hitherto unprecedented levels of demand with price increases following suit due to the phylloxera attack in France, Germany and Austria. The region increased its production in raisins, but it never became a monoculture in this crop either.[68] When vines in France and subsequently in central Europe too recovered fully, high tariffs dropped prices precipitously as these important markets in essence closed their doors. In this conjuncture, cultivators, advance purchasers, exporters, creditors and a whole host of people involved in this trade suffered and of course some must have gone bankrupt. For the region as a whole, however, there were valonia, barley, opium and figs, as well as carpets and tobacco, to save the day allowing İzmir to record growth in trade in the 1890s.

The steady growth in the world economy, evident in the empire, too, led the cotton production and export trade sectors to register continuous growth in the 1900s. However, this should be qualified as follows: cotton would remain a visible export in the region's profile; its close communication channels with the US market would become even stronger, thus allowing the region to be better connected through an important global produce. Any movement in prices in the US cotton supply market would be nearly instantaneously recorded in İzmir; the cotton futures market was one of the strongest in the city. In 1911 cotton was considered by experts and pundits alike in Anatolia as probably the most profitable crop in the world, whose value was likely to grow even more.[69] In terms of bales exported, the years 1908–12 saw an annual average

---

64   PP, A&P, vol. LXXVII, Trade Report for İzmir, 1874 (London, 1875); and PP, A&P, vol. LXXXIII, Trade Report for İzmir, 1876 (London, 1877).

65   AMAE, CCC, vol. 54, Pellissier, İzmir, 13 May 1882 to Foreign Affairs Minister, Paris.

66   PP, A&P, vol. LXXIII, Trade Report for İzmir, 1877–1881 (London, 1883).

67   PP, A&P, vol. LXXXI, Trade Report for İzmir, 1888 (London, 1889); see also, PP, A&P, vol. LXXXVIII, Trade Report for İzmir, 1890 (London, 1890–1891).

68   Frangakis-Syrett, "XVIII. Yüzyıl Başından, XX. Yüzyıl Başlarına Kadar Krala Gemiyle İzmir'den Giden Sultaniye Kuru Üzüm İhracatı", pp. 125–9.

69   HC of C Bulletin, Istanbul, Year 11, 1 January 1911. On similar sentiments concerning cotton within the business circles of İzmir, see also HC of C Bulletin, Year 6, Istanbul, 11 February 1906; HC of C Bulletin, Year 7, Istanbul, 13 January 1907; HC of C Bulletin, Year 9,

of less than 40,000 bales – certainly, not a large amount.[70] However, it was an improvement on earlier decades: in 1879–92, there was annual average of 24,000 bales being exported of all qualities.[71] The increase in the 1900s reflected the growing global demand for cotton, even when American cotton production was robust and even more if it had suffered from adverse weather conditions, which the savvy cultivators of western Anatolia evidently sought to gain from. Overall, the lower average of annual cotton exports did coincide with the Great Depression that by the 1880s was dampening demand in the West for raw materials as well as the extraordinary opportunities for profit that raisins offered in the late 1880s and early 1890s.[72] Yet, as was almost typical in the commodities export trade sector of İzmir, 1884 and 1885 saw robust cotton exports of 51,000 and 42,000 bales respectively with cotton becoming the third export of the region in value during those years, although not surprisingly raisins were the first export and bigger in value, by far.[73]

The positive terms of trade that western Anatolia and in fact the Ottoman empire as a whole, experienced for most of the nineteenth century allowed capital accumulation to occur and gave options for its exporters too, for western imported goods, primarily textiles, fell in price as increased cost efficiencies in production and transportation lowered their costs whilst Ottoman exports of primarily raw materials and foodstuffs continued to fetch high prices. This allowed the Ottoman domestic market to grow, and was equally the case for its agricultural sector. However, it hit the local manufacturing economy especially badly.[74] The growth in local manufacture in western Anatolia that eyewitness accounts offer for the 1770s to the 1820s was not evident for the next almost 50 years. As greater productivity and costs reductions were no longer possible

---

Istanbul, 7 March 1909. See also, *PP, A&P*, vol. LXV, Trade Report for İzmir, 1882–1885 (London, 1886).

70   *PP, A&P*, vol. XCVIII, Trade Report for İzmir, 1908 (London, 1909); *PP, A&P*, vol. CIII, Trade Report for İzmir, 1909 (London, 1910); *PP, A&P*, vol. C, Trade Report for İzmir, 1909–1911 (London, 1911–1912); *PP, A&P*, vol. XCV, Trade Report for İzmir, 1912–1913 (London, 1914).

71   *PP, A&P*, vol. LXXIII, Trade Report for İzmir, 1877–1881 (London, 1883); *PP, A&P*, vol. LXV, Trade Report for İzmir, 1882–1885 (London, 1886); *PP, A&P*, vol. LXXXVI, Trade Report for İzmir, 1885–1886 (London, 1887); *PP, A&P*, vol. LXXXI, Trade Report for İzmir, 1888 (London, 1889); *PP, A&P*, vol. LXXXVIII, Trade Report for İzmir, 1890 (London, 1890–1891); *PP, A&P*, vol. LXXXIV, Trade Report for İzmir, 1891 (London, 1892); *PP, A&P*, vol. XCVII, Trade Report for İzmir, 1892 (London, 1892–1893).

72   *PP, A&P*, vol. LXXXI, Trade Report for İzmir, 1888 (London, 1889); *PP, A&P*, vol. LXXXVIII, Trade Report for İzmir, 1890 (London, 1890–1891); *PP, A&P*, vol. LXXXIV, Trade Report for İzmir, 1891 (London, 1892); *PP, A&P*, vol. XCVII, Trade Report for İzmir, 1892 (London, 1892–1893).

73   *PP, A&P*, vol. LXV, Trade Report for İzmir, 1882–1885 (London, 1886).

74   AMAE, CCC, vol. 51, Economic Report on İzmir, for 1867.

in the western manufacturing sector, which led, amongst other factors, to the nineteenth century Great Depression, western textiles rose in price. At the same time, demand in the western markets for western Anatolian cotton as raw material decreased. The combined effect of these forces was the regeneration of the local cotton textile manufacturing sector serving not only the domestic market but also regional markets abroad.[75]

Conclusion

Looking at the nineteenth and twentieth centuries overall, and in seeking to understand what made western Anatolia able to remain competitive as well as sustain the potential of wild swings in the cotton trade, we would perhaps do best to see it within the context of the approach the region's economic actors took to production and trade. Their knowledge of cotton – which they had dealt in since the eighteenth century – coupled with their understanding of how competitive and volatile markets functioned, at home and abroad, gave them valuable experience in how to do well within such markets, when the pace and scope of economic activity quickened, as the nineteenth century progressed, offering both high profits and risks. Their experience stood them well particularly as far as cotton was concerned, for the global nature of cotton was both the source of its profitability but also of its volatility, both of which did not *only* depend on the weather but on a whole host of other factors that had to do with multiple global economies as well as national and international political conditions. Certainly cotton was not unique in offering such challenges. As the world economy became better inter-connected, these were conditions that any goods that were *truly globally* traded could potentially face. However, those dealing in cotton, at any stage of production, faced a whole host of such risks and those who did well in it had to know how to strategize.

Indeed, some of those strategies were in many respects features of the region's economy: a diversified agricultural production and a high level of connectivity to the (inter)-national channels of communication and an open business environment attuned to change. In order to operate effectively, the region's exporters and cultivators sought to inform themselves as to where and how to best place their exports either in markets where they were already established, or how to pursue new market opportunities. İzmir was one of the first to enter into regular trading contacts with the Americans in the late

---

75   Quataert, *Ottoman Manufacturing in the Age of the Industrial Revolution*, pp. 1–20, 52–9, 92–104; see also Issawi, *The Economic History of Turkey, 1800–1914*, pp. 298–314.

eighteenth and early nineteenth centuries. Everyone had to be involved – merchants, money lenders, small and large-scale cultivators, intermediaries of all sorts, ship brokers and insurance agents, all of whom invariably handled different stages of the process. In seeking to hedge against downward cycles in the global (and potentially domestic) consumption markets for cotton, they chose to remain producers and exporters of an array of goods, rather than cotton only, for which western Anatolia had acquired brand recognition in the global markets. These numbered at different times in the course of the nineteenth and early twentieth centuries over a dozen different commodities, half as many as in the eighteenth century: from cotton, opium, raisins, figs (amongst other dried fruit) and carpets to wool, valonia, barley (amongst other cereals), silk, leeches, liquorice paste and madder roots. Although Britain was clearly the region's most important trading partner in the nineteenth and early twentieth centuries, just as France had been in the previous century, the region's entrepreneurs maintained links with multiple trading partners at all times. Aware of the power of advertising, even more so as the nineteenth century came to a close, they used this medium to enter new markets. They were apparently successful, as indicated by their entry into the Japanese, Australian and Chinese markets a few years before the First World War, which was applauded in the local business press. Most of the time, they were well-informed in the new ways of doing business and open to implementing them. For instance, in 1908 and 1912, respectively, two 'conglomerates', in the parlance of the time, were established through the merging of a large number of local businesses in the sectors of carpet manufacturing and carpet exporting as well as in the fig preparation and exporting trade; both conglomerates did very well.[76]

Through long-standing visibility in the markets they had acquired valuable expertise in gaging the cotton supply markets, as far as that was possible. Aware of the potential for overstocking of markets abroad – and potentially at home too –, they sought to pre-empt them by switching half-way through the year cotton with raisins, for instance, two crops where soil preparation allowed this. The unpredictability of weather in some respect also balanced out profits and losses; a bumper harvest in cotton for instance may have led to losses for advance purchasers but not for cultivators; low harvests increased prices and potentially helped cultivators rather than merchants who may

---

76   Frangakis-Syrett, Elena, "Modernity from below: the Amalgamated Oriental Carpet Manufacturers Ltd. of Izmir, 1907–1922", *Perspectives on Global Development and Technology*, 14/4 (2015), 413–29; and Frangakis-Syrett, Elena, "British economic activities in Izmir in the second half of the nineteenth century and in the early twentieth centuries", *New Perspectives on Turkey*, 5–6 (1991), pp. 205–6, 210–14.

have had to forgo fulfilling orders and/or getting more business. Through a close watch of the weather at specific times of the year (almost an obsession in İzmir) they sought to predict demand for cotton. Judging from lively press coverage of the weather they were equally aware that predictions were often wrong: weather could suddenly improve or the reverse. By the 1900s, direct communication channels effectively monitored cotton price movements. This meant that any changes in the US Stock Exchanges (New York, New Orleans), or any news coming out of Washington D.C., which could affect prices, were registered almost instantaneously in the market of İzmir and soon thereafter in the hinterland. Of course the above are but an indication of the state of the region's agricultural and commercial sectors, given so as to better contextualize the trends in the production and trade of cotton in western Anatolia in the late Ottoman period spanning from the eighteenth to the early twentieth centuries. Furthermore, in the course of the nineteenth century and in many respects from the middle of the eighteenth century, cotton became one of the main vehicles for bringing İzmir and Anatolia into the global capitalist system of supply and demand, a phenomenon that was part of a larger economic process that affected the Ottoman empire more broadly and one which the region actively and, judging from cotton, successfully participated in.

CHAPTER 6

Working, Marketing and Consuming Ottoman Copper – with a Special Emphasis on Female Involvement

Suraiya Faroqhi

In the Ottoman context, studies dealing with metals made into objects, rather than with raw material sent to the mint, are not very common. Even personal ornaments made of precious metals have attracted only a limited amount of attention, although samples possessed by people outside the Ottoman court have survived, albeit in limited numbers. In the case of females we find earrings, necklaces, bracelets and jewelled headdresses, while males owned ornamented weapons as well as horse-gear with silver inlays. Presumably, scholars have held back because it is very difficult to interpret the written documentation relevant to metalwork – if it even exists. The refining of copper and the products of coppersmiths remain in limbo as well, apart from a number of catalogues describing items in public museums and private collections.[1]

This neglect is all the more remarkable as copper stands out by its striking colour and sheen; and several alloys containing this metal feature eye-catching hues, including bright blue and grass green. Among Ottoman authors, the traveller Evliya Çelebi (1611–after 1683) did however take note of the fact that copper derivatives coloured the items with which they came into contact; and he recorded that older men, who had for many years refined or otherwise worked with copper, possessed beards of a blue, green or yellow hue.[2] Presumably,

---

1   Kayaoğlu, İzzet Gündağ, *Tombak* (Istanbul: Dışbank, 1992), the pieces shown were loans by collectors and/or items that the auctioneer Antik A.Ş. had sold at auction; Özkan, Özlem (For Askeri Müze), *Askeri Müze Tombak Eserler Kataloğu* (Istanbul: Askeri Müze ve Kültür Sitesi Komutanlığı, 2001); Belli, Oktay and Gündağ Kayaoğlu, *Trabzon'da Türk Bakırcılık Sanatının Tarihsel Gelişimi/ The Historical Development of Coppersmithing in Trabzon* (Istanbul: Arkeoloji ve Sanat Yayınları, 2002); Atasoy, Sümer, *Geleneksel Bakır Kaplar – Semahat ve Nusret Arsel Koleksiyonu / Traditional Copperware – Semahat & Nusret Arsel Collection* (Istanbul: Sadberk Hanım Müzesi, 2014); Uğurluer, Murat, *Osmanlı Dönemi Gaziantep Bakırcılığı* (Gaziantep: MCG Kültür ve Sanat Yayınları, 2015); Kuşoğlu, Mehmet Zeki, *The Ottoman Touch: Traditional Decorative Arts and Crafts* (New York, London, Frankfurt/Main, Cairo: Blue Dome, 2015).
2   Evliya Çelebi b. Derviş Mehemmed Zıllı, *Evliya Çelebi Seyahatnâmesi, Topkapı Sarayı Bağdat 304 Yazmasının Transkripsyonu –Dizini*, vol. 1, ed. Robert Dankoff, Seyit Ali Kahraman and Yücel Dağlı (Istanbul: Yapı Kredi Yayınları, 2006), p. 309.

seventeenth-century refiners and coppersmiths knew about the dangers of poisoning involved in their work; but Evliya Çelebi did not say anything about this issue.[3]

Since the uses of copper and copper derivatives are very numerous, it is impossible to discuss all the attendant problems in a single chapter: even so, we do attempt to fill some of the more obvious gaps. In the first section of this study, we focus on the competition for access to copper in the Ottoman world of the 1600s, 1700s, and the first half of the nineteenth century, conflicts of interest that involved persons and institutions holding power on the one hand, and 'ordinary, unprivileged' subjects on the other. As noted, the relevant sources, documentary and material, are often difficult to interpret; thus, to facilitate evaluation we include some source-critical considerations. Apart from the written record, we dwell upon some of the surviving copper vessels made for customers outside the Ottoman palace; these pieces date mostly to the years before and after 1800.

A brief survey of the uses of copper in the civilian, unprivileged sector of Ottoman society serves as a prelude to the major concern of this study, namely the different ways in which women might establish connections to the world of copper and copperware. In this context, we discuss the manner in which females might obtain – or fail to obtain – access to copper pots and pans. We then proceed to the practical and spiritual uses to which Ottoman females might put their copperware. As the last point, we discuss the activities of a certain prominent woman of late eighteenth-century Tokat, who as the administrator of a pious foundation (*vakıf, evkaf*), attempted to ensure the payment of revenues generated by local copper smelting. A short conclusion sums up the results.

Competition over Copper

The Ottoman military consumed large quantities of copper, as cannons were often of bronze and copper is the major ingredient in this alloy. In addition, the early Ottoman mints produced copper coins (*mangır*) for small everyday transactions. Especially in the fifteenth and sixteenth centuries, these coins

---

3   For the relevant knowledge of twentieth-century artisans see Batur, Sabahattin, "Une recherche sur le tombak ou dorure au mercure", in *Seventh International Congress of Turkish Art*, ed. Tadeusz Majda (Warsaw: Polish Scientific Publishers, 1990), pp. 43–8.

were much in demand, before – in and after 1585 – the *akçe* lost much of its value in a series of devaluations.[4] From the late sixteenth century onward, the *akçe* thus took over the role previously played by copper coinage, making the latter largely non-functional.

A century later, however, when the Ottoman treasury ran out of bullion during the long war against the Habsburgs (1683–99), the sultans' administration began to re-issue copper coins, this time in large quantities. However, given the frequency of counterfeiting, after a few years, in 1693, the administration gave up on this policy, and only employed copper for monetary purposes again during the Tanzimat period (1839–76).[5] In the nineteenth century, unworked copper garnered official attention for another reason as well, as for a short time the product of Anatolian mines attracted foreign purchasers and thus became a source of much needed revenue.[6] However, in the present study, we do not deal with exports but with the domestic uses of copper.

In the period under study, roughly speaking from the 1580s to 1850, copper pots and pans served for the daily food consumption of the rich, and in addition, as the treasured valuables of less wealthy people. Furthermore, the pious might donate certain vessels to a dervish lodge, where the cooks used them to prepare food for visitors and residents. Occasionally, the records of pious foundations noted that the *şeyh* of a certain lodge had decided to sell some of the copper owned by his foundation. Likely, numerous donations had resulted in a store of copperware far larger than that needed by the dervishes and their guests.

Householders had their copper pots, pans and other cooking equipment covered with a layer of tin to avoid food poisoning. Moreover, perhaps some Ottoman men and women liked to give their better quality dishes a silvery sheen. Larger bowls and ewers were in use for washing; and copper vats an indispensable and costly investment in dyers' workshops, with the relevant artisans often pooling their capital for this purpose.[7] Before the 1800s, the

4   Pamuk, Şevket, *A Monetary History of the Ottoman Empire* (Cambridge: Cambridge University Press, 2000), pp. 136–40.

5   Tekin, Oğuz, "Mangır", in *Türkiye Diyanet Vakfı İslâm Ansiklopedisi*, vol. 27 (2003), p. 568.

6   Bragg, John K., *Ottoman Notables and Participatory Politics: Tanzimat Reform in Tokat, 1839–1876* (London, New York: Routledge, 2014), p. 152.

7   Faroqhi, Suraiya, "Between collective workshops and private homes: places of work in eighteenth-century Bursa", in Faroqhi, Suraiya, *Stories of Ottoman Men and Women: Establishing Status, Establishing Control* (Istanbul: Eren, 2002), pp. 235–43.

registers enumerating the property of deceased persons frequently listed copper vessels as individual items, sometimes noting the presence of lids to cover pots and kettles. By the mid-nineteenth century, however, it became common merely to record the total weight of the copperware at issue.[8]

Given the preliminary and provisional character of our findings, we cannot say for sure that this change in recording practice indicated that throughout Anatolia, copperware had become more accessible and thus probably cheaper. After all, many examples of copperware merely recorded by weight come from inventories compiled in Tokat, a town on the Erzurum-Istanbul route, which even in the 1900s had a reputation for manufacturing these goods. Therefore, copperware may simply have been more common in Tokat than elsewhere.[9] However, I would posit that in parts of Anatolia at least, consumers of the late 1800s and early 1900s purchased more copper than their ancestors of the sixteenth or seventeenth century had done; and this tendency continued until stainless steel and – for the shallow pocket – aluminium pots became available during the later twentieth century.

Thus, we observe a competition over copper between the subject population, wealthy and poor, on the one hand and the Ottoman administrative cum military apparatus on the other. At certain times, the sultans' mints entered the picture too. Practical concerns were surely in the foreground; but to some extent, a 'demonstration effect' was at issue as well. Wealthy subjects liked their copperware gilded (*tombak*), surely a manner of showing off wealth and status. While the administration forbade this practice, the prohibition must have been difficult to enforce, especially in outlying locales.[10] We may wonder when and where provincials decorated their guest rooms with tinned and gilded copperware, and under which circumstances they considered it prudent to bury these valuables in gardens and courtyards.

---

8   See the numerous inventories analyzed in Bragg, *Ottoman Notables*.

9   For a twentieth-century photograph of a Tokat coppersmith, compare Faroqhi, Suraiya, *Towns and Townsmen of Ottoman Anatolia, Trade, Crafts, and Food Production in an Urban Setting 1520–1650* (Cambridge: Cambridge University Press, 1984), p. 182. The picture is the work of Sevgi Aktüre (Middle East Technical University, Ankara); and once again I thank her for sharing it.

10   Devlet Arşivleri, Osmanlı Arşivi, Istanbul [hereafter BOA], Mühimme Defteri 26, no. 621 (983/1574–75), p. 219; Melikian-Chirvani, Assadullah Souren, "Recherches sur l'école du bronze ottoman au XVIe siècle", *Turcica*, 6 (1975), 146–67.

Evaluating Sources: How to Make Texts and Objects
More Accessible

Presumably, one reason why historians have neglected copper, despite its obvious importance, is its softness and fragility, so that items made of this material easily deteriorate. In such cases, the owner(s) might ask a coppersmith to restore the item in question; and some surviving pieces do indeed show traces of repairs, sometimes by inexpert hands. However, the owner might prefer to have the smith melt down the damaged pot or pan altogether. He/she might then buy a new one, made from the recycled material. Or else the customer might prefer to acquire a completely new item, paid for in part by the money that he/she had received for the copper contained in the damaged piece. The Ottoman authorities sometimes forbade coppersmiths to use copper described as 'old', in the vessels that they manufactured. Probably, the tin coats on kitchenware meant that recycled copper contained a sizeable quantity of tin; and many coppersmiths may not have told their customers what they were getting.[11] However, Evliya Çelebi has recorded that in the mid-1600s, there were workshops operating in several towers of the Istanbul city walls, where specialist refiners prepared used copper for recycling.[12] As the traveller does not say that this activity was illegal, presumably standards in his time were more flexible than they were to be in later years.

As 'recycling' was a simple process, it is rare to find copperware from the 1500s or 1600s, apart from some high-quality items used in the sultans' palace; and this situation must have contributed to the very moderate interest that twentieth- and twenty-first century scholars have shown in copperware. In this context, it is noteworthy that when publishing the collection of copper items brought together by Nusret and Semahat Arsel, the art historian Sümer Atasoy has defined this assemblage as "closed"; put differently, the collectors are not

---

11   BOA, Maliye Ahkam Defteri [hereafter MAD] 9983 (1171/1757–58), p. 211. This text is the confirmation of an order issued in the name of Mahmud I and dated to 1165 (1751–52). In turn, the command of 1751–52 reiterates an order from the year 1114 (1702–03). The first prohibition, if indeed it is the first, thus goes back to the year in which Ahmed III (r. 1703–30) came to the throne after a major rebellion, the so-called Edirne Vak'ası. As the commands of every sultan lost all validity with the ruler's death or deposition, the beneficiaries of such orders had to ensure that the successor, once enthroned, confirmed the previous rulings. In the 1700s, officials used to compile special and often voluminous registers of older commands confirmed by the reigning sultan.

12   Evliya Çelebi, *Seyahatnâmesi*, I, p. 308.

in the market for new pieces. Probably, given the constant recycling of copper-ware, the Arsel family does not expect that in the foreseeable future, interest-ing pieces will appear on the antiques market.[13]

Ethnographic and archaeological data are indispensable for making sense of the information conveyed by Ottoman archival records. Studies dealing with towns in which coppersmiths are active, or in which they still operated until a few decades ago, often contain descriptions of decorative motifs and types of vessels produced, and discuss the technologies favoured by local mas-ters as well.[14]

For historians studying the use of Ottoman copper, Hungary is something like a promised land. For many years, Hungarian archaeologists have included Ottoman finds in their studies rather than discarding these items as 'recent', as was customary in quite a few formerly Ottoman regions until a few years ago. Hungarian scholars have thus unearthed a sizeable number of Ottoman copper vessels, which now often appear in exhibition catalogues.[15] Apart from excavations for purely scholarly purposes, archaeologists in Hungary have made use of digs preparatory to a variety of public works; and particularly the excavations intended to deepen the riverbed of the Danube have yielded quite a few pieces of Ottoman copperware. It is intriguing to observe that quite a few items found in Hungary feature shapes and decorations typical of the eighteenth century, although after 1699 this area had passed into the hands of the Habsburgs and was no longer part of the Ottoman empire. Apparently, Ottoman copperware continued to interest wealthy Hungarians for some time after the peace of Karlowitz.

In addition, Hungarian museums have acquired quite a few pieces once assembled by private collectors in the nineteenth and early twentieth

---

13   Atasoy, *Geleneksel Bakır Kaplar*. Certain pieces from the Sadberk Hanım Museum appear in a publication by Bodur, Fulya, *Türk Maden Sanatı: The Art of Turkish Metalworking* (Istanbul: Türk Kültürüne Hizmet Vakfı, 1987); by contrast the book by Erginsoy, Ülker, *İslam Maden Sanatının Gelişmesi* (Istanbul: Kültür Bakanlığı Yayınları, 1978) deals only with the pre-Ottoman period.

14   Belli and Kayaoğlu, *Trabzon'da Türk Bakırcılık*; Uğurluer, *Gaziantep Bakırcılığı*. For the Balkans compare Koneska, Elizabeta, "Coppersmiths and tinsmiths from Kruševo (Macedonia) settling and working in other towns on the Balkan Peninsula", in *Ottoman Metalwork in the Balkans and in Hungary*, ed. Ibolya Gerelyes and Maximilian Hartmuth (Budapest: Hungarian National Museum, 2015), pp. 133–44.

15   Gerelyes, Ibolya and András Csonka, *Oszmán-Török rézmüvesség (XVI–XIX. Század)/ Ottoman-Turkish Coppersmith's Art 16th to 19th Centuries* (Budapest: Magyar Nemzeti Múzeum, 1997); Gerelyes and Hartmuth, *Ottoman Metalwork*.

centuries; these items are quite often imports from Anatolia and the Balkans.[16] However, in Hungary only noblemen and a few wealthy merchants had enough money to acquire Ottoman copperware, which was definitely a luxury. By contrast, as we have seen, in certain Anatolian towns of the nineteenth century, even large quantities of copperware were quite affordable. When reflecting on this diversity, we do, however, need to keep in mind that the men and women whose property made it into the estate inventories compiled by the scribes of Anatolian shari'a courts were usually part of local elites, for only families with a significant amount of property would have spent money, often in sizeable amounts, on registering the goods and chattels of their deceased relatives.

It is not always easy to assign certain styles of copperware to a particular town or region. In Anatolia and in the Balkans, many communities have migrated in the course of the sixteenth, seventeenth and eighteenth centuries; and if these groups contained coppersmiths, the relevant artisans travelled along with their fellow townspeople or villagers. In addition, many coppersmiths migrated as groups of colleagues or as families, often over long distances, in their never-ending quest for customers. These kinds of migrations have mainly interested scholars dealing with the Balkans. Thus for example the Vlachs (in Turkish Eflak) migrant herders, whom we may regard as the Christian counterpart to the Muslim *yürük*s, were especially famous for their skills as coppersmiths. In Bosnia, the standard term for 'coppersmith' even acquired a secondary meaning, namely "a member of the Vlach community".[17] Vlach coppersmiths quite often combined their artisanal work with trade, dealing mostly in unworked copper. Some of these merchants prospered; and in Belgrade, there survives a large building, put up in the early twentieth century by a successful coppersmith.[18] Other artisans practicing this trade, not all of them Vlachs, worked in northern Greece. As for Macedonia, in this region, copper workshops flourished well into the 1950s.

Remarkably, in the middle of the twentieth century, just before many Muslims inhabiting the (former) republic of Yugoslavia migrated to Turkey, the manufacture of copperware flourished for what was seemingly the last time. Perhaps the future migrants wanted to take a piece of the old country along with them. Others may have thought that good quality copperware would be saleable in Turkey. However, as consumers' habits have changed over the last few decades, today the trade in copperware is of marginal significance.

---

16   Gerelyes, Ibolya, "Ottoman metalwork at the Hungarian National Museum: issues regarding origins and dating", in Gerelyes and Hartmuth, *Ottoman Metalwork*, pp. 79–96.
17   Koneska, "Coppersmiths and tinsmiths", p. 136.
18   Koneska, "Coppersmiths and tinsmiths", p. 134.

Traditional coppersmiths retain only a small niche market in Turkey; and in Cairo as well, coppersmiths working for the tourist market apparently do not feel that their craft has a bright future.[19]

Dating copper vessels, which rarely feature inscriptions of any kind, is difficult as well. When dating is at issue, even scholars very familiar with the material have sometimes changed their minds. Thus the Hungarian scholar Alexander Fodor (1941–2014), in a posthumously published article, declared that he now thought that a copper bowl, which he had once dated to the nineteenth century, is more likely a work of the 1500s or 1600s.[20]

Apart from surviving objects and information derived from interviews with twentieth-century artisans, Ottoman archival sources are important to the present project, as they reflect the procedures by which artisans and merchants secured unworked copper.[21] In addition, if lucky, the researcher may locate some information on manufacturing techniques and the sale of the final product. In the case of Istanbul, the lists of administratively determined prices (*narh*) are especially helpful, as they list the different vessels produced by coppersmiths, sometimes even detailing ornaments whose presence or absence might influence the price permitted to the seller.[22] As purchasing power in Istanbul was far superior to the financial means of customers in provincial towns, the manufacturers of up-market goods produced outside of the capital frequently made special efforts to acquaint Istanbul customers with the goods that they could offer.

However, as people of modest incomes might buy cooking pots made of copper as well, the detailed Istanbul price register of 1640 contains a separate record of "copper pots for poor people"; for this purpose, the manufacturers employed waste copper.[23] We find further information on copperware in the *Vilayet Ahkam Defterleri* (Registers of sultans' commands sent to the provinces), which contain a subdivision dealing with the four administrative units comprising Ottoman Greater Istanbul, namely the walled city, Galata, Üsküdar, and Eyüp. These registers contain numerous regulations concerning craft practice,

---

19   Kickinger, Claudia, "Relations of production and social conditions among coppersmiths in contemporary Cairo", in *Crafts and Craftsmen of the Middle East, Fashioning the Individual in the Muslim Mediterranean*, ed. Suraiya Faroqhi and Randi Deguilhem (London: I.B. Tauris, 2005), pp. 285–307.

20   Fodor, Alexander, "An Ottoman magic bowl from Istanbul", in Gerelyes and Hartmuth, *Ottoman Metalwork*, pp. 59–78, see pp. 73 and 75.

21   For an introduction, compare Faroqhi, *Towns and Townsmen*, pp. 171–90.

22   Kütükoğlu, Mübahat, *Osmanlılarda Narh Müessesesi ve 1640 Tarihli Narh Defteri* (Istanbul: Enderun Kitabevi, 1983), pp. 195–6.

23   Kütükoğlu, *Osmanlılarda Narh Müessesesi*, p. 195.

with some valuable texts referring to coppersmiths.[24] The post-mortem inventories, previously introduced, also contain references to copperware owned by different sections of the population. Scribes serving the four *kadıs* of Istanbul, Galata, Üsküdar, and Eyüp compiled the inventories of ordinary subjects, while a special office holder, known as the *askeri kassam*, handled the confiscation of the inheritances left by the sultan's servitors, the *askeri*. We can find copperware in many of these registers.

Where narrative sources are at issue, as noted, we need to refer to the work of Evliya Çelebi, while constantly deepening our awareness of the many problems of source criticism posed by this ever-curious and creative traveller. Especially his account of Istanbul artisans is indispensable to the social historian, and in the present context, his work is of particular value as it includes observations on coppersmiths not available elsewhere.[25] The abiding problem is that historians have not found any archival documents recording the artisans' parade of 1638 that Evliya Çelebi has elaborately described. Even so, Ottoman and foreign observers have recorded many similar parades taking place throughout the seventeenth and eighteenth centuries, and while Evliya Çelebi's figures remain subject to caution, there is no reason to doubt that parades of the type that he has recorded enlivened the difficult existences of Istanbul's inhabitants.

Producing Copperware, in the Balkans – and Especially in Anatolia

In the Ottoman Balkans, copper mines were quite numerous, particularly between Alacahisar/ Kruševac (Serbia) and Novo Brdo (Kosovo). Other mines were in today's Bosnia, near Kreševo and Srebrenića. In today's northern Greece, the mines of Sidrekapsi (Siderokausia in Greek) were important mainly for silver and (some) gold. Even so, for the most part, these mines produced copper as well as silver; and Halil İnalcık has suggested that from the 1300s to the early 1500s, these resources were a major reason for the sultans to prioritize the conquest of the Balkans.[26]

In Anatolia, the northern section of the province of Kastamonu had been producing copper already before the Ottoman conquest. The mines of Küre-i

24   Kal'a, Ahmet, *et al.* (eds.), *İstanbul Külliyatı: İstanbul Ahkâm Defterleri*, 10 vols. (Istanbul: İstanbul Araştırmaları Merkezi, 1997–98), vol. I, Kal'a, Ahmet, *et al.* (eds.), *İstanbul Külliyatı: İstanbul Ahkâm Defterleri İstanbul Esnaf Tarihi I* (Istanbul: İstanbul Araştırmaları Merkezi, 1997).

25   Evliya Çelebi, *Seyahatnâmesi*, I, compare the detailed index.

26   Hartmuth, Maximilian, "Mineral exploitation and artistic production in the Balkans after 1250", in Gerelyes and Hartmuth, *Ottoman Metalwork*, pp. 97–110, see pp. 100 and 102.

Mamure had been a significant resource in the sixteenth century, but given the technological limitations of the period, by the late 1600s, they were no longer very productive.[27] An Ottoman observer, whose report has survived as part of Katip Çelebi's *Cihannüma*, reported that the mines were prone to flooding. Moreover, the slaves working in this location were in very poor health and gave off a bad smell, probably due to gas poisoning. By the late eighteenth and early nineteenth centuries, the Küre mine was no longer in use; local smelters only used ore previously mined, probably of low metal content, rejected by previous smelters and thus remaining on the ground. Only in the twentieth and especially the twenty-first century, computer technology has permitted the renewed exploitation of the Küre mines. Copper now emerges from ore mined in locations nearly 1000 metres underground, supposedly, machinery under remote control rather than human beings now do much of the work.[28]

While in the eighteenth century, Küre was no longer a major source of copper, the region as a whole still produced a certain amount of this metal. After all, a command of the sultan, dated to the beginning 1700s, recorded that Istanbul coppersmiths and traders were in the habit of dealing in copper from "Kastamonu ve Tokad ve Belğrad ve Bosna".[29] Therefore, the bureaucrats who wrote this order must have assumed that in contemporary Istanbul, not all the copper in the market came from the Balkans, and metal from northern Anatolia remained available.

However, shortages were probably common; and individual artisans found ways of ensuring supplies and acquiring more copper than their guild was willing to assign them. They thus purchased copper unbeknownst to their guild elders, in places where official control was difficult or impossible. Commands by the sultan that prohibited this practice sometimes included the order to notify not only the elders of the coppersmiths' guild, but also the head of the kettle makers (*kazgancıbaşı*), of all copper-related transactions. Officially, it was the role of these guild headmen, who were often palace officials as well, to facilitate control by the authorities; but it is difficult to say to what extent ordinary artisans obeyed the sultan's injunctions.

While the productivity of the Kastamonu mines regressed, the mines of Ergani and Keban, both located near Diyarbakır (Diyarbekir), now gained in importance. A register from the late 1700s, available in print, throws some light

---

27   Faroqhi, *Towns and Townsmen*, pp. 172–88.
28   http://www.madencilik-turkiye.com/haberler/haberdetay/1459 (accessed on 20 June 2017).
29   BOA, MAD No. 9983 (1171/1757–58), p. 211.

on their functioning.[30] At this time, potential revenue farmers probably did not have much information about the problems involved in running the mine. Therefore, they did not submit any bids; and as customary in such cases, the Ottoman financial bureaucracy had appointed a salaried official (*emin*) who kept detailed records of expenses and revenues. A growing demand for copper in Istanbul was the reason for this revival of the mine and the concomitant appointment of the *emin*. For in those same years, Sultan Selim III (r. 1789–1807) was intent on reforming the Ottoman army, and this enterprise involved the local manufacture of different, European-style weapons, for which gun-smiths required copper.[31]

In Tokat, as noted a town manufacturing copperware for the civilian market, the increase in army requisitions led to a serious conflict. On one side, there were the demands of the *emin* in charge of supplying the central administration and on the other, opposing his demands as best they could, we find the merchants selling copper to the local coppersmiths as well as the guild heads representing these artisans.[32]

The situation in Tokat had become even more difficult because the Ottoman administration had first instituted life-long tax farms (*malikane*), which included the revenues payable by the workshops of copper smelters, and later on had entrusted certain pious foundations active in the locality with revenues derived from copper smelting. As a result, a large group of real or potential actors with an interest in the business was active in Tokat, and it was often impossible to decide which of the many – and often contradictory – demands of these people were legally justified and/or realistic. In the years before and after 1800, the representatives of the central state usually gained the upper hand, but only after loud and often violent protests on the part of foundation administrators, copper merchants and coppersmiths. In the mid-nineteenth century, the government gradually abolished *malikane*s; and in addition, many pious foundations lost part of their revenues or even disappeared because of confiscation. Moreover, for a short time, as we have seen, demand from indus-trializing Europe resulted in an export boom in copper, so that the traders and artisans of Tokat must have had even more trouble in securing this essential

---

30   Yüksel, Hasan, *Osmanlı Döneminde Keban Ergani-Madenleri: 1776–1794 Tarihli Maden Emini Defteri* (Sivas: n.p., 1997).

31   Shaw, Stanford J., *Between Old and New: The Ottoman Empire under Selim III 1789–1807* (Cambridge, MA: Harvard University Press, 1971), pp. 140–1; Duman, Yüksel, "Textiles and Copper in Ottoman Tokat 1750–1840", Ph.D. Dissertation, Binghamton University, 1998, pp. 189–210.

32   Duman, "Textiles and Copper", pp. 174–251.

metal. However, the boom was short-lived, as in the world market, cheaper copper from the Americas soon marginalized the Anatolian product.[33]

Despite these difficulties, partly due to oscillations in world trade, the coppersmiths of Tokat continued to manufacture pots, plates and pans for the local and regional market. Though complaining about the scarcity of raw material, these men even managed to turn out the large kettles needed by local textile dyers. Thus, the manufacture of copperware in Tokat retained considerable vitality; and local consumption must have been significant, as the *kadı* registers of this town show that in terms of monetary value, vessels and other implements manufactured from copper made up an appreciable share of the possessions left by the town's deceased. By the mid-1800s, copperware amounted to at least 5.8 per cent of the estates left by Tokat Muslims. In the case of non-Muslims, the percentage amounted to 4.7 and was thus slightly lower.[34] We can only speculate about the reasons for this difference. Perhaps non-Muslims were less of a presence among coppersmiths, so that in this group, we find fewer inventories of shops as opposed to household goods: most shops probably contained more copperware than did ordinary kitchens. In addition, we may hypothesize that Tokat's non-Muslims possessed more goods and chattels than their Muslim fellow townspeople, and therefore their copperware made up a smaller percentage of their total estates. However, other, unknown reasons may be involved too, and/or our sample is simply not large enough to exclude the factor of mere chance.

Concerning seventeenth-century Istanbul, Said Öztürk has authored an extremely detailed study of post mortem estates, and his work allows us to attempt a comparison with the data that John K. Bragg has made available for Tokat. However, there are certain caveats: bureaucratic practice in the 1600s was certainly different from that current in the Tanzimat period; and in terms of local practices, there may have been subtle differences between the two places as well. Therefore, we need to approach the percentages calculated for both Istanbul and Tokat with a good deal of caution. Even so, these figures are worth thinking about: for in the Istanbul estate inventories, the monetary value of kitchen utensils, which must have consisted largely of copper, amounted only to 1.6 per cent. Professional cooks typically left estates in which copperware was more prevalent and made up 3.2 per cent of the total inheritances.[35]

33   Bragg, *Ottoman Notables*, pp. 140–77.

34   Bragg, *Ottoman Notables*, p. 151.

35   Öztürk, Said, *Askeri Kassama Ait Onyedinci Asır İstanbul Tereke Defterleri (Sosyo-Ekonomik Tahlil)* (Istanbul: OSAV, 1995), p. 186.

Even in this group, copperware was thus of less significance than it was to be in nineteenth-century Tokat.

Intriguingly, in the estates of Istanbul women of the seventeenth century, copperware was far more important than in the estates of the total population, put differently, of males and females combined. In the post-mortem inventories of women's goods, the percentage amounted to 3.5 and thus was even somewhat higher than that calculated for professional cooks. Unfortunately, in this respect a comparison with the situation in Tokat is impossible, as Bragg has not included any information about copperware owned by people running cook-shops.

Women and Copper: a Question of Privilege

While historians have long accepted that in many cultures textiles are part of the female domain, metals are normally associated with men. After all, female spinners, weavers and embroiderers occur in the Ottoman world as elsewhere; but women working in mines and at smelting ovens are virtually unknown. Furthermore, metals are the raw material of arms; and in the Ottoman world, women did not hunt or fight, although for instance in Mughal and post-Mughal India, princesses who did both these things are on record in texts and especially images.[36] Thus, at first glance, it seems outlandish to associate Ottoman women and copper.

However, given the scarcity of direct testimonies on Ottoman women, who after all made up one half of the sultans' subjects, it is surely useful to try an oblique approach, by reconstructing the life-worlds of females including the material goods, to which they did, or did not, have access. These goods include foods, textiles, jewellery, real estate, and – of course – cash. Historians have at least partially investigated the textile sector; and the houses owned by women in medium-sized Anatolian towns, including Ankara and Kayseri have attracted some attention too.[37] More recently, several studies of female jewellery have

---

36 For a portrait of Nur Jahan (1577–1645) with a gun compare Beach, Milo Cleveland, *The New Cambridge History of India: Mughal and Rajput Painting* (Cambridge: Cambridge University Press, 1992), no. 69, p. 96. Her spouse the emperor Jahangir wrote appreciatively about her marksmanship.

37 Faroqhi, Suraiya, *Men of Modest Substance, House Owners and House Property in Seventeenth-Century Ankara and Kayseri* (Cambridge: Cambridge University Press, 1987), pp. 150–201; Faroqhi, Suraiya, "Women, wealth and textiles in 1730s Bursa", in *Living the Good Life: Consumption in the Qing and Ottoman Empires of the Eighteenth Century*, ed. Elif Akçetin and Suraiya Faroqhi (Leiden: Brill, 2017), pp. 213–35.

become available.[38] However, given the great diversity not only between individual regions but more specifically, between Istanbul and Anatolian towns, it is clear that much work remains undone. In particular, we have limited information on the extent to which the high status of a father or husband had an impact on the material goods available to a young girl or married woman.

Thus, the present study of women's access to copper goods is merely a small contribution to the much more encompassing topic of women and their insertion into the Ottoman material world: a piece of glass or stone that should find a place in the mosaic that we are constructing. After all, a good deal of female sociability revolved around the public bath, where many women would have used bowls made of copper or copper alloys. Furthermore, in households without slaves – and that was the vast majority of the population – cleaning and cooking was mostly the work of women. It is an intriguing question, how often these female cleaners and cooks owned their 'means of production'. Or else, they may have worked with items belonging to their husbands.

There is good reason for assuming, for instance, that with respect to female ownership of copperware, certain provincial cities differed substantially from seventeenth-century Istanbul. For in a broadly based study of kitchenware used in late seventeenth- and early eighteenth-century Damascus, Colette Establet and Jean-Paul Pasqual have shown that while most kitchenware was indeed in the hands of women, copperware was an exception. As ewers, dishes, pots and pans made of this material were rather expensive the kitchenware owned by men was twice as valuable as that owned by women. However, while female owners of copperware were a minority, this group was still of some importance: among the 294 persons leaving copperware to their heirs, there were 83 women, who thus made up 28 per cent of the total.[39]

In some towns and at certain times, women may have viewed the ownership of copperware as a status symbol: this type of property could apparently stand for the responsibilities and rights of a woman enjoying a certain status, as the mistress of her household. In a recent study, Beshara B. Doumani has focused on a pious foundation instituted by a woman named Maryam 'Anklis, who

---

38   İrepoğlu, Gül, *Imperial Ottoman Jewellery: Reading History through Jewellery*, trans. Feyza Howell (Istanbul: BKG, 2012); Establet, Colette, "Les bijoux dans l'empire ottoman au XVIIIᵉ siècle: l'exemple damascène", *Turcica*, 43 (2011), 207–29; Türkoğlu, Sabahattin, *Tarih Boyunca Anadolu'da Takı ve Kuyumculuk Kültürü/ Jewel and Jewellery Culture in Anatolia throughout History* (Istanbul: İstanbul Kuyumcuları Odası and Lidya, 2014).

39   Establet, Colette and Jean-Paul Pasqual, "Cups, plates and kitchenware in late seventeenth and early eighteenth-century Damascus", in *The Illuminated Table, the Prosperous House, Food and Shelter in Ottoman Material Culture*, ed. Suraiya Faroqhi and Christoph Neumann (Istanbul: Orient-Institut, 2003), pp. 185–97.

lived in Tripoli (Lebanon) and disposed of her possessions in 1840.[40] Maryam particularly insisted on gifting several cooking pots made of copper – together with their lids – to her two daughters, and Doumani has interpreted this emphasis as a symbolic gesture. If we remember that Damascus and Tripoli belong to the same cultural region, it makes sense to assume that Maryam wanted to establish her two daughters as women of property and prestigious mistresses of their households, who differently from many Damascene women could run their everyday lives without recourse to the copperware owned by their husbands.

Acquiring Copperware: Practical and Spiritual Purposes

Less prestigious women might acquire copperware too. Sometimes the artisans, often migratory, who tinned copper vessels, must have offered a few pieces for sale. After all, the profits from the tinning of copperware were small and difficult to foresee; and in addition, for many women it was difficult to leave the house, so that salespeople must have visited them at home if possible. Such migratory tradespeople often did not belong to the relevant guilds and therefore needed to conduct their business as unobtrusively as possible.[41] Especially poor women will thus have bought some low-quality copperware 'on the sly'.

Women bought copperware from established artisans as well, as apparent from a very interesting text, which Ahmet Kal'a and his collaborators have located and published.[42] In 1759, negotiations about the installation of a new shop for copperware were in progress; the location envisaged was in Tophane, near the Istanbul cannon foundry that had given its name to the venue. Nowadays, Tophane is in the very centre of the city. In the 1700s, however, the location was on the margins of Galata, in part because the foundry was a major fire hazard.

Previously, the inhabitants of Tophane and the shopkeepers already established in this locality had agreed that a shop selling copperware was lacking but highly desirable. However, two persons objected and finally the local *kadı* had to decide the case. The latter called in a large number of witnesses, all of them Muslims, who confirmed that there was no shop selling copperware in

40   Doumani, Beshara B., *Family Life in the Ottoman Mediterranean: A Social History* (Cambridge: Cambridge University Press, 2017), p. 7.
41   BOA, MAD 9983, p. 211.
42   Kal'a, *et al., İstanbul Ahkâm Defterleri*, I, pp. 245–6.

Tophane. According to the witnesses, in winter, when storms were frequent, this situation made life difficult for the elderly, poor people living alone, and women. Both the judge and the central administration accepted that this was a valid argument; and in due course, a coppersmith probably set up shop in this place.

The formulaic statement that vulnerable people needed shops near their homes is quite familiar from petitions asking for sales-points offering bread or vegetables. However, while especially the poor probably bought foodstuffs on a daily basis, presumably they did not need to visit a copper shop quite that often.[43] Whatever the situation, for our purposes it is worth retaining that the judge, the witnesses and the officials serving the central administration all agreed that the routines of modest women included visits to a coppersmith's shop.

Can inscriptions tell us which kinds of copperware were most likely to be in the possession of women? Unfortunately, few copper vessels have inscriptions mentioning the names of the owners, be they males or females. Moreover, the value of many existing inscriptions is dubious. In 1970s Ankara for example, salespeople anxious to make their pots and pans more saleable were likely to add inscriptions, a fact well known to customers looking for copperware produced in the late Ottoman empire, at that time defunct for only half a century. However, we have at least two nineteenth-century inscriptions naming female owners, which connoisseurs have accepted as genuine; and non-specialists can only accept their judgement.[44]

One of these inscriptions decorates an elegant and costly set of ewer and flat bowl (leğen-ibrik), made of gilt copper (tombak). This item served personal hygiene, as the flat saucer-like bowl obviously served to hold soap (sabunluk); the manufacturer and/or the owner seemingly wanted to stress that the two pieces formed a set. The inscription features the date of 1222/1807, the name of the owner being Kamer Hatun; unfortunately, we do not know the place of manufacture or purchase. Dated to 1279/1862, the second item is much simpler and coated all over with tin. The small bowl once belonged to a woman named Münyab Hanım, who probably used it in her bath. In this instance too, we do not know the place of manufacture or purchase.[45] Leğen-ibrik sets and bowls for use in the bath could be the property of either men or women.

In this context, the so-called 'magic bowls' are of special interest because they sometimes feature inscriptions referring to specifically feminine

---

43   Kal'a, et al., İstanbul Ahkâm Defterleri, 1, p. 158.
44   Bodur, Türk Maden Sanatı, pp. 131 and 125.
45   Atasoy, Geleneksel Bakır Kaplar.

problems.[46] Often made of copper or copper alloys, these items were popular throughout the Islamic world, supposedly because they provided healing while helping people perform good deeds and avoid misfortunes. Many magic bowls shown in contemporary museums or on offer in the antique trade – if genuine – are Iranian and date to the Safavid period (1501–1722); others come from India. Early variants feature stylised depictions of people and animals. In later periods, patrons preferred prayers, pious sayings and *surahs* from the Qur'an; if the manufacturers had skilled calligraphers at their disposal, these craftspeople had occasion to show their skills. Men and women seem to have interpreted certain magical signs shown on these bowls as symbols of the universe, while they regarded the hexagram, popular as a decorative motif all over the Ottoman world, as the seal of Solomon.

Among bowls of this kind, Ottoman items were a minority, but they did exist. When hoping to benefit from them, people drank water from their 'magic bowls', and if they needed help in giving birth, it was customary to colour the water with saffron. Bowls of this kind had been in use in Mesopotamia in early Islamic times; and the list of illnesses and misfortunes against which water drunk from these bowls supposedly was helpful, did not greatly change either. After all, most of these dangers were universal and birthing problems a major risk well into the twentieth century.

Shortly before his death, the Hungarian art historian Alexander Fodor had re-examined a copper bowl of supposedly magical properties, covered by a thin layer of tin. As noted, in the early 2010s he considered this piece as dating to the sixteenth or seventeenth century. From our point of view, the date is perhaps of secondary significance, but it is important that Fodor assigned this piece to Istanbul; among other considerations, he arrived at this conclusion because the inscriptions insistently emphasized Sunni right belief.[47] In addition, Fodor observed that the manufacturer or patron envisaged a female public: for the inscription promised help against troubles among married people and furthermore, mediation if the arrangement of a marriage turned out to be difficult. However, Fodor concluded that help with difficult births was *the* major reason for manufacturing the item at issue. Without any reference to the

---

46   Savage-Smith, Emilie, "Magic-medicinal bowls", in *Science, Tools & Magic, Part One, Body and Spirit, Mapping the Universe*, ed. Francis Maddison and Emilie Savage-Smith (London: The Nour Foundation with Azimuth Editions and Oxford University Press, 1997), pp. 72–100. A magic bowl made out of an alloy containing copper, dated to 565/1169, is in Leoni, Francesca (ed.), *Power and Protection: Islamic Art and the Supernatural* (Oxford: Ashmolean Museum, 2016), p. 60.

47   Fodor, "An Ottoman magic bowl".

owner, we cannot be completely sure that the bowl had belonged to a woman. However, on balance, this is the most likely solution.

Female Agency in a Different Key: a *Vakıf* Administrator Demanding Copper-Based Revenues

Sources permitting some insight into the lives of Ottoman women before the 1850s being scanty, it makes sense to collect and synthesize even small nuggets of information that allow us a glimpse of the *condition féminine*, Ottoman style. In this sense, the petition of the female administrator of a pious foundation in the copper-manufacturing town of Tokat is particularly intriguing. As we have seen, several pious foundations in this town possessed large shares in the revenues generated by the local smelting ovens, until the central government took over smelting in the 1790s. Presumably, the founders had intended to supply mosques, dervish lodges and other pious works with reliable sources of income.

Unfortunately, we have little background information about Tokat *evkaf*; even so, it is clear that the *vakıf* set up by Ebubekir Ağazade el-hac Mustafa, also known as Ebubekirzade, was of some importance. El-hac Mustafa probably had connections to the prominent family of Tokat notables known as the Katıroğulları, whose members frequently named their sons Ebubekir.[48] In the 1790s, when the Ottoman government was taking over copper smelting from local pious foundations, the administrator of the *vakıf* was a female, Şerife Fatma by name, who claimed descent from the Prophet Muhammad, and apparently, managed to retain control of the foundation for several decades. In terms of Islamic law, there was no reason to prevent a woman from exercising this office, although among the numerous administrators of Ottoman pious foundations, women were probably a small minority.[49] Surviving documents show that many people establishing pious foundations preferred men as administrators, although they might concede that if no male descendants existed, females might take over.[50] We thus encounter a paradoxical situation:

---

48   Duman, "Textiles and Copper", p. 204.

49   Yediyıldız, Bahaeddin, *Institution du Vaqf au XVIIIᵉ siècle en Turquie: étude socio-historique* (Ankara: Ministère de la Culture, 1990), while including many pious foundations established by females, does not discuss the role of women in *vakıf* administration.

50   On female administrators compare Baer, Gabriel, "Women and waqf: an analysis of the Istanbul *tahrîr* of 1546", in *Studies in Islamic Society: Contributions in Memory of Gabriel*

in the dervish milieu, succession to the office and charisma of a *şeyh* was strictly patrilineal; but at the same time and in the same institution, a woman might hold the purse strings.

Şerife Fatma had complained that the foundation of Ebubekirzade, for which she was responsible, in 1795 had not received the revenue from copper smelting to which the institution possessed a legal title. The sum of money at issue was modest, amounting to 1,500 *guruş*.[51] Şerife Fatma had addressed her complaint to Katıroğlu Lütfullah, presumably a scion of the family to which the original founder had once belonged. At this time, Katıroğlu Lütfullah was the acting governor of Tokat province; but his position was rather insecure, because as we have seen, the government in Istanbul demanded the delivery of large quantities of copper, and local merchants and coppersmiths were protesting against these impositions. Probably, the governor needed to mediate between the two parties; but he had almost no cash at his disposal.

Katıroğlu Lütfullah thus asked Şerife Fatma to discuss the matter with a certain Yusuf Ziya Paşa; since 1785, put differently for the past ten years, this man had been the sultan's officer in charge of mining affairs (*maden-i hümayun emini*). Furthermore, the paşa owned shares in the smelting and refining works located in the city of Diyarbakır (Diyarbekir).[52] In fact, Şerife Fatma managed to procure an order enjoining Yusuf Ziya Paşa to pay the money claimed by the foundation, at least for the year of 1796. We do not know what had happened to the 1,500 *guruş* payable in 1795.

Interestingly, the reason for the sultan's generosity was that Şerife Fatma was "a helpless woman".[53] Perhaps she had used her position as a 'poor female' as a bargaining chip when dealing with the sultan and the *maden-i hümayun emini*. Or else the sultan and his governor had tried to use the case as a legitimizing ploy. In the tense situation arising from government demands for more copper, it may have been good for 'public relations' to aid a woman who may have been 'helpless' but enjoyed good political connections on the local level. We do not know how the story ended; but as the government's demands were unrelenting, the long-term chances of a local pious foundation were probably not good.

Baer, ed. Gabriel A. Warburg and Gad G. Gilbar (Haifa: Haifa University Press, 1984), pp. 9–28.

51 Duman, "Textiles and Copper", p. 206.
52 Duman, "Textiles and Copper", pp. 190 and 196.
53 Duman, "Textiles and Copper," p. 215.

In Conclusion

It is not easy to draw hard and fast conclusions from these scattered pieces of evidence, and we urgently need to strengthen our source base. Where the trade in copper and the consumption of copperware are at issue, we have to cover the eighteenth century much more energetically than we have done to date. After all, now that some historians accept that before the Russo-Ottoman war of 1768–74, there was an albeit modest expansion of production and trade in many Ottoman provinces, it makes sense to look at the consumer goods available to the better off inhabitants of places like Bursa, Damascus or Cairo.[54] Likely, the constant wars of the late 1700s and early 1800s completely destroyed this limited but (probably) growing consumption, just as the wars that ended the Ottoman Empire and established the Republic of Turkey annihilated the expanded consumption in certain parts of the late Ottoman orbit, which had made the Hamidian period into a modest version of the *belle époque*.[55] Şükrü Hanioğlu has concluded that there was little change in Istanbul consumption patterns during the second half of the eighteenth century.[56] Even so, in the opinion of the present author, this judgement should not deter us from study-ing eighteenth-century consumption in greater detail; and the purchase and use of copperware is only one among several possibilities.

As for the role of women in consumption, the good news is that we now have a great many studies on Ottoman post mortem inventories. However, they mostly concern the possessions of males, as the latter are richer in content and allow more far-reaching conclusions. Post mortem inventories of wealthy women exist as well, and historians have studied some of them.[57] However, wealthy women sometimes did not own much kitchenware, perhaps because they did not do their own cooking. Thus, when in a pioneering work, Ömer Lütfi Barkan published and examined about 90 post mortem inventories of the 1500s and 1600s, he chose to study only three inventories belonging to females, although his statistical summaries show that women's inventories made up

---

54   Genç, Mehmet, "Osmanlı Ekonomisi ve Savaş", *Yapıt*, 49/4 (1984), 52–61; 50/5 (1984), 86–93; French version: "L'économie ottomane et la guerre au XVIIIème siècle", *Turcica*, 27 (1995), 177–96.

55   Boyar, Ebru and Kate Fleet, *A Social History of Ottoman Istanbul* (Cambridge: Cambridge University Press, 2010), pp. 271–327.

56   Hanioğlu, Şükrü, *A Brief History of the Late Ottoman Empire* (Princeton: Princeton University Press, 2010), pp. 27–33.

57   For a modest beginning see Faroqhi, Suraiya, "Two women of substance", in *Festgabe an Josef Matuz, Osmanistik, Turkologie, Diplomatik*, ed. Christa Fragner and Klaus Schwarz (Berlin: Klaus Schwarz Verlag, 1992), pp. 37–56 and Faroqhi, Suraiya, "Women, wealth and textiles in 1730s Bursa", in Akçetin and Faroqhi, *Living the Good Life*, pp. 213–35.

about one third of the total number on record.[58] When selecting inventories for full publication, Barkan quite obviously preferred the wealthy ones; and the three women that he included, probably owed this distinction to the rich jewellery that they had once possessed.

Moreover, when dealing with large groups of post mortem inventories, historians of a statistical mind set have rarely paid much attention to the specific concerns of women. Thus, the broadly based works of Öztürk, Establet, and Pasqual contain only a small amount of information on the female half of the populations at issue.[59]

For historians trying to assess the activities open to women, regional and local differences are another source of difficulty. After all, we can no longer assume that Istanbul practices were identical to those prevailing in Tokat or Damascus. Perhaps more importantly, it is often difficult to interpret the figures that we do possess: Öztürk has shown that when measured in money terms, the percentage of kitchen- and copperware among the possessions of seventeenth-century Istanbul women was relatively high. However, from the tables published by this author, we cannot determine whether these Istanbul women actually owned many copper pots and pans. For as women were – and are – generally poorer than their menfolk, the percentage calculated by Öztürk may only signify that given the lower value of females' estates, copperware made up a more important percentage of the total. Given current interest in the study of post mortem inventories, we may get closer to answering this question in the future.

At the same time, I hope that this study of copper, trade and material culture has some relevance for gender studies as well. Admittedly, the concerns and problems of women that the 'magic bowl' investigated by Fodor alludes to, appear only as ritualized formulas in an inscription whose date remains doubtful. Even so, the bowl is precious, as concrete threats inherent in giving birth are not often covered by Ottoman sources, apart from specialized medical

---

58   Barkan, Ömer Lütfi, "Edirne Askeri Kassam'ına ait Tereke Defterleri (1545–1659)", *Belgeler*, 3/5–6 (1966), 1–479.

59   Öztürk, *Tereke Defterleri*; Establet, Colette and Jean-Paul Pascual, *Familles et fortunes à Damas, 450 foyers damascains en 1700* (Damascus: Institut français de Damas, 1994); Establet, Colette and Jean-Paul Pascual, *Ultime voyage pour la Mecque: les inventaires après décès de pelerins morts à Damas vers 1700* (Damascus: Institut français de Damas, 1998); Establet, Colette and Jean-Paul Pascual, *Des tissus et des hommes, Damas vers 1700* (Damascus: Institut français d'études arabes de Damas, 2005); Establet, Colette and Jean-Paul Pascual, *La gent d'état dans la société ottomane damascène: les 'askar à la fin du XVIIᵉ siècle* (Damascus: Presses de l'Ifpo, 2011).

literature – and a few observations by Evliya Çelebi, alert as ever.[60] Moreover, the possession of copperware could be a status symbol, showing that a given woman was the mistress of her household. With patience and perseverance, material culture – copperware included – thus will allow us to broaden our vision of the life worlds of Ottoman townswomen.

---

60   For an example compare Dankoff, Robert, *The Intimate Life of an Ottoman Statesman: Melek Ahmed Pasha 1588–1662 as Portrayed in Evliya Çelebi's Book of Travels (Seyahat-name): with an Historical Introduction by Rhoads Murphey* (Albany, N.Y.: State University of New York Press, 1991), p. 231.

CHAPTER 7

The Cihanbeyli and the Sheep Trade: from Provisionism and Semi-Nomadism to Liberal Economy and Sedentarisation

Yonca Köksal and Mehmet Polatel

Providing the food supply of the imperial capital was a major concern for the Ottoman state, and trade networks of basic food supplies such as grains and meat were oriented from provinces to Istanbul. Scholars usually focus on Rumeli as a source of meat supply for the imperial capital, and they rarely pay attention to the Anatolian meat supply and animal trade to Istanbul.[1] This chapter analyses the crucial role of one of the Anatolian tribes, the Cihanbeyli, in animal trade and meat provisioning of Istanbul. It argues that the Cihanbeyli tribe's involvement in the animal trade was continuous and spread over a long time period from the late eighteenth to the late nineteenth century. A semi-nomadic Kurdish tribe that circulated between winter and summer pastures in the province of Ankara, the Cihanbeyli emerged as the main supplier of sheep for Istanbul when the Rumelian meat supply decreased in this period.

Animal trade and meat provisioning faced challenges in the nineteenth century: firstly, the Ottoman state gradually adopted liberal economic policies after the Treaty of Baltalimanı (1838). The meat provisioning of Istanbul residents came to an end in 1857, but the provisioning of the army and the imperial palace continued until the very end of the empire. Secondly, as part of the centralization project of the state, tribes were settled in Anatolia. The sedentarization of the Cihanbeyli started in 1840 and ended in the 1850s. Both changes had major implications for the animal trade of the Cihanbeyli. Although some provisioning policies continued in the supply of meat, the adoption of free trade policies meant a more competitive market. Settlement scattered the Cihanbeyli households spreading them over several villages and decreased the power of the tribal chief over the animal trade. Donald Quataert has argued

---

1 See Uzun, Ahmet, *İstanbul'un İaşesinde Devletin Rolü: Ondalık Ağnam Uygulaması (1783–1857)* (Ankara: Türk Tarih Kurumu Basımevi, 2006); Türkhan, Mehmet Sait, "18. Yüzyılın İkinci Yarısında İstanbul'un Et İaşesinin Temini: Hassa Kasabbaşılık Kurumu", Ph.D. Dissertation, Marmara Üniversitesi, Istanbul, 2006; Greenwood, Anthony, "Istanbul's Meat Provisioning: A Study of the Celepkeşan System", Ph.D. Dissertation, University of Chicago, 1988.

that, with the adoption of liberal economic policies, Ottoman manufacturing was transformed from guild organization to more disorganized forms adopted in non-guild shops in urban areas and in homes in both rural and urban areas.[2] This chapter argues that a similar kind of transformation from an organized sheep trade represented by the head trader into a disorganized trade carried out by individual merchants can be seen in the case of the Cihanbeyli as a result of tribal settlement and free market policies.

In this chapter we will first discuss how a well-organized sheep trade was established between the Cihanbeyli and the imperial capital in the late eighteenth and early nineteenth centuries. The creation of a new position called 'head trader' of the tribe who was responsible for collection, transportation, and sale of sheep and animal quotas that were set in the 1800s, systematized the Cihanbeyli's animal trade and increased the quantity of animals sold and transported to Istanbul. The chapter will then discuss hardships that the Cihanbeyli faced in the Tanzimat era. Archival documents show that the Cihanbeyli failed to fulfil the quota of animals that they were required to send to Istanbul and were not able to pay their related debts to local and foreign merchants in the 1840s. The Ottoman state pushed for both tribal settlement and increasing animal supply of the tribe to the imperial capital in this period. The final section of the chapter will discuss the outcomes of these state policies between the 1860s and 1890s. The animal trade changed its form after sedentarization: it became more diffused and localized to villages. Quotas, that is the requirement for a certain number of animals to be sent to Istanbul, disappeared when free trade policies dominated the market. Despite these changes, animal trade was still conducted by the Cihanbeyli tribe until the end of the nineteenth century. Tribal members actively negotiated with the Ottoman state and wanted to have a representative in Istanbul to regulate and organize the animal trade in this period.

There are few studies on the meat provisioning and animal trade to Istanbul, and those that exist focus on earlier centuries (from the sixteenth to the eighteenth centuries) and on the European territories of the Ottoman empire. These studies have shown that the Ottoman state actively regulated animal trade to Istanbul first through the *celepkeşan*[3] system in the fifteenth and sixteenth centuries, and later through a form of tax farming, and finally

---

2   Quataert, Donald, *The Ottoman Empire, 1700–1922* (Cambridge: Cambridge University Press, 2000), pp. 110–39.

3   *Celepkeşan*s were wealthy people in the Rumelian provinces appointed as sheep dealers to provide a certain number of sheep to Istanbul, Greenwood, "Istanbul's Meat Provisioning: A Study of the Celepkeşan System", pp. 62–155.

through a special animal tax called *ondalık ağnam*[4] established in 1783. These studies rarely mention the Anatolian meat supply, although sheep were sent from Anatolia to the imperial palace as early as the fifteenth century.[5] In the sixteenth century, the Ottoman state demanded animals from Diyarbakır, and from the Yeniil and Bozok tribes when there was a shortage in the Rumelian meat supply.[6] By the eighteenth century, the Anatolian meat supply was expanded to western, central, and eastern Anatolia.[7]

In the existing literature, the Anatolian supply is considered temporary, only required in times of shortages in the Rumelian supply.[8] Increasingly in the eighteenth century, the Ottoman state demanded animals from Anatolia in a systemic way as a result of territorial losses in Rumeli and continuous wars with the Habsburgs and the Russians. In 1783, *ondalık ağnam*, a specific tax taken from 1/10 of animals for the meat supply of Istanbul, was imposed in Rumeli, and a year afterwards a similar tax called *bedel-i ağnam* was introduced in the Anatolian meat supply to Istanbul. The head butcher in Istanbul (*hassa kasapbaşı*) was responsible for organizing the collection of the tax and the transportation of animals. In 1857, the *bedel-i ağnam* and *ondalık ağnam* taxes were abolished, and a single animal tax was imposed.[9] This elimination of the special taxes for the meat provisioning of Istanbul and the earlier decision to abolish the head butcher position meant a symbolic end to meat provisioning. Instead of earlier policies of keeping meat prices low for Istanbul residents, meat prices were left free to fluctuate to be determined by market forces. The Ottoman state continued to supply the needs of the imperial palace and the army, meaning that attempts to control meat prices and ensure a continuous meat supply for Istanbul continued to a limited extent. After 1857, tax farmers (*mültezims*) of the animal tax were made responsible for buying and

---

4 See Uzun, *İstanbul'un İaşesinde Devletin Rolü*, pp. 57–120.

5 Bilgin, Arif, "Osmanlı Sarayının İaşesi", Ph.D. Dissertation, Marmara Üniversitesi, 2000, p. 210.

6 Kala, Ahmet, "Osmanlı Devleti'nde İstanbul'un Et İhtiyacının Temini İçin Kurulan Kasap ve Celep Teşkilatları (XVI, XVII ve XVIII. Asırlarda)", Ph.D. Dissertation, İstanbul Üniversitesi, 1985, p. 5.

7 Erzurum, Ankara, Muğla, Niğde and Adana were among the regions that sent sheep to Istanbul. See Faroqhi, Suraiya, *Towns and Townsmen of Ottoman Anatolia: Trade, Crafts, and Food Production in an Urban Setting, 1520–1650* (Cambridge: Cambridge University Press, 1984), pp. 274–5 and Türkhan, "18. Yüzyılın İkinci Yarısında İstanbul'un Et İaşesinin Temini", p. 43.

8 The two major works on the topic, both Greenwood, "Istanbul's Meat Provisioning: A Study of the Celepkeşan System", and Uzun, *İstanbul'un İaşesinde Devletin Rolü*, focus on the Rumelian supply and mention the Anatolian stock only in times of decrease in the Rumelian supply.

9 Uzun, *İstanbul'un İaşesinde Devletin Rolü*, p. 56.

transporting animals to Istanbul. Free market mechanisms were supposed to work here when the tax farmer and sheep owners negotiated and consented to the price. In practice, tax farmers forcefully obtained sheep when their owners were unable to pay the animal taxes. Thus in Erzincan in the 1870s, for example, tax farmers travelled with drovers (*celeps*) and bought sheep at lower prices when the owners failed to pay their animal taxes.[10]

Another challenge for the meat provisioning and animal trade was the Ottoman state policy of tribal settlements. Different from earlier settlement attempts, the Tanzimat policies aimed at eliminating the mobility of tribes. Therefore, the nomadic tribes that circulated in vast regions and the semi-nomadic tribes that migrated between their winter and summer pastures were all subject to settlement in permanent villages. Settlement policy was not limited to rebellious tribes, but also included nomadic groups from Bosnia to Central Anatolia and from Mount Kozan to the River Jordan. Once the tribal groups were settled, either by force or negotiation, they were provided with incentives such as tax exemptions to encourage them to become involved in agricultural production.

How did the Cihanbeyli's animal trade respond to these changes? Like all other Anatolian tribes, the Cihanbeyli was exempt from the *bedel-i ağnam* tax. In the early nineteenth century the Ottoman state tied the Cihanbeyli into a special agreement and required them to send a certain number of animals to Istanbul. The number of animals that the tribe traded increased during the Tanzimat era. The adoption of free market policies meant the end of some measures that were used to encourage the Cihanbeyli to orient their animal trade to Istanbul. For example, the Cihanbeyli were exempt from passage fees and taxes for their animals moving to Istanbul, and these free passage privileges came to an end during the Tanzimat.[11] The competitive market that emerged after 1857 also meant the elimination of the required quota of animals to be sent to Istanbul and introduced the possibility for the Cihanbeyli traders of diverting their animals to other cities. However, continuation of provisioning policies for the army and the imperial palace required the Ottoman state to concern itself with meat prices and animal trade. In the absence of strictly provisionist policies such as required quotas of animals, the Ottoman state had to find new ways to keep meat prices low and ensure a constant supply of animals. We argue that ending the organized form of the tribal trade and

---

10   Yarman, Arsen (ed.), *Palu-Harput 1878: Çarsancak, Çemişkezek, Çapakçur, Erzincan, Hizan ve Civar Bölgeler*, vol. II (Istanbul: Derlem Yayınları, 2010), p. 385.

11   Devlet Arşivleri, Osmanlı Arşivi, Istanbul [hereafter BOA], DH.MKT. 2558/4, 8 Teşrin-i evvel 1317 (21 October 1901).

favouring trade carried out by individual merchants reduced the negotiating power of the tribal merchants. This became a new state strategy for keeping meat prices low in Istanbul.

Sedentarization of the Cihanbeyli also presented various advantages and disadvantages for the animal trade. Studies on tribal settlements in the nineteenth century usually emphasize the disruption of nomadic and semi-nomadic tribes of agricultural production, such as plundering of villages and robbing peasants, and state concerns for generating more taxation revenue and military conscription. Such studies have not addressed the disadvantages that might emerge with the disappearance of tribes' earlier economic functions, such as stock farming and transportation.[12]

The scattered settlement of the Cihanbeyli over several villages challenged the organization of the animal trade as a tribal activity. The abolition of the head trader position which made it difficult to defend the rights of tribal merchants was an example of this challenge to the tribe's animal trade. Sedentarization also meant an end to the mobility of animals between winter and summer pastures which was crucial for sheep breeding. Despite these challenges, the Ottoman state needed to provide regular meat supply to the imperial palace and the army, and therefore it adopted measures to support animal breeding during the settlement of the tribe. Land was distributed to the settled members of the tribe and exemptions from animal and agricultural taxes were granted for three years.[13] How the Cihanbeyli traded animals, responded to the major changes brought about by settlement and liberal economic policies, and negotiated with Ottoman state authorities over the nineteenth century will be analysed in the following pages.

The Cihanbeyli in the Sheep Trade before the Tanzimat

By the end of the eighteenth century there was a well-defined trade network from the Cihanbeyli tribe to the imperial capital. According to Ahmet Uzun, there was an increase in demand for mutton from the Cihanbeyli tribe throughout the early nineteenth century in the context of the Rumelian meat

---

12   Köksal, Yonca and Mehmet Polatel, "A tribe as an economic actor: the Cihanbeyli tribe and the meat provisioning of İstanbul in the early Tanzimat era", *New Perspectives on Turkey*, 61 (2019), 1–27.

13   Köksal, Yonca, "Coercion and mediation: centralization and sedentarization of tribes in the Ottoman empire", *Middle Eastern Studies*, 42/3 (2006), p. 479.

supply's decline.[14] Archival documents show that a constant meat supply from the Cihanbeyli tribe was already well established by the late eighteenth century. As early as 1792, the Cihanbeyli brought to Istanbul 8,300 Karaman sheep, while the remaining 71,000 *kızıl* (red) sheep were on their way to Istanbul – a good round sum of 80,000 sheep.[15] The Cihanbeyli tribe was also responsible for collecting sheep from other tribes in the region.[16] The head of the tribe, Alişan Bey, was to collect them under the scrutiny of the district governor who was a member of the prominent Cabbarzade dynasty. A marshal (*mübaşir*) was also appointed to check the collection of 80,000 sheep.[17] In 1804, a member of the Cihanbeyli tribe, Hacı Osman Oğlu, collected 30,000 to 40,000 sheep from Ilgaz, but failed to bring them to Istanbul. When they arrived in Bolu, the sheep were diverted to various regions such as Eskişehir, Bursa and İzmid where prices were higher. The state wrote several petitions to force the sheep to be collected and brought to Istanbul.[18] Provisioning policies meant keeping meat prices lower in the imperial capital than in other cities, so that ordinary residents could afford to buy meat. Therefore, it was attractive for butchers and traders to sell sheep in other Anatolian cities in order to generate a higher profit margin. The Ottoman state provided several incentives, such as a reduction in transportation taxes to the providers and drovers of sheep to Istanbul. From time to time, the state used force to prevent the diversion of sheep to other provinces, as seen in the imperial orders.[19]

The Cihanbeyli were integrated into the vast animal trade network not only as drovers and breeders, but also by being held responsible for maintaining secure passage of sheep from Erzurum. The distant province of Erzurum contributed to the meat supply of the imperial capital. A special kind called *kızıl* (red) sheep was brought from Erzurum.[20] In 1813, it was noted that the sheep from Erzurum should be recorded separately from those that were to be brought by the Cihanbeyli and Zeyveli tribes, although the number of sheep was not mentioned.[21] Since sheep from Erzurum travelled a long distance,

---

14   The Cihanbeylis were required to send 80,000 sheep in 1800. The number increased to 100,000 in 1835. See Uzun, *İstanbul'un İaşesinde Devletin Rolü*, p. 21.

15   BOA, HAT 195/9666, 29 Zilhicce 1206 (18 August 1792).

16   These tribes were the Seyfhanlı, Atmanlı, Şeyh Bezenli, Zeyveli, Mikailli and Kikelli. See BOA, C.BLD. 151/7522, 29 Zilkade 1216 (2 April 1802).

17   BOA, C.BLD. 151/7522, 29 Zilkade 1216 (2 April 1802).

18   BOA, AE.SSLM. III 254/14738, 29 Zilhicce 1218 (10 April 1804).

19   For example, drovers from the Cihanbeyli tribe demanded the release of their sheep which were held in İnegöl by the governor; this was immediately rejected. See BOA, C.BLD. 103/5133, 29 Cemaziülahır 1226 (21 July 1811).

20   BOA, AE.SSLM. III 102/06205, 21 Rebiülevvel 1219 (30 June 1804).

21   BOA, C.BLD. 103/5150, 29 Receb 1228 (28 July 1813).

their security was of major concern. On their way to Istanbul, the drovers of Erzurum sheep had been attacked by members of the Cihanbeyli and other tribes. The head of the Cihanbeyli, Alişan Bey, was then made responsible for the security of Erzurum sheep by means of an imperial order.[22]

In the early nineteenth century, the Cihanbeyli role in the meat supply became institutionalized with the appointment of the head of the tribe as the head trader responsible for the collection and transportation of sheep to Istanbul. The appointment of a head trader shows that the constant supply of the Cihanbeyli sheep necessitated an official contact person to regulate this trade between the head butcher (*hassa kasapbaşı*) in Istanbul and the tribe. A title of privilege (*berat*) granted the collection of 100,000 sheep from eight tribes in the Ankara region to the Cihanbeyli tribe, and the head of the tribe, Alişan Bey, was appointed head trader in 1825.[23] This *berat* institutionalized the sheep trade and marked the crucial role of the tribal chief in it.[24]

There is evidence that the title of head trader (*tacirbaşı*) existed before this *berat*. In fact, there was competition among different tribes to receive this title. A head trader (*tacirbaşı/tüccarbaşı*) position appears in archival documents towards the end of the 1810s. In 1819, a conflict between Mehmed Bey from the Şeyh Bezenli tribe and Alişan Bey, the head of the Cihanbeyli, occurred because of this title. The Şeyh Bezenli tribe seemed to be the second largest tribe among the eight tribes responsible for bringing 100,000 sheep to Istanbul.[25] Mehmed Bey of the Şeyh Bezenlis claimed to be the head trader ("devlet-i aliyye tacir başısı benim diyerek"). His claim was refuted by local state officials, and he was arrested. Alişan Bey's title was reassured, but apparently there existed anxiety about the timing of the meat supply. Istanbul needed this meat before the start of the month of Ramazan. Alişan and the headmen of the tribes were gathered and advised to collect and send the sheep before that month. They were warned not to divert them to other cities on the way to Istanbul.[26] Preventing the smuggling of sheep was a major concern for the state when the meat prices in other cities were higher than in Istanbul. The head trader was a contentious

---

22   BOA, AE.SSLM. III 254/14704, 29 Zilhicce 1206 (18 August 1792).
23   Starting with Mahmud II's reign, Ottoman merchants (*hayriye tüccarı*) were granted trade privileges (*berat*s) to encourage both international and domestic trade. Okyar, Osman, "Tanzimat Ekonomisi Hakkındaki Karamsarlık Üzerine", in *Tanzimat'ın 150. Yıldönümü Uluslararası Sempozyumu* (Ankara: Türk Tarih Kurumu Basımevi, 1994), pp. 243–54.
24   The *berat* issue emerged in a later document asking for a copy in 1883, since the original one had been lost in a fire. BOA, Y.PRK.AZJ. 6/103, 11 Cemaziülahır 1300 (19 April 1883).
25   The eight tribes were the Cihanbeyli, Şeyh Bezenli, Zeyveli, Mikailli, Geyikli, Atmanlı, Terkanlı and Siganlı.
26   BOA, AE.SMHD.II 23/1393, 11 Şaban 1234 (5 June 1819).

position: different tribal leaders competed to become the head trader, and the issue of smuggling and illegal sale in provinces with higher meat prices was always part of this trade.

The Tanzimat, the Cihanbeyli and the Sheep Trade

The combination of two major processes of the Tanzimat, the introduction of a liberal economy and the sedentarization of tribes, deeply influenced and transformed the role of the Cihanbeyli in the sheep trade to Istanbul. This was not a quick transformation, but rather a gradual process in which the form and volume of the Cihanbeyli animal trade changed especially after the 1860s. Interestingly, during and after the Tanzimat the Cihanbeyli tribe continued to play a role in that trade, to varying degrees. Until 1857, the continuation of provisionist policies meant that the Cihanbeyli continued to be significant in the meat supply to Istanbul and in the 1840s the number of sheep sent by the Cihanbeyli tribe was around 120,000.[27] Estimates for the total meat consumption of early-nineteenth-century Istanbul display a wide range, between 600,000 and 1,800,000 sheep.[28] Thus, the Cihanbeyli tribe itself was required to maintain a minimum of 6.6 percent and a maximum of 20 percent of the meat supply to the imperial capital. The 1857 regulation that ended the provisionist policies in Istanbul's meat supply coincided with the attempts to sedentarize the Cihanbeyli in the 1850s. Even after they were settled, the tribe continued to be involved in the meat trade, although the form of the trade and the amount of sheep changed significantly.

Let us first look at the early Tanzimat years (1839–57) to analyse the impact of changing state policies. On 10 April 1840, an imperial order was released in response to the demands of the headmen (muhtars) of the Cihanbeyli tribe, requesting that Alişan Bey, a young boy of twelve years old, be made the new head of the tribe (mir-i aşiret) and head trader (tacirbaşı) for the sheep trade. Alişan Bey was the son of Halil Bey and nephew of Ömer Bey, the previous two heads of the tribe, now deceased. He was also the grandson of the famous Alişan Bey, the previously mentioned head of the tribe and head trader.[29] This request was accepted, and Alişan Bey emerged as a key actor both in the tribal settlement and sheep trade during the early Tanzimat era. He held enormous power in the twelve years during which he ruled the tribe

---

27   BOA, C.BLD. 37/1836, 14 Safer 1265 (21 January 1848).
28   Greenwood, "Istanbul's Meat Provisioning: A Study of the Celepkeşan System", p. 19.
29   BOA, C.DH. 108/5351, 7 Safer 1256 (10 April 1840).

(1840–52), in the absence of strongly defined divisions and local headmen in the Cihanbeyli tribe.

A mechanism for sedentarization in the province of Ankara was the formation of a separate administrative unit called *müstakil muhassıllık* for tribes.[30] In this system, a tribal chief was appointed director or chieftain (*müdür* or *mir*), subordinate to the state-appointed governor of the tribe (*kaymakam* or *muhassıl*). Tribal governors were not subordinated to the local administrators of nearby towns and districts, and they enjoyed a privileged status of unchecked power, while the Ottoman state was able to keep a close eye on the tribe by controlling their appointment. In the period of the Cihanbeyli administration, Alişan Bey ruled alongside the tribe's governor (*kaymakam*). The governor depended on Alişan Bey's support, as he was an outsider and had little knowledge about tribal relations. Alişan Bey was willing to cooperate with the state since this provided him with benefits such as tax collection and an entourage of state troops. Ultimately, the state gave Alişan Bey a pay raise and a medal for his success in the settlement of the Cihanbeyli.

Alişan Bey had administrative, security and financial duties as tribal chief, in addition to his role as the head trader of sheep. For example, he was responsible for preventing tribal members from acting aggressively towards the local residents of Sivas.[31] He was also responsible for controlling the illegal activities of the tribes under Cihanbeyli jurisdiction.[32] More importantly, his financial duties included the collection and transportation of sheep to Istanbul. This necessitated a vast network of trade that encompassed not only tribal members and state authorities, but also merchants who provided funding for the collection of sheep. The repayment of the funds received from these merchants was also his responsibility.

As part of sedentarization, the Ottoman state gradually appointed headmen to their localities and later dismissed Alişan Bey. The state secured Alişan Bey's acceptance of dismissal from the chieftainship by granting him a state post in 1852.[33] The dismissal of Alişan Bey was an important step towards the sedentarization of the Cihanbeyli. In 1860, the separate administrative unit of

---

30   The settlement of the Cihanbeyli tribe has been analysed in Köksal, "Coercion and mediation: centralization and sedentarization of tribes in the Ottoman empire", pp. 481–3. The paragraphs below about the settlement of the Cihanbeyli include a summary of the passages on their settlement.

31   BOA, A.MKT. 39/85, 3 Rebiülahir 1264 (9 March 1848).

32   BOA, Ayniyat Defteri 402, 21 Zilkade 1262 (10 November 1846), pp. 143–5; BOA, Ayniyat Defteri 403, Zilkade 1262 (14 November 1846), pp. 14, 25.

33   Alişan was described as the local governor of the town of Kırşehir, not far from his tribal lands. BOA, Ayniyat Defteri 428, 4 Rebiülevvel 1269 (16 December 1852), p. 90.

the Cihanbeyli was abolished, and the tribal units were incorporated into the towns and villages where they resided.[34] Several units of the tribe were settled in villages in the town of Esbikeşan in the province of Konya, but the majority were settled in the district of Koçgiri in Sivas.[35]

In the 1840s, there erupted a debt crisis involving Cihanbeyli tribes and a Russian merchant named David Savalan which might have contributed to Alişan's dismissal in the 1850s. The tribe had received a credit of 2,100,000 piasters from Savalan in the 1840s to cover their expenses related to the sheep trade with Istanbul. As they failed to pay the debt on time, a multi-layered conflict emerged between the tribes, the Sublime Porte, local authorities, the Russian consulate, and David Savalan. Upon the non-payment of the debt, backed by the Russian consulate, Savalan sent several petitions and memoranda concerning this matter to the Ottoman government while pushing for the payment of the sum by confiscating sheep traded by Cihanbeyli. This process threatened the meat provisioning of Istanbul as Savalan also confiscated sheep sent to Istanbul. The Porte tried to ensure the meat supply of Istanbul, which was in jeopardy because of this crisis, and sent officials to the region to oversee the trade and the payment process in order to achieve this end. The crisis was finally resolved in the early 1850s, but even after this period there were traders who had no ties with Cihanbeyli and whose sheep had been confiscated by Savalan for their debt. Their complaints and efforts to obtain compensation continued in the 1850s.[36] This debt crisis shows the importance of the sheep trade of the Cihanbeyli for the meat supply of Istanbul.

The Cihanbeyli and the Sheep Trade after 1857

Beginning in the late 1850s, several developments shifted the social and political context concerning the Cihanbeyli and their sheep trade. After the abolition of *ondalık ağnam* and the measures that had been established to secure meat provisions for the capital, the Sublime Porte did not conduct agreements with the Cihanbeyli to secure the meat provisioning. In addition to these changes in economic policies, important political and social developments concerned the Cihanbeyli such as the removal of Alişan Bey from his post, the sedentarization of the tribe and the abolition of the Cihanbeyli as an administrative unit.

---

34   BOA, C.ML. 3026, 17 Cemaziülahır 1276 (11 January 1860).
35   BOA, Ayniyat Defteri 463, 7 Cemaziülevvel 1279 (31 October 1862), pp. 156–7.
36   Köksal and Polatel, "A tribe as an economic actor: the Cihanbeyli tribe and the meat provisioning of İstanbul in the early Tanzimat era".

The aim of this section is to examine the extent to which these developments affected the tribe's sheep trade.

Documents from the Ottoman archives indicate that the Cihanbeyli continued to be involved in sheep trade in the decades that followed the sedentarization of the tribe and the transformation of the central government's economic policies. Even though they were settled, the Cihanbeyli did not lose their tribal identity and claimed their tribal titles in archival documents. Tribesmen continued to transfer thousands of sheep to Istanbul and other cities on an annual basis. In the late 1880s, the number of sheep that Cihanbeyli tribesmen annually brought to Istanbul was around 300,000.[37] This indicates that the Cihanbeyli not only continued sheep trade in this period, but even increased the volume of their trade.

Although the Cihanbeyli continued their sheep trade, there were important changes in the way in which it was conducted. The Cihanbeyli lost some of their earlier privileges that came with the provisionist policies. As noted in the previous section, the agreement between the central government and the Cihanbeyli (berat) provided them with the right to free passage. Cihanbeyli tribesmen transferring sheep from Anatolia to Istanbul were not subject to passage fees. After the end of the provisionist policies, the Cihanbeyli tribesmen lost this right. This presumably increased the cost of transporting sheep for the Cihanbeyli. An order sent by the ministry of the interior to the governorate of Hüdavendigar in 1901 exemplifies the effects of this situation. This order stated that Cihanbeyli tribesmen from Konya used the pastures within a royal farm (çiftlik-i hümayun) while transporting their sheep to Istanbul and for this usage paid a considerable sum to the farm's directorate. Upon the complaints of the Cihanbeyli merchants, the Sublime Porte reduced the fee for using the pastures during transport.[38]

While the cost of animal trade increased with the elimination of earlier privileges such as exemption from passage taxes, another important change concerning the Cihanbeyli sheep trade in this period was the abolition of the title of head trader. Until 1883, the Sublime Porte had bestowed this title on a person from among the Cihanbeyli. The head trader was responsible for overseeing the tribe's sheep trade in the capital. Until his dismissal from the chieftainship, Alişan Bey held this title, which was later awarded to other members of the tribe. Until sedentarization, the head trader position was granted to the tribal chief. After the settlement, these two were separated, and the head

---

37   BOA, DH.MKT. 1444/60, 11 Ağustos 1303 (23 August 1887).
38   BOA, DH.MKT. 2558/4, 8 Teşrin-i evvel 1317 (21 October 1901).

trader was recorded in archival documents as residing in Istanbul[39] near the
animal market.[40] The head trader had the power of negotiation with the state
authorities in Istanbul for the quantity of animals and meat prices in the name
of the tribe. This position was an example of an organized trade activity, in
which the tribal representative had some power to negotiate state demands.

After the 1860s, there occurred several crises concerning this position. In
1861, the representatives of the merchants of the tribes tied to the Cihanbeyli
submitted a petition to the Porte, demanding the removal of the head trader,
Süleyman Ağa, from this position. They claimed that he paid the *celep*s less
than the worth of the sheep they had brought to the capital and thus embezzled a considerable sum. They also claimed that the head trader was not a
competent person, noting that he owed debts to various merchants.[41] In 1863,
the state removed Süleyman Ağa from this position. By 1867, another person,
also named Süleyman, was given this title.[42] Yet, struggles over the head trader
title continued in the years that followed. Some traders petitioned the Sublime
Porte for the re-appointment of the former head trader. In 1871, the former head
trader Süleyman Ağa himself submitted a petition, grounding his demand to
be re-appointed on the demands of these traders. He claimed that the current
head trader was carrying out trade in an irregular way and that the merchants
could not collect their money on time, underlining that such irregularities
affected the sheep trade carried out by the tribe. He promised to ensure the
sale of sheep at reasonable rates, should he be re-assigned, and offered to pay
50,000 piasters to the treasury within five years for the re-appointment.[43] In
1883, the council of state abolished the title of head trader, citing the embezzlement cases involving the head traders as the reason. After the title of head
trader had been abolished, the representatives of the Cihanbeyli tribes submitted another petition, demanding its restitution. This petition, which was
also signed by Alişan's son, noted that the head trader was a historical position established by Sultan Mahmud II and facilitated the tribe's sheep trade.
According to the petitioners, this position was the primary means of the sheep

---

39   The residence of the head trader is recorded as Uzunçayır or İbrahim Ağa Çayırı in Üsküdar
       in some documents. See BOA, Y.PRK.AZJ. 6/103, 11 Zilkade 1300 (13 September 1883) and
       BOA, MVL. 378/2, 14 Rebiülahir 1278 (19 October 1861).
40   However, there were exceptions: Alişan Bey's son, Ömer, claimed to hold both the posi-
       tions of tribal chief and head trader based on the earlier *berat*. Ömer had a representative
       in Istanbul, Ali, who acted as the head trader in his name. See BOA, Y.PRK.AZJ. 6/103, 11
       Zilkade 1300 (13 September 1883).
41   BOA,MVL. 378/20, 14 Rebiülahir 1278 (19 October 1861).
42   BOA, MVL. 552/64, 7 Receb 1284 (4 November 1867).
43   BOA, DH.MKT. 1311/114, 15 Kanun-ı sani 1286 (27 January 1871).

trade of the Cihanbeyli. The petitioners claimed that the simple tribesmen, who lacked the skills to navigate large cities, would experience enormous losses in the absence of a head trader, that even the transportation process would become more difficult and that the meat supply of Istanbul would be put in jeopardy.[44]

The abolition of the head trader position meant less negotiation power for the Cihanbeyli traders, which would reduce meat prices and profit of the traders. Since the elimination of provisionist policies, such as requiring a certain quota of animals to be sent from the Cihanbeyli, the Ottoman state had perhaps found a new means to keep meat prices low through eliminating the head trader. Eliminating the organized form of the trade, symbolized in the position of head trader, would keep the prices low both for the Istanbul residents and for the imperial palace and the army.

Following the abolition of the head trader position, the responsibility of overseeing the Cihanbeyli sheep trade was given to a *kotra* (pen for small animals) officer, Ali Rıza Efendi. In 1886, Ali Rıza Efendi was also removed from this post.[45] Upon his removal, Ankara's Kurdish tribes involved in the sheep trade submitted a petition, demanding his reinstatement. The ministry of the interior consulted the *Şehremaneti* (municipality of Istanbul). The *Şehremaneti* informed the ministry that Kurdish tribesmen transporting sheep to Istanbul had limited knowledge of trade in large cities and were manipulated by traders and merchants in the capital. According to the *Şehremaneti*, Ali Rıza Efendi had defended the rights of the tribesmen and to ensured that the sheep were not sold below the minimum prices established by law. On this basis, the *Şehremaneti* supported the demands of the tribal leaders and argued that the restitution of the position of head trader would be appropriate. This demand was further supported by the administrative council of Ankara, which submitted an *ilam* on the same lines. Upon the petition of the tribal leaders and the decisions taken by different official bodies including the *Şehremaneti* and the administrative council of Ankara, the council of state once again took this matter under review. In 1887, it decided that reinstating the position of head trader would lead to an increase in meat prices in the capital. Moreover, a head trader appointed by the state would appropriate a portion of the sums that rightfully belonged to the sheep owners, according to the members of the council of state. Thus, the demand for the re-establishment of this position was rejected. In rejecting this demand, it was stated that the tribal merchants could appoint trustees who would oversee the sheep trade in the capital

---

44   BOA, Y.PRK.AZJ. 6/103, 11 Cemaziülahır 1300 (19 April 1883).
45   BOA, DH.MKT. 1426/99, 22 Ramazan 1304 (14 June 1887).

and facilitate their operations, but that these trustees could not be given official status.[46]

In the years that followed, the Cihanbeyli were not able to obtain head trader status again. We were not able to find any archival document related to the Cihanbeyli sheep trade to Istanbul after 1901. This hints at several possibilities, one of which is that the Cihanbeyli might have ended its animal trade to Istanbul. Especially after the abolition of the head trader, a collectively organized trade in the name of the tribe might have diminished significantly. Another possibility is that animal trade to Istanbul decreased significantly during the war years. Both the Balkan Wars and World War I oriented meat supply to the needs of the army, and there was a shortage of basic food items including grain and meat in Istanbul during the war years.[47] Thus, very much as was the case in the rest of Anatolia, the Cihanbeyli might not have enough animals to send to Istanbul. There is also the possibility that sheep were still sent to Istanbul, but not recorded or recorded in uncatalogued documents that we have no access to in the Ottoman archives.

Other archival sources show that the sheep trade continued to be an important socio-economic activity in the region until the end of the nineteenth century. Although we do not have specific numbers for the Cihanbeyli sheep trade, trade reports of the British Consulate in Ankara provide detailed information about the number of sheep, along with export numbers for the province. In the 1890s, sheep were one of the main exports of Ankara, and raising and trading sheep was the main source of income of many people living in the region. In this period, around 1,500,000 sheep were raised in the province. A million of these were consumed within the province, while the rest were exported to other provinces. Around 700,000 of the sheep in the province were raised in the district of Ankara.[48] Animal husbandry in the region generated a significant tax income as well. In the 1890s, the *ağnam* tax collected in Ankara was generally around 10 million piasters.[49]

---

46   BOA, DH.MKT. 1444/60, 11 Ağustos 1303 (23 August 1887).

47   Toprak, Zafer, *İttihat Terakki ve Cihan Harbi: Savaş Ekonomisi ve Türkiye'de Devletçilik* (İstanbul: Kaynak Yayınları, 2016), pp. 175–6.

48   "Report on the trade and agriculture of the consular district of Angora for the year 1895", *Diplomatic and Consular Reports on Trade and Finance. Turkey: Report for the Year 1895 on the Agriculture of Angora* (Foreign Office, Annual Series, no. 1739) (London: Harrison and Sons, 1896), p. 14.

49   *Ankara Vilayetine Mahsus Salname* (Ankara: Matbaa-ı Vilayet, 1307/1891), p. 298; *Ankara Vilayetine Mahsus Salname* (Ankara: Matbaa-ı Vilayet, 1311/1893), p. 305; and *Ankara Vilayetine Mahsus Salname* (Ankara: Matbaa-ı Vilayet, 1318/1900), p. 121.

A significant development that affected the region's socio-economic life in the 1890s was the construction of the railway. From Istanbul, the railway reached Ankara in 1893 and Konya in 1896. As the train did not run at night, the journey from Ankara to Istanbul took two days. A train was run daily backwards and forwards between these two destinations, carrying passengers and goods, as well as animals.[50] The introduction of this new means of transportation significantly changed socio-economic life in the region. One of the most striking effects of the railway's introduction was the increase in grain export. As grain producers gained the ability to sell their products in new markets, grain prices doubled.[51] This also affected the distribution of the tax income in the region. The share of the *aşar* in Ankara's total tax income increased significantly in these years, while the share of the *ağnam* tax declined.[52]

While it had tremendous effects on grain production and trade, the railway did not lead to a transformation in sheep production and trade to the same degree. Some traders began to use the railway as early as 1893. Normally, 90 sheep were transported in a wagon, and a drover was allowed to accompany the transported animals free of charge. In this first year, the number of sheep transported to Istanbul via the railway amounted to 8,550.[53] This was a very small percentage of the number of all sheep exported from Ankara to Istanbul in 1893 – that is, around 200,000.[54] In 1894 and 1895, there was no significant increase in the number of sheep transported by rail.[55]

---

50   "Report on the trade and agriculture of the consular district of Angora for the year 1893", *Diplomatic and Consular Reports on Trade and Finance. Turkey: Report for the Year 1893 on the Trade and Agriculture of Angora* (Foreign Office, Annual Series, no. 1368) (London: Harrison and Sons, 1894), p. 8.

51   "Report on the trade and agriculture of the consular district of Angora for the year 1893", p. 2, and *Diplomatic and Consular Reports on Trade and Finance. Turkey: Report on the Agricultural Condition of the Vilayet of Angora* (Foreign Office, Annual Series, no. 1624) (London: Harrison and Sons, 1895), p. 2.

52   *Ankara Vilayetine Mahsus Salname* (1307), p. 298; *Ankara Vilayetine Mahsus Salname* (1311), p. 305; *Ankara Vilayetine Mahsus Salname* (1318), p. 305; and *Ankara Vilayeti Salnamesi* (Ankara: Matbaa-ı Vilayet, 1325/1907), p. 328.

53   "Report on the trade and agriculture of the consular district of Angora for the year 1893", p. 3.

54   "Report on the trade and agriculture of the consular district of Angora for the year 1894", *Diplomatic and Consular Reports on Trade and Finance. Turkey: Report for the Year 1894 on the Agriculture of Angora* (Foreign Office, Annual Series, no. 1505) (London: Harrison and Sons, 1895), p. 2.

55   "Report on the trade and agriculture of the consular district of Angora for the year 1894", p. 8, and "Report on the trade and agriculture of the consular district of Angora for the year 1895", p. 15.

A decision of the ministry of finance, dated 1893, indicates that several state agencies tried to promote the transportation of sheep by rail, through reducing the cost of transportation. According to the ministry, conveying the sheep to their destination by road carried a high cost and led to losses due to the hardships of the journey. The ministry noted that this also negatively affected the treasury. According to the ministry of forests, mines and agriculture, a price reduction would lead to an increase in the sheep export from Ankara to Istanbul and a decline of meat prices in the capital, as well as contribute to the welfare of sheep owners and the development of agriculture and animal husbandry in the region. Moreover, this would enable these sheep merchants to compete with merchants who exported sheep from abroad. In line with these considerations, the ministry of finance requested the ministry of trade and public works to undertake the necessary measures.[56] British trade reports indicate that the Ottoman agencies trying to promote the use of the railway might have had one other consideration. The agreement between the Anatolia Railway Company and the Porte included a kilometre guarantee. If ticket receipts did not exceed a certain number, the tithes of the province of Ankara would be left to the company. This might have further motivated Ottoman state agencies to promote the use of the railway. The company also established a special tariff for promoting the transportation of sheep and cattle by large-scale merchants. For instance, when a shipper sent 10 wagons of sheep by railway, there was a reduction of 10 percent. For shippers who sent 76 wagon loads of sheep, the reduction was 24 percent.[57]

According to British trade reports, the number of sheep exported from Ankara to Istanbul amounted to 200,000 in the early 1890s. In 1894, there was a steep decline in this number, with a drop to 40,000. Disturbances related to the Armenian question and a bad harvest affected the socio-economic life in the region in a negative way.[58] These developments might have contributed to this decline. In the late 1890s, the number of sheep exported from Ankara to Istanbul was unable to recover or reach its pre-1894 level. In the years of 1897 and 1898, this number was 120,000 and 100,000, respectively.[59] Despite

---

56   BOA, BEO. 336/25164, 30 Teşrin-i sani 1309 (12 December 1893).
57   "Report on the trade and agriculture of the consular district of Angora for the year 1894",
      pp. 6–7.
58   "Report on the trade and agriculture of the consular district of Angora for the year 1895",
      pp. 1–2, 11.
59   "Report on the trade and commerce of Angora and district for the year 1897", *Diplomatic
      and Consular Reports Turkey. Report for the Year 1897 on the Trade and Commerce of
      Angora and District* (Foreign Office, Annual Series, no. 1505) (London: Harrison and Sons,
      1898), p. 10 and "Report on the trade and commerce of Angora and district for the year

this decline, raising and trading sheep continued to constitute important economic activities in the region; by 1907, the number of sheep raised in the province of Ankara was around 1.5 million.[60]

Conclusion

This article has focused on a neglected topic, that is the Anatolian meat supply to Istanbul and the role of the tribes in it. In contrast to the studies which
argue that the Anatolian meat supply was a temporary solution and a remedy
only used in times of shortages in the Rumelian meat supply, our findings show
that, whether settled or not, tribes had always been part of Anatolian trade
and production in the Ottoman empire. The Cihanbeyli role in supplying meat
to the imperial capital was already well-established through the position of
head trader in the 1810s. The tribe continued to be a crucial economic actor in
providing Istanbul's meat, even under the pressure of sedentarization and free
trade policies.

In the nineteenth century, the Ottoman state started to see nomadic and
semi-nomadic tribes as a security concern, disrupting economic activity and
in need of state control. This chapter has shown that the Ottoman state's need
to control and settle the Cihanbeyli tribe co-existed with another and somewhat contradictory need, that of a continuous meat supply from the tribe to
Istanbul. The well-established animal trade network which included various
social actors such as foreign traders, state officials, non-Muslim moneylenders,
tribal chiefs, drovers and graziers meant that the animal trade of the Cihanbeyli
was not a small-scale local trade. Rather, it was part of a larger imperial network of animal trade in Anatolia. Therefore, the nineteenth century challenges
of sedentarization and the end of provisioning not only affected the tribe, but
they also placed important constraints on the meat supply of Istanbul.

These two major processes in the nineteenth century, sedentarization and
liberal policies, did not eliminate the role of the Cihanbeyli in sheep trade, but
transformed the form and volume of the trade. Until 1857, the old practices of
providing meat supply for Istanbul continued, demonstrating that the shift to
free trade policies did not easily eliminate provisionism when it came to the
capital's food supply. The annual sheep export of the Cihanbeyli to Istanbul
constantly increased from 80,000 in 1792 to 300,000 in 1883. Then there was

---

1898", *Diplomatic and Consular Reports Turkey. Report for the Year 1898 on the Trade and
Commerce of Angora and District* (London: Harrison and Sons, 1899), p. 9.
60   *Ankara Vilayeti Salnamesi* (1325), pp. 118, 330–1.

a gradual decrease to 100,000 sheep sent from the Ankara region to Istanbul annually in 1898. After the abolition of the *ondalık ağnam* in 1857, there occurred changes in the organization of the trade. The head trader position, which had been held by the tribal chief of the Cihanbeyli, was eliminated. The head trader had exercised power in negotiating high prices for the sheep. With his elimination, the bargaining power of the tribe decreased, and the price of sheep could be kept low, which was advantageous for the state and Istanbul residents, but problematic for the Cihanbeyli traders and producers.

CHAPTER 8

The Draw of the Lottery: *Piyango*, Profit and Politics in Early Twentieth-Century İzmir

Ebru Boyar

In September 1902, a story entitled "Piyango" (Lottery) was published in an Istanbul journal *İrtika*. This was the story of İsmail, a young man in his twenties, "cheerful and outgoing by nature and a bit of a spendthrift",[1] who bought a lottery ticket, numbered 404, in the İzmir Hamidiye Sanayi Mektebi Piyangosu (the İzmir Hamidiye Artisanal School Lottery). As he waited impatiently for the draw to be held in İzmir, İsmail indulged in "sweet, sweet daydreams", promising presents to all the people in his household. When the day of the draw arrived, İsmail, in a state of agitation, pressured his brother, who was none other than the narrator of the story, for news of the results, as he was working in a publishing house. But the brother's response was not helpful: "News! How would I have news! You'll just have to be patient [until] the numbers of the lottery drawn in İzmir get to Istanbul". Unhappy, İsmail snapped "What patience! I'm going to have trouble even just sleeping until I get the news".

He therefore set out to find the results on his own. He checked the newspapers; "talking to each and every one of the *sarraf*s [money changers] in Istanbul who sold İzmir lottery tickets, he checked whether the numbers had arrived from İzmir". Finally, on Friday he got hold of the results in a prominent Istanbul newspaper *Sabah*, and was delighted to find that his ticket number 404 had won a prize of 270 *kuruş*. On the same day, over the moon, and somewhat smug, İsmail, before even getting the prize money in his hand, immediately borrowed ten *kuruş* from his mother, promising to pay her back at 100 per cent interest (one *mecidiye*), and took various people, including his brother, to a pleasure ground for a lavish meal. He spent the whole day contemplating how he was going to spend his 270 *kuruş*. He decided to buy a suit and a pair of shoes, as well as paying his mother back one *mecidiye*. That evening he shared the news about his good fortune in the neighbourhood coffee house. But, on Saturday, when İsmail went to collect his prize money from the *sarraf* in Karaköy, from whom he had bought his lottery ticket, he received only 28

---

1 Kızanlıklı Mehmed Ali, "Küçük Hikaye: Piyango", *İrtika*, 181–33 (16 Cemaziülahır 1320/6 Eylül 1318/19 September 1902), p. 313.

kuruş. It transpired that the value of his ticket was one eighth of a full lottery ticket, the *sarraf* pointing out to him the 1/8 marked on the corner of the ticket. The prize was therefore divided into eight shares (although in the story it was not explained what happened to the remaining 5.5 *kuruş*; perhaps the *sarraf* received a percentage from the prize as a handling charge). Although İsmail had not received what he had dreamt about, this was not an impediment to him trying his luck again. Like every hopeful gambler, İsmail, who had already spent most of his prize money, decided to keep his last ten *kuruş* to buy a new lottery ticket, rather than paying his debt to his mother.

Living in Istanbul, İsmail tied his 'sweet dreams' of easy money to the İzmir Hamidiye Sanayi Mektebi Piyangosu. This lottery was first organized in 1890, authorized by Governor Halil Rıfat Paşa, who had first obtained permission from the sultan.[2] It had been organized regularly since 1899 to finance the expenses of the İzmir Hamidiye Sanayi Mektebi, an artisanal school which was established in 1868. Originally called İzmir Islahhanesi (or sometimes İzmir Mektebi-i Sanayi), a free boarding school for poor boys, the name was later changed in 1891 to the Hamidiye Mektebi-i Sanayi, popularly known as the İzmir Hamidiye Sanayi Mektebi, in honour of Sultan Abdülhamid II.[3] The fame and popularity of this lottery spread well beyond the borders of İzmir, a popularization in which the local government and the local press played a crucial role. It was the governor of Aydın, Kıbrıslı Kamil Paşa, who had been the grand *vezir* between 1885 and 1891 and in 1895 and who had then fallen from the sultan's grace and been exiled to İzmir as the governor of the province of Aydın in 1895,[4] who had permitted the regular organization of this cash lottery and had acted as its 'patron'. He used some of the lottery income for funding the building and maintenance of the İzmir Gureba Hastanesi (İzmir Pauper Hospital), the first Muslim hospital in the town, which accepted both Muslim and non-Muslim patients.[5] The İzmir press encouraged people to buy tickets in the İzmir Hamidiye Sanayi Mektebi Piyangosu. The İzmir newspaper *Hizmet* urged its readers on 26 Kanun-ı evvel 1305 (7 January 1890): "rather than giving our money abroad" by eagerly purchasing European lottery tickets, "or, in

---

2   Tunçay, Mete, *Türkiye'de Piyango Tarihi ve Millî Piyango İdaresi* (Ankara: Milli Piyango İdaresi Yayını, 1993), p. 81.

3   Koyuncu-Yakın, Gülnaz, *İzmir Sanayi Mektebi (Mithatpaşa Endüstri Meslek Lisesi) (1868–1923)* (İzmir: İzmir Valiliği, 1997), pp. 16 and 22–3.

4   Kırmızı, Abdulhamit, *Abdülhamid'in Valileri. Osmanlı Vilayet İdaresi 1895–1908* (Istanbul: Klasik, 2007), p. 101.

5   Dursun, M. Kamil, *İzmir Hatıraları*, ed. Ünal Şenel (İzmir: Akademi Kitabevi, 1994), pp. 24–5.

truth, transferring it in this way to foreign works, let us contribute to the development of charitable institutions in our country".[6]

The Irresistible Attraction of Easy Money: Lotteries in the Ottoman Empire

Lotteries became increasingly popular among the Ottoman population throughout the nineteenth century. Providing a well-informed history of the lottery from the Roman empire to modern times in Europe, Ebüzziya Tevfik, like his Ottoman contemporaries, linked the arrival of all novel evils from Europe to the 'ill-omened' Crimean War (1853–56), the war which had brought with it the influx of thousands of European soldiers, European cash and goods into Ottoman lands, including the lottery.[7] In fact, the lottery did not make its first appearance with the Crimean War, for the Ottomans had become acquainted with it earlier. As early as 1792, in his *sefaretname*, Ebubekir Ratıp Efendi, who was sent to Vienna as ambassador, had given information about the lottery in Hungary and argued for the possible benefits of a lottery to the Ottoman treasury if such a venture were organized in the Ottoman empire.[8] By the mid-1850s, the lottery had become a part of Ottoman social life and an economically lucrative business venture, to such an extent that foreign nationals sought lottery concessions and foreign lotteries found customers within the empire.[9]

There was, however, a major problem about the lottery: it was, in essence, a form of gambling, which was religiously, morally and legally unacceptable. Ebüzziya Tevfik condemned the lottery, describing it as "the contagious disease of civilization that pervades the nineteenth century".[10] Despite all condemnation and attempts to ban lotteries in the empire as early as 1848,[11] the late Ottoman state's position towards the lottery was ambiguous: on one hand, it was condemned and banned, but on the other, the lottery was lucrative for the state as it brought much needed cash into the state coffers and produced

---

6   Quoted in Koyuncu-Yakın, *İzmir Sanayi Mektebi*, p. 76.
7   Ebüzziya Tevfik, "Piyango", *Mecmua-i Ebüzziya*, 3/27 (Gurre-i Safer 1300/12 December 1882), p. 843.
8   Tunçay, *Türkiye'de Piyango Tarihi*, p. 28.
9   Tunçay, *Türkiye'de Piyango Tarihi*, pp. 75–80; Tızlak, Fahrettin, "Osmanlı Toplumuna Şans Oyunlarının Girişi", *XV. Türk Tarih Kongresi. Kongreye Sunulan Bildiriler, 11–15 Eylül 2006*, 4. Cilt, 3. Kısım (Ankara: Türk Tarih Kurumu Basımevi, 2010), pp. 1885–8 and 1892–5.
10   Ebüzziya Tevfik, "Piyango", p. 838.
11   Tızlak, "Osmanlı Toplumuna Şans Oyunlarının Girişi", p. 1879.

a revenue that could be used to serve public interest. Furthermore, there were already many Ottoman lottery enthusiasts and if there were no state-sanctioned and controlled lotteries, then such people would either buy foreign lottery tickets or invest in illegally organized lotteries.[12]

The solution for this dilemma was found by the Tanzimat Dairesi (Danıştay, the Council of State) in 1883. Accordingly, while lotteries organized for private benefit or interest were legally forbidden, lotteries organized "for public need and benefit among the religious community" were allowed.[13] In this way, both cash lotteries and those whose prizes were goods became legally, politically and socially acceptable, once they were tied to charitable acts, acts that would bring social benefit. Such lotteries were first organized by non-Muslims or foreign nationals in the empire, as well as international companies, but were then followed by those organised by Muslims and state institutions.[14] For instance, in October 1880, one of the lottery draws organized by the Osmanlı Bankası (the Ottoman Bank) was an "international lottery" for the benefit of the victims of the famine in Anatolia.[15] Almost two decades later, Abdülhamid II became the patron of the İane Sergisi Piyangosu of 1898–99, a cash and goods lottery organized for the benefit of the wounded soldiers and families of those who had lost their lives during the Ottoman-Greek War of 1897.[16]

Although, these charity lotteries were socially and politically acceptable, what made them popular was not people's charitable motives. People did not need to buy lottery tickets in order to support charitable causes as there was a very well-established charity system in the Ottoman empire. In the second half of the nineteenth century, specific public campaigns were even organized to collect donations.[17] The popularity of lotteries, thus, stemmed from the search for easy money and the dreams which such money could fuel, as in the case of İsmail. This was a universal desire, and Ottoman lotteries had followers not only among Ottoman subjects but also among foreigners living in the empire. The English woman Dorina L. Neave, whose father was in the British diplomatic service and who lived in Istanbul until 1907, related how she and an American friend had visited a fortune teller who told them, among other things, that they "held in the family three original "lots Turcs" (Lottery tickets)

12   Tızlak, "Osmanlı Toplumuna Şans Oyunlarının Girişi", pp. 1880–5 and 1888–92.

13   Tunçay, *Türkiye'de Piyango Tarihi*, p. 51.

14   Özbek, Nadir, "Philanthropic activity, Ottoman patriotism, and the Hamidian regime, 1876–1909", *International Journal of Middle East Studies*, 37/1 (2005), pp. 64–5.

15   *La Turquie*, 14/246, Sunday, 24 and Monday, 25 October 1880.

16   Tunçay, *Türkiye'de Piyango Tarihi*, pp. 92–8.

17   Boyar, Ebru and Kate Fleet, *A Social History of Ottoman Istanbul* (Cambridge: Cambridge University Press, 2010), pp. 78–9.

that would be best burned, as they would never been drawn", a prophesy which had apparently come true.[18]

In his column *Şehir Mektupları* (City Letters) in the newspaper *Malumat*, Ahmet Rasim, adopting his usual sarcastic tone, commented on the commotion created by the İane Sergisi Piyangosu among the people of Istanbul, who were impatiently waiting for the draw. The dreams of people from all walks of life, who, perhaps, did not even know the reason for this lottery or were not interested, were infused with the phantasy of the first prize, which was 1,000 Ottoman lira.[19]

The Lottery Business of İzmir

There was obviously a high demand for lotteries in the late Ottoman empire. Unlike one-off lotteries such as the İane Sergisi Piyangosu, the İzmir Hamidiye Sanayi Mektebi Piyangosu was a high-prized regular lottery with a good reputation. But it was not the only regular lottery in İzmir. Among the various lotteries, the İzmir Musevi Eytam Mektebi ve Hastanesi Piyangosu (the İzmir Jewish School for Orphans and Hospital Lottery), organized by the Jewish community, also appeared regularly and had a reputation beyond İzmir. Indeed, in the late nineteenth century and early twentieth century, İzmir became the centre of cash prize 'charity' lotteries popular not only in İzmir, where there was already a well-established gambling culture,[20] but in all Ottoman territories. Lotteries organized in İzmir set an example for similar ventures in other provincial centres of the empire. These lotteries developed into very profitable business ventures, involving many actors not only in İzmir but also beyond.

Over the years, the İzmir lotteries had been systemized and turned into professional financial ventures, which were run according to legal rules, and had gained an empire-wide credibility and popularity. Once an organizing board of an institution or a community got the permit to organize a lottery from the local administrative council, the board of the institution signed a contract with an organizer, called a "kollektör" (from French *collecteur*). This *kollektör*, in return for a sizeable percentage from the lottery revenue, printed lottery tickets, organized their sale, collected ticket fees and made sure that the prize money was ready to be paid before each draw by depositing the necessary

---

18   Neave, Dorina L., *Twenty-Six Years on the Bosphorus* (London: Grayson & Grayson, 1933), pp. 132–3.

19   Ahmet Rasim, *Şehir Mektupları*, ed. Nuri Akbayar (Istanbul: Oğlak, 2005), letter 21, p. 77.

20   Beyru, Rauf, *19. Yüzyılda İzmir'de Yaşam* (Istanbul: Literatür Yayınları, 2000), pp. 138–40.

sum in the Osmanlı Bankası.[21] One of the characteristics of these regular cash lotteries was that one series (*tertib*) was made up of multiple draws (*keşide*) spread over several months.

One of the most important aspects of this process was to make sure that as many tickets as possible were sold since this would increase the profit of both organizers and the institution. A successful sale operation required a network of people who would sell tickets not only in İzmir, but beyond. The main professionals selling lottery tickets were *sarraf*s, who also sold foreign lottery tickets in the empire. The main agent of the İzmir Hamidiye Sanayi Mektebi Piyangosu in Istanbul was Abram L. Papadopoulou (in French rendering Abraham L. Papadopoulo) who, among other financial transactions, "sells wholesale and retail tickets of the İzmir Sanayi Mektebi Piyangosu".[22] *Tickets* handled by Papadopoulou in Istanbul were sold by various sub-agents, who were also described as "kollektör efendiler" and whose names and the addresses of their shops were listed. These people were not only responsible for the sale of lottery tickets but also dealt with any complaints, which were to be directed to their shops.[23] Furthermore, by 1906, there were those who sold the tickets in the streets (*ayak satıcıları*), presumably like today's lottery ticket street peddlars.[24] Even well before 1906, by the beginning of the twentieth century, at least in İzmir, the lottery ticket seller (*piyangocu*) seems to have become a recognized occupation according to the *bedel-i askeri defteri* (the register of the tax paid in place of military service) for the Jewish population dated 1316 (1900). According to this registration, there was one *piyangocu* registered in Hahambaşı *mahalle* (modern Güzelyurt), a specific occupation distinct from *sarraflık* (the profession of money-changer).[25]

One of the most important parts of the lottery business was advertising both to lure customers and also to inform them about the process. Newspapers played a crucial role in the popularization of lotteries not only by providing detailed information about prizes, draw dates and those involved in the process, but also by creating trust in these lotteries because people believed that

---

21   Tunçay, *Türkiye'de Piyango Tarihi*, p. 81.

22   "İzmir Hamidiye Sanayi Mektebi Menfaatine Aid Olmak Üzere Hükümet-i Seniyenin Müsadesiyle Ayrıca Programda Gösterilen Tarihlerde Yedi Kurada Keşide Edilecek Dokuzuncu Piyangonun Talimatıdır", in Devlet Arşivleri, Osmanlı Arşivi, Istanbul [hereafter BOA], Y.PRK. MF. 5/8, p. 12, [13 Şaban 1322].

23   BOA, Y.PRK. MF. 5/8, pp. 11–12, [13 Şaban 1322].

24   BOA, BEO. 2781/208556, 20 Şubat 1321.

25   Arıkan, Zeki, "1316 (1900) Tarihli Askeri Bedel Cetveline Göre İzmir Yahudileri", in *İzmirli Olmak. Sempozyum Bildirileri 22–24 Ekim 2009* (İzmir: İzmir Büyükşehir Belediyesi, 2010), p. 306.

such lotteries could not be scams since they appeared in trusted newspapers. Apart from newspapers, agents who sold lottery tickets published individual multi-lingual booklets or handbills explaining draws, prizes, prices and the process. Papadopoulou's above-mentioned detailed multi-lingual booklet (Ottoman, French, Greek and Armenian), was prepared in order to inform and to attract customers. It explained that half of all 14,000 printed tickets would win, the price of a full ticket (*tam bilet*) was four *mecidiye*, the ticket fee was to be paid before the draw, and that those who wanted to buy lottery tickets after the first and subsequent draws, had to pay for the previous draws, too.[26]

It seems that there was a competition between the İzmir Hamidiye Sanayi Mektebi Piyangosu and the Musevi Eytam Mektebi ve Hastanesi Piyangosu. Although financially the latter was smaller and less prominent, it, too, was very popular and also sold outside the province of Aydın. The handbill printed by the main agents of this lottery in Istanbul for 1904, Devidas and Ventura, stated that the number of the tickets printed for this draw was 6,000, that one full ticket was four *mecidiye*, and that not half, as was the case with the İzmir Hamidiye Sanayi Mektebi Piyangosu, but all of the tickets would win something. The handbill gave the specific addresses of those who sold these tickets but also added that the lottery tickets would also be sold in the shops of the *sarraf*s in Galata and Istanbul.[27] Stiff competition and high profit margins forced the agents to find ways to promote the lotteries. Papadopoulou, hence, further promised that a free one-off promisary note would be given for a Rumeli Railway bond to those who bought a full Hamidiye lottery ticket at his offices.[28]

Lottery tickets themselves, however, were the main source of information. Unlike the modern national lottery (Milli Piyango) tickets in today's Turkey, the early twentieth-century Hamidiye Sanayi Mektebi Piyangosu tickets were awash with information not only about the price of the ticket (full or in part), and the date of the draw, but also about the value of all prizes, such information being provided in a variety of languages. The ticket of the İzmir Hamidiye Sanayi Mektebi Piyangosu from 15 June 1904 was in five languages, Ottoman, French, Armenian, Greek and Hebrew. Tickets could carry further information added after printing, as evidenced by the seal of the main distributer in Istanbul, Papadopoulou, and the note that it was only sold for "this draw".[29]

---

26   BOA, Y.PRK. MF. 5/8, p. 12, [13 Şaban 1322].
27   BOA, Y.PRK. DH. 13/13, [1904].
28   BOA, Y.PRK. MF. 5/8, p. 10, [13 Şaban 1322].
29   For a copy of this lottery ticket dated 2 Haziran 1320/15 June 1904, see BOA, Y. PRK. MF. 5/7.

This care to inform customers was essential as lottery tickets were not cheap. Comparing the prices for main foodstuffs in this period with lottery ticket prices gives an idea about the real value of such tickets. In 1900, one kilogramme of bread cost 1.25 *kuruş* and one kilogramme of sugar cost 2.1 *kuruş*, while in 1906, the price of bread increased to 1.50 and of sugar to 2.25 *kuruş*.[30] The price of a ticket in the İzmir Hamidiye Sanayi Mektebi Piyangosu in the ninth series (*tertib*) and third draw (*keşide*), dated 2 Haziran 1320/ 15 June 1904, was 1.5 *mecidiye* (30 *kuruş*) (although the price of the ticket was only a half *mecidiye* for those who had bought the initial tickets), and this price was only for a 1/8th ticket, a full lottery ticket costing two lira, 20 *kuruş*. Such a high price for a full ticket shows why lottery tickets were divided into smaller shares, thus making them more affordable to people from lower income brackets who would be more willing to invest their money even for small prizes. It was for this reason that there was a great deal of care to over-inform buyers through multiple channels in order to prevent any complaints. Even so, there was still the possibility of a buyer's failing to understand about the nature of the lottery, as was evidenced by the case of İsmail, who received much less prize money than he had expected as he had failed to understand the real value of his lottery ticket.

By 1904, there was a well-organized lottery sector in İzmir, which accrued a healthy financial accumulation. The December 1904 report of İbrahim Edhem Efendi, who was a member of the Meclis-i Maliye (The Financial Committee) and was sent to İzmir to inspect the İzmir Hamidiye Sanayi Mektebi Piyangosu, gives a clear picture of the financial size of this lottery from its inception to the end of the ninth *tertib*. According to this report, the total revenue of the lottery was 44,393,000 *kuruş*, of which 28,097,000 *kuruş* was spent for prizes (*ikramiye*) and *amorti* (the smallest amount of prize money paid out which equated to the value of the ticket). *Kollektör*s, here organizers, received 9,836,000 *kuruş*, while the share of the school was 6,458,750 *kuruş*.[31] But, the income of the school related to the lottery was not limited to the school's share from the total revenue. *Kollektör*s gave 243,170 *kuruş* to the school, although the nature of this transaction is not clear, and the school also won *ikramiye* and *amorti* from the tickets bought in the name of the school (the ethical nature of such purchases was not questioned by İbrahim Edhem Efendi). Another important point

---

30   Eldem, Vedat, *Osmanlı İmparatorluğu'nun İktisadi Şartları Hakkında Bir Tetkik* (Ankara: Türk Tarih Kurumu Basımevi, 1994), p. 134.

31   BOA, Y.A. HUS. 482/66, 8 Kanun-ı evvel 1320.

noted in this report was that over the years, ticket prices, the number of tickets printed and the share of the school from the lottery revenue had increased.[32]

The End of the Ottoman Provincial Cash Lotteries

The increasing monetary value of the İzmir lotteries had a downside, for it resulted in the central government becoming increasingly interested in such provincial lotteries and, indeed, İbrahim Edhem Efendi's mission was the result of the centre's decision to keep a close eye on İzmir's lotteries in general, and the Hamidiye Sanayi Mektebi Piyangosu in particular. The centre's interest eventually resulted in the sultan's wish to ban all cash lotteries in the empire. On 13 Mart 1322 (26 March 1906), Abdülhamid II issued an *irade* and ordered "the total and complete prohibition of all lotteries, whether the lottery which is created by the Ziraat Bankası for *muhacirs* [refugees, in particular here from Crete], or the lotteries created, earlier for the İzmir, Thessaloniki (Selanik) and Bursa artisanal schools (*sanayi mektepleri*) and the İzmir Jewish school (*Musevi mektebi*) and which continue today".[33] As will be explained below, although this decision would be shortly altered, the İzmir cash lotteries, together with other provincial cash lotteries, would be banned until 1909.

According to Koyuncu-Yakın, the reason behind the decision to ban the İzmir Hamidiye Sanayi Mektebi Piyangosu was connected to the coded telegraph from the grand *vezir*'s office to Kamil Paşa, which was dated 24 Kanun-ı evvel 1321 (6 January 1906).[34] This telegraph alleged that information had been received that those organizing Hamidiye Sanayi Mektebi and Yahudi Eytam Mektebi lotteries (who though not named in the telegraph were Mardoches Levy (Mordehey Levi Efendi) and Benyamin Devidas (Bünyamın Devidas Efendi)), were funding "the seditious Armenian committees and the Alliance Israélite Society" from their shares in these lotteries. Such use of money collected within the Ottoman empire, was, the telegraph noted, completely unacceptable. Added to this, the telegraph referred to the corruption within the lotteries, which had earlier prompted the order that the lotteries be organized for the benefit of the Hamidiye Hicaz Railway.[35]

---

32   BOA, Y.A. HUS. 482/66, 8 Kanun-ı evvel 1320.
33   BOA, İ. HUS. 139/109, 13 Mart 1322 and 30 Muharrem 1324.
34   Koyuncu, Gülnaz, "İzmir Sanayi Mektebi Piyangosu", *Tarih ve Toplum*, 18/107 (November 1992), p. 282.
35   BOA, BEO. 2735/205105, 24 Kanun-ı evvel 1321.

Accepting Koyuncu-Yakın's reasoning, Mete Tunçay argued that "every type of lottery including the İzmir lottery" was banned "probably due to such rumours".[36] Although Koyuncu-Yakın and Tunçay were correct that the ban was imposed because of the İzmir lotteries, their linking the ban to the allegations put forward in the telegraph sent from the grand *vezir's* office to Kamil Paşa fails to reveal the real reason behind this ban. Regardless of what was alleged in the telegraph, the actual reason was very much related to Governor Kamil Paşa himself and to the high monetary value of the İzmir lotteries, which was a factor that was used effectively against the governor by his political rivals.

In January 1903, Avlonyalı Mehmed Ferid Paşa was appointed as the grand *vezir*, replacing Said Paşa.[37] This appointment sealed not only the fate of Kamil Paşa as the governor of Aydın but also the fate of provincial lotteries under Abdülhamid II. Kamil Paşa, on many occasions, accused Ferid Paşa of being instrumental in his removal from the province of Aydın in January 1907[38] and even, according to H.A. Cumberbatch, the British consul in İzmir, "looked upon the manner of his dismissal as an act of personal vindictiveness on the part of the Grand Vizier".[39] Avlonyalı Mehmed Ferid Paşa perceived Kamil Paşa as a political rival. Although the sultan had exiled Kamil Paşa to İzmir, he continued to ask his advice about political matters,[40] even, as claimed by Kamil Paşa, offering the grand vizierate to him once more in 1903 – an occurrence heard about by Ferid Paşa – before changing his mind.[41] Perhaps this change of mind related to the fact that Kamil Paşa had never managed entirely to regain the sultan's trust as Abdülhamid had continued to be very suspicious of the *paşa's* good relations with the Europeans, especially with the British.

Ferid Paşa was not shy of using Abdülhamid II's increasing suspicion of Kamil Paşa's motives and his relations with the foreign counsels and representatives in İzmir. Abdülhamid II's Mabeyn-i Hümayun Başkatibi (the sultan's chief private secretary) Tahsin Paşa, who was not very flattering about either Kamil Paşa or Ferid Paşa, revealed Ferid Paşa's role in Kamil Paşa's removal from the governorship of Aydın:

---

36   Tunçay, *Türkiye'de Piyango Tarihi*, p. 82.

37   Kırmızı, Abdulhamit, *Avlonyalı Ferid Paşa. Bir Ömür Devlet* (Istanbul: Klasik, 2014), p. 223.

38   See for example, Kırmızı, *Avlonyalı Ferid Paşa*, p. 331.

39   From H.A. Cumberbatch, İzmir, The National Archives, London [hereafter TNA], FO 424/212, p. 29, 18 January 1907.

40   From H.A. Cumberbatch, İzmir, TNA, FO 424/212, p. 30, 18 January 1907.

41   Kırmızı, *Avlonyalı Ferid Paşa*, pp. 334–6.

While, on the one hand, Ferid Paşa, engaged in friendly correspondence with the İzmir governor Kamil Paşa, feeding him implications and innuendos about the palace, he continued, on the other, to present to the sultan suspicions about Kamil Paşa's circumstances and activities, making it inappropriate for him to remain in İzmir. The sultan was fundamentally of the same opinion. Kamil Paşa's excessive liking for the English had caused Sultan Hamid's loss of confidence [in him]. Ferid Paşa, knowing this, totally played on the sultan's views and inclinations against Kamil Paşa. In the end Sultan Hamid decided to remove Kamil Paşa from İzmir and to appoint him to a more secure location.[42]

Due to the byzantine workings of the *Babıali* of Abdülhamid II, Tahsin Paşa's accusations should perhaps be taken with a pinch of salt. According to Tevfik Bey (Biren), who succeeded Avlonyalı Ferid Paşa as the governor of Konya, Tahsin Paşa was instrumental in Ferid Paşa's appointment as the grand *vezir* since both Tahsin Paşa and Ferid Paşa were united in their hostility towards Arab İzzet Holo Paşa (Ahmad Izzet Pasha al-Abed), who was the confidant of the sultan.[43] But this short-lived pragmatic alliance did not turn into true affection. According to Ferid Paşa's son, his father disliked Tahsin Paşa so much that he nick-named him "Kara Tahsin" (Black Tahsin), not only because of his dark complexion, but also because "this man, who was fearful for his position and who had unlimited ambitions, was hostile to [my] father".[44]

Accepting Tahsin Paşa's allegations, Uzunçarşılı argued that Ferid Paşa, exploiting the *jurnal*s (reports of informers), "had not neglected to stir up Abdülhamid" against Kamil Paşa.[45] Before the appointment of Ferid Paşa as the grand *vezir*, there was already a continuous stream of *jurnal*s sent to Istanbul, by people such as the assistant governor Hasan Bey, the military commander

---

42   Tahsin Paşa, *Abdülhamit. Yıldız Hatıraları*, ed. Kudret Emiroğlu (Ankara: İmge Kitabevi, 2008), p. 150.

43   Hürmen, Fatma Rezan (ed.), *Bürokrat Tevfik Biren'in II. Abdülhamid, Meşrutiyet ve Mütareke Hatıraları*, two vols. (Istanbul: Pınar Yayınları, 2006), vol. I, p. 254.

44   Tansu, Samih Nafiz (ed.), *Madalyonun Tersi. Anlatan: Sadrazam Avlonyalı Ferid Paşa'nın Oğlu Celâleddin Paşa (Velora)* (Istanbul: Gür Kitabevi, 1970), p. 32.

45   Uzunçarşılı, İsmail Hakkı, "Sadr-ı Âzâm Kâmil Paşa'nın Siyasî Hayatı İsimli Eser Dolayısile II Abdülhamid Döneminde Kâmil Paşa", *Belleten*, 19/74 (1955), p. 212. The hostility of Avlonyalı Ferid Paşa towards Kamil Paşa was noted by Süleyman Kani İrtem, too. "Saray ve Babıâlinin İçyüzü: Kâmil Paşa'nın Izmir Ingiliz Konsoloshanesine İlticası", *Akşam*, press cutting from Taha Toros Arşivi, Dosya No: 32-Kamil Paşa'lar ve Kıbrıslı Sadrazam Kamil Paşa at http://openaccess.marmara.edu.tr/handle/11424/120957.

of the İzmir divisional army General Tevfik Paşa and the customs officer Giritli Ferid, a protégé of Tatar Şakir Paşa, one of the sultan's *aide-de-camp*s. Giritli Ferid provided information, which was personally submitted to the sultan by Tatar Şakir Paşa himself.[46] The predecessor of Ferid Paşa, Said Paşa who was another rival of Kamil Paşa, had attempted to use the allegations which appeared in such *jurnal*s to remove Kamil Paşa, but had been unsuccessful.[47] What enabled Ferid Paşa to succeed in removing Kamil Paşa was *zeistgeist*. According to one of the important legal figures of the period Necmeddin Molla (Kocataş), the period when Ferid Paşa was the grand *vezir*

> coincided exactly with the time in which, with his fears for his life and his throne, all balance and moderation in Abdülhamid's decisions and actions was disappearing. In this period informing (*jurnalcilik*) became so wide spread that occurrences of the head of a family who had led an honourable life being taken from his house in the middle of the night because of a *jurnal* and, usually without any legal investigation or action, passing several years in a police cell and being exiled to some part of Anatolia or to a desert in Africa were daily events.[48]

Although Kocataş stressed that Ferid Paşa did not sanction such exiles and even learned about them after they had happened, this did not mean that he did not effectively use *jurnal*s against Kamil Paşa.[49]

The biographer of Avlonyalı Ferid Paşa, Abdulhamit Kırmızı, stressed the role of the grand *vezir* in the removal of Kamil Paşa from Aydın, noting that "the beginning of the quarrel that ended with the dismissal of Kamil Paşa from the position of governor of Aydın at the beginning of 1907 can be dated to 1904, that is at the time when Ferid Paşa had been grand *vezir* for a year and Kamil Paşa had been the governor of Aydın for nearly nine years".[50] During this period, the allegations against Kamil Paşa had reached such a level that he was even accused of conspiracy against the state. Giritli Ferid, in one of his *jurnal*s, accused Kamil Paşa of "considering himself the khedive of the province of Aydın and of calling himself in this manner",[51] claiming in effect that

---

46   Bayur, Hilmi Kamil, *Sâdrazam Kâmil Paşa Siyasi Hayatı* (Ankara: Sanat Kitabevi, 1954), pp. 192–8; Uzunçarşılı, "Sadr-ı Âzâm Kâmil Paşa'nın Siyasî Hayatı", *passim*.

47   İnal, İbnülemin Mahmud Kemal, *Osmanlı Devrinde Son Sadrazamlar*, four vols., second edition (Istanbul: Milli Eğitim Basımevi, 1965), vol. III, p. 1380.

48   İnal, *Osmanlı Devrinde Son Sadrazamlar*, III, p. 1608.

49   İnal, *Osmanlı Devrinde Son Sadrazamlar*, III, p. 1608.

50   Kırmızı, *Avlonyalı Ferid Paşa*, p. 331.

51   Bayur, *Sâdrazam Kâmil Paşa Siyasi Hayatı*, p. 195.

he wanted to set up an autonomous government in İzmir.[52] According to Uzunçarşılı, this *jurnal* must have been effective in the centre's decision not to provide modern martini rifles to replace the old ones in the hands of gendarme who had been handicapped in their fight against bandits, since Istanbul had concerns that Kamil Paşa might use these modern weapons in order to create an autonomous region for himself. Kamil Paşa even wrote a complaint to the sultan concerning the *Babıali*'s not listening to him, and about his enemies' spreading slanderous gossip about him when he, "in this time of difficulty and confusion", was facing the continuation of the Armenian sedition, banditry and financial hardship in the province.[53]

At exactly the same time, the control of the İzmir lotteries came onto the agenda of the central government. The İzmir lotteries were significant for Kamil Paşa for they alleviated some of his financial difficulties by providing an autonomous revenue source away from the clutches of Istanbul. By 1905, the financial situation in the province of Aydın was so dire and the central government was siphoning off so much of the revenue of the province to the centre that a British consular report sent to the ambassador Sir Nicholas O'Conor stated that "all this money is remitted to Constantinople nothing being allowed to be retained for public works, such as prisons, schools, roads etc. and very little indeed for the payment of salaries which are several months in arrears. Requests made by the 'Defterdars' for grants towards such payments are taken no notice of but imperative orders for more money are received instead".[54]

This situation made the income from the lotteries essential for financing some of the public works in the province. It was for this reason that the ending of the lottery was not welcomed by Kamil Paşa who had to be ingenious in finding alternative sources of revenue for public services, as was the case in his proposal to impose taxes on the brothels of İzmir to finance a much needed syphilis hospital in the city.[55] The İzmir Hamidiye Sanayi Mektebi Piyangosu, apart from financing the school itself, became an important source of income to fund the İzmir Gureba Hastanesi.[56]

---

52   Uzunçarşılı, "II Abdülhamid Döneminde Kâmil Paşa", p. 212.

53   Uzunçarşılı, "II Abdülhamid Döneminde Kâmil Paşa", p. 212, note 9.

54   From H.A. Cumberbatch, the consul general, İzmir to Sir Nicholas O'Conor, the ambassador, Istanbul in *Smyrna and Trebizond. Received and Sent, 1905*, TNA, FO 195/2209, 28 March 1905.

55   For details see Boyar, Ebru, "Profitable prostitution: state use of immoral earnings for social benefit in the late Ottoman empire", *Bulgarian Historical Review*, 1–2 (2009), 143–57.

56   Dursun, *İzmir Hatıraları*, p. 25.

The allegations put forward in the coded telegraph mentioned above were part of an on-going smear campaign organized by various local officials and by Istanbul against Kamil Paşa whose control of sizeable autonomous lottery funds was used to increase suspicions of his political motives in the eyes of the sultan. The Alliance Israélite Universelle schools, including the one in İzmir, which in 1908, had 351 female and 312 male students,[57] did not have an antagonistic relationship with the Ottoman authorities. According to Avigdor Levy, "crucial to the successful operations of the Alliance was the attitude of the Ottoman authorities. In spite of their French orientation, the Alliance schools were set up as local community institutions, and unlike other European schools, they did not request the protection of foreign powers. Their curricula stressed modernity and Ottoman patriotism and they were seen, therefore, by the Ottoman authorities as complementing the work of the state schools".[58]

Halid Ziya Uşaklıgil, a contemporary native of İzmir, complemented the education of the Alliance school in the city and contrasted its quality of education with the local *rüştiye*, which he attended. The only criticism he levelled at the students of the Alliance Israélite Universelle school was that "there is only one thing they don't know: Turkish ... Even if they did know a little, it was the fashion not to seem to".[59] Not only Turkish, but also Judaeo-Spanish, too, was not considered highly in the Alliance schools.[60] The school, which functioned openly, survived with the support of the local Jewish community and it should therefore not be surprising to see that Levy and Devidas had assisted the school. They were, however accused of aiding Armenian terrorists, who were active in İzmir and its surroundings in that period. Given that Levy and Devidas were members of the Jewish community of İzmir which had a patriotic loyalty to the Ottoman state, this seems somewhat unlikely and the accusation was perhaps aimed more at undermining the success of Kamil Paşa and his son Said Bey in uncovering "the Armenian Dynamite Plot", as the English called it, in İzmir and Manisa in the summer of 1905. Said Bey uncovered explosives to be used for attacks on government offices including

---

57   Rodrigue, Aron, *French Jews, Turkish Jews. The Alliance Israélite Universelle and the Politics of Jewish Schooling in Turkey, 1860–1925* (Bloomington and Indianapolis: Indiana University Press, 1990), p. 91.

58   Levy, Avigdor, "Introduction", in *The Jews of the Ottoman Empire*, ed. Avigdor Levy (Princeton, N.J.: the Darwin Press, 1994), pp. 113–14.

59   Uşaklıgil, Halit Ziya, *Kırk Yıl*, ed. Nur Özmel Akın (Istanbul: Özgür, 2008), p. 160.

60   Nahum, Henri, *İzmir Yahudileri. 19.–20. Yüzyıl*, trans. Estreya Seval Vali (Istanbul: İletişim Yayınları, 2000), p. 113.

the Public Debt Administration Office and the Osmanlı Bankası.[61] After this success, Said Bey was made a *paşa* due to services rendered.[62] With the reinstatement of the provincial lotteries in 1909, Levy and Devidas continued to organize the re-named İzmir Sanayi Mektebi Piyangosu and now their names even appeared on the lottery tickets.[63] This shows that Levy and Devidas were still trusted Ottoman citizens by the then local authorities.

Of course, one should also bear in mind that not only Kamil Paşa and his son, but also Levy and Devidas might have been the targets of *jurnal*s of those who were envious of the amount of money these *kollektör*s had made from these lotteries. It was known that Kamil Paşa was not given to taking rumours and *jurnal*s seriously. According to one anecdote, Kamil Paşa had received a very detailed *jurnal* against a Jew, listing allegations about this man's many activities against the Ottoman state and *millet*. After reading this report from beginning to end, Kamil Paşa had noted at the end of the *jurnal*: "since it is impossible the said Jew would have been able to do all this, just file the document!"[64] Given that since the governor himself was thus liable to be deaf to the allegations against these two *kollektör*s, informers might have instead approached Istanbul and in this way sought to damage both the *kollektör*s and the governor.

Discrediting a Governor: Kamil Paşa and the Corruption Charges

In contrast to Abdülhamid's apparent wish to ban the lottery, Grand Vezir Avlonyalı Ferid Paşa's policy was geared towards gaining control of it and directing its profits into the central government's coffers, which were always in need of cash. At the same time, the grand *vezir* used the lottery issue to undermine Kamil Paşa's position in Aydın, gradually increasing the pressure on the governor and accusing him of exceeding his authority and even implying his involvement in corruption. It is therefore evident that what pushed Istanbul to end the local lotteries was not the corruption allegations and conspiracy theories about Armenians and Jews but its desire to seize control of these assets, as well as to further discredit Kamil Paşa.

---

61 From J.H. Monahau, İzmir to O'Conor, Istanbul, TNA, FO, 195/2209, 15 August 1905; 22 August 1905; 25 August 1905; 26 August 1905; 30 August 1905; 4 September 1905; 7 September 1905; 22 September 1905. There is also an extract from *Ahenk* about the matter and its translation into English attached to the letter dated 26 August.

62 From J.H. Monahau, İzmir to O'Conor, Istanbul, TNA, FO, 195/2209, 10 October 1905.

63 Tunçay, *Türkiye'de Piyango Tarihi*, pp. ix–x.

64 Dursun, *İzmir Hatıraları*, p. 32.

Allegations about irregularities, corruption and the misappropriation of funds related to the İzmir lotteries were not new and Abdülhamid II was well aware of such allegations since he was receiving *jurnals* from different sources. The lucrative nature of the İzmir Hamidiye Sanayi Mektebi Piyangosu was not only known to the central government but also to shrewd businessmen who were in hot pursuit of it. The local press even reported the arrival of the well-known merchant Nemlizade Hasan Tahsin Paşa in İzmir in 1317 (1901).[65] Hasan Tahsin Paşa was a member of the well-known merchant family, the Nemlizades from Trabzon. In 1893 he settled in Istanbul where he ingratiated himself with the palace. He generously contributed to the 1898 İane Sergisi and even provided money for its lottery, and, due to services rendered, was rewarded by the sultan with the bestowal of the title of *paşa*. According to Cora, "Tahsin Paşa turned his "charity" into a lucrative investment and established himself as an exemplary Ottoman entrepreneur".[66] Nemlizade Hasan Tahsin Paşa put forward a bid for the organization of the fourth *tertib* of the İzmir Hamidiye Sanayi Mektebi Piyangosu by offering that his share of the revenue be 18 per cent, three points lower than the 21 per cent offered by the Jewish organizers who had already undertaken the organization of the previous lottery. But in the end, it was not Hasan Tahsin Paşa's bid but that of the previous organizers which was accepted and they organized the fourth *tertib* of the lottery for the Sanayi Mektebi.

What is interesting here is not that there was more than one bidder for such a lucrative venture, but that a letter of complaint was sent to Yıldız Palace claiming corruption and bribery, the main culprits being Said Bey, the son of Governor Kamil Paşa, and the Vilayet Mektupçusu (the chief secretary of the province) Ahmed Bey. In this letter, which claimed that Hasan Tahsin Paşa's motive for this bid was doing "good for the school", it was alleged that from the beginning of the setting up of this lottery until the present, a consortium of Jews had taken over the running of the lottery in return for a 21 per cent share of the revenue, and "in response for this self sacrifice as an act of thanks, 400 lira have been presented by the consortium, which money was divided between the son of the protector of the province [i.e. governor] Said Bey and Vilayet Mektupçusu Ahmed Bey". Therefore, in order not to lose this 'gift', Said Bey and Ahmed Bey did everything possible to prevent Hasan Tahsin

---

65   *Ahenk*, 2 Mayıs 1317 (15 May 1901), quoted in Koyuncu, "İzmir Sanayi Mektebi Piyangosu", p. 280.

66   Cora, Yaşar Tolga, "a Muslim great merchant [*tüccar*] family in the late Ottoman empire: a case study of Nemlizades, 1860–1930", *International Journal of Turkish Studies*, 19/1–2 (2013), pp. 16–17, the quotation is from p. 17.

Paşa from winning the bid.[67] Although the pious nature of Nemlizade Hasan Tahsin Paşa was questionable, he was, without doubt, a cunning businessman in pursuit of profit and obviously saw the great money-making potential of the İzmir Hamidiye Sanayi Mektebi Piyangosu. In 1905, he succeeded in becoming the organizer of the Bursa Sanayi Mektebi Piyangosu (Bursa Artisanal School Lottery),[68] which was among the local lotteries cancelled by the sultan's order a year later.

In 1900, a year before Nemlizade Hasan Tahsin Paşa's failed bid for the lottery, another letter was sent to Yıldız Palace accusing Said Bey of unsavoury dealings including obtaining bribes from brothels in Kordonboyu, and, in particular, his use of the İzmir Hamidiye Sanayi Mektebi Piyangosu for his own personal gain. According to this letter, which also claimed that the İzmir government was in the hands of the son of the governor, Said Bey, in cooperation with the school's honourary president (*nazır-ı fahri*) Ahmed Esad Efendi, embezzled 10,000 lira of the 60,000 lira of ticket sales. This, according to the letter, was common knowledge among the entire population of İzmir for "it circulated in the mouths of all the people".[69] It later transpired that neither Said Bey nor Ahmed Esad Efendi was investigated, and it was only in 1902 that Ahmed Esad was accused by the provincial administration of embezzlement of the school lottery funds and removed from his position.[70]

Such allegations about Said Bey were not uncommon. Indeed, Said Bey was Kamil Paşa's Achilles heel. Kamil Paşa's local and Istanbul opponents continuously brought forward allegations about Said Bey's ill doings to undermine the governor's position and prestige. In May 1904, Grand Vezir Ferid Paşa complained to the sultan about Said Bey's "participation" in the governing of the province.[71] Two years later, in September 1906, he took aim at Kamil Paşa's age and his son and son-in-law. Noting that Kamil Paşa was nearly 80, an advanced age at which one needed to take care, he drew attention to "the extension of the hand of interference" into the government of the province and "the procuring of illegitimate interests" by those around him, including his son Said Bey, now Paşa, and his son-in-law Faik Paşa.[72] Furthermore, Said Bey was accused of receiving bribes from Çakırcalı Mehmed Efe, the legendary bandit in the

67   BOA, Y.PRK. AZJ. 43/6, 28 Eylül 1317.

68   Cora, "a Muslim great merchant [*tüccar*] family in the late Ottoman empire", p. 19.

69   BOA, Y.PRK. AZJ. 41/16, 23 Teşrin-i evvel 1316.

70   Özeçoğlu, Halil, "Modernleşme Sürecinde İzmir'de Müslim ve Gayrimüslimlerin Eğitimine Karşılaştırmalı Bir Yaklaşım (1856–1908)", Ph.D. Dissertation, Dokuz Eylül Üniversitesi, İzmir, 2009, pp. 139–40.

71   Kırmızı, *Avlonyalı Ferid Paşa*, p. 332.

72   Quoted in Kırmızı, *Avlonyalı Ferid Paşa*, pp. 333–4.

province of Aydın, resulting in Kamil Paşa's failure effectively to strive to sub-
due Çakırcalı. This allegation was used as the strongest pretext for removing
Kamil Paşa from his post.[73] These allegations were even published in European
newspapers, and according to Koloğlu, "those who knew Abdülhamid's sen-
sitivities about the European press, once more began to use them for their
own interests".[74] While Kamil Paşa vehemently denied such allegations,[75] Said
Bey pointed out that the reasons for failing to capture Çakırcalı were the old
rifles used by the gendarme, and the assistance given by those who abetted
the bandits. He further accused Commander Tevfik Paşa of not taking his job
seriously but instead using all his energy to undermine Kamil Paşa due to his
"personal jealousy".[76]

Even the British developed an aversion to Said Bey, despite the fact that Kamil
Paşa was a good thing for the British. His pro-English reputation was very well-
known. The dragoman of the British embassy in Istanbul, G.H. Fitzmaurice
called him: "English Kiamil", alluding to Kamil Paşa's reputation among the
Ottomans.[77] In 1909, French Ambassador Jules Cambon, commenting on the
character of Kamil Paşa, who was then grand *vezir* for the third time, did not
miss his Anglophile predilection, describing him as "a very upright man, but
old, imperious, obstinate and anglophile".[78] Even after his death, the British
remembered him as a great friend of Britain. The governor of Cyprus, Ronald
Storrs, who restored Kamil Paşa's grave remembered him at the opening cere-
mony for the newly-restored grave in 1927 as "a fervent and utterly enlightened
patriot and a stalwart and enlightened friend of England".[79]

The bad reputation of his son Said Bey, however, was not lost on the
British. Describing Said Bey as the "favourite son" of Kamil Paşa, who had
22 children,[80] the British consul general in İzmir, Cumberbatch, reported to the

73   Bayur, *Sâdrazam Kâmil Paşa Siyasi Hayatı*, pp. 199–211; İnal, *Son Sadrazamlar*, III, p. 1381.

74   Koloğlu, Orhan, *Avrupa'nın Kıskacında Abdülhamit* (Istanbul: İletişim Yayınları, 2005),
      p. 305.

75   Bayur, *Sâdrazam Kâmil Paşa Siyasi Hayatı*, p. 208.

76   Quoted from Said Bey's notes by his brother Hilmi Kamil Bayur in *Sâdrazam Kâmil Paşa
      Siyasi Hayatı*, p. 205.

77   Gooch, G.P. and Harold Temperley (eds.), *British Documents on the Origins of the War
      1898–1914. Vol. V the Near East, the Macedonian Problem and the Annexation of Bosnia
      1903–9* (London, 1928, reprinted by London: Johnson Reprint Company, 1967), p. 270.

78   From M. Jules Cambon, French ambassador in Berlin to M. Pichon, the minister of foreign
      affairs, 7 January 1909, in *Documents diplomatiques français (1871–1914), tome XI (15 Mai
      1907–8 Février 1909)* (Paris: Imprimerie Nationale Alfred Costes, 1950), p. 1019.

79   Quoted in Özoran, Beria Remzi, "Sadrazam Kâmil Paşa- İngiliz Dostları- Kıbrıs'taki
      Mezarı", *Türk Kültürü*, 105/9 (1971), p. 761.

80   Bayur, Hilmi Kamil, "Osmanlı İmparatorluğunda 4 Defa Sadrazam Olan Kıbrıslı Kâmil
      Paşa'nın Özel Hayatı", p. 48, note 1, at Taha Toros Arşivi, Dosya No: 32-Kamil Paşa'lar ve
      Kıbrıslı Sadrazam Kamil Paşa, at http://openaccess.marmara.edu.tr/handle/11424/120957.

British ambassador O'Conor in Istanbul that: "It is alleged, I think truthfully, that every official in the civil service has to make some contribution towards his private income if he wishes to maintain his post, whilst on the other hand anyone needing assistance, whether for good or evil, has recourse to Said Bey's powerful 'protection' which has its price".[81] Cumberbatch's not very flattering view of Said Bey was no secret. Although more restrained in his official report about Kamil Paşa's taking refuge in the British consulate,[82] Cumberbatch was not as restrained in talking to the legendary Gertrude Bell, whom he met in İzmir in April of 1907. According to Bell's diary entry, while "Kiamil was an excellent Vali and very pro English", his son was not very much liked: "Kiamil has a son, Said Pasha, who was born the same day as Burhan ed Din and has been treated as his foster brother and given every rank which he received. This young man is a rogue, weak and in bad hands; he was used as a spy against his father by the Palace Clique".[83] This "Palace Clique", led by Ferid Paşa was seen as responsible for the operation against Kamil Paşa and, by implication, Bell accused Said Bey of conspiring against his own father. All this information could only have come from Cumberbatch, who could have liberally passed on the rumours about Kamil Paşa and his son to Bell in an informal environment.

This attitude to Said Bey became a part of the British official trope. After Kamil Paşa's removal from the office of governorship, a British report, commenting on Kamil Paşa's services in the province of Aydın, revealed the reason for the British dislike of Said Bey:

> His administration of this important province during the past eleven years has been consistently creditable, the only blemish upon it being the misplaced confidence which he appears to repose in his son Said and his son-in-law Faik Pasha, both of whom are corrupt and unscrupulous to the last degree. The former, who is nominally in the navy, attained the rank of Bear-Admiral, with the title of Pasha, on account of the activity which he displayed in connection with the discovery of bombs at Smyrna in August 1905. He is also one of the principal agents of the Palace in the conduct of the Pan-Islamic and anti-English agitation in Egypt.[84]

---

81   From H.A. Cumberbatch, the consul general, İzmir to Sir Nicholas O'Conor, the ambassador, Istanbul in *Smyrna and Trebizond. Received and Sent*, 1905, TNA, FO 195/2209, 28 March 1905. For another reference about the bad reputation of Said Bey, see from J.H. Monahua, İzmir to O'Conor, Istanbul, TNA, FO 195/2209, 22 August 1905.

82   From H.A. Cumberbatch, İzmir, TNA, FO 424/212, p. 29, 18 January 1907.

83   *Diaries*, 2/4/1907, available at http://gertrudebell.ncl.ac.uk/diary_details.php?diary _id=513.

84   Gooch and Temperley, *British Documents on the Origins of the War 1898–1914. Vol. V the Near East*, p. 20.

Obviously, this portrait of Said Bey was not accepted by all the British. In handling the Armenian plot in 1905, according to Monahau, the British acting consul general at that time, "Said Bey's evil reputation is referred to in Mr. Consul General Cumberbatch's despatch number 15 of March 28 1905 but I have not heard of him or any other Turkish officials having been guilty of malpractices such as extortion in this matter".[85] But the bad reputation of Said Bey still lingered in the British minds. In 1909, Edward Grey, who was the British foreign secretary, wrote to G. Lowther, about his contrasting feelings about Kamil Paşa and his son: "I liked Kiamil, because he seemed to me a man of character and honesty, and a fine old fellow, though by all accounts his son appears to be a scoundrel".[86] Aubrey Herbert, who shared this sentiment, described newly-resurrected Grand Vezir Kamil Paşa in 1909 as "the liberal, the anglophile, who had been photographed with King Edward (his chief asset in Turkey) and the father of rascal Said" who "was made Grand Vizier to propitiate Great Britain. He was a friend of the Embassy, and in Turkey he was credited with no power of action apart from Fitzmaurice".[87]

Corruption allegations and irregularities, however, were not limited to Said Bey's ill doings and the İzmir Hamidiye Sanayi Mektebi Piyangosu, for such allegations were also directed at other charitable lotteries organized especially by non-Muslim communities in the city. For instance, on 22 Şubat 1318 (7 March 1903), Minister of Internal Affairs Mehmed Memduh Paşa sent a coded telegraph to the province of Aydın enquiring about the lottery organized by the Greek community to fund the building of the "Aya Katerina" Church. The ministry learned about this venture from the hand-bills (ilan varakaları) which arrived at the post office, a strategic location kept under very strict surveillance by the ministry of internal affairs. Memduh Paşa asked officials in the province of Aydın whether this lottery was organized in accordance with "the customary official authorisation". The reply of the provincial government to this question revealed that these cash lotteries could be not only financial ventures open to corruption but could also lead to splits and rifts among the various religious communities and the society in general. A commission made up entirely of the members of the Greek community had organized this lottery for 12 years to build the "Aya Katerina" Church. However, "since it would have been possible to build several churches with the money collected from the draws of

85   From J.H. Monahau, İzmir to O'Conor, Istanbul, TNA, FO, 195/2209, 10 October 1905.
86   Gooch and Temperley, *British Documents on the Origins of the War 1898–1914, Vol. V The Near East*. p. 319.
87   Herbert, Aubrey, *Ben Kendim. A Record of Eastern Travel*, ed. Desmond MacCarthy (London: Hutchinson & Co., 1924), p. 271.

the lottery which had taken place in the 12-year period [in which it had been going], the continuation of the lottery made no sense and it had therefore been stopped for the last four years".[88]

The concern related to this lottery was not only limited to the fact that the money collected for the purpose of building a church should have been more than sufficient. There was also a rumour among the Greek community, which reached the ears of the Ottoman local government, that 8,000 lira from the revenue of the lottery had gone "missing" before the recent Ottoman-Greek War. Although this "missing" money created an uproar among the Greeks, they did not officially bring this to the attention of the local government. No official inspection, therefore, was conducted into the matter. Due to the questionable past of the lottery, once the local government learned that the tickets of this lottery had been sent to other provinces to be sold, contrary to the existing ban, it requested other provinces to get hold of these tickets and destroy them, arrested the members of lottery commission and sent all revenue and expense accounts of the lottery (from its inception) to the police for inspection. All these measures were not, however, sufficient for the Aydın provincial government. The person held responsible for this affair, not directly but because he had lost control of his flock, was the bishop of İzmir, Basileios (active between 1885 and 1910), who spent his entire time in Istanbul as he was a member of the Holy Synod. The provincial government wanted the patriarch to replace the bishop with somebody who would be worthy of the respect of both the Ottoman government and the Greek community.[89]

What changed with Ferid Paşa's becoming the grand *vezir* and taking active interest in the workings of the İzmir lotteries was that the central government now directly pursued such corruption allegations targeting not individuals or religious communities, but the provincial governor, Kamil Paşa, himself. According to Biren, putting financial pressure on and sending inspectors to the provinces of which the governors were his political rivals was Ferid Paşa's *modus operandi*. Biren, who was one of the three governors Ferid Paşa had targeted, the other two being Kamil Paşa and the governor of Beirut Halil Bey, claimed that one of his acquittances in Istanbul had informed him that Ferid Paşa had striven to persuade the sultan to remove these three from their posts to no avail. In the end, he had used the "issue of financial hardship", the issue which bothered the sultan the most, and had persuaded him to send financial inspection committees, whose members had been selected personally by the grand *vezir*, to the provinces to make sure that they would send "the amount

88   BOA, Y.EE. KP. 18/1749, 25 Şubat 1318 and 12 Zilhicce 1320.
89   BOA, Y.EE. KP. 18/1749, 25 Şubat 1318 and 12 Zilhicce 1320.

of money necessary to the centre".[90] Ferid Paşa had used the lottery issue with the same strategy in mind.

On 25 Mart 1320 (7 April 1904), Grand Vezir Ferid Paşa asked the minister of internal affairs to provide information for the investigation conducted by Şura-i Devlet (the Council of State) about "the corruption in the collection and expenditure of the revenues of the lottery which had been drawn for the benefit of the general revenues of the İzmir [Hamidiye] Sanayi Mektebi and the activities of the school", an allegation which was brought to the attention of the government by the investigation commission of the Cezair-i Bahr-i Sefid province. The reason why the grand *vezir* asked for this information was related to the fact that the aforementioned school was "directly" under the administration of the province of Aydın and hence under the jurisdiction of the ministry of internal affairs.[91] The ministry of internal affairs was, however, reluctant to conduct any investigation to obtain the information requested by the grand *vezir*. Using rather convulsed language, the ministry claimed that it could not conduct such an investigation and that *Şura-i Devlet* should do it itself.[92] This rejection by the ministry of internal affairs cannot be explained by any financial or other incapacity of the ministry's, as claimed in the response, but should be read as Minister of Internal Affairs Memduh Paşa's rejection of being a part of Ferid Paşa's ploy against Kamil Paşa, as Memduh Paşa himself, too, was a political rival of Ferid Paşa about whom he was busy complaining to the sultan.[93]

This investigation was nevertheless conducted during the 10th *tertib* of the lottery and, on an imperial order, the above-mentioned İbrahim Edhem Efendi, was sent to İzmir to check the finances of the İzmir Hamidiye Sanayi Mektebi Piyangosu and to write a report about his findings. This appointment was even announced by the local İzmir newspaper *Ahenk*.[94] The grand *vezir*, in his letter to the palace, summarized İbrahim Edhem Efendi's report providing not only the financial figures but also his own personal views about the malfunctioning of the lottery, not because İbrahim Edhem Efendi accused anybody directly of corruption but because he commented on the spending of the money of the school, on how the school's share was not high enough and claimed that "the money that formed the greatest part of the general revenue of the lottery" served "the interests of the *kollektör*s rather than those of the school". İbrahim Edhem Efendi then suggested that in order to increase

90   Hürmen, *Bürokrat Tevfik Biren'in II. Abdülhamid, Meşrutiyet ve Mütareke Hatıraları*, I, pp. 288–9.
91   BOA, DH. MKT. 843/54, 25 Mart 1320 and 20 Muharrem 1322.
92   BOA, DH. MKT. 843/54, 8 Nisan 1320 and 3 Safer 1322.
93   Kırmızı, *Avlonyalı Ferid Paşa*, pp. 349–55.
94   Koyuncu, "İzmir Piyangosu", p. 281.

the school's share, decrease the control of *kollektörs* and capitalize on the high popular interest in this lottery, an interest which he described as "an extremely strong demonstration of demand", felt not only among the people of İzmir and its surroundings but also by the foreigners, an organising committee should be established which would control the operation, and would thus decrease the responsibilities of *kollektörs* whose position would then be no more than ticket sellers. This would increase the school share of the lottery revenue which could then also be used to sponsor the development of other artisanal schools in the empire and even to finance building new ones. Since the lottery's income would be used outside the province of Aydın, "the inhabitants of other provinces too would participate in the purchasing of tickets".[95] Although İbrahim Edhem Efendi's report did not implicate anybody directly, it provided sufficient ammunition to be used by Ferid Paşa against Kamil Paşa and the İzmir Hamidiye Sanayi Mektebi Piyangosu. Ferid Paşa made no comment at the end of his letter apart from noting that this report was the result of an "impartial investigation".[96]

In May 1905, there was yet another lottery investigation. This time the target was the lottery regularly organized for the benefit of the İzmir Musevi Eytam Mektebi ve Hastanesi. As can be construed from a series of documents from Governor Kamil Paşa, Minister of Internal Affairs Memduh Paşa and the Şura-i Devlet Tanzimat Dairesi, the main question was whether the provincial government of Aydın had exceeded its authority. The ministry of internal affairs had received correspondence from the province of Adana enquiring about the authority of the province of Aydın. A Jew living in Mersin, whose identity was not disclosed to the ministry of internal affairs, had published a handbill (*ilanat*) about the "lottery with seven draws" organized for the benefit of the İzmir Musevi Eytam Mektebi ve Hastanesi. The provincial government of Adana, which had obtained a copy of this handbill, enquired whether the tickets of this lottery, which was organized with official permission from the province of Aydın, could be sold outside the boundaries of the Aydın province. The ministry of trade and public works added another question to this investigation and asked whether the province of Aydın had exceeded its authority by issuing a permit for the organization of a lottery exceeding 50,000 *kuruş*.[97] According to the decision taken by the Şura-i Devlet Tanzimat Dairesi in 1883, permits for lotteries with a value up to 50,000 *kuruş* were to be issued by the local governments while those for lotteries for any figure higher than

---

95   BOA, Y.A. HUS. 482/66, 8 Kanun-ı evvel 1320 and 14 Şevval 1322.
96   BOA, Y.A. HUS. 482/66, 8 Kanun-ı evvel 1320 and 14 Şevval 1322.
97   BOA, ŞD. 2748/47, 20 Mayıs 1321 and 8 Rebiülahir 1323.

50,000 *kuruş* should be issued by the ministry of trade and public works, i.e. the central government.[98] According to the allegations, the Meclis-i İdare-i Vilayet (the administrative council of the province) of Aydın had issued a permit for a lottery valued at 50,000 *kuruş*, while tickets printed for this lottery were worth around 30,000 lira.[99]

The response to these allegations came from Kamil Paşa. While Kamil Paşa did not comment on whether tickets for the lottery could be sold outside his province or not, as this was not the question directed to him but to the central government as underlined by Memduh Paşa in his letter to the grand *vezir*,[100] he set out to prove that the province did not exceed its authority by issuing a permit for a lottery over 50,000 *kuruş*. As explained by Kamil Paşa, the permit for this lottery issued by the Meclis-i İdare-i Vilayet did not exceed the 50,000 *kuruş* rule. For this lottery, 3,000 tickets were printed and 65 per cent of the income to be accrued from the sale of these tickets was allocated as *amorti* and *ikramiye* to those whose numbers were drawn, 25 per cent was to be paid to sellers and the remaining ten per cent was to be used to cover the printing expenses of tickets, the stamp fee of the Public Debt Administration and 500 lira to be paid to the Hamidiye Hicaz Railway. Once all these expenses were extracted, the remainder would provide only 50,000 *kuruş* for each establishment since from previous experience, only half of the tickets would in fact be sold.[101] Persuaded by Kamil Paşa's response, the Şura-i Devlet Tanzimat Dairesi decided that indeed the Meclis-i İdare-i Vilayet's permit did not breach the legal requirement.[102]

Regardless of all these failed attempts by Istanbul to uncover Kamil Paşa's alleged ill doings, in the end, on 8 Teşrin-i evvel 1321 (21 October 1905), utilising an *irade*, the palace moved to direct control of both the Hamidiye Sanayi Mektebi and Musevi Eytam Mektebi lotteries in İzmir. The reason for this manoeuvre was explained as being due to the fact that since the lottery was for the benefit of the İzmir Hamidiye Sanayi Mektebi and the Musevi Eytam Mektebi, its drawing, the total amount of money obtained and the reason for and the manner of the expenditure were all "unknown to the centre". Using this as a pretext, Istanbul sought to take control of these two lucrative ventures. Accordingly, the sultan wanted stamps of 40 *para* to be attached to the tickets for the "benefit of the illustrious line", i.e., the building of Hamidiye

---

98   Tunçay, *Türkiye'de Piyango Tarihi*, p. 51.
99   BOA, ŞD. 2748/47, 13 Haziran 1321 and 22 Rebiülahir 1323.
100   BOA, ŞD. 2748/47, 13 Haziran 1321 and 22 Rebiülahir 1323.
101   BOA, ŞD. 2748/47, 11 Mayıs 1321.
102   BOA, ŞD. 2748/47, 13 Haziran 1321 and 22 Rebiülahir 1323.

Hicaz Railway, the expenses of which were on the increase. The profit from the draws would be transferred to the office for the financial management of the line, a new financial administration which was set up under the auspices of the ministry of trade and public works on 15 Haziran 1319 (28 June 1903), once "the genuine expenses" of the two schools and the Gureba Hastanesi had been ascertained.[103]

The reference to "the genuine expenses" was a clear indication of the centre's distrust of the declared needs of these schools and the Gureba Hastanesi. By doing so, these two big İzmir lotteries were, in essence, turned into lotteries for the benefit of the Hamidiye Hicaz Railway, an enterprise described by *Servet-i Fünun* as "the greatest work of charity",[104] the funding of which was a substantial burden for the Ottoman economy. The government strove to fund the project with domestic resources, of which public donations, voluntary or involuntary, formed a large part. According to Kamil Paşa, the 12th *tertib* of the İzmir Hamidiye Sanayi Mektebi Piyangosu, the first draw of which was to be held on 15 Şubat 1321 (28 February 1906) was organized "for the benefit of the Hicaz Railway".[105] Apparently, the lottery income was not small. According to an undated financial table from an official publication on the Hicaz Railway dated 1324, the income accrued from the lottery tickets for the railway was 103,375 *kuruş* and two *para*.[106]

Obviously, Istanbul was not satisfied with simply controlling the schools' share of these two big and regular İzmir lotteries but wanted to control them totally. This was what lay behind the addition of allegations of sedition against Levy and Devidas to the already existing allegations about the misuse of the funds accrued from the lotteries in the document dated 24 Kanun-ı evvel 1321 referred by both Koyuncu-Yakın and Tunçay. The allegations about misuse of these funds had already become the pretext for the transfer of the lottery funds to the coffers of the Hamidiye Hicaz Railway. As revealed by İbrahim Edhem Efendi's inspection report, the volume of the İzmir Hamidiye Sanayi Mektebi Piyangosu was such that, in a period of increasing financial pressure from Istanbul on the province of Aydın together with the sultan's increasing distrust of Kamil Paşa, it was not easy for the centre to ignore. In its dire need of cash, Istanbul's eyes drifted to the İzmir lotteries and it used corruption, irregularity and political conspiracy charges as pretexts to take direct control of all revenue accrued from the lotteries. It can hardly be a coincidence therefore,

---

103   BOA, İ. HUS. 134/80, 8 Teşrin-i evvel 1321 and 22 Safer 1323.

104   Quoted in Boyar and Fleet, *A Social History of Ottoman Istanbul*, p. 288.

105   BOA, Y.EE. KP. 27/2676, 14 Şubat 1321.

106   *Hicaz Demiryolu Lahiyası* (Dersaadet: Servçin Matbaası, 1324), [table IV].

that a couple weeks after these serious accusations against Levy and Devidas, the Ziraat Bankası Piyangosu (the Lottery of the Agricultural Bank) was set up, with the permission of the sultan, with the declared intention of financing the settlement of refugees.[107] According to the regulation (*nizamname*) dated 12 Kanun-ı sani 1321 (25 January 1906), this lottery was based in Istanbul and was to be organized by a committee made up of representatives of the Ziraat Bankası, the Osmanlı Bankası, the ministry of finance and the Divan-ı Muhasebat (today's Sayıştay, the audit office).[108]

Once the Ziraat Bankası Piyangosu was established, the grand *vezir's* office created a pretext for banning İzmir and other cash lotteries in the empire, according to which the Ziraat Bankası Piyangosu was a "general lottery", that is empire-wide, and so "there was no longer any need for other lotteries".[109] The grand *vezir's* office immediately ordered both the province of Aydın and the lottery *kollektörs* to stop the draws. Obliged to accept the pretext that there was no space for another "general" lottery, the ministry of trade and public works wanted at least the completion of the ongoing lotteries, the revenues of which were to be transferred to the Hamidiye Hicaz Railway project. The reason for this request was related not only to the fact that the completion of these lotteries was "indispensable" for the financing of the railway but also to the fact that it was necessary to maintain "the respect and trust of the population".[110]

Oblivious to these points, two days later, a letter sent from the grand *vezir's* office to the province of Aydın and the ministry of trade and public works on 8 Şubat 1321, clearly stated that the setting up of the Ziraat Bankası Piyangosu, described as "a general lottery", obviated the need for any other lottery. The grand *vezir* thus ordered the provincial government and the ministry that "henceforth no drawing of the lottery was to be permitted". The only exception to this order was that the first draw of the 12th *tertib* of the İzmir Hamidiye Sanayi Mektebi Piyangosu that was scheduled for the 15th of Şubat 1321 would be held. Specifically written for the İzmir Hamidiye Sanayi Mektebi Piyangosu and the Musevi Eytam Mektebi ve Hastanesi Piyangosu, this order specified that the ongoing Musevi Eytam Mektebi ve Hastanesi Piyangosu of which three out of seven draws had been already held, was to be halted, too. The order also made the point that the end of the Hamidiye Sanayi Mektebi Piyangosu would not harm either the school itself or the Gureba Hastanesi, for

---

107   BOA, BEO. 2782/208610, 6 Şubat 1321 and 25 Zilhicce 1323.

108   Tunçay, *Türkiye'de Piyango Tarihi*, p. 99.

109   BOA, BEO. 2766/207389, 8 Şubat 1321 and 27 Zilhicce 1323; BOA, BEO. 2782/208610, 6 Şubat 1321 and 25 Zilhicce 1323.

110   BOA, BEO. 2782/208610, 6 Şubat 1321 and 25 Zilhicce 1323.

while the former had income from rents accrued from the properties bought with the lottery money, the later had sufficient funds to survive.[111] The school did indeed have a substantial number of moveable and immoveable properties including three boats bought in 1904.[112] Before totally banning the İzmir lotteries, the grand *vezir* had already been busy hindering ticket sales. On 1 Şubat 1321 (14 February 1906), the grand *vezir*'s office urged the ministry of the trade and public works to ban the sale of lottery tickets of the İzmir Sanayi Mektebi and Yahudi Mektebi in the province of Hüdavendigar,[113] which already had its own cash lottery organized for the benefit of the Bursa Sanayi Mektebi by Nemlizade Hasan Tahsin Paşa.

Kamil Paşa wrote a letter to the grand *vezir* on 14 Şubat 1321 (27 February 1906), in which he carefully failed to engage with the 8th of Şubat order of the grand *vezir*. After noting that the first draw of the İzmir Hamidiye Mektebi Piyangosu would happen the next day, he mentioned that a rumour had reached his ears that Istanbul might ban it. Unable to object to the decision to impose a total ban, the governor tried to persuade Istanbul to postpone the announcement of the ban of the İzmir Hamidiye Sanayi Mektebi Piyangosu, the 12th *tertib* of which was for the benefit of the Hicaz Railway and which, according to the timetable which had been announced, was to be drawn the next day. Claiming that the immediate implementation of this ban would harm the populace – i.e. those lottery ticket holders who had bought tickets as they had already been in circulation, as well as those who were involved in the organization and sale of tickets –, he argued that it would result in a considerable loss of revenue of c. 5000 lira for the Hamidiye Hicaz Railway and would damage the Ziraat Bankası Piyangosu.[114] Although Istanbul did not stop the first draw which was to be held on 15 Şubat 1321, the remaining draws were terminated.

Kamil Paşa persisted and continued to appeal to the grand *vezir*. A few days later, the governor officially replied to the order of the grand *vezir* dated 8 Şubat. At the beginning of his reply, Kamil Paşa countered the somewhat scathing remarks of the grand *vezir*'s office about the more than sufficient funds of the İzmir Hamidiye Sanayi Mektebi and the Gureba Hastanesi by pointing out the difference between the conditions of the İzmir Hamidiye Sanayi Mektebi and the Gureba Hastanesi now and their conditions six or seven years ago,

111   BOA, BEO. 2766/207389, 8 Şubat 1321 and 27 Zilhicce 1323.
112   Özeçoğlu, "Modernleşme Sürecinde İzmir'de Müslim ve Gayrimüslimlerin Eğitimine Karşılaştırmalı Bir Yaklaşım (1856–1908)", pp. 136–7.
113   BOA, BEO. 2761/207024, 1 Şubat 1321 and 20 Zilhicce 1323.
114   BOA, Y.EE. KP. 27/2676, 14 Şubat 1321.

conditions which had improved enormously thanks to the lottery. After listing the material cost of this ban, he requested that the grand *vezir* either ban
it before its first draw was held or postpone the ban until the completion of
the whole *tertib*.[115] Kamil Paşa's appeal was a little odd considering that the
first draw of the 12th *tertib* had been already held, so in reality, Kamil Paşa
wanted to force the grand *vezir*'s hand to adopt the second option, i.e. to postpone the ban until the end of the 12th *tertib*. A day later, Kamil Paşa appealed
to the ministry of trade and public works, which had direct legal authority over
the lottery organizations, by pointing out the financial damage that would be
caused by the decision of the immediate ban of the İzmir Hamidiye Sanayi
Mektebi Piyangosu.[116] The ministry, which was already in favour of at least the
completion of the ongoing lotteries, once more wrote to the grand *vezir*'s office
repeating Kamil Paşa's appeal and his reasoning,[117] but the grand *vezir* was ada-
mant and on 2 Mart 1322 (15 March 1906) he replied to the ministry's appeal
repeating the original order that after the first draw of the Hamidiye Sanayi
Mektebi Piyangosu on 15 Şubat, this lottery was to be prohibited as was that for
the Musevi Eytam Mektebi, and instructed the ministry to repeat this order to
Kamil Paşa.[118] The İzmir lotteries thus came to an end with this final order and
Istanbul took full control of this lucrative Anatolian financial venture.

Before the ink was dry on the instructions sent to the ministry of trade and
public works, a day later, on 3 Mart 1322 (16 March 1906) Abdülhamid II, however, set out to ban all lotteries, including the Ziraat Bankası Piyangosu. The
sultan ordered Meclis-i Mahsusa-i Vükela, the council of ministers headed by
Grand Vezir Ferid Paşa, to conduct a discussion with the aim of "agreeing the
adopting of a decision by the state with the object of banning the lotteries".
The order drew attention to the "noteworthy" fact that the drawing of lotteries was in essence illegitimate, "as is known", the people were being duped,
there was unacceptable behaviour in İzmir and other regions in relation to
this activity, and that a significant number of documents related to the lottery
was in the possession of one person.[119] Considering that Abdülhamid II was
the sultan who had legalized the lottery and had even become a patron of the
1898–99 İane Sergisi Piyangosu, his moral reasoning here sounds both belated
and insincere. As the İzmir lotteries had already been terminated, the second
reason, too, looks questionable. What seems clear, however, is that the sultan

---

115   BOA, BEO. 2781/208556, 20 Şubat 1321.
116   BOA, BEO. 2781/208556, 21 Şubat 1321.
117   BOA, BEO. 2781/208556, 23 Şubat 1321 and 12 Muharrem 1324.
118   BOA, BEO. 2781/208556, 2 Mart 1322 and 19 Muharrem 1324.
119   BOA, İ. HUS. 139/69, 3 Mart 1322 and 20 Muharrem 1324.

was over-worked on by the grand *vezir* and others concerning the nature of cash lotteries, in particular those in İzmir. This, thus, produced a response in excess of what they had wanted: the removal of Kamil Paşa's financial resource in the form of the lottery, now banned, and the control by Istanbul of the lottery in general, not the outright ban of all lotteries which the sultan was now moving to.

Upon receiving this order, the grand *vezir*'s office wrote an addendum to the above-mentioned *tezkere* sent on 2 Mart 1322 to the ministry of trade and public works. Although the *tezkere* started with the full reiteration of the sultan's *irade* of 3rd of Mart, the grand *vezir*, in essence, ignoring the sultan's order for a total ban, stressed the existence of the Ziraat Bankası Piyangosu for the settlement of refugees, which thus did away with the need for the Musevi Eytam Mektebi and Hamidiye Sanayi Mektebi lotteries and asked the ministry to warn the provincial government of Aydın to ensure that the Hicaz Railway share from the İzmir Hamidiye Sanayi Mektebi Piyangosu was transferred to the financial administration of the railway.[120] The grand *vezir*, in essence, had manipulated Abdülhamid II's order to ensure the full obedience of the ministry of trade and public works which was unhappy about the banning of the İzmir lotteries before the completion of their ongoing *tertib*s. On 12 Mart 1322 (25 March 1906), the end of the İzmir lotteries was made public in a news item published in *Ahenk* which stated that "it has been officially announced that the lotteries organized for our city's Hamidiye Sanayi Mektebi and the Jewish orphanage and hospital will be abolished and henceforth there will be no drawing of the aforementioned lotteries".[121] Nevertheless, the sultan, apparently, was not pleased with Ferid Paşa's partial ban on cash lotteries, keeping the Ziraat Bankası Piyangosu exempt, and insisted on a ban of all empire-wide cash lotteries as stipulated in his *irade* of 13 Mart 1322 (26 Mart 1906).[122]

Persuading the Sultan: Istanbul's Need for Cash

As a reaction to the sultan's insistence, the Meclis-i Mahsusa-i Vükela requested the sultan to reconsider his decision to impose a total ban. The council praised the sultan's *irade* banning the lotteries of İzmir, Thessaloniki and Bursa, describing the sultan's decision as "entirely wise and sound". But, at the same time, the council subtly pointed out that the lotteries of İzmir and Thessaloniki,

---

120   BOA, BEO. 2782/208610, 4 Mart 1322 and 21 Muharrem 1324.
121   Quoted in Koyuncu, "İzmir Sanayi Mektebi Piyangosu", p. 281.
122   BOA, İ. HUS. 139/109, 13 Mart 1322 and 30 Muharrem 1324.

which were initially organized for charitable purposes, had already been banned due to corruption, while the lottery in Bursa had too been banned earlier. The objection of the council was, thus, about the banning of the Ziraat Bankası Piyangosu organized for the benefit of refugees. Already put in motion, tickets for this lottery had been printed and sold in the capital and the provinces. This ban, hence, would, both cause loss to those buying the tickets and hinder the settlement of refugees as there was no other way of meeting the expenses of settling them. Furthermore, there was a foreseeable danger that the lack of a domestic lottery would encourage Ottoman subjects to buy foreign lottery tickets.[123]

The authorities had already been trying to fend off the foreign lottery threat in the empire by preventing the sale of foreign lottery tickets. The grand *vezir*'s office, for example, sent a coded telegram to the province of Aydın on 24 Ağustos 1320 (6 September 1904) urging the governor to take every precaution to prevent the sale of tickets for the lottery which was organized in support of the finances of the Greek national navy and which the Greek foreign ministry encouraged Greeks living in the Ottoman empire to buy. While the Ottoman Greek population's providing charitable donations for schools and churches was acceptable, its providing funds for the strengthening of the naval force of a foreign country was not. Thus, given that this activity was contrary to the political and economic interests of the Ottoman state, the governor of Aydın was ordered to prevent the sale.[124] In a similar vein, the minister of internal affairs, Memduh Paşa, had earlier warned Kamil Paşa about the circulation of a sizeable number of tickets of a lottery organized in support of the Greek army and navy and asked him not to allow the sale of such tickets.[125] The question of foreign lotteries was sometimes further complicated by the involvement of foreign subjects and Ottoman authorities had to deal with foreign embassies and consulates in their pursuit of forbidden foreign lottery tickets. On 7 February 1907, the *mutasarrıf* of Beyoğlu, Hamdi Bey, wrote in Italian and Ottoman to ask the Italian consulate to send an official from the consulate to be present while Ottoman authorities opened a safe belonging to an Italian subject, Guiseppe Matalon, who was employed in stock market business and shared an office in Galata (69 in Hubar Han) with a German subject, Baruch, who was in possession of foreign lottery tickets the circulation of which was forbidden in the Ottoman empire. In the Italian version of the letter, the *mutasarrıf* made the reason for this search clear, for he referred to "having

---

123   BOA, İ. TNF. 15/14, 19 Mart 1322 and 7 Safer 1324.
124   BOA, Y.EE. KP. 22/2158, 24 Ağustos 1320.
125   BOA, Y.EE. KP. 24/2311, 2 Şubat 1320.

now learnt that there are other similar tickets in the safe of the Italian subject Giuseppe Matalon".[126]

All in all, having a domestic cash lottery had its advantages for the Ottoman empire, advantages of which the sultan now needed to be persuaded. Assuring the sultan that the "methods of execution" of the lottery organized by the Ziraat Bankası were not open to abuse, the Meclis-i Mahsusa-i Vükela requested the sultan to allow the continuation and completion of at least the ongoing *tertib* of the Ziraat Bankası Piyangosu.[127] On 28 March 1322 (10 April 1906), the sultan revised his order for a total ban, adding a marginal note to the grand *vezir's* cover letter for the Meclis-i Mahsusu Vükela's report and allowed the continuation of the Ziraaat Bankası Piyangosu,[128] which was organized regularly until 1909 as the only nation-wide legal cash lottery held in the empire.

Grand Vezir Avlonyalı Ferid Paşa's desire was not to ban all cash lotteries, but to use the dubious practices concerning the İzmir lotteries against Kamil Paşa as ammunition in his operation to remove him from Aydın, and also to move control of lottery operations from the provinces to Istanbul. The wisdom of this move was made clear as people, driven along by "man's refusal to accept the conclusion of mathematical proof",[129] as the British novelist Evelyn Waugh was to put it in 1930 referring to the casino at Monte Carlo, continued to play the lottery and to provide cash for the government coffers.

---

126   İstanbul Büyükşehir Belediyesi (İBB) Atatürk Kitaplığı, Istanbul, Bel_Mtf_046721, 23 Kanun-ı sani 1322, 22 Zilhicce 1324, and 5 February 1907.

127   BOA, İ. TNF. 15/14, 19 Mart 1322 and 7 Safer 1324.

128   BOA, İ. TNF. 15/14, 19 Mart 1322 and 7 Safer 1324 and the date of the marginal note is 28 Mart 1322 and 16 Safer 1324.

129   Waugh, Evelyn, *Labels. A Mediterranean Journal* (London: Penguin Books, 2011), p. 42.

CHAPTER 9

The Fabric of *Nizam*: Uncertainty and the Activation of Economic Norms in Nineteenth-Century Provincial Contexts

Marc Aymes

Economic dealings rely, in one way or another, on an ordering scheme of things. That is because the economy literally means the need to put one's house in order, to bring *nomos* to reign over the *oikos*. Thus, it implies some kind of 'embeddedness' of economic activities into hierarchies of value that are topics of consensus and conflict.

This, in a nutshell, is what 'political economy' is about. Several contributors to this volume (and to the conference upon which the volume is based) mentioned it in turn. But as the chapters show, Ottoman historians have been opting for highly heterogeneous approaches to the topic. While some foreground the assessment of revenues and supplies, others, including the present author, highlight issues of regulation and knowledge – what one may also call the activation of economic norms.

Be this as it may, the economy is not only about order: it is also framed at least as much by the occurrence of uncertainty – whenever an incident causes the *nomos* to become defective and the *oikos* to stand idle. Studying the various techniques which undergird economic settlements therefore involves close examination of the ways in which they may be found wanting.

The present chapter aims to situate this conundrum of uncertainty and the activation of economic norms in nineteenth-century Ottoman provincial contexts. Starting in the 1820s, the Ottoman state developed procedures of control over production and trade that entailed the deployment of regulations of all sorts. Still the "Tanzimat economy experience", as Donald Quataert once put it, could also be seen as "one of compromise, incorporating innovation but retaining much of the earlier methods of agricultural and industrial production".[1] Such an "experience" hence allowed for the coexistence of several normative or practical patterns of economic regulation.

---

1 Quataert, Donald, "Main problems of the economy during the Tanzimat period", in *150. Yılında Tanzimat*, ed. Hakkı Dursun Yıldız (Ankara: Türk Tarih Kurumu Basımevi, 1992), p. 214.

Let us try and explore some of these ambivalent patterns of economic regulation that seem to have prevailed at the time. As amply illustrated elsewhere in this volume, today's approaches to the social and economic history of the Ottoman empire greatly differ from what garnered consensus some decades ago.[2] Meticulous scholarship applied to an ever-growing diversity of sources has changed our understanding of the Ottoman 'political economy'. More specifically, since the indexing of documents from the Ottoman ministry of finance still goes on in Istanbul, a critical reshuffle of our ways to approach the empire's last and 'longest century' is to be expected in the near future. Yet the cumulative growth of available data should not deter scholars from close reading at length, for even a few documents among those (we think) we already know can make a difference. Hence the methodological commitment adopted in the following pages: no more than two different files from the Ottoman archives held in Istanbul will be examined. One relates to an early Tanzimat affair; the other to an end-of-century case. This wide interval of time may incidentally help us question the chronological modes of uncertainty management that have been ruling supreme among professional historians.

Trust in a *Nizam* Nowhere to Be Found

This idea of order and reorganisation
is an old one within the Ottoman state;
it has to do with custom law.[3]

Whenever Ottoman regulators meant to speak of their business, they referred to *nizam*. To historians of the nineteenth century this almost automatically involves dealing with the Tanzimat, i.e. the vast body of regulatory "reorganisations" undertaken by the Ottoman administrative elites from the 1840s onwards. Classic scholarly accounts of the Tanzimat have identified them with top-down reform aiming at the centralisation and standardisation of imperial policies.[4] Yet in economic matters Tanzimat endeavours unfolded (starting from the Anglo-Ottoman Convention of 1838) with the Ottoman authorities

---

2 Cf. *V. Milletlerarası Türkiye Sosyal ve İktisat Tarihi Kongresi: Tebliğler. Marmara Üniversitesi Türkiyat Araştırma ve Uygulama Merkezi, İstanbul 21–25 Ağustos 1989* (Ankara: Türk Tarih Kurumu Basımevi, 1990).

3 İnalcık, Halil, "Sened-i İttifak ve Gülhane Hatt-ı Hümâyûnu", *Belleten*, 28/112 (1964), p. 617: "Bu nizam ve tanzim fikri Osmanlı devletinde örfi hukuka bağlı eski bir fikirdir".

4 A condensed formulation is to be found in Karpat, Kemal, "The transformation of the Ottoman state, 1789–1908", *International Journal of Middle East Studies*, 3/3 (1972), especially

moving towards the easing of trade restrictions. So in a seemingly paradoxical way the urge to "reorganise" went hand in hand with *laissez-faire laissez-passer* policies. One may think of these as two distinct realms: top-down order in the state administration on the one hand; bottom-up *laissez-faire* in the economy on the other. What then about occurrences of *nizam* that had precisely to do with the organisation of economic activities?

Such is the case in the document that we are about to quote at length, a petition (*arzuhal*) dated late 1845–early 1846 and signed by several cloth printers (*basmacı*) from Cyprus.[5] I will now provide a tentative translation of the text, interspersed with notes and comments.

Petition

> Excellency my fortunate, graceful and abundantly compassionate master and sultan, may he be strong with fortune and felicity!
>
> This is the petition of your humble slaves: being part of the cloth-printing trade of the island of Cyprus we spent years working as apprentice and assistant craftsmen. Then after five, ten or fifteen years each of us managed, under His Royal Excellency's favour-dispensing aegis, to become masters. We know all about the art of cloth-printing. We own our workshops and shops. We buy the fabric; we print on demand. And so your humble slaves have always earned enough, be it from owners of merchandise or from the sales of products, to maintain their wives and children.

This first part of the petition is thus devoted to stressing how much compliant with the rules of their craft the signatories have been. Quoting how long it took them to become their own masters, in particular, comes as an apposite way to assert the legitimacy of their achievements: in short, it aims to impart political value to economic success. Indeed, their insistence that they "spent years" as

---

pp. 251–6. For a more recent account of related scholarship see Köksal, Yonca, "Tanzimat ve Tarih Yazımı", *Doğu-Batı*, 51 (2010), pp. 197–220.

5   Devlet Arşivleri, Osmanlı Arşivi, Istanbul [hereafter BOA], A.}DVN. 14/16, late 1261/early 1262 (late 1845/early 1846). See pp. 221–4 for facsimiles and a full-text transliteration of the petition along with its marginal annotations. For a study on craftsmen's petitions before the nineteenth century see Faroqhi, Suraiya, "Guildsmen complain to the sultan: artisans' disputes and the Ottoman administration in the 18th century", in *Legitimizing the Order: The Ottoman Rhetoric of State Power*, ed. Hakan Karateke and Maurus Reinkowski (Leiden: Brill, 2005), pp. 177–93.

subaltern trainees (*öteden-berü*) purposefully quotes a cornerstone argument of the Ottoman traditionalist repertoire of power.[6] The Cypriot cloth printers hence make their claims depend on the activation of norms that aim to dispel uncertainty not only in the realms of trade but also, more fundamentally, for the sake of maintaining socio-political order.[7]

After aptly providing its readers with such value-laden background information, the petitioners set about presenting their case itself:

> Now, rich and prominent members of the trade come up saying: "the cloth printing business is ours, we will not let you print merchandise from other people". Their attempted unfair meddling and interference contradicts the custom of the place and contravenes the benevolent rules of the reorganisations. As a result, this situation has caused wrong.

As it turns out the case revolves around a quite common kind of argument: members of the same trade contend for control over output and yields. Neither does the petitioners' plea take any unexpected path:

> Our hopes rest on His Excellency's sublime acts of kindness: our supplication is that an illustrious order from His Grand Vizierial Excellency, including an insert about the prohibition of monopolies, be written and sent to the council of the locality and other requisite addressees, along with your servants, the trade's *şeyh* and the country's canonical counsel, so as to prevent and forbid the ongoing intrusions of those [aforesaid] people. In this matter the order and decree belong to His Excellency whence benevolence proceeds.

Confronted with the attempted monopolisation of their business by some of the *esnaf*'s commanding figures, the petitioners again point to the activation of norms both economic and political: their supplication actually argues for the

---

6 Aymes, Marc, *"Un grand progrès – sur le papier". Histoire provinciale des réformes ottomanes à Chypre au XIXᵉ siècle* (Paris, Louvain and Walpole, MA.: Peeters, 2010), pp. 40–51. On 'traditionalism' as a constituent of the Ottoman political economy see Genç, Mehmet, *Osmanlı İmparatorluğunda Devlet ve Ekonomi* (Istanbul: Ötüken, 2000).

7 See İnalcık, Halil, "Şikâyet Hakkı: 'Arz-ı hâl ve 'Arz-ı mahzarlar", *Osmanlı Araştırmaları*, 7–8 (1988), 33–54; Avcı, Yasemin, Vincent Lemire and Ömür Yazıcı Özdemir, "Collective petitions ('arż-ı maḥżar) as a reflective archival source for Jerusalem's networks of citadinité in the late 19th century", in *Ordinary Jerusalem 1840–1940: Opening New Archives, Revisiting a Global City*, ed. Angelos Dalachanis and Vincent Lemire (Leiden: Brill, 2018), pp. 161–85.

mere implementation of whatever anti-trust measures the Ottoman government had agreed to legalise earlier on.[8] The text thus bespeaks the petitioners'
keen awareness that rules previously ingrained in *esnaf* organisations, such as
holding a shop by patent or warrant (*gedik*), were now being subsumed under
the "kind of monopoly" general heading.[9] The express wish that "an insert
about the prohibition of monopolies" ("inhisar maddesinin memnu'iyeti
derci") be attached to the besought order shows the Cypriot cloth printers'
familiarity with the paper procedures that accompanied newly issued regulations at the time. This up-to-date knowledge works as an instrument to impart
a sense of certainty to their case, and eventually better support their claims.

Follow-ups

Beside the text of the petition is a series of annotations flanked by paraphs
and signatures (*pençe*). Although not systematically dated they outline the
document's travels from one office clerk to the other in Istanbul.[10] These
"follow-ups" (*mu'amelat*) lasted for a week or so, and were committed to paper
in chronological order, top to bottom and continuing on the back side. Their
careful reading makes it possible to better understand how the Ottoman officials interpreted the petitioners' request, how they sought to provide it with a
satisfactory answer – and how, eventually, the norms firmly counted upon by
the provincial cloth printers proved more elusive than expected among the
Porte's *nizam* enforcers.

The first question prompted by the reception of the petition was basic to
the point of being intriguing: "Is there any kind of *nizam* in there? Let this be
enquired from the imperial council". Clearly then, the preliminary search for
a *nizam* of some sort appeared requisite before the Ottoman authorities could

---

8   On the revocation of trade monopolies see for instance BOA, HAT. 382/20601, 29 Zilhicce
       1255 (4 March 1840).
9   Cf. BOA, A.}M. 2/57, 29 Zilhicce 1261 (29 December 1845): "Gedik maddesinin mazarr-ı
       tazammünisi bir nev'-i inhisar dimek olub bu ise şer'en ve kanunen tacviz olunur mev-
       addan olmadığına ve inhisardan kurtarılarak [...]". On *gedik* see Faroqhi, Suraiya, "The
       fieldglass and the magnifying lens: Ottoman studies of crafts and craftsmen", *The Journal
       of European Economic History*, 20/1 (1991), 29–57; Akarlı, Engin Deniz, "Gedik: A bundle of
       rights and obligations for Istanbul artisans and traders, 1750–1840", in *Law, Anthropology
       and the Constitution of the Social: Making Persons and Things*, ed. Alain Pottage and Martha
       Mundy (Cambridge and New York: Cambridge University Press, 2004), pp. 166–200.
10   Cf. İnalcık, Halil, "Osmanlı Bürokrasisinde Aklâm ve Muamelât", *Osmanlı Araştırmaları*, 1
       (1980), 1–14.

take any tentative steps to meet the petitioners' expectations. Immediately underneath this energetic query, one or several pens – a careful handwriting followed by more harshly drawn final words – recorded the answer, including a stipulation of where to look next:

> No *nizam* whatsoever is to be found on this matter in the Imperial Council's records. To begin with a check from the accounts of expenses and revenues would be needed. Once His fortunate Excellency shall be cognizant thereof, the order shall belong to my illustrious Sultan.

So the quest for *nizam* began. As per the aforesaid recommendation the petition was forwarded to the ministry of finance: "Let the situation and requisite be enquired from the accounts of expenses and revenues. 7 M[uharrem] [1]262 [5 January 1846]". The sought-after *nizam* might, one seemed to hope, be couched in figures as well as in legal terms. Norms could therefore be uncovered by excavating the recesses of financial registers. This attempt nevertheless proved of little avail:

> Upon transmission of the accounts records of expenses no explicit entry whatsoever could be retrieved regarding the said matter. As per the commanding order pertaining thereto information ought to be extracted from the accounts records of revenues. Annotations could also be requested from the accounts of mortmain estates and government annuities. In this matter the order shall belong to His Excellency my illustrious and generous Sultan. On 15 Muharrem 1262 [13 January 1846].

A clerk in charge of the accounts books of revenues took over, with no more fruitful results:

> Regarding the requested matter, no explicit reference to a *nizam* whatsoever could be found in the accounts of revenues either. The order shall belong to His Excellency my illustrious and generous master. On 17 M[uharrem] 1262 [15 January 1846].

"Let the situation be enquired from the registries of mortmain estates and government annuities", a quick pen added in the right-hand margin. Maybe these, as the clerks at the accounts office of expenses had dared suggest, could come up to the expected positive outcome. Although this seemed to be a promising idea at first, eventually the answer was a clear "no" again:

Records of the noble decrees regarding the trade *nizam* of the cloth printers based in Istanbul and Üsküdar do appear in the accounts registers
of mortmain estates; yet based on the wording of the petition no record
has been found regarding the trade *nizam* of the cloth printers in Cyprus.
The order shall belong to His Excellency my illustrious master. On 22
M[uharrem] 1262 [20 January 1846].

This note differs from the others on at least two accounts, thus providing significant additions to our understanding of the case. First, it shows what ratio-
nale had been behind the string of annotations all along. Ottoman officials
looking for *nizam* were not acting on a mere hunch: such a set of rules did exist
somewhere, namely among "the cloth printers based in Istanbul and Üsküdar",
and they had been duly registered. The only difficulty was to find where. But
sooner or later this record would be located, and based on that expected discovery, the Sublime Porte clerks contemplated an exercise in extrapolation: if
such rules were in force by the Bosphorus, a similar framework might exist in
Cyprus as well.

Yet here the mortmain estates clerk provides us with a second crucial piece
of information: *nizam*, he contended, is not something to extrapolate from; it
is a local rule, and shall remain so. In itself this contention is remarkable: other
clerks from the Ottoman administration, as the document makes amply apparent, were content simply to get through the register-trawling routine without
daring to comment on its premise nor to cast doubt on its outcome. By contrast, the annotating clerk turned this register-centred philology on its head:
he argued that one should not extrapolate from records found in the *defter*s,
but rather make one's conclusions rest on "the wording of the petition" itself
("ber mantuk-ı 'arzuhal"). In short, he claimed, there is no better source than
local informants. And since those most directly affected by the matter at hand
did not explicitly mention any kind of *nizam* to support their plea, one could
doubt the relevance of the search for *nizam* in the first place. As per this logical
empiricist stance, no explicit reference to *nizam* means no *nizam* at all.

A fellow clerk from the registry of government annuities nevertheless rep-
licated the ordered search logic with all due docility. It comes as little surprise
that he came to similarly inconclusive results:

Upon transmission of the accounts records of government annuities
one found no explicit entry whatsoever regarding the said *nizam*. The
order shall belong to His Excellency my illustrious and generous Sultan.
On 26 Muharrem 1262 [24 January 1846].

The search for registered records hence came to an end. Yet annotations continued on the back. The main, longer one was – judging by the handwriting (with harshly drawn final words) and *pençe* – from the same official who at the imperial council had sent the petition out for circulation in the first place. Now that the document finally came back to him, he drafted a full recap of the case.[11]

Recap and Recommendation
First comes a summary of the petition itself:

> The petitioners are part of the cloth-printing trade of the island of Cyprus. Each and every one of them have become past masters in the aforesaid craft. It has been quite a long time since they managed to handle their duty and craft to perfection. They are no immature practitioners. And in this way their aforesaid trade has always earned them enough to maintain their wives and children. Yet some in the trade told them: "we won't let you", and tried to prevent them from practising. Based on this explanation the purport of the petition consists of a supplication that an illustrious order from His Excellency prevent and forbid this.

To be sure, this summarising procedure was regulation in the Ottoman chancery at the time. Yet here this (not so) short abstract also signified a manifest departure from the call to rely on "the wording of the petition" emphasised above. Thus, as a comparison of the two successive annotations makes clear, summarising actually involved a great deal of paraphrasing, which brought about a significant shift from precise "wording" ("mantuk") to more general "purport" ("me'al").

This shift also showed in the annotation's following section. Drawing on the little information collected so far, it provided the reader with a series of questions piling up all the conjectures accumulated on this case:

> Why are the petitioners being prevented from practising in this way? Is it because of their immaturity? Is it because of some kind of *nizam* amongst them, based on certain customs of the place, which the petitioners

---

11   A mention in the top left-hand corner on the back of the document refers to the intervention, on 10 Muharrem 1262, of a palace servant called "the coffee master Mehmed Ağa" ("hademeden ser-kahve Mehmed Ağa fi 10 M 62"). His exact involvement in the follow-up process remains to be ascertained at this point.

contravened? Or is it because some people among them have been ran-
corous and spiteful?

Here again, reference to "the purport of the petition" left much room for para-
phrase and interpretation. While the petitioners had chosen to complain
about a situation that, in their own words, "contradict[ed] the custom of the
place and contravene[d] the benevolent rules of the reorganisations", the final
summary hypothesised about regulations that they themselves might have
breached. More importantly perhaps: whereas the petitioners appealed to
tanzimat along with "the custom of the place", the final summary conjectured
about *nizam* by affixing it to that very custom, thus corroborating the view
(explicitly held by another Sublime Porte official above) that *nizam* could not
but stem from local usage. The "reorderings" of rule notwithstanding, "order"
was expected to remain local through and through.[12]

This commitment to local knowledge also permeated the recommendation
added at the end of the annotation:

> The matter shall be investigated in due course by the [local] council,
> in the presence of the warden and foreman of the aforesaid trade and
> of other tradesmen, then communicated in writing by means of round
> robin and judicial report to the royal abode of imperial majesty. Let it
> be contingent on His Highness's views to have this request for informa-
> tion finely written in an illustrious order. Once His fortunate Excellency
> shall be cognizant thereof, the order shall belong to my illustrious Sultan.
> On 28 Muharrem 262 [26 January 1846].

Such was indeed the outcome of these lengthy consultations: "Request for
information to be written accordingly". It all ended (as far as this document
is concerned) with the Istanbul authorities asking locals for additional spe-
cifics, as per their understanding of *nizam* as local ruling. Ironically perhaps,
while their search for *nizam* aimed to rein in uncertainty, this uncertainty
management rested on local information – hence, on the provincial diffrac-
tion thereof. Trust in *nizam* somehow ended up enhancing uncertainty rather
than curtailing it.

---

12   For further references to *nizam* as locality-based in earlier contexts see Bağış, Ali İhsan,
      *Osmanlı Ticaretinde Gayri Müslimler: Kapitülasyonlar – Avrupa Tüccarları – Beratlı
      Tüccarlar – Hayriye Tüccarları* (1750–1839) (Ankara: Turhan Kitabevi, 1983), p. 42. Cf.
      Philliou, Christine, "Mischief in the old regime: provincial dragomans and social change
      at the turn of the nineteenth century", *New Perspectives on Turkey*, 25 (2001), 103–21.

Normalised at Last? Liquid Samples and the Provincial 'Predicament'

A document alone, however close the reading might be, remains a 'local' arte-fact, and seldom tells a general rule. Common scholarly wisdom knows better how to crystallise generalisations. Often this involves emphasising the proces-sual quality of history. Chronological thinking, abhorrence of anachronism, are the primary hallmarks of this generalisation pattern. By this standard oper-ating procedure, suffice it to say that the Cypriot petition dated back to the early years of the Tanzimat period. In other words, the case took place at the very beginning of the Ottoman path to modernity. Later on, one may add, the "well-protected" and "well-connected" domains followed a historical course that synchronised with that of other European polities.[13] The late nineteenth century could thus be presumed to better match the bureaucratic ideal-type of tighter centralisation and enhanced standardisation. At long last the uncer-tainty management techniques of Ottoman authorities may thus have ceased to rely on the local iridescence of *nizam*.

The methodology adopted in this chapter therefore needs further elabora-tion. Discreet close reading may not significantly affect established generalisa-tions. What will be of use is close reading in combination with cross-reading. Let us for instance consider a report dated 1894, sent by the Ottoman com-missioner for duties and taxes (*Rüsumat Emini*) to the ministry of the Interior (*Dahiliye Nezareti*). By sheer chronological standards, we could reasonably expect the reordering effect of decades of centralisation to make itself clearly felt. When superimposed on the mid-century petition, though, it provides a slightly different view from that bird's eye chronology, one that departs from its implicit linearity. What this reading causes, in sum, is more uncertainty.

The first half of the report should be read as a compilation of previous cor-respondence, all duly paraphrased by the present clerk:

> Excellency my fortuned Lord,
>   It has been decided that Trieste rums and Agia Mavra wines shall, on arrival, be inspected, and treated in the light of the reports drawn up about their purity. The illustrious Governorate-General of Ioannina has

---

13   See Deringil, Selim, *The Well-Protected Domains: Ideology and the Legitimation of Power in the Ottoman Empire* (London: I.B. Tauris, 1998); Firges, Pascal, Tobias Graf, Christian Roth and Gülay Tulasoğlu (eds.), *Well Connected Domains: Towards an Entangled Ottoman History* (Leiden: Brill, 2014).

however informed the Preveza Directorate of Duties and Taxes that due to a lack of analysis instruments this decision was difficult to implement, and consequently samples would be sent to the Threshold of Felicity to be analysed there by the [School of] Medicine.

Such is the purport of the Ioannina governor's recommendation, and at first the centralisation-cum-standardisation scenario seems to fully play out here: because of defective technical means at the provincial level, the task of checking and analysing imported rums and wines should be a job for the Sublime Porte.

And yet the commissioner for duties and taxes begged to differ. Such a course of action, he pointed out, would bring about more problems than it actually aimed to solve:

> In a memorandum dated May 9 of the year 1307, my humble Commission informed the illustrious Ministry of Your Grand Vizierial Excellency of the resultant predicament, setting out in detail the measures required to be rid of it. The said memorandum noted that wine from Agia Mavra reached Preveza by sailing ship. But from the time when a sample is sent by the abovementioned Directorate to the [School of] Medicine, and the information about its purity is sent back, nearly a year passes. The boat cannot remain immobilized for so long. It was thus agreed that this way of conducting inspections would not be authorized.

In a nutshell, sailing to Istanbul with the liquid samples on board, then waiting for the analyses to be delivered, would be a waste of time. (One may here conjecture that the *emin* skirted round other issues such as the preservation of the product itself.) A surest way hence was to reach out to the local authorities so as to "learn" (*ögrenilüb*) what they had been up to:

> The memorandum indicated that, under these conditions, a request for information had been sent out to the Directorates for Duties and Taxes, to establish the promptest way to handle the matter. The idea was to learn from the local authorities how they managed to carry out inspection operations of liquids known to reach them so as to put an end to this sort of predicament. In the light of their responses, it was established that, in all places, it is the municipal doctors who carry out the business of inspection, and that Customs rely on their reports in carrying out procedures. In İzmir however, given the particular importance of the task and the fact that no chemist is available, the work of inspection cannot be freed from these predicaments and amalgamations.

Local knowledge and decision-making thus ruled supreme. Even in a port-city as large as İzmir, where tighter government supervision would have been expected, it lacked the means to implement a coordinated inspection policy.

The author of the document then proceeded to add a further layer to his compilation of reports. In so doing he explicated the more specific circum-stances and the political background that made this situation become a matter of concern in the first place:

> Under the terms of the sublime memorandum presently received from the illustrious Ministry of the Exterior, dated 23 Kanun-i ṣani of the year 1309, the Greek Embassy stated that Greek wines transported from the Seven Islands to the Governorate-General of Ioannina were refused import. The embassy called for this ban to be lifted, arguing that it con-travened the clauses of agreements concluded and the interests of trade. As the said memorandum ordered to take the necessary steps in this mat-ter, in response it was reported and related that the ban in question did not apply absolutely but concerned wines which, on inspection, were clearly shown to be noxious. Predicaments may arise during this inspec-tion, and supposing that such gave rise to the present complaint, it would be natural to inform His sublime Grand Vizierial Excellency, so that the necessary steps be taken for the said predicaments to be shortly removed.

As could be expected from the foreign affairs services, key to the argument here was the concern not to ruffle any Greek feathers, with care taken not only over "the interests of trade" ("menafi'-i ticariye") but also over "agreements concluded" ("mu'ahedat"). When stating that "the ban in question did not apply absolutely" ("memnu'iyet-i mebhusin 'anha suret-i mutlakada mevzu' olmayub"), the Ottoman commissioner was careful to stress that it was, in other words, not an embargo to be applied for political reasons. This somewhat specious argument could ultimately be considered a matter of normalization: there was nothing specific to the Greek merchandise, the report basically argued, import inspection was a standard measure. Yet since the ban applied to specific products on inspection, its implementation could not solely rely on top-down blanket norms, and had to remain a local measure to be taken on a case-by-case basis:

> Given this situation, the proper functioning of affairs requires that local authorities attach supplementary importance to inspection operations. They shall be careful and attentive via the intermediary of municipal doctors as to how well these are conducted and supervised. In the event that certain are not convinced by the doctor's report, and call for an

inspection of samples by the [School of] Medicine, these shall be sent to my humble Commission by the local Directorate of Duties and Taxes. The cost of the analysis fees shall be appended, to be paid solely by the owners [of the merchandise]. In large cities such as İzmir where the presence of a chemist is required, particular care shall be taken to find the means to do so.

Supposing that this is consistent with Your ministerially protective Excellency's sublime decree, the requisite descriptions shall be duly sent out to the local authorities. The decision taken should be ordered and communicated to your humble servant so that the customs administrations may also be informed. Such is the request, following the declaration to the Committee for Taxation, audaciously submitted. On this subject the order and decree belong to His Excellency who is the fount of authority. 19 Şevval [1]311 and 13 Nisan 1310.

Quoting this piece in full makes the difficulty of reading tangible. The matter treated was recounted in snatches, against a backdrop of platitudes. Its convoluted phraseology notwithstanding, the compilation of reports gathered here brings to light the concrete traces left by the standardization, or at least harmonization, of the Ottoman administration's practical formalities. We could, in a sense, speak of a certain "centralization of knowledge".[14] But we should not therefore deduce that the Sublime Porte had become the dream bureaucracy of some compact and unified rational-legal elite. Though centralized, government knowledge was still disseminated across multiple lower-level networks of knowledge and recommendations. Only in the event of "predicaments" or disputed findings were appeals to be addressed to Istanbul. But in the general (and generic) case, it was up to the local authorities to monitor ongoing inspections. So what we find here again is a quintessentially provincial procedure. Uncertainty management relied on patterns both devolved and scattered, in a manner very much similar to that of *nizam* earlier on.

Close Reading and the Longue Durée of Historical Thinking

"Order" is no abstract concept: it shows in practice; it relies on implementation. The use of such wording may itself lend credence to an understanding

---

14   Hanssen, Jens, "Practices of integration – center-periphery relations in the Ottoman empire", in *The Empire in the City: Arab Provincial Capitals in the Late Ottoman Empire*, ed. Jens Hanssen, Thomas Philipp and Stefan Weber (Beirut: Ergon Verlag, 2002), p. 64.

long dominant in Ottoman studies when approaching nineteenth-century contexts, one that viewed *nizam* as a top-down pattern and *tanzimat* as a linear, inexorable process. Yet the two documents analysed in this chapter point to a different understanding: each occurrence of *nizam* relied on what one may call a "trial of explicitness", namely "a situation in which uncertainty arises about the agency of parties at stake, a situation which calls for a collective investigation in order to settle the state of affairs", and which therefore interweaves institutional, technical and diplomatic issues.[15] Even though such trials did not always develop in full view, still the close analysis of available sources may help highlight how uncertainty participated in the ordering of economic regulation, i.e. both the design of norms and their activation.[16] This regulation thus appears 'deconcentrated' into multiple provincial processes and devices of uncertainty management, all through the end of the 'long' nineteenth century.

Historical scholarship too has its explicitness trials. By way of conclusion, let us carry out yet another close reading experiment, based on two exemplary sets related to the matter at hand: *nizam* and *tanzimat* as modes of uncertainty management. Our first set includes the "*tanzīmāt*" entry in the *Encyclopaedia of Islam*'s second edition as a key reference. While the time of actual writing may have predated the year of publication, and although the author's *magnum opus* on *Reform in the Ottoman Empire* was published at a much earlier date, still it remains striking that this later account of *tanzimat* scholarship persisted in identifying "the general nature of the reform period" with "the effort to strengthen the central government and to increase its control over the provinces".[17] This was, moreover, no isolated occurrence: later encyclopaedic endeavours quietly relayed the deep conviction that "reforms allowed the Ottoman state to have greater control over its own provinces with greater administrative efficiency, technological capability, and international legitimacy".[18] More importantly still, such assertions bear no little resemblance to views published some 40 years earlier, such as the following:

---

15   Muniesa, Fabian and Dominique Linhardt, "Trials of explicitness in the implementation of public management reform", *Critical Perspectives on Accounting*, 22/6 (2011), p. 551.

16   Stanziani, Alessandro, *Histoire de la qualité alimentaire (XIXᵉ–XXᵉ siècle)* (Paris: Seuil, 2005), p. 15. See Levi, Giovanni, *Inheriting Power: the Story of an Exorcist* (Chicago: University of Chicago Press, 1988).

17   Davison, Roderic H., "Tanẓīmāt", *The Encyclopaedia of Islam*, 2nd ed., ed. P. Bearman, Th. Bianquis, C.E. Bosworth, E. van Donzel and W.P. Heinrichs (Leiden: Brill, 1960–2006), vol. X (2000), pp. 201–2. See Davison, Roderic H., *Reform in the Ottoman Empire 1856–1876* (Princeton: Princeton University Press, 1963).

18   Aydın, Cemil, "Reform", in *Encyclopedia of the Ottoman Empire*, ed. Gábor Ágoston and Bruce Masters (New York: Facts on File, 2009), p. 485.

The whole assumption of the *Tanzimat* was that reform meant codifi-
cation, systematization, and control, even in those areas where actual
reforms were not needed. [...] The local autonomy allowed in the old system was replaced by central regulations applied more and more in all
parts of the empire regardless of local conditions.[19]

Late-1960s modernisation theories of *tanzimat* thus carried over, as it were,
to early-twenty-first-century historiography. Regardless of the chronologies
of scholarship, *nizam* continued to be viewed as a pattern of regulation that
aimed at "autocracy and centralization".[20]

Our second set implies a quite different understanding of how the Tanzimat
related to uncertainty management and local knowledge. On the one hand
is yet another encyclopaedic entry devoted to the Tanzimat, whose conclud-
ing remarks start as follows: "From a general perspective one may say that
the Tanzimat reforms were not so much planned and programmed as aimed
to meet practical needs".[21] On the other hand is an analysis, published 50
years earlier, of what prompted nineteenth-century Ottoman leaders such as
Mustafa Reşid Paşa to promote reformist principles such as those of the 1839
Gülhane rescript:

As he put forward these principles Reşit Pasha did not retreat into theo-
retical realms, nor did he use a political philosophy or the theory of natural rights as starting points: he only used these as practical means to
reach determined ends.[22]

The similarity between these two quotations, separate as they may be in
chronological order, is again striking. It points to a "longue durée" of historical

---

19   Shaw, Stanford, "Some aspects of the aims and achievements of the nineteenth-century
      Ottoman reformers", in *Beginnings of Modernization in the Middle East: The Nineteenth
      Century*, ed. William R. Polk and Richard Chambers (Chicago and London: University of
      Chicago Press, 1968), p. 33.
20   Shaw, "Some aspects of the aims and achievements of the nineteenth-century Ottoman
      reformers", p. 32.
21   Akyıldız, Ali, "Tanzimat", *Türkiye Diyanet Vakfı İslâm Ansiklopedisi*, vol. 40 (2011), pp. 1–10,
      here p. 9: "Genel olarak değerlendirildiğinde Tanzimat reformlarının planlı ve programlı
      olmaktan ziyade pratik ihtiyaçlara cevap verebilecek bir karakter gösterdiği söylenebilir".
22   İnalcık, "Sened-i İttifak ve Gülhane Hatt-ı Hümâyûnu", p. 620: "Reşit Paşa bu prensipleri
      ileri sürerken nazariyâta kaçmıyor, bir siyasî felsefeden, tabiî haklar nazariyesinden
      hareket etmiyor, bunları ancak belirli gayelere erişmek için pratik tedbirler olarak ele
      alıyordu". As shown by one of his previous texts on the meaning of the reforms, İnalcık
      linked the practical aims of the reformists to economic issues in the first place: İnalcık,
      Halil, "Tanzimat Nedir?", *Tarih Araştırmaları*, 1 (1941), 237–63.

thinking that does not necessarily evolve along the chronological categories otherwise promoted by the rules of the historian's craft. A better understanding of this longue durée would require more close and cross-reading to be on order.

Documents

Petition by a Group of Cypriot Cloth Printers, Est. Late 1261 / Early 1262 [Late 1845 / Early 1846] (BOA, A.}DVN. 14/16)

Facsimiles

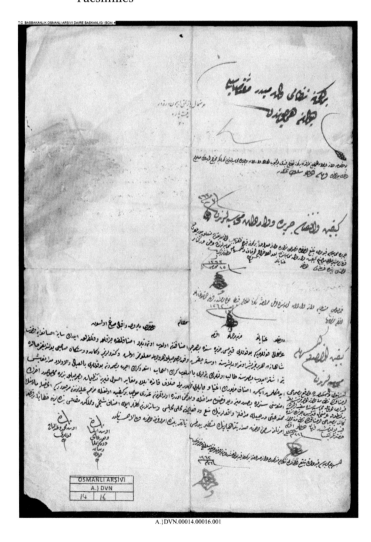

A.}DVN.00014.00016.001

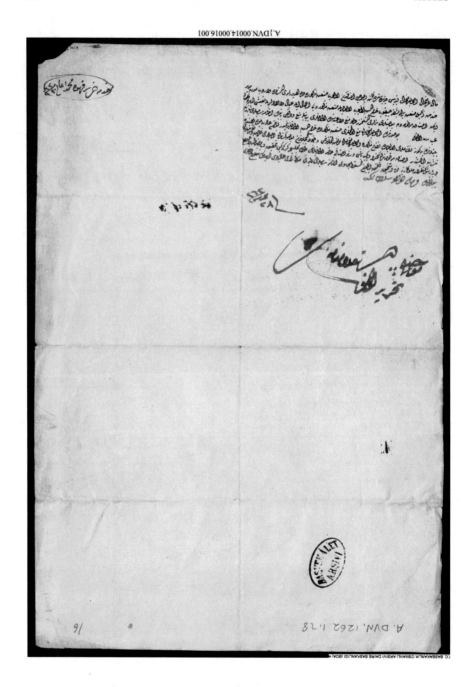

Full Text Transliteration

Devletlü ʿināyetlü mezīd-i merḥametlü efendim sulṭānım ḥażretleri bā devlet
ü iḳbāl ṣaġ olsun

ʿArżuḥāl-ı ḳullarıdır ki bu ḳulları Ḳıbrıs cezīresinde başmacı eṣnāfından olub
öteden-berü eṣnāflıḳda çıraḳlıḳ ve ḳalfalıḳ ederek sāye-i iḥsān-vāye-i ḥażret-i
şāhānede her birimiz beşer onar on beşer sene usta çıḳmış ve fenn-i başmacılıḳ
her vechile maʿlūmumuz olmuş ve kendülerimiz dükkān ve dest-gāh ṣāḥibi
bulundığımız ḥālde bez iştirā edüb başmasına ṭaleb olanlarıñ bezleri başılub
gerek eṣḥāb-ı emtiʿa ve gerek ücret-i başmadan bu ḳulları biʾl-ʿıyāl veʾl-evlād
medār-ı taʿayyüş edegelmiş iken eṣnāf-ı mezbūruñ aġniyā ü bāyları ẓuhūr
birle ḥilāf-ı ḳāʾide-i bilād [*sic*, for *ḳāʾide-i bilād*] ve muġāyir-i uṣūl-i ḥayriyye-i
tanẓīmāt başmacılıḳ bizlere maḥṣūṣdur āḫarıñ emtiʿasını sizlere başdırmayız
deyü fużūlī müdāḫale ve taʿarruż üzere olduḳlarından ġadrı mūcib bir keyfiyet olmaġla merāḥim-i ʿaliyyelerinden mercūdur ki inḥiṣār māddesiniñ
memnūʿiyeti derciyle müdāḫale-i vāḳiʿeleriniñ menʿ ü defʿiçün maḥali meclisi
ve sāʾir lāzım gelenler ile eṣnāf şeyḫi ve memleket müftisi bendelerine ḫiṭāben
bir ḳıṭʿa emirnāme-i sāmī-i ḥażret-i ṣadāret-penāhīleriniñ tasṭīr buyrulması
niyāzımız bābında emr ü fermān ḥażret-i veliyyiʾl-iḥsānıñdır

Bende	Bende
usta Meḥmed	usta İlyā ve Yorġākī
ve ʿAbdülbāḳī	ve diger İlyā ve
ḳulları	zimmiyān ḳulları*

Follow-up Annotations in the Right-Hand Margin

Bir gūne niẓāmı var mıdır muḳteżāsıyla Divan-ı hümāyūnʾdan

Bu ḫuṣūṣa dāʾir Divan-ı hümāyūn ṭarafından bir gūne niẓām ḳaydı bulun-
mayub evvelen vāridāt ve cerīde muḥāsebelerinden görülmege muḥtāc edügi
maʿlūm-ı devletleri buyrulduḳda fermān devletlü sulṭānımıñdır

Keyfiyet ü iḳtiżāsı cerīde ve vāridāt muḥāsebelerinden fī 7 M[uḥarrem] 262

---

* According to the writing rules common to collective representations such as *arzuhal*s or
*mahzar*s, the signatures are to be read from left to right, as indicated. I thank Elias Kolovos
for helping solve reading issues here.

Cerīde muḥasebesi ḳuyūdı teblīġ olunduḳda ḥuṣūṣ-ı mezbūre dā'ir ṣarāḥaten
bir gūne ḳayda ẓafer-yāb olunamadığından müte'alliḳ buyurılan fermān-ı
müşīrīleri mūcebince keyfiyet vāridāt muḥāsebesinden ba'de'l-iḫrāc evḳāf ü
eshām muḥāsebelerinden daḫī der-kenār olunması bābında fermān devletlü
'ināyetlü sulṭānım ḥażretleriñdir fī 15 Muḥarrem 1262

Ḥuṣūṣ-ı müsted'aya dā'ir vāridāt muḥāsebesinde daḫī ṣarāḥaten bir gūne
niẓām ḳaydı bulunamamışdır fermān devletlü 'ināyetlü efendim ḥażretler[iñ]
dir fī 17 M[uḥarrem] 1262

Keyfiyet evḳāf ü eshām muḥāsebelerinden

İstānbūl ve Üsküdār'da vāḳi' başmacı eşnāfınıñ niẓāmına dā'ir evāmir-i
şerīfe ḳayıdları evḳāf muḥāsebesinde muḳayyedler ise de ber manṭūḳ-ı 'arżuḥāl
Ḳıbrıs cezīresinde kā'in başmacı eşnāfınıñ niẓāmına dā'ir ḳayıd bulunmamışdır
fermān devletlü efendim ḥażretleriniñdir fī 22 M[uḥarrem] 1262

Eshām muḥāsebesi ḳuyūdātı teblīġ olunduḳda niẓām-ı mezḳūre dā'ir
ṣarāḥaten bir gūne ḳayıd bulunmamışdır fermān devletlü 'ināyetlü sulṭānım
ḥażretleriniñdir fī 26 M[uḥarrem] 1262

Overleaf Recap and Recommendation

Me'āl-i 'arżuḥāl eṣḥāb-ı 'arżuḥāl Ḳıbrıs cezīresinde kā'in başmacı eşnāfından
olub ṣan'at-ı mezḳūrede her birerleri ustada varub müddet-i medīd ḫidmet ve
tekmīl-i ṣan'at birle başḳa [sic, probably for başa] çıḳub ḫām-dest olmayub ol-
vechle ṣanat-ı mezḳūreyi i'māl ile 'ıyāl ü evlādlarıyla ta'ayyüş edegelürler iken
eşnāf-ı mezḳūreden ba'żıları sizleri işletmeyiz deyü men' dā'iyesinde olduḳları
beyānıyla men' ü def'i bābında emirnāme-i sāmīleri niyāzından 'ibāret olmaġla
bu ṣūretde eṣḥāb-ı 'arżuḥāliñ men' olunmaları ṣan'at-ı mezḳūrde ḫām-dest
olduḳlarından-mıdır ba'żı 'ādet-i belde üzere beynlerinde bir gūne niẓāmları
olub-da niẓām-ı mezḳūra eṣḥāb-ı 'arżuḥāliñ muḫālefet etmelerinden-mi ve
yāḫūd içlerinden ba'żı kesānıñ icrā-yı ġaraż ü nefsāniyetlerinden-mi neş'et
eylemişdir eşnāf-ı merḳūmeniñ ketḫüdā ve yıġıd [sic] başı ve sā'ir eşnāfı ḥāżır
olduḳları ḥālde meclisce geregi gibi taḥḳīḳ ve bā mażbaṭa ve i'lām der-bār-ı
şevket-ḳarār-ı mülūkāneye inhā ve tenmīḳ ḳılınmaḳ içün isti'lām-cāvi
emirnāme-i sāmīleri tasṭīri menūṭ-ı rey'-i 'alīleri edügi ma'lūm-ı devletleri
buyrulduḳda fermān devletlü sulṭānımıñdır

Mūcebince isti'lām-nāmesi taḥrīr olunur

Report from the Commissioner in Charge of Duties and Taxes, Sent to the Ministry of Interior Affairs, Dated 19 Şevvāl 1311 and 13 April 1310 [25 April 1894] (BOA, DH.MKT. 235/9, #4)
Facsimile

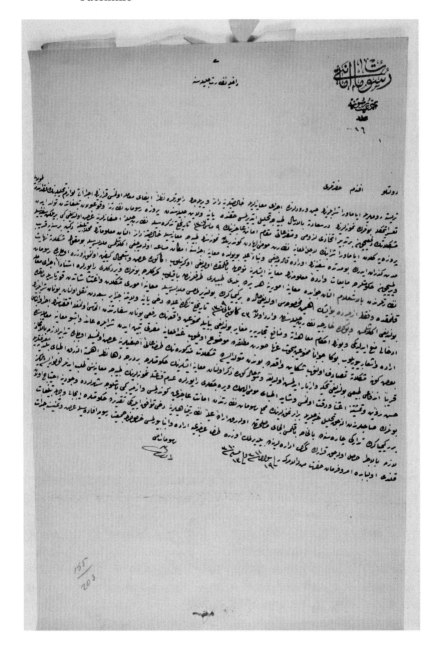

Full Text Transliteration

Devletlü efendim ḥażretleri

Triyeste romlarıyla Ayāmāvra şarāblarınıñ ḥīn-i vürūdlarında icrā-yı
muʿāyeneleriyle ḥāliṣiyetlerine dāʾir virilecek rāporatlara [sic] naẓaren īfā-yı
muʿāmele olunması ḳarārınıñ icrāʾatı levāzım-ı taḥlīliyyeniñ fıḳdānından ṭolayı
taʿassür etmekle bunlarıñ nümūneleriniñ Dersaʿādetʾe biʾl-irsāl Ṭıbbiyeʾce
taḥlīl etdirilmesi ḥaḳḳında Yānya vilāyet-i celīlesinden Preveza rüsūmāt
neẓāretine vuḳūʿbulan teblīġātdan tevellüd eden müşkilātıñ defʿiçün bir
tedbīr ittiḫāẕı lüzūmı ve müteferriʿātı maḳām-ı emānet-i ʿācizīniñ 9 Māyıs
sene 1307 tārīḫli teẕkiresiyle neẓāret-i celīle-i āṣafānelerine ʿarż olundıġı gibi
bir yelken sefīnesiyle Prevezaʾya gelen Ayāmāvra şarābınıñ li-ecliʾl-muʿāyene
neẓāret-i mūmāileyhādan gönderilen nümūnesiniñ Ṭıbbiyeʾce muʿāyenesiyle
ḥāliṣiyetine dāʾir alınan maʿlūmātıñ maḥaline teblīġine degīn bir seneye ḳarīb
müddet güẕerān ederek bu müddetde sefīneniñ orada ḳalamayacaġı ve bināʾen
ʿaleyhi bu yolda muʿāyene icrāsına imkān-ı müsāʿid olamayacaġı añlaşılması
mülābesesiyle bu maḳūle müşkilāta nihāyet virilmesiçün ḥükūmetlerce
māʾıʿāt-ı vāride-i maʿlūmeniñ muʿāyene işlerine ne-vechle baḳılmaḳda
oldıġı ögrenilüb aña göre ʿarż ve istiʿcāl-i keyfiyet olunmaḳ üzere ol-bābda
rüsūmat neẓāretlerinden biʾl-istiʿlām alınan cevābda muʿāyene umūrına
her yerde beledī ṭabībleri ṭaraflarından baḳılub gümrüklerce bunlarıñ vir-
dikleri rāporlara istināden icrā-yı muʿāmele ḳılınmaḳda ve faḳaṭ İzmīrʾde bu
işiñ ehemmiyet-i maḥṣūṣesi oldıġı ḥālde bir kīmiyā-geriñ bulundırılmaması
mülābesesiyle muʿāyene umūrı müşkilāt ü iġtişāşātdan ḳurtarılamamaḳda
bulundıġı añlaşılmış ve bu kere Ḫāriciye neẓāret-i celīlesinden vārid olan 23
Kānūn-ı s̱ānī sene 1309 tārīḫli teẕkire-i ʿaliyyede daḫī Yānya vilāyetine Cezāʾir-i
sebʿaʾdan naḳl olunan Yūnān şarāblarınıñ idḫāli menʿ edildigi ve bunuñ
aḥkām-ı muʿāhedāta ve menāfiʿ-i ticāriyyeye bulundıġı beyānıyla memnūʿiyet-i
vāḳiʿeniñ refʿi Yūnān sefāretinden iltimās olunmaġla iḳtiżāsınıñ icrā ü inbāsı
irāde ve işʿār buyurılub buña cevāben memnūʿiyet-i mebḥūsin ʿanhā ṣūret-i
muṭlaḳada mevżūʿ olmayub ʾindiʾl-muʿāyene mażarratı tebeyyün eden
şarāblara ʿāʾid ve işbu muʿāyene muʿāmelesinde baʿżı gūne müşkilāta teşādüf
olunub şikāyet-i vāḳiʿe de bundan mütevellid ise de müşkilāt-ı mezkūreniñ
ṭaraf-ı ʿālī-i āṣafīlerine ʿarż olunmasıyla ol-bābda tedābīr-i lāzıme biʾl-ittiḫāẕ
ḳarīben indifāʿı ṭabīʿī bulundıġı taḥkiye ü izbār edilmiş oldıġına ve şu ḥāle göre
ẕikr olunan muʿāyene işleriniñ ḥükūmetlerce bir derece daha naẓar-ı ehem-
miyete alınarak ettibāʿ-ı belediyye maʿrifetiyle ḥüsn-i rüʾyet ü temşiyetine
iʿtinā ve diḳḳat olunması ve şāyed ettibāʿ-ı mūmāileyhumuñ virecekleri
rāporlara ʿadem-i ḳanāʿatla nümūnelerinin Ṭıbbiyeʾce muʿāyenesini ṭaleb eden-
ler olur ise yalñız bunlarıñ ṣāḥiblerinden alınacaḳ taḥlīl ḫarclarıyla berāber

nümūneleriniñ maḥallī rüsūmāt neẓāretinden emānet-i ʿācizīye gönderilmesi
ve İzmīr gibi başluca şehirlerde vücūdına iḥtiyāc olan birer kīmiyā-geriñ
tedārügi çāresine de bi'l-ḫaṣṣa baḳılması ilcā-yı maṣlaḥatdan olaraḳ irāde-i
ʿaliyye-i neẓāret-penāhīlerine daḫī tevāfuḳ eyledigi taḳdīrde ḥükūmetlere
īcābı vechle teblīġāt-ı lāzıme bi'l-icrā ḥāṣıl olacaḳ ḳarārıñ gümrük idārelerine
de bildirilmek üzere ṭaraf-ı ʿācizīye irāde ve inbā buyrulması ḫuṣūṣunuñ
Cemʿiyet-i rüsūmiyye ifādesiyle ʿarż ü temennīsine cürʾet ḳılındı ol-bābda emr
ü fermān ḥażret-i men lehi'l-emriñdir fī 19 Şevvāl 311 ve 13 Nīsān 1310

Bibliography

Primary Sources

Archives

Archives de la Chambre de Commerce de Marseille, Marseilles (ACCM), France

Archives du Ministère des Affaires Étrangères, Paris (AMAE), France

Archives Nationales, Paris (ANF), France

Archivio di Stato di Genova (ASG), Italy

Centre des Archives Diplomatiques, Nantes, Ministère des Affaires Étrangères (CADN, MAE), France

Devlet Arşivleri, Osmanlı Arşivi, Istanbul (BOA), Turkey

Gertrude Bell Archive Online (http://gertrudebell.ncl.ac.uk/), Newcastle University, Newcastle, UK

İstanbul Büyükşehir Belediyesi (İBB) Atatürk Kitaplığı Online (http://ataturkkitapligi.ibb.gov.tr/ataturkkitapligi/index.php), Turkey

Taha Toros Arşivi Online (http://openaccess.marmara.edu.tr/handle/11424/120957), Turkey

Tapu ve Kadastro Genel Müdürlüğü, Ankara (TK), Turkey

The National Archives, London (TNA), UK

Newspapers and Journals

Hellenic Chamber of Commerce Bulletin (*HCofC Bulletin*)

La Turquie

Published

166 Numaralı Muhâsebe-i Vilâyet-i Anadolu Defteri (937/1530) *Hüdâvendigâr, Biga, Karesi, Saruhân, Aydın, Menteşe, Teke, Alâiye Livâları* (Ankara: Osmanlı Arşivi Daire Başkanlığı, 1995).

387 Numaralı Muhâsebe-i Vilâyet-i Karaman ve Rûm Defteri (937/1530) *I: Konya, Bey-Şehri, Ak-Şehir, Larende, Ak-Saray, Niğde, Kayseriyye ve İç-İl Livâları* (Ankara: Osmanlı Arşivi Daire Başkanlığı, 1996).

387 Numaralı Muhâsebe-i Vilâyet-i Karaman ve Rûm Defteri (937/1530) *II: Amasya, Çorumlu, Sivas-Tokat, Sonisa-Niksar, Karahisar-ı Şarkî, Canik, Trabzon, Kemah, Bayburd, Malatya, Gerger-Kahta ve Divriği-Darende Livâları* (Ankara: Osmanlı Arşivi Daire Başkanlığı, 1997).

438 Numaralı Muhâsebe-i Vilâyet-i Anadolu Defteri (937/1530) *I: Kütahya, Karahisâr-ı Sâhip, Sultanönü, Hamîd ve Ankara Livâları* (Ankara: Osmanlı Arşivi Daire Başkanlığı, 1993).

998 Numaralı Muhâsebe-i Vilâyet-i Diyar-i Bekr ve Arab ve Zü'l-Kadriyye Defteri (937/1530)
I: Âmid, Mardin, Sincar, Musul, Arapkir, Ergani, Çirmük, Siverek, Kiğı, Çemişkezek,
Harput, Ruha, Ana-Hit ve Deyr-Rahbe Livâları ile Hısn-ı Keyf ve Siird Kazaları
(Ankara: Osmanlı Arşivi Daire Başkanlığı, 1998).

998 Numaralı Muhâsebe-i Vilâyet-i Diyar-i Bekr ve Arab ve Zü'l-Kadriyye Defteri (937/1530)
II: Âmid, Mardin, Sincar, Musul, Arapkir, Ergani, Çirmük, Siverek, Kiğı, Çemişkezek,
Harput, Ruha, Ana-Hit ve Deyr-Rahbe Livâları, ile Hısn-ı Keyf ve Siird Kazaları
(Ankara: Osmanlı Arşivi Daire Başkanlığı, 1999).

Ahmet Rasim, Şehir Mektupları, ed. Nuri Akbayar (Istanbul: Oğlak, 2005).

Ainsworth, William Francis, Travels and Researches in Asia Minor, Mesopotamia,
Chaldea, and Armenia, two vols. (London: John W. Parker, 1842).

Akgöz, Alaaddin (ed.), Kanunî Devrine Ait 939–941 / 1532–1535 Tarihli Lârende [Karaman]
Şer'iye Sicili Özet-Dizin-Tıpkıbasım (Konya: Tablet Kitabevi, 2006).

Andreasyan, Hrand D. (trans.), Polonyalı Bir Seyyahın Gözünden 16. Asır Türkiyesi
Polonyalı Simeon (Istanbul: Köprü Kitapları, 2016).

Ankara Vilayetine Mahsus Salname (Ankara: Matbaa-ı Vilayet, 1307/1891).

Ankara Vilayetine Mahsus Salname (Ankara: Matbaa-ı Vilayet, 1311/1893).

Ankara Vilayetine Mahsus Salname (Ankara: Matbaa-ı Vilayet, 1318/1900).

Ankara Vilayeti Salnamesi (Ankara: Matbaa-ı Vilayet, 1325/1907).

Anonymi descriptio Europae orientalis imperium Constantinopolitanum, Albania,
Serbia, Bulgaria, Ruthenia, Ungaria, Polonia, Bohemia. Anno MCCCVIII exarata, ed.
Dr. Olgierd Górka (Kraków: Gebethner et Socii, 1916, reprinted by Pranava Books,
India).

Aşıkpaşazade, Die Altosmanische Chronik des Aşıkpaşazāde, ed. Fredrich Giese (Leipzig,
1929, reprinted Osnabrük: Otto Zeller Verlag, 1972).

Atasoy, Sümer, Geleneksel Bakır Kaplar – Semahat ve Nusret Arsel Koleksiyonu /
Traditional Copperware – Semahat & Nusret Arsel Collection (Istanbul: Sadberk
Hanım Müzesi, 2014).

Ayn Ali Efendi, Kavânîn-i Âl-i Osman der Hülâsa-i Mezâmin-i Defter-i Dîvân, ed. Tayyib
Gökbilgin (Istanbul: Enderun Kitabevi, 1979).

Bacqué-Grammont, Jean-Louis, "Un rapport inédit sur la révolte anatolienne de 1527",
Studia Islamica, 62 (1985), 155–71.

Badoer, Giacomo, Il Libro dei Conti di Giacomo Badoer (Costantinopoli 1436–1440),
ed. Umberto Dorini and Tommaso Bertelè (Rome: Istituto Poligrafico dello Stato,
Libreria dello Stato, 1956).

Balard, Michel, Gênes et l'Outre-Mer I. Les actes de Caffa du notaire Lamberto di
Sambuceto 1289–1290 (Paris and the Hague: Mouton and Co., 1973).

Balard, Michel, Angeliki L. Laiou and Catherine Otten-Froux, Les Italiens à Byzance et
présentation de documents (Paris: Publications de la Sorbonne, 1987).

Balbi, Giovanna and Silvana Raiteri, *Notai genovesi in oltremare. Atti rogati a Caffa e a Licostomo (sec. XIV)* (Bordighera: Istituto Internazionale di Studi Liguri, 1973).

Balletto, Laura, *Notai genovese in oltremare. Atti rogati a Laiazzo da Federico di Pizzalunga (1274) e Pietro di Bargone (1277, 1279)* (Genoa: Università di Genova, 1989).

Barbaro, Nicolò, "Giornale dell'assedio di Costantinopoli", in *La caduta di Costantinopoli. Le testimonianze dei contemporanei*, vol. I, ed. Agostino Pertusi (Milan: Mondadori, 1999), pp. 8–38.

Barkan, Ömer Lütfi, *XV ve XVI inci Asırlarda Osmanlı İmparatorluğunda Ziraî Ekonominin Hukukî ve Malî Esasları. I. Kanunlar* (Istanbul: Bürhaneddin Matbaası, 1943).

Barkan, Ömer Lütfi, "Edirne Askeri Kassam'ına ait Tereke Defterleri (1545–1659)", *Belgeler*, 3/5–6 (1966), 1–479.

Barkan, Ömer Lütfi, "Türkiye'de İmparatorluk Devirlerinin Büyük Nüfus ve Arazi Tahrirleri ve Hakana Mahsus İstatistik Defterleri I", *İstanbul Üniversitesi İktisat Fakültesi Mecmuası*, 1 (1940–1941), 20–59.

Barkan, Ömer Lütfi, "Türkiye'de İmparatorluk Devirlerinin Büyük Nüfus ve Arazi Tahrirleri ve Hakana Mahsus İstatistik Defterleri II", *İstanbul Üniversitesi İktisat Fakültesi Mecmuası*, 2 (1940–1941), 214–47.

Ibn Battuta, *Voyages d'Ibn Batoutah*, vol. II, trans. and ed. C. Defrémery and R. Sanguinetti (Paris: L'Imprimerie Impériale, 1854).

Baykal, Bekir Sıtkı (ed.), *Peçevi İbrahim Efendi Peçevi Tarihi*, vol. II (Istanbul: Kültür ve Turizm Bakanlığı Yayınları, 1982).

Beldiceanu-Steinherr, Irene and Jean-Louis Bacqué-Grammont, "A propose de quelques causes de malaises sociaux en Anatolie centrale aux XVIᵉ et XVIIᵉ siècles", *Archivum Ottomanicum*, 7 (1982), 71–115.

Belgrano, L.T., "Cinque documenti genovesi-orientali", *Atti della Società Ligure di Storia Patria*, 17 (1885–1886), 221–51.

Belgrano, L.T., "Prima serie di documenti riguardanti la colonia di Pera", *Atti della Società Ligure di Storia Patria*, 13 (1877), 97–336.

Biren, Tevfik, *Bürokrat Tevfik Biren'in II. Abdülhamid, Meşrutiyet, ve Mütareke Hatıraları*, two vols., ed. Fatma Rezan Hürmen (Istanbul: Pınar Yayınları, 2006).

Bratianu, G.I., *Actes des notaires génois de Péra et de Caffa de la fin du treizième siècle 1281–1290* (Bucharest: Cultura Nationala, 1927).

Brown, Adna, *From Vermont to Damascus* (Boston: Geo. H. Ellis, 1895).

Chalkokondyles, *Historiarum Libri Decem*, ed. I. Bekker (Bonn: E. Weber, 1843).

Chalkokondyles, *The Histories*, two vols., trans. Anthony Kaldellis (Cambridge, Mass.: Harvard University Press, 2014).

Chrysostomides, Julian (ed.), *Monumenta Peloponnesiaca. Documents for the History of the Peloponnese in the 14th and 15th Centuries* (Camberely: Porphyrogenitus, 1995).

Cunningham, A.B. (ed.), "The journal of Christophe Aubin: a report of the Levant trade in 1812", *Archivum Ottomanicum*, 8 (1983), 5–131.

Dankoff, Robert and Sooyong Kim (trans. and commentary), *An Ottoman Traveller. Selections from* The Book of Travels *of Evliya Çelebi* (London: Eland, 2011).

Dennis, G.T., "The Byzantine-Turkish Treaty of 1403", *Orientalia Christiana Periodica*, 33 (1967), 72–88.

Desimoni, C. and L.T. Belgrano, "Atlante idrografico del medio evo posseduto dal Prof. Tammar Luxuro", *Atti della Società Ligure di Storia Patria*, 5 (1867), 1–168.

Dincer, Celal, "Osmanlı Vezirlerinden Hasan Fehmi Paşa'nın Anadolu'nun Bayındırlık İşlerine Dair Hazırladığı Lâyiha", *Belgeler*, 5–8/9–12 (1968–71), 153–232.

Diplomatic and Consular Reports on Trade and Finance. Turkey: Report for the Year 1893 on the Trade and Agriculture of Angora (Foreign Office, Annual Series, no. 1368) (London: Harrison and Sons, 1894).

Diplomatic and Consular Reports on Trade and Finance. Turkey: Report for the Year 1894 on the Agriculture of Angora (Foreign Office, Annual Series, no. 1505) (London: Harrison and Sons, 1895).

Diplomatic and Consular Reports on Trade and Finance. Turkey: Report on the Agricultural Condition of the Vilayet of Angora (Foreign Office, Annual Series, no. 1624) (London: Harrison and Sons, 1895).

Diplomatic and Consular Reports on Trade and Finance. Turkey: Report for the Year 1895 on the Agriculture of Angora (Foreign Office, Annual Series, no. 1739) (London: Harrison and Sons, 1896).

Diplomatic and Consular Reports Turkey. Report for the Year 1897 on the Trade and Commerce of Angora and District (Foreign Office, Annual Series, no. 1505) (London: Harrison and Sons, 1898).

Diplomatic and Consular Reports Turkey. Report for the Year 1898 on the Trade and Commerce of Angora and District (London: Harrison and Sons, 1899).

Documents diplomatiques français (1871–1914), tome XI (15 Mai 1907–8 Février 1909) (Paris: Imprimerie Nationale Alfred Costes, 1950).

Doukas, *Decline and Fall of Byzantium to the Ottoman Turks*, trans. H.J. Magoulias (Detroit: Wayne State University Press, 1975).

Doukas, *Historia Byzantina*, ed. Immanuel Bekker (Bonn: E. Weber, 1834).

Dursun, M. Kamil, *İzmir Hatıraları*, ed. Ünal Şenel (İzmir: Akademi Kitabevi, 1994).

Ebüzziya Tevfik, "Piyango", *Mecmua-i Ebüzziya*, 3/27 (Gurre-i Safer 1300/ 12 December 1882), 838–43.

Ender, Celil, Üstün Erek and Gültekin Teoman, *Candaroğulları Beyliği (İsfendiyaroğulları Beyliği) Paraları Kataloğu* (Istanbul: Ender Nümismatik Yayınları, 2003).

Evliya Çelebi b. Derviş Mehemmed Zıllı, *Evliya Çelebi Seyahatnâmesi, Topkapı Sarayı Bağdat 304 Yazmasının Transkripsyonu –Dizini*, vol. 1, ed. Robert Dankoff, Seyit Ali Kahraman and Yücel Dağlı (Istanbul: Yapı Kredi Yayınları, 2006).

Eyice, Semavi, "Amasra'da Cenova Hâkimiyeti Devrine Ait Bir Armalı Levha", *Belleten*, 65 (1953), 27–40.

Gölpınarlı, Abdülbaki, *Alevî-Bektâşî Nefesleri* (Istanbul: Remzi Kitabevi, 1963).

Gooch, G.P. and Harold Temperley (eds.), *British Documents on the Origins of the War 1898–1914. Vol. V the Near East, the Macedonian Problem and the Annexation of Bosnia 1903–9* (London, 1928, reprinted by London: Johnson Reprint Company, 1967).

Güney, Eflatun Cem (ed.), *Halk Şiiri Antolojisi. Başlangıçtan Bugüne Türk Şiiri: 2* (Istanbul: Varlık Yayınları, 1959).

Habesci, Elias, *État actuel de l'empire ottoman*, two vols. (Paris: Lavillette, 1792).

Herbert, Aubrey, *Ben Kendim. A Record of Eastern Travel*, ed. Desmond MacCarthy (London: Hutchinson & Co., 1924).

Hezarfen, Ahmet (ed.), *Rumeli ve Anadolu Âyan ve Eşkiyası. Osmanlı Arşiv Belgeleri* (Istanbul: Kaynak Yayınları, 2002).

Hicaz Demiryolu Lahiyası (Dersaadet: Serviçin Matbaası, 1324).

İnalcık, Halil, "Adâletnâmeler", *Belgeler*, 2/3–4 (1965), 49–162.

Işık, Ali (ed.), *Vali İngiliz Sait Paşa'nın Konya Günleri* (Konya and Istanbul: Çizgi Kitabevi, 2018).

Joliffe, Thomas Robert, *Narrative of an Excursion from Corfu to Smyrna* (London: Printed for Black, Young and Young, 1827).

Kal'a, Ahmet, *et al.* (eds.), *İstanbul Külliyatı: İstanbul Ahkâm Defterleri*, 10 vols. (Istanbul: İstanbul Araştırmaları Merkezi, 1997–1998).

Kal'a, Ahmet, *et al.* (eds.), *İstanbul Külliyâtı: İstanbul Ahkâm Defterleri İstanbul Esnaf Tarihi I* (Istanbul: İstanbul Araştırmaları Merkezi, 1997).

Kastritsis, Dimitri K. (trans.), *An Early Ottoman History. The Oxford Anonymous Chronicle (Bodleian Library, Ms Marsh 313)* (Liverpool: Liverpool University Press, 2017).

Kızanlıklı Mehmed Ali, "Küçük Hikaye: Piyango", *İrtika*, 181–33 (16 Cemaziülahır 1320/6 Eylül 1318/19 September 1902), 313.

Kocatürk, Vasfi Mahir (ed.), *Şiir Defteri. Yunus Emre'den Bugüne Kadar Türk Edebiyatının Her Çeşitten Güzel Şiirleri* (Ankara: Edebiyat Yayınevi, 1965).

Kritoboulos, *History of Mehmed the Conqueror. By Kritovoulos*, trans. Charles T. Riggs (Princeton: Princeton University Press, 1954).

Kütükoğlu, Mübahat, "1624 Sikke Tashihinin Ardından Hazırlanan Narh Defterleri", *Tarih Dergisi*, 34 (1983–1984), 123–82.

Kütükoğlu, Mübahat, *Osmanlılarda Narh Müessesesi ve 1640 Tarihli Narh Defteri* (Istanbul: Enderun Kitabevi, 1983).

Lubenau, Reinhold, *Reinhold Lubenau Seyahatnamesi. Osmanlı Ülkesinde 1587–1589*, two vols., trans. Türkis Noyan (Istanbul: Kitap Yayınevi, 2012).

Lüdeke, Christoph Wilhelm, *Türklerde Din ve Devlet Yönetimi. İzmir ve İstanbul 1759–1768*, trans. Türkis Noyan (Istanbul: Kitap Yayınevi, 2013).

Luttrell, Anthony and Elizabeth A. Zachariadou (eds.), *Sources for Turkish History in the Hospitallers' Rhodian Archive 1389–1422* (Athens: National Hellenic Research Foundation Institute for Byzantine Research, 2008).

Manfroni, C., "Le relazioni fra Genova, l'impero Bizantino e i Turchi", *Atti della Società Ligure di Storia Patria*, 28 (1896), 575–856.

Morozzo della Rocca, Raimondo, "Notizie da Caffa", in *Studi in onore di Amintore Fanfani III. Medioevo* (Milan: A. Giuffrè, 1962), pp. 266–95.

Neave, Dorina L., *Twenty-Six Years on the Bosphorus* (London: Grayson & Grayson, 1933).

Neşri, *Kitâb-ı Cihan-nümâ. Neşri Tarihi*, vol. 1, ed. Faik Reşit Unat and Mehmed A. Köymen (Ankara: Türk Tarih Kurumu Basımevi, 1987).

Noiret, H. (ed.), *Documents inédits pour servir à l'histoire de la domination vénitienne en Crète de 1380 à 1485* (Paris: E. Thorin, 1892).

Orhonlu, Cengiz (ed.), *Osmanlı Tarihine Âid Belgeler Telhîsler (1597–1607)* (Istanbul: Edebiyat Fakültesi Basımevi, 1970).

Özkan, Özlem, *Askeri Müze Tombak Eserler Kataloğu* (Istanbul: Askeri Müze ve Kültür Sitesi Komutanlığı, 2001).

Öztürk, Said (ed.), *Askeri Kassama Ait Onyedinci Asır İstanbul Tereke Defterleri (Sosyo-Ekonomik Tahlil)* (Istanbul: OSAV, 1995).

Panaretos, Michael, "On the emperors of Trebizond", in *Two Works on Trebizond. Michael Panaretos, Bessarion*, ed. and trans. Scott Kennedy (Cambridge, Mass.: Harvard University Press, 2019).

Pegolotti, *Fr Balducci Pegolotti, La Pratica della Mercature*, ed. A. Evans (Cambridge, Mass.: The Medieval Academy of America, 1936).

Petti Balbi, Giovanna (ed.), *Georgii et Iohannis Stellae, Annales genovenses* (Bologna: Zanicelli, 1975).

Promis, Vincenzo (ed.), "Continuazione della cronaca de Jacopo da Varagine dal MCCXCVII al MCCCXXXII", *Atti della Società Ligure de Storia Patria*, 10 (1874), 493–511.

Promontorio, Iacopo de, *Die Aufzeichnungen des Genuesen Iacopo de Promontorio-de Campis über den Osmanenstaat um 1475*, ed. Franz Babinger (Munich: Verlag der Bayerischen Akademie der Wissenschaften, 1957).

Rauwolff, Leonhart, *Itinerary into the Eastern Countries*, trans. Nicholas Staphorst, in *A Collection of Curious Travels and Voyages* (London: Mr. John Ray, 1705).

Rougon, R., *Smyrne. Situation commerciale et économique des pays compris dans la circonscription du consulat général de France (Vilayeti d'Aidin, de Konieh et des Iles)* (Paris-Nancy: Berger-Levrault et Cie, 1892).

Rubruck, William, *The Journal of William of Rubruck to the Eastern Parts of the World 1253–55*, ed. and trans. William Woodville Rockhill (London: The Hakluyt Society, 1900).

Schiltberger, Johann, *The Bondage and Travels of Johann Schiltberger, A Native of Bavaria, in Europe, Asia and Africa, 1396–1427*, trans. J. Buchan Telfer (London: The Hakluyt Society, 1879).

Serristori, Luigi, *Illustrazione di una carta del Mar Nero del 1351 e ricordi sul Caucaso, sulla Spagna, sul Marocco ... Con tavole* (Florence: Società Editrice Fiorentine, 1856, reprinted by British Library, Historical Prints Editions, 2011).

Silay, Kemal, "Ahmedī's history of the Ottoman dynasty", *Journal of Turkish Studies. Türklük Bilgisi Araştırmaları*, 16 (1992), *Richard Nelson Frye Festschrift I*, ed. Şinasi Tekin and Gönül Alp Tekin, pp. 129–200.

Sullivan, James, *Diary of a Tour in the Autumn of 1856* (Printed for Presentation to his Friends, April 1857).

Tafur, Pero, *Travels and Adventures, 1435–1439*, trans. and ed. Malcolm Letts (London: George Routledge and Sons, 1926).

Tahsin Paşa, *Abdülhamit. Yıldız Hatıraları*, ed. Kudret Emiroğlu (Ankara: İmge Kitabevi, 2008).

Tansu, Samih Nafiz (ed.), *Madalyonun Tersi. Anlatan: Sadrazam Avlonyalı Ferid Paşa'nın Oğlu Celâleddin Paşa (Velora)* (Istanbul: Gür Kitabevi, 1970).

Tavernier, John-Baptiste, *The Six Voyages of John Baptista Tavernier* (London, 1678).

Thiriet, F., *Régestes des délibérations du Sénat de Venise concernant la Romanie*, three vols. (Paris: Mouton, 1958–1961).

Tournefort, Joseph Pitton de, *A Voyage into the Levant* (London, 1718).

al-'Umari, "Notice de l'ouvrage qui a pour titre Masalek alabsar fi memalek alamsar, Voyages des yeux dans les royaumes des différentes contrées (ms. arabe 583)", ed. E. Quatremère, in *Notices et Extraits des mss. de la Bibliothèque du Roi*, vol. XIII (Paris, 1838), pp. 334–81.

Uşaklıgil, Halit Ziya, *Kırk Yıl*, ed. Nur Özmel Akın (Istanbul: Özgür, 2008).

Villani, Giovanni, *Nuova Cronaca* (Parma: Guanda, 1991).

Waugh, Evelyn, *Labels. A Mediterranean Journal* (London: Penguin Books, 2011).

Yaman, Talat Mümtaz, "Küre Bakır Madenine Dair Vesikalar", *Tarih Vesikaları*, 1/4 (1941), 266–82.

Yarman, Arsen (ed.), *Palu-Harput 1878: Çarsancak, Çemişkezek, Çapakçur, Erzincan, Hizan ve Civar Bölgeler*, vol. II (İstanbul: Derlem Yayınları, 2010).

Yaşar, Yücel and Selami Pulaha (eds.), *I. Selim Kanunnameleri (1512–1520)* (Ankara: Türk Tarih Kurumu Basımevi, 1995).

Yörük, Doğan (ed.), *3 Numaralı Konya Şer'iye Sicili (987–1330 / 1579–1912) (Transkripsiyon ve Dizin)* (Konya: Palet Yayınları, 2013).

Yüksel, Hasan, *Osmanlı Döneminde Keban Ergani-Madenleri: 1776–1794 Tarihli Maden Emini Defteri* (Sivas: n.p., 1997).

Zachariadou, Elizabeth A., *Trade and Crusade: Venetian Crete and the Emirates of Menteshe and Aydin (1300–1415)* (Venice: Istituto Ellenico di Studi Bizantini e Postbizantini di Venezia, 1983).

Secondary Sources

Abdel Nour, Antoine, *Introduction à l'histoire urbaine de la Syrie ottomane (XVIᵉ– XVIIIᵉ siècle)* (Beirut: Librairie Orientale, 1982).

Acun, Fatma, *Karahisar-ı Şarkî ve Koyulhisar Kazaları Örneğinde Osmanlı Taşra İdaresi (1485–1569)* (Ankara: Türk Tarih Kurumu Basımevi, 2006).

Acun, Fatma, "The other side of the coin: tax exemptions within the context of Ottoman taxation history", *Bulgarian Historical Review*, 1–2 (2002), 125–39.

Àgoston, Gàbor, "Early modern Ottoman and European gunpowder technology", in *Multicultural Science in the Ottoman Empire*, ed. Ekmeleddin İhsanoğlu, Efthymios Nicolaïdis and Konstantinos Chatzis (Turnhout: Brepols, 2003), pp. 13–27.

Àgoston, Gàbor, "Firearms and military adaptation: the Ottomans and the European military revolution, 1450–1800", *Journal of World History*, 25/1 (2014), 85–124.

Àgoston, Gàbor, *Guns for the Sultan. Military Power and the Weapons Industry in the Ottoman Empire* (Cambridge: Cambridge University Press, 2005).

Ak, Mehmet, "Osmanlı Devleti'nde Veba-i Bakarî (Sığır Vebası)", *Ankara Üniversitesi Osmanlı Tarihi Araştırma ve Uygulama Merkezi Dergisi*, 39 (2016), 215–40.

Akarlı, Engin D., "Economic policy and budgets in Ottoman Turkey, 1876–1909", *Middle Eastern Studies*, 28/3 (1992), 443–76.

Akarlı, Engin Deniz, "Gedik: A bundle of rights and obligations for Istanbul artisans and traders, 1750–1840", in *Law, Anthropology and the Constitution of the Social: Making Persons and Things*, ed. Alain Pottage and Martha Mundy (Cambridge and New York: Cambridge University Press, 2004), pp. 166–200.

Akçetin, Elif and Suraiya Faroqhi (eds.), *Living the Good Life: Consumption in the Qing and Ottoman Empires of the Eighteenth Century* (Leiden: Brill, 2017).

Akdağ, Mustafa, *Celâlî İsyanları 1550–1603* (Ankara: Ankara Üniversitesi Basımevi, 1963).

Akdağ, Mustafa, *Türkiye'nin İktisadi ve İçtimai Tarihi* (Ankara: Türk Tarih Kurumu Basımevi, 1959).

Akder, A. Halis, "Yirminci Yüzyılın Başında Çukurova'ya Pamuk Ekmenin Maliyeti", in *Osmanlı'nın Peşinde bir Yaşam. Suraiya Faroqhi'ye Armağan*, ed. Onur Yıldırım (Ankara: İmge Kitabevi Yayınları, 2008), pp. 221–69.

Akyıldız, Ali, "Tanzimat", *Türkiye Diyanet Vakfı İslam Ansiklopedisi*, vol. 40 (2011), pp. 1–10.

"Ankara", *Yurt Ansiklopedisi*, vol. I (Istanbul: Anadolu Yayıncılık, 1981), pp. 511–13.

Arıkan, Zeki, "1316 (1900) Tarihli Askeri Bedel Cetveline Göre İzmir Yahudileri", in *İzmirli Olmak. Sempozyum Bildirileri 22–24 Ekim 2009* (İzmir: İzmir Büyükşehir Belediyesi, 2010), pp. 296–316.

Artuk, İbrahim, "I. Murad'ın Sikkelerine Genel Bir Bakış 761–792 (1359–1389)", *Belleten*, 46/184 (1982), 787–93.

Artuk, İbrahim, "Karesi-oğulları Adına Basılmış Olan İki Sikke", *İstanbul Üniversitesi Edebiyat Fakültesi Tarih Dergisi*, 33 (1980–1981), 283–90.

Avcı, Yasemin, Vincent Lemire and Ömür Yazıcı Özdemir, "Collective petitions ('arż-ı maḥżar) as a reflective archival source for Jerusalem's networks of citadinité in the late 19th century", in *Ordinary Jerusalem 1840–1940: Opening New Archives, Revisiting a Global City*, ed. Angelos Dalachanis and Vincent Lemire (Leiden: Brill, 2018), pp. 161–85.

Aydın, Cemil, "Reform", in *Encyclopedia of the Ottoman Empire*, ed. Gábor Ágoston and Bruce Masters (New York: Facts on File, 2009), pp. 484–6.

Aymes, Marc, *"Un grand progrès – sur le papier". Histoire provinciale des réformes ottomanes à Chypre au XIXᵉ siècle* (Paris, Louvain and Walpole, MA.: Peeters, 2010).

Baer, Gabriel, "Women and waqf: an analysis of the Istanbul tahrîr of 1546", in *Studies in Islamic Society: Contributions in Memory of Gabriel Baer*, ed. Gabriel A. Warburg and Gad G. Gilbar (Haifa: Haifa University Press, 1984), pp. 9–28.

Bağış, Ali İhsan, *Osmanlı Ticaretinde Gayri Müslimler: Kapitülasyonlar – Avrupa Tüccarları – Beratlı Tüccarlar – Hayriye Tüccarları (1750–1839)* (Ankara: Turhan Kitabevi, 1983).

Bakhit, Muhammad Adnan, *The Ottoman Province of Damascus in the Sixteenth Century* (Beirut: Librairie du Liban, 1982).

Balard, Michel, "The Greeks of Crimea under Genoese rule in the XIVth and XVth centuries", *Dumbarton Oaks Papers*, 49 (1995), 23–32.

Balard, Michel, "Notes sur la fiscalité génoise à Caffa au XVe siècle", *Bulletin de la Société Nationale des Antiquaires de France* (1993), 224–41.

Balard, Michel, *La Romanie génoise (XIIᵉ–début du XVᵉ siècle)*, two vols. (Genoa: Società Ligure di Storia Patria, and Paris: École Française de Rome, 1978).

Banat, Rabih and Amézianne Ferguène, "La production et le commerce du textile à Alep sous l'empire ottoman: une forte contribution à l'essor économique de la ville", *Histoire, Économie et Sociétés*, 2 (2010), 9–21.

Barkan, Ö. Lütfi, "Çiftlik", *İslam Ansiklopedisi, İslâm Âlemî Coğrafya, Etnoğrafya ve Biyografya Lügatî*, ed. Adnan Adıvar, *et al.* (Istanbul: Milli Eğitim Basımevi, 1940–1988), vol. III, pp. 392–7.

Barkan, Ö. Lütfi, "Osmanlı İmparatorluğu'nda Çiftçi Sınıfların Hukukî Statüsü", *Ülkü Mecmuası*, 9/49, 50, 53; 10/56, 58, 59 (1937).

Barkan, Ömer Lütfi, "Tarihî Demografi Araştırmaları ve Osmanlı Tarihi", *Türkiyat Mecmuası*, 10 (1953), 1–26.

Barkan, Ömer Lütfi, "Türk-İslam Toprak Hukuku Tatbikatının Osmanlı İmparatorluğunda Aldığı Şekiller: Malikâne-Divânî Sistemi", *Türk-Hukuk ve İktisat Tarihi Mecmuası*, 2 (1939), 119–84.

Barkan, Ö. Lütfi, "Türkiye'de İmparatorluk Devirlerinin Büyük Nüfus ve Arazi Tahrirleri ve Hakana Mahsus İstatistik Defterleri I", *İstanbul Üniversitesi İktisat Fakültesi Mecmuası*, 2/1 (1940), 20–59.

Barkan, Ö. Lütfi, "Türkiye'de İmparatorluk Devirlerinin Büyük Nüfus ve Arazi Tahrirleri ve Hakana Mahsus İstatistik Defterleri II", *İstanbul Üniversitesi İktisat Fakültesi Mecmuası*, 2/2 (1941), 214–47.

Barkan, Ö. Lütfi, *Türkiye'de Toprak Meselesi* (Istanbul: Gözlem Yayınları, 1980).

Barker, Hannah, *That Most Precious Merchandise. The Mediterranean Trade in Black Sea Slaves, 1260–1500* (Philadelphia: University of Pennsylvania Press, 2019).

Basso, Enrico, "Gli atti di Giovanni de Labaino (1410–1412): note su una fonte inedita per la storia di Caffe e del Mar Nero", in *Море и берега К 60-летию Сергея Павловича Карпова от коллег и учеников*, ed. Rustam Shukurov (Moscow: INDRIK, 2009), pp. 501–18.

Basso, Enrico, *Genova: un impero sul mare* (Cagliari: Consiglio Nazionale delle Ricerche, Istituto sui Rapporti Italo-Iberici, 1994).

Basso, Enrico, "Genova e gli Ottomani nel XV secolo: gli "itali Teucri" e il Gran Sultano", in *L'Europa dopo la Caduta di Costantinopoli: 29 maggio 1453. Atti del XLIV Convegno Storico Internazionale* (Spoleto: Fondazione Centro Italiano di Studi sull'Alto Medioevo, 2008), pp. 375–410.

Basso, Enrico, "El sistema de puertos genoveses entre el mediterráneo y el mar negro", in *Navegación y puertos en época medieval y moderna*, ed. Adela Fábregas García (Granada: Grupo de Investigación Toponimia, Historia y Arqueología del Reino de Granada, 2012), pp. 103–61.

Batizi, Zoltán, "Mining in medieval Hungary", in *The Economy of Medieval Hungary*, ed. József Laszlovszky, Balázs Nagy, Péter Szabó and András Vadas (Leiden: Brill, 2018), pp. 166–81.

Batur, Sabahattin, "Une recherche sur le tombak ou dorure au mercure", in *Seventh International Congress of Turkish Art*, ed. Tadeusz Majda (Warsaw: Polish Scientific Publishers, 1990), pp. 43–8.

Bayur, Hilmi Kamil, *Sâdrazam Kâmil Paşa Siyasi Hayatı* (Ankara: Sanat Kitabevi, 1954).

Beach, Milo Cleveland, *The New Cambridge History of India: Mughal and Rajput Painting* (Cambridge: Cambridge University Press, 1992).

Beckert, Sven, "Emancipation and empire: reconstructing the world wide web of cotton production in the age of the American Civil War", *American Historical Review*, 109/5 (2004), 1405–38.

Beldiceanu-Steinherr, Irène, "Fiscalité et formes de possession de la terre arable dans l'Anatolie préottomane", *Journal of the Economic and Social History of the Orient,* 19/3 (1976), 233–312.

Belli, Oktay and Gündağ Kayaoğlu, *Trabzon'da Türk Bakırcılık Sanatının Tarihsel Gelişimi/ The Historical Development of Coppersmithing in Trabzon* (Istanbul: Arkeoloji ve Sanat Yayınları, 2002).

Beyru, Rauf, *19. Yüzyılda İzmir'de Yaşam* (Istanbul: Literatür Yayınları, 2000).

Bilgin, Arif, "Osmanlı Sarayının İaşesi", Ph.D. Dissertation, Marmara Üniversitesi, 2000.

Bodur, Fulya, *Türk Maden Sanatı: The Art of Turkish Metalworking* (Istanbul: Türk Kültürüne Hizmet Vakfı, 1987).

Bölükbaşı, Ömerül Faruk, "Mangır", in *Encyclopaedia of Islam, Three,* ed. Kate Fleet, Gudrun Krämer, Denis Matringe, John Nawas and Everett Rowson (Leiden: Brill, 2007–), online http://dx.doi.org/10.1163/1573-3912_ei3_COM_36161.

Bostan, İdris, *Osmanlı Bahriye Teşkilatı: XVII. Yüzyılda Tersâne-i Âmire* (Ankara: Türk Tarih Kurumu Basımevi, 1992).

Boulanger, Robert, *Turkey: Hachette World Guides,* trans. J.S. Hardman (Paris: Hachette, 1970).

Boyar, Ebru, "Ottoman expansion in the East", in *The Cambridge History of Turkey, Volume 2. The Ottoman Empire as a World Power, 1453–1603,* ed. Suraiya Faroqhi and Kate Fleet (Cambridge: Cambridge University Press, 2013), pp. 74–140.

Boyar, Ebru, "Profitable prostitution: state use of immoral earnings for social benefit in the late Ottoman empire", *Bulgarian Historical Review,* 1–2 (2009), 143–57.

Boyar, Ebru, "Public good and private exploitation: criticism of the tobacco Régie in 1909", in *The Ottomans and Trade,* ed. Ebru Boyar and Kate Fleet (*Oriente Moderno,* 25/1, 2006) (Rome, 2006), pp. 193–200.

Boyar, Ebru and Kate Fleet, *A Social History of Ottoman Istanbul* (Cambridge: Cambridge University Press, 2010).

Bragg, John K., *Ottoman Notables and Participatory Politics: Tanzimat Reform in Tokat, 1839–1876* (London and New York: Routledge, 2014).

Bratianu, G.I., *Recherches sur le commerce génois dans la mer noire au xiiie siècle* (Paris: Libraire Orientaliste Paul Geuthner, 1929).

Bryer, Anthony, "Greeks and Türkmen: the Pontic exception", *Dumbarton Oaks Papers,* 29 (1975), 113–48.

Bryer, Anthony and David Winfield, *The Byzantine Monuments and Topography of the Pontos,* vol. I (Washington D.C.: Dumbarton Oaks, 1985).

Çınar, Hüseyin and Osman Gümüşçü, *Osmanlıdan Cumhuriyete Çubuk Kazası* (Ankara: Bilge Yayınevi, 2002).

Cohen, Amnon and Bernard Lewis, *Population and Revenue in the Towns of Palestine in the Sixteenth Century* (Princeton: Princeton University Press, 1978).

Cook, M.A., *Population Pressure in Rural Anatolia, 1450–1600* (London and New York: Oxford University Press, 1972).

Cora, Yaşar Tolga, "a Muslim great merchant [tüccar] family in the late Ottoman empire: a case study of Nemlizades, 1860–1930", *International Journal of Turkish Studies*, 19/1–2 (2013), 1–29.

Coşgel, Metin M., "Efficiency and continuity in public finance: the Ottoman system of taxation", *International Journal of Middle East Studies*, 37/4 (2005), 567–86.

Coşgel, Metin M., "Ottoman tax registers (tahrir defterleri)", *Historical Methods*, 37/2 (2004), 87–100.

Coşgel, Metin and Boğaç Ergene, *The Economics of Ottoman Justice. Settlement and Trial in the Sharia Courts* (Cambridge: Cambridge University Press, 2016).

Coşgel, Metin M. and Thomas J. Miceli, "Risk, transaction costs, and tax assignment: government finance in the Ottoman empire", *Journal of Economic History*, 65/3 (2005), 806–21.

Coşgel, Metin M., Thomas J. Miceli and Jared Rubin, "The political economy of mass printing: legitimacy and technological change in the Ottoman empire", *Journal of Comparative Economics*, 40/3 (2012), 357–71.

Dalachanis, Angelos and Vincent Lemire (eds.), *Ordinary Jerusalem 1840–1940: Opening New Archives, Revisiting a Global City* (Leiden: Brill, 2018).

Danişmend, İsmail Hakkı, "Eski Türk Ordusunun Silah ve Teknik Üstünlüğü", in Danişmend, İsmail Hakkı, *Tarihi Hakikatler* (Istanbul: Bilgeoğuz, 2016), pp. 253–7.

Dankoff, Robert, *The Intimate Life of an Ottoman Statesman: Melek Ahmed Pasha 1588–1662 as Portrayed in Evliya Çelebi's Book of Travels (Seyahat-name): with an Historical Introduction by Rhoads Murphey* (Albany, N.Y.: State University of New York Press, 1991).

Davison, Roderic H., *Reform in the Ottoman Empire 1856–1876* (Princeton: Princeton University Press, 1963).

Davison, Roderic H., "Tanzīmāt", *The Encyclopaedia of Islam*, 2nd ed., ed. P. Bearman, Th. Bianquis, C.E. Bosworth, E. van Donzel and W.P. Heinrichs (Leiden: Brill, 1960–2006), vol. 10 (2000), pp. 201–9.

Deletant, Dennis, "Genoese, Tatars and Rumanians at the mouth of the Danube in the fourteenth century", *The Slavonic and East European Review*, 62/4 (1984), 511–30.

Doumani, Beshara B., *Family Life in the Ottoman Mediterranean: A Social History* (Cambridge: Cambridge University Press, 2017).

Duman, Yüksel, "Textiles and Copper in Ottoman Tokat 1750–1840", Ph.D. Dissertation, Binghampton University, 1998.

Eldem, Vedat, *Osmanlı İmparatorluğu'nun İktisadi Şartları Hakkında Bir Tetkik* (Ankara: Türk Tarih Kurumu Basımevi, 1994).

Emecen, Feridun M., *Doğu Karadeniz'de İki Kıyı Kasabasının Tarihi Bulancak-Piraziz* (Istanbul: Kitabevi, 2005).

Emecen, Feridun M., *XVI. Asırda Manisa Kazası* (Ankara: Türk Tarih Kurumu Basımevi, 1989).

Erder, Leila, "The measurement of preindustrial population changes. The Ottoman empire from the 15th to the 17th century", *Middle Eastern Studies*, 11 (1975), 284–301.

Erdoğan [Özünlü], Emine, "Ankara'nın Bütüncül Tarihi Çerçevesinde Ankara Tahrir Defterleri'nin Analizi", Ph.D. Dissertation, Gazi Üniversitesi, 2004.

Ergenç, Özer, *XVI. Yüzyılda Ankara ve Konya* (Ankara: Ankara Enstitüsü Vakfı Yayınları, 1995).

Erginsoy, Ülker, *İslam Maden Sanatının Gelişmesi* (Istanbul: Kültür Bakanlığı, 1978).

Establet, Colette, "Les bijoux dans l'empire ottoman au XVIIIᵉ siècle : l'exemple damascène", *Turcica*, 43 (2011), 207–29.

Establet, Colette and Jean-Paul Pasqual, "Cups, plates and kitchenware in late seventeenth and early eighteenth-century Damascus", in *The Illuminated Table, the Prosperous House, Food and Shelter in Ottoman Material Culture*, ed. Suraiya Faroqhi and Christoph Neumann (Istanbul: Orient-Institut, 2003), pp. 185–97.

Establet, Colette and Jean-Paul Pascual, *Familles et fortunes à Damas, 450 foyers damascains en 1700* (Damascus: Institut français de Damas, 1994).

Establet, Colette and Jean-Paul Pascual, *La gent d'état dans la société ottomane damascène: les 'askar à la fin du XVIIᵉ siècle* (Damascus: Presses de l'Ifpo, 2011).

Establet, Colette and Jean-Paul Pascual, *Des tissus et des hommes, Damas vers 1700* (Damascus: Institut français d'études arabes de Damas, 2005).

Establet, Colette and Jean-Paul Pascual, *Ultime voyage pour la Mecque: les inventaires après décès de pelerins morts à Damas vers 1700* (Damascus: Institut français de Damas, 1998).

Faroqhi, Suraiya, "Between collective workshops and private homes: places of work in eighteenth-century Bursa", in Faroqhi, Suraiya, *Stories of Ottoman Men and Women: Establishing Status, Establishing Control* (Istanbul: Eren, 2002), pp. 235–43.

Faroqhi, Suraiya, "The fieldglass and the magnifying lens: Ottoman studies of crafts and craftsmen", *The Journal of European Economic History*, 20/1 (1991), 29–57.

Faroqhi, Suraiya, "Guildsmen complain to the sultan: artisans' disputes and the Ottoman administration in the 18th century", in *Legitimizing the Order: The Ottoman Rhetoric of State Power*, ed. Hakan Karateke and Maurus Reinkowski (Leiden: Brill, 2005), pp. 177–93.

Faroqhi, Suraiya, *Men of Modest Substance, House Owners and House Property in Seventeenth-Century Ankara and Kayseri* (Cambridge: Cambridge University Press, 1987).

Faroqhi, Suraiya, "Onyedinci Yüzyıl Ankara'sında Sof İmalatı ve Sof Atölyeleri", *İstanbul Üniversitesi İktisat Fakültesi Mecmuası*, 41/1–4 (1985), 237–59.

Faroqhi, Suraiya, "Ottoman Population", in *The Cambridge History of Turkey, Volume 2. The Ottoman Empire as a World Power, 1453–1603*, ed. Suraiya Faroqhi and Kate Fleet (Cambridge: Cambridge University Press, 2013), pp. 356–403.

Faroqhi, Suraiya, "Rural society in Anatolia and the Balkans during the sixteenth century, I", *Turcica*, 9/1 (1977), 161–95.

Faroqhi, Suraiya, "Sixteenth century periodic markets in various Anatolian sancaks", *Journal of the Economic and Social History of the Orient*, 22/1 (1979), 32–80.

Faroqhi, Suraiya, *Stories of Ottoman Men and Women: Establishing Status, Establishing Control* (Istanbul: Eren, 2002).

Faroqhi, Suraiya, "Taxation and urban activities in sixteenth-century Anatolia", *International Journal of Turkish Studies*, 1/1 (1979–80), 19–53.

Faroqhi, Suraiya, "Textile production in Rumeli and the Arab provinces: geographical distribution and internal trade (1560–1650)", *Osmanlı Araştırmaları/ The Journal of Ottoman Studies*, 1 (1980), 61–83.

Faroqhi, Suraiya, "Towns, agriculture and the state in sixteenth-century Ottoman Anatolia", *Journal of the Economic and Social History of the Orient*, 33 (1990), 125–56.

Faroqhi, Suraiya, "Town officials, timar-holders, and taxation: the late sixteenth-century crisis as seen from Çorum", *Turcica*, 18 (1986), 53–82.

Faroqhi, Suraiya, *Towns and Townsmen of Ottoman Anatolia: Trade, Crafts, and Food Production in an Urban Setting, 1520–1650* (Cambridge: Cambridge University Press, 1984).

Faroqhi, Suraiya, "Two women of substance", in *Festgabe an Josef Matuz, Osmanistik, Turkologie, Diplomatik*, ed. Christa Fragner and Klaus Schwarz (Berlin: Klaus Schwarz Verlag, 1992), pp. 37–56.

Faroqhi, Suraiya, "Vakıf administration in sixteenth century Konya: the zaviye of Sadreddin-i Konevi", *Journal of the Economic and Social History of the Orient*, 17/2 (1974), 145–72.

Faroqhi, Suraiya, "Women, wealth and textiles in 1730s Bursa", in *Living the Good Life: Consumption in the Qing and Ottoman Empires of the Eighteenth Century*, ed. Elif Akçetin and Suraiya Faroqhi (Leiden: Brill, 2017), pp. 213–35.

Faroqhi, Suraiya and Randi Deguilhem (eds.), *Crafts and Craftsmen of the Middle East, Fashioning the Individual in the Muslim Mediterranean* (London: I.B. Tauris, 2005).

Faroqhi, Suraiya and Kate Fleet (eds.), *The Cambridge History of Turkey, Volume 2. The Ottoman Empire as a World Power, 1453–1603* (Cambridge: Cambridge University Press, 2013).

Faroqhi, Suraiya and Christoph Neumann (eds.), *The Illuminated Table, the Prosperous House, Food and Shelter in Ottoman Material Culture* (Istanbul: Orient-Institut, 2003).

Fleet, Kate, "Caffa, Turkey and the slave trade: the case of Battista Macio", in *Europa e Islam tra i Secoli XIV e XVI. Europe and Islam between 14th and 16th Centuries*, ed. Michele Bernardini, Clara Borrelli, Anna Cerbo and Encarnación Sánchez Garcia (Naples: Istituto Universitario Orientale. Collana "Matteo Ripa" XVIII, 2002), pp. 373–89.

Fleet, Kate (ed.), *The Cambridge History of Turkey. Volume 1. Byzantium to Turkey 1071–1453* (Cambridge: Cambridge University Press, 2009).

Fleet, Kate, *European and Islamic Trade in the Early Ottoman State: The Merchants of Genoa and Turkey* (Cambridge: Cambridge University Press, 1999).

Fleet, Kate, "Ottoman grain exports from western Anatolia at the end of the fourteenth century", *Journal of the Economic and Social History of the Orient*, 40/3 (1997), 283–93.

Fleet, Kate, "The Turkish economy, 1071–1453", in *The Cambridge History of Turkey. Volume 1. Byzantium to Turkey 1071–1453*, ed. Kate Fleet (Cambridge: Cambridge University Press, 2009), pp. 227–65.

Fodor, Alexander, "An Ottoman magic bowl from Istanbul", in *Ottoman Metalwork in the Balkans and in Hungary*, ed. Ibolya Gerelyes and Maximilian Hartmuth (Budapest: Hungarian National Museum, 2015), pp. 59–78.

Fragner, Christa and Klaus Schwarz (eds.), *Festgabe an Josef Matuz, Osmanistik, Turkologie, Diplomatik* (Berlin: Klaus Schwarz Verlag, 1992).

Frangakis-Syrett, Elena, "XVII. Yüzyıl Başından, XX. Yüzyıl Başlarına Kadar Krala Gemiyle İzmir'den Giden Sultaniye Kuru Üzüm İhracatı", in *Üzümün Akdeniz'deki Yolculuğu. Konferans Bildirileri,* ed. Ertekin Akpınar and Ekrem Tükenmez (İzmir: İzmir Akdeniz Akademisi, 2017), pp. 121–31.

Frangakis-Syrett, Elena, "British economic activities in Izmir in the second half of the nineteenth century and in the early twentieth centuries", *New Perspectives on Turkey*, 5–6 (1991), 191–227.

Frangakis-Syrett, Elena, "Commerce in the eastern Mediterranean from the eighteenth to the early twentieth centuries: the city-port of Izmir and its hinterland", *International Journal of Maritime History*, 10/2 (1998), 125–54.

Frangakis-Syrett, Elena, *The Commerce of Smyrna in the Eighteenth Century, 1700–1820* (Athens: Centre for Asia Minor Studies, 1992).

Frangakis-Syrett, Elena, "L'économie de l'Anatolie occidentale, 1908–1918", in *La Turquie entre trois mondes: actes du Colloque International de Montpellier, 5, 6 et 7 octobre 1995,* ed. Marcel Bazin, Salgur Kançal, Roland Perez and Jacques Thobie (Paris: L'Harmattan, 1998), pp. 239–48.

Frangakis-Syrett, Elena, "The making of an Ottoman port: the quay of Izmir in the nineteenth century", *The Journal of Transport History*, 22/1 (2001), 23–46.

Frangakis-Syrett, Elena, "Modernity from below: the Amalgamated Oriental Carpet Manufacturers Ltd. of Izmir, 1907–1922", *Perspectives on Global Development and Technology*, 14/4 (2015), 413–29.

Frangakis-Syrett, Elena, *The Port-City in the Ottoman Middle East at the Age of Imperialism* (Istanbul: The Isis Press, 2017).

Frangakis-Syrett, Elena, *Trade and Money: The Ottoman Economy in the Eighteenth and Early Nineteenth Centuries* (Istanbul: The Isis Press, 2007).

Fukasawa, Katsumi, *Toilerie et commerce du Levant, d'Alep à Marseille* (Paris: Editions du Centre national de la recherche scientifique, 1987).

Genç, Mehmet, "L'économie ottomane et la guerre au XVIIIème siècle", *Turcica*, 27 (1995), 177–96.

Genç, Mehmet, "Osmanlı Ekonomisi ve Savaş", *Yapıt*, 49/4 (1984), 52–61; 50/5 (1984), 86–93.

Genç, Mehmet, *Osmanlı İmparatorluğunda Devlet ve Ekonomi* (Istanbul: Ötüken, 2000).

Gerelyes, Ibolya, "Ottoman metalwork at the Hungarian National Museum: issues regarding origins and dating", in *Ottoman Metalwork in the Balkans and in Hungary*, ed. Ibolya Gerelyes and Maximilian Hartmuth (Budapest: Hungarian National Museum, 2015), pp. 79–96.

Gerelyes, Ibolya and András Csonka, *Oszmán-Török rézmüvesség (XVI–XIX. Század)/ Ottoman-Turkish Coppersmith's Art 16th to 19th Centuries* (Budapest: Magyar Nemzeti Múzeum, 1997).

Gerelyes, Ibolya and Maximilian Hartmuth (eds.), *Ottoman Metalwork in the Balkans and in Hungary* (Budapest: Hungarian National Museum, 2015).

Gökçe, Turan, *XVI. ve XVII. Yüzyıllarda Lâzıkıyye (Denizli) Kazâsı* (Ankara: Türk Tarih Kurumu Basımevi, 2000).

Göyünç, Nejat, "XVI. Yüzyılda Güney-Doğu Anadolu'nun Ekonomik Durumu", in *Türkiye İktisat Tarihi Semineri, Metinler, Tartışmalar, 8–10 Haziran 1973*, ed. Osman Okyar and Ünal Nalbantoğlu (Ankara: Hacettepe Üniversitesi, 1975), pp. 71–98.

Göyünç, Nejat, *XVI. Yüzyılda Mardin Sancağı* (Ankara: Türk Tarih Kurumu Basımevi, 1991).

Göyünç, Nejat and Wolf-Dieter Hütteroth, *Land an der Grenze: Osmanische Verwaltung im heutigen türkisch-syrisch-irakischen Grenzgebiet im 16. Jahrhundert* (Istanbul: Eren Yayıncılık, 1997).

Greenwood, Anthony, "Istanbul's Meat Provisioning: A Study of the Celepkeşan System", Ph.D. Dissertation, University of Chicago, 1988.

Griswold, William J., *The Great Anatolian Rebellion, 1000–1020/1591–1611* (Berlin: Klaus Schwarz Verlag, 1983).

Güçer, Lütfi, *XVI ve XVII. Asırlarda Osmanlı İmparatorluğu'nda Hububat Meselesi ve Hububattan Alınan Vergiler* (Istanbul: İstanbul Üniversitesi Yayınları, 1964).

Güran, Tevfik, *19. Yüzyılda Osmanlı Tarımı Üzerine Araştırmalar* (Istanbul: Eren Yayıncılık, 1998).

Hanioğlu, Şükrü, *A Brief History of the Late Ottoman Empire* (Princeton: Princeton University Press, 2010).

Hanssen, Jens, "Practices of integration – center-periphery relations in the Ottoman empire", in *The Empire in the City: Arab Provincial Capitals in the Late Ottoman Empire*, ed. Jens Hanssen, Thomas Philipp and Stefan Weber (Beirut: Ergon Verlag, 2002), 49–74.

Hartmuth, Maximilian, "Mineral exploitation and artistic production in the Balkans after 1250", in *Ottoman Metalwork in the Balkans and in Hungary*, ed. Ibolya Gerelyes and Maximilian Hartmuth (Budapest: Hungarian National Museum, 2015), pp. 97–110.

Hasluk, F.W., "Genoese heraldry and inscriptions at Amasra", *Annual of the British School at Athens*, 17 (1910–1911), 132–44.

Heyd, Wilhelm, *Histoire du commerce du Levant au moyen-âge*, vol. II (Leipzig: Otto Harrassowitz, 1886).

Heywood, Colin, "Between historical myth and 'mytho-history'. The limits of Ottoman history", *Byzantine and Modern Greek Studies*, 12 (1988), 315–45.

Heywood, Colin, "Notes on production of fifteenth-century Ottoman cannon", in Heywood, Colin, *Writing Ottoman History: Documents and Interpretations* (Aldershot: Ashgate, 2002), XVI, pp. 3–9.

Hinz, Walter, *İslâm'da Ölçü Sistemleri*, trans. Acar Sevim (Istanbul: Marmara Üniversitesi Yayınları, 1990).

Imber, Colin, "The legend of Osman gazi", in *The Ottoman Emirate (1300–1389)*, ed. Elizabeth Zachariadou (Rethymnon: Crete University Press, 1993), pp. 67–75.

Imber, Colin, *The Ottoman Empire 1300–1481* (Istanbul: The Isis Press, 1990).

İnal, İbnülemin Mahmud Kemal, *Osmanlı Devrinde Son Sadrazamlar*, four vols., second edition (Istanbul: Milli Eğitim Basımevi, 1965).

İnalcık, Halil, "Bursa and the commerce of the Levant", *Journal of the Economic and Social History of the Orient*, 3/2 (1960), 131–47.

İnalcık, Halil, "A case study of the village microeconomy: villages in the Bursa sancak, 1520–1593", in İnalcık, Halil, *The Middle East and the Balkans under the Ottoman Empire. Essays on Economy and Society* (Indiana: Indiana University Turkish Studies, 1993), pp. 161–76.

İnalcık, Halil, "The emergence of big farms, çiftliks: state, landlords and tenants", in *Landholding and Commercial Agriculture in the Middle East*, ed. Çağlar Keyder and Faruk Tabak (Albany, N.Y.: State University of New York Press, 1991), pp. 17–34.

İnalcık, Halil, "Introduction to Ottoman metrology", *Turcica*, 15 (1983), 311–42.

İnalcık, Halil, "Köy, Köylü ve İmparatorluk", in *V. Milletlerarası Türkiye Sosyal ve İktisat Tarihi Kongresi-Tebliğler (İstanbul, 21–25 Ağustos 1989)* (Ankara: Türk Tarih Kurumu Basımevi, 1990), pp. 1–11.

İnalcık, Halil, "Mehmet the Conqueror (1432–1481) and his time", *Speculum*, 35/3 (1960), 408–27.

İnalcık, Halil, "Osmanlı Bürokrasisinde Aklâm ve Muamelât", *Osmanlı Araştırmaları*, 1 (1980), 1–14.

İnalcık, Halil, *Osmanlı İmparatorluğu Toplum ve Ekonomi* (Istanbul: Eren Yayıncılık, 1993).

İnalcık, Halil, "Osmanlılarda Raiyyet Rüsumu", *Belleten*, 23/92 (1959), 575–610.

İnalcık, Halil, *The Ottoman Empire: The Classical Age 1300–1600* (London: Phoenix, 2000).

İnalcık, Halil, "The question of the closing of the Black Sea under the Ottomans", Αρχεῖον Πόντου, 35 (1979) [Athens], 74–110.

İnalcık, Halil, "Rice cultivation and the *çeltükçi reaya* system in the Ottoman empire", *Turcica*, 14 (1982), 69–141.

İnalcık, Halil, "Sened-i İttifak ve Gülhane Hatt-ı Hümâyûnu", *Belleten*, 28/112 (1964), 603–22.

İnalcık, Halil, "Şikâyet Hakkı: 'Arz-ı hâl ve 'Arz-ı mahzarlar", *Osmanlı Araştırmaları*, 7–8 (1988), 33–54.

İnalcık, Halil, "Tanzimat Nedir?", *Tarih Araştırmaları*, 1 (1941), 237–63.

İnalcık, Halil and Donald Quataert (eds.), *An Economic and Social History of the Ottoman Empire, 1300–1914* (Cambridge: Cambridge University Press, 1994).

İrepoğlu, Gül, *Imperial Ottoman Jewellery: Reading History through Jewellery*, trans. Feyza Howell (Istanbul: BKG, 2012).

İslamoğlu-İnan, Huri, *State and Peasant in the Ottoman Empire. Agrarian Power Relations and Regional Economic Development in Ottoman Anatolia during the Sixteenth Century* (Leiden: Brill, 1994).

İslamoğlu-İnan, Huri, "State and peasants in the Ottoman empire: a study of a peasant economy in north-central Anatolia during the sixteenth century", in *The Ottoman Empire and the World Economy*, ed. Huri İslamoğlu-İnan (Cambridge: Cambridge University Press, 1987), pp. 101–59.

İslamoğlu, Huri and Suraiya Faroqhi, "Crop patterns and agricultural production trends in sixteenth-century Anatolia", *Review (Fernand Braudel Center)*, 2/3 (1979), 401–36.

Issawi, Charles, *The Economic History of Turkey, 1800–1914* (Chicago: University of Chicago Press, 1980).

Kala, Ahmet, "Osmanlı Devleti'nde İstanbul'un Et İhtiyacının Temini İçin Kurulan Kasap ve Celep Teşkilatları (XVI, XVII ve XVIII. Asırlarda)", Ph.D. Dissertation, İstanbul Üniversitesi, 1985.

Kankal, Ahmet, *XVI. Yüzyılda Çankırı* (Çankırı: Çankırı Belediyesi Kültür Yayınları, 2009).

Karamustafa, Ahmet T., "Kaygusuz Abdal: a medieval Turkish saint and the formation of vernacular Islam in Anatolia", in *Unity in Diversity. Mysticism, Messianism and the Construction of Religious Authority in Islam*, ed. Orkhan Mir-Kasimov (Leiden: Brill, 2013), pp. 329–42.

Karpat, Kemal, "The transformation of the Ottoman state, 1789–1908", *International Journal of Middle East Studies*, 3/3 (1972), 243–81.

Karpov, Serghej Pavlovič, "Una famiglia nobile del mondo coloniale genovese: i Di Negro, mercanti e "baroni" dei Grandi Comneni di Trebisonda", in *Oriente e occidente tra medioevo ed età moderna. Studi in onore di Geo Pistarino*, ed. Laura Balletto (Genoa: Glauco Brigati, 1997), vol. II, pp. 587–604.

Karpov, S.P., "The grain trade in the southern Black Sea region: the thirteenth to the fifteenth century", *Mediterranean Historical Review*, 8/1 (1993), 55–71.

Karpov, Sergej Pavlovič, *L'impero di Trapezunda, Venezia Genova e Roma 1204–1461. Raporti politici, diplomatici e commerciali* (Rome: İl Veltro Editrice, 1986).

Karpov, S.P., *Итальянские морские республики и Южное Причерноморье в XIII–XV вв.: проблемы торговли* (Moscow: Izd-vo MGU, 1990).

Karpov, S.P., "New documents on the relations between the Latins and the local populations in the Black Sea area (1392–1462)", *Dumbarton Oaks Papers*, 49 (1995), 33–41.

Katsiardi-Hering, Olga, Τεχνίτες και τεχνικές βαφής νημάτων (Athens: Herodotos, 2003).

Kayaoğlu, İzzet Gündağ, *Tombak* (Istanbul: Dışbank, 1992).

Keyder, Çağlar and Faruk Tabak (eds.), *Landholding and Commercial Agriculture in the Middle East* (Albany, N.Y.: State University of New York Press, 1991).

Khvalkov, Evgeny, *The Colonies of Genoa in the Black Sea Region. Evolution and Transformation* (New York and Abingdon, Oxon: Routledge, 2018).

Kickinger, Claudia, "Relations of production and social conditions among coppersmiths in contemporary Cairo", in *Crafts and Craftsmen of the Middle East, Fashioning the Individual in the Muslim Mediterranean*, ed. Suraiya Faroqhi and Randi Deguilhem (London: I.B. Tauris, 2005), pp. 285–307.

Kimble, George H.T., "The Laurentian world map with special reference to its portrayal of Africa", *Imago Mundi*, 1 (1935), 29–33.

Kırmızı, Abdulhamit, *Abdülhamid'in Valileri. Osmanlı Vilayet İdaresi 1895–1908* (Istanbul: Klasik, 2007).

Kırmızı, Abdulhamit, *Avlonyalı Ferid Paşa. Bir Ömür Devlet* (Istanbul: Klasik, 2014).

Koç, Yunus, *XVI. Yüzyılda Bir Osmanlı Sancağı'nın İskân ve Nüfus Yapısı* (Ankara: Kültür Bakanlığı Yayınları, 1988).

Koç, Yunus, "Zirai Tarih Araştırmalarında Ölçü Tartı Birimleri Sorunu: Bursa Müddü Örneği", *Uluslararası Kuruluşunun 700. Yıl Dönümünde Bütün Yönleriyle Osmanlı Devleti Kongresi, Konya, 7–9 Nisan 1999* (Konya: Selçuk Üniversitesi Basımevi, 2000), pp. 541–6.

Köksal, Yonca, "Coercion and mediation: centralization and sedentarization of tribes in the Ottoman empire", *Middle Eastern Studies*, 42/3 (2006), 469–91.

Köksal, Yonca, "Tanzimat ve Tarih Yazımı", *Doğu-Batı*, 51 (2010), 193–214.

Köksal, Yonca and Mehmet Polatel, "A tribe as an economic actor: the Cihanbeyli tribe and the meat provisioning of İstanbul in the early Tanzimat era", *New Perspectives on Turkey*, 61 (2019), 1–27.

Koloğlu, Orhan, *Avrupa'nın Kıskacında Abdülhamit* (Istanbul: İletişim Yayınları, 2005).

Koneska, Elizabeta, "Coppersmiths and tinsmiths from Kruševo (Macedonia) settling and working in other towns on the Balkan Peninsula", in *Ottoman Metalwork in the Balkans and in Hungary*, ed. Ibolya Gerelyes and Maximilian Hartmuth (Budapest: Hungarian National Museum, 2015), pp. 133–44.

Korobeinikov, D.A., "The revolt of Kastamonu, c. 1291–1293", *Byzantinische Forschungen*, 28 (2004), 87–118.

Koyuncu, Gülnaz, "İzmir Sanayi Mektebi Piyangosu", *Tarih ve Toplum*, 18/107 (November 1992), 278–83.

Koyuncu-Yakın, Gülnaz, *İzmir Sanayi Mektebi (Mithatpaşa Endüstri Meslek Lisesi) (1868–1923)* (İzmir: İzmir Valiliği, 1997).

Kurmuş, Orhan, *Emperyalizmin Türkiye'ye Girişi* (Istanbul: Bilim Yayınları, 1974).

Kurt, Yılmaz, "XVI. Yüzyıl Adana Tarihi", Ph.D. Dissertation, Hacettepe Üniversitesi, 2002.

Kurt, Yılmaz, *Çukurova Tarihinin Kaynakları*, III (Ankara: Gurup Matbaacılık, 2005).

Kuşoğlu, Mehmet Zeki, *The Ottoman Touch: Traditional Decorative Arts and Crafts* (New York, London, Frankfurt/Main and Cairo: Blue Dome, 2015).

Lapidus, Ira, *Muslim Cities in the Later Middle Ages* (Cambridge: Harvard University Press, 1967).

Lee, Young-Suk, "Why did they admire the machinery? Rethinking intellectuals' view from the perspective of the competition between English cotton goods and Indian handicraft ones in the early Industrial Revolution", *The East Asian Journal of British History*, 5 (2016), 151–60.

Leoni, Francesca (ed.), *Power and Protection: Islamic Art and the Supernatural* (Oxford: Ashmolean Museum, 2016).

Levi, Giovanni, *Inheriting Power: the Story of an Exorcist* (Chicago: University of Chicago Press, 1988).

Levy, Avigdor, "Introduction", in *The Jews of the Ottoman Empire*, ed. Avigdor Levy (Princeton: the Darwin Press, 1994), pp. 1–150.

Levy, Avigdor (ed.), *The Jews of the Ottoman Empire* (Princeton: the Darwin Press, 1994).

Liaou, Angeliki E., *Constantinople and the Latins. The Foreign Policy of Andronicus II, 1282–1328* (Cambridge, Mass.: Harvard University Press, 1972).

Lindner, Rudi Paul, "Anatolia, 1300–1451", in *The Cambridge History of Turkey. Volume I. Byzantium to Turkey 1071–1453*, ed. Kate Fleet (Cambridge: Cambridge University Press, 2009), pp. 102–37.

Lowry, Heath W., "The Ottoman tahrîr defterleri as a source for social and economic history: pitfalls and limitations", in Lowry, Heath W., *Studies in Defterology: Ottoman Society in the Fifteenth and Sixteenth Centuries* (Istanbul: Isis Press, 1992), pp. 3–18.

Lowry, Heath W., *Studies in Defterology: Ottoman Society in the Fifteenth and Sixteenth Centuries* (Istanbul: Isis Press, 1992).

Maddison, Francis and Emilie Savage-Smith (eds.), *Science, Tools & Magic, Part One, Body and Spirit, Mapping the Universe* (London: The Nour Foundation with Azimuth Editions and Oxford University Press, 1997).

Maden, Fahri, "XVIII. Yüzyıl Sonu XIX. Yüzyıl Başlarında Kastamonu'da Esnaf Grupları Zanaatkârlar ve Ticari Faliyetler", *Karadeniz Araştırmaları*, 15 (2007), 149–67.

Maifreda, Germano, *From Oikonomia to Political Economy. Constructing Economic Knowledge from the Renaissance to the Scientific Revolution* (Farnham: Ashgate, 2012).

Mansel, Philip, *Levant: Splendour and Catastrophe on the Mediterranean* (New Haven, CT.: Yale University Press, 2011).

Masters, Bruce, "Aleppo: the Ottoman empire's caravan city", in Eldem, Edhem, Daniel Goffman and Bruce Masters, *The Ottoman City between East and West: Aleppo, Izmir, and Istanbul* (Cambridge: Cambridge University Press, 1999), pp. 17–78.

Masters, Bruce, *The Origins of Western Economic Dominance in the Middle East: Mercantilism and the Islamic Economy in Aleppo, 1600–1750* (New York and London: New York University Press, 1988).

McGowan, Bruce, "Food supply and taxation on the Middle Danube 1568–1579", *Archivum Ottomanicum*, 1 (1969), 139–96.

Melikian-Chirvani, Assadullah Souren, "Recherches sur l'école du bronze ottoman au XVIᵉ siècle", *Turcica*, 6 (1975), 146–67.

Micklewright, Nancy, "London, Paris, Istanbul and Cairo: fashion and international trade in the 19th century", *New Perspectives on Turkey*, 7 (1992), 125–36.

Muniesa, Fabian and Dominique Linhardt, "Trials of explicitness in the implementation of public management reform", *Critical Perspectives on Accounting*, 22/6 (2011), 550–66.

Nagata, Yuzo, *Tarihte Âyânlar-Karaosmanoğulları Üzerine Bir İnceleme* (Ankara: Türk Tarih Kurumu Basımevi, 1997).

Nahum, Henri, *İzmir Yahudileri. 19.-20. Yüzyıl*, trans. Estreya Seval Vali (Istanbul: İletişim Yayınları, 2000).

Necipoğlu, Gülru, *The Age of Sinan: Architectural Culture in the Ottoman Empire* (London: Reaktion Books, 2005).

Okyar, Osman, "Tanzimat Ekonomisi Hakkındaki Karamsarlık Üzerine", in *Tanzimat'ın 150. Yıldönümü Uluslararası Sempozyumu* (Ankara: Türk Tarih Kurumu Basımevi, 1994), pp. 243–54.

Orbay, Kayhan, "Bursa'da II. Murad Vakfı'nın Mali Tarihi (1608–1641)", *İstanbul Üniversitesi İktisat Fakültesi Mecmuası*, 61/2 (2011), 239–322.

Orbay, Kayhan, "Celâlîs recorded in the account books", *Rivista degli studi orientali*, 78/1–2 (2004), 71–83.

Orbay, Kayhan, "Financial development of the waqfs in Konya and the agricultural economy in the Central Anatolia (late sixteenth–early seventeenth centuries)", *Journal of the Economic and Social History of the Orient*, 55 (2012), 74–116.

Orbay, Kayhan, "Osmanlı İmparatorluğu'nda Tarımsal Üretkenlik Üzerine Tetkikat ve Notlar", *Belleten*, 81/292 (2017), 787–856.

Orhonlu, Cengiz and Turgut Işıksal, "Osmanlı Devrinde Nehir Nakliyatı Hakkında Araştırmalar Dicle ve Fırat Nehirlerinde Nakliyat", *İstanbul Üniversitesi Edebiyat Fakültesi Tarih Dergisi*, 13/17–18 (March 1962–September 1963), pp. 77–103.

Öz, Mehmet, "XV–XVI. Yüzyıllar Anadolu'nda Tarım ve Tarım Ürünleri", *Kebikeç-İnsan Bilimleri Dergisi*, 23 (2007), 111–28.

Öz, Mehmet, *XV–XVI. Yüzyıllarda Canik Sancağı* (Ankara: Türk Tarih Kurumu Basımevi, 1999).

Öz, Mehmet, "XVI. Yüzyıl Anadolu'sunda Köylülerin Vergi Yükü ve Geçim Durumu Hakkında Bir Araştırma", *Osmanlı Araştırmaları – The Journal of Ottoman Studies*, 17 (1997), 77–90.

Öz, Mehmet, "XVI. Yüzyılda Anadolu'da Tarımda Verimlilik Problemi", *XIII. Türk Tarih Kongresi – Ankara, 4–8 Ekim 1999 – Kongreye Sunulan Bildiriler*, vol. 3/3 (Ankara: Türk Tarih Kurumu Basımevi, 2002), pp. 1643–51.

Öz, Mehmet, "Bozok Sancağında İskân ve Nüfus, 1539–1642", *XII. Türk Tarih Kongresi, Bildiriler (Eylül 1994)*, vol. 3 (Ankara: Türk Tarih Kurumu Basımevi, 2000), pp. 787–94.

Öz, Mehmet, "Osmanlı Klasik Döneminde Tarım", *Osmanlı*, vol. 3, ed. Güler Eren, Kemal Çiçek and Cem Oğuz (Ankara: Yeni Türkiye Yayınları, 1999), pp. 66–73.

Öz, Mehmet, "Tahrir Defterlerinin Osmanlı Tarihi Araştırmalarında Kullanılması Hakkında Bazı Düşünceler", *Vakıflar Dergisi*, 22 (1991), 429–39.

Özbek, Nadir, "Philanthropic activity, Ottoman patriotism, and the Hamidian regime, 1876–1909", *International Journal of Middle East Studies*, 37/1 (2005), 59–81.

Özcan, Ruhi, "Arşiv Belgeleri Diliyle Su Değirmenleri (Âsiyâb)", *Ankara Üniversitesi Osmanlı Tarihi Araştırma ve Uygulama Merkezi Dergisi*, 40 (2016), 195–203.

Özdeğer, Mehtap, *15–16. Yüzyıl Arşiv Kaynaklarına Göre Uşak Kazasının Sosyal ve Ekonomik Tarihi* (Istanbul: Filiz Kitabevi, 2001).

Özeçoğlu, Halil, "Modernleşme Sürecinde İzmir'de Müslim ve Gayrimüslimlerin Eğitimine Karşılaştırmalı Bir Yaklaşım (1856–1908)", Ph.D. Dissertation, Dokuz Eylül Üniversitesi, İzmir, 2009.

Özel, Oktay, *The Collapse of Rural Order in Ottoman Anatolia* (Leiden: Brill, 2016).

Özel, Oktay, "Population changes in Ottoman Anatolia during the 16th and 17th centuries: the 'demographic crisis' reconsidered", *International Journal of Middle East Studies*, 36/2 (2004), 183–205.

Özoran, Beria Remzi, "Sadrazam Kâmil Paşa- İngiliz Dostları- Kıbrıs'taki Mezarı", *Türk Kültürü*, 105/9 (1971), 756–62.

Pamuk, Şevket, *A Monetary History of the Ottoman Empire* (Cambridge: Cambridge University Press, 2000).

Panza, Laura, "Globalization and the Near East: a study of cotton market integration in Egypt and western Anatolia", *The Journal of Economic History*, 73/3 (2013), 847–72.

Pares, Richard, *Colonial Blockades and Neutral Rights, 1739–1763* (Oxford: Clarendon Press, 1938).

Paviot, Jacques, "Le séjour de l'ambassade de Geoffroy de Langley à Trebizonde et à Constantinople en 1291", *Médiévales*, 12 (1987), 47–54.

Peacock, Andrew, "Sinop: a frontier city in Seljuk and Mongol Anatolia", *Ancient Civilizations from Scythia to Siberia*, 16 (2010), 103–24, and 537.

Philips, J.R.S., *The Medieval Expansion of Europe* (Oxford: Oxford University Press, 1998).

Philliou, Christine, "Mischief in the old regime: provincial dragomans and social change at the turn of the nineteenth century", *New Perspectives on Turkey*, 25 (2001), 103–21.

Polat, Süleyman, "The economic consequences of the Celali revolts: the destruction and re-establishment of the state's taxation organisation", *Turkish Historical Review*, 4/1 (2013), 57–82.

Quataert, Donald, "Clothing laws, state and society in the Ottoman empire, 1720–1829", *International Journal of Middle East Studies*, 29/3 (1997), 403–25.

Quataert, Donald, "Main problems of the economy during the Tanzimat period", in *150. Yılında Tanzimat*, ed. Hakkı Dursun Yıldız (Ankara: Türk Tarih Kurumu Basımevi, 1992), pp. 211–18.

Quataert, Donald, *The Ottoman Empire, 1700–1922* (Cambridge: Cambridge University Press, 2000).

Quataert, Donald, *Ottoman Manufacturing in the Age of the Industrial Revolution* (Cambridge: Cambridge University Press, 1993).

Raymond, André, "The population of Aleppo in the 16th and 17th Centuries", *International Journal of Middle East Studies*, 16/4 (1984), 447–60.

Riello, Giorgio, *Cotton: the Fabric that Made the Modern World* (Cambridge: Cambridge University Press, 2013).

Riello, Giorgio, "Cotton: the making of a modern commodity", *East Asian Journal of British History*, 5 (2016), 135–49.

Rodrigue, Aron, *French Jews, Turkish Jews. The Alliance Israélite Universelle and the Politics of Jewish Schooling in Turkey, 1860–1925* (Bloomington and Indianapolis: Indiana University Press, 1990).

Savage-Smith, Emilie, "Magic-medicinal bowls", in *Science, Tools & Magic, Part One, Body and Spirit, Mapping the Universe*, ed. Francis Maddison and Emilie Savage-Smith (London: The Nour Foundation with Azimuth Editions and Oxford University Press, 1997), pp. 72–100.

Schindel, Nikolaus, "The earliest Ottoman copper coin?", *Numismatic Circular*, 120/4 (2014), 137–9.

Setton, Kenneth M., *The Papacy and the Levant (1204–1571). Volume II. The Fifteenth Century* (Philadelphia: The American Philosophical Society, 1978).

Shaw, Stanford J., *Between Old and New: The Ottoman Empire under Selim III 1789–1807* (Cambridge, M.A.: Harvard University Press, 1971).

Shaw, Stanford, "Some aspects of the aims and achievements of the nineteenth-century Ottoman reformers", in *Beginnings of Modernization in the Middle East:*

The Nineteenth Century, ed. William R. Polk and Richard Chambers (Chicago and London: University of Chicago Press, 1968), pp. 29–39.

Shimizu, Yasuhisa, "On the operation and supervision of the muḳâṭa'a system under the Ottoman empire during the late sixteenth century: an analysis of documents related to the finance department of Ḥaleb", reprinted from *Memoirs of the Research Department of the Toyo Bunko*, no. 69 (Tokyo: The Toyo Bunko, 2011).

Shimizu, Yasuhisa, "Practices of tax farming under the Ottoman empire in Damascus Province", in *Tax Farm Register of Damascus Province in the Seventeenth Century: Archival and Historical Studies*, ed. Yuzo Nagata, Toru Miura, and Yasuhisa Shimizu (Tokyo: The Toyo Bunko, 2006), pp. 23–52.

Shukurov, Rustam, "Foreigners in the empire of Trebizond (the case of Orientals and Latins)", in *At the Crossroads of Empires: 14th–15th Century Eastern Anatolia. Proceedings of the International Symposium Held in Istanbul, 4th–6th May 2007* (Istanbul: Institut français d'études anatoliennes-Georges Dumézil, 2012), pp. 71–84.

Shukurov, Rustam, "Trebizond and the Seljuks (1204–1299)", *Mésogeios*, 25–26 (2005), 71–136.

Şimşirgil, Ahmet, "Osmanlı Taşra Teşkilâtında Tokat (1455–1574)", Ph.D. Dissertation, Marmara Üniversitesi, 1990.

Solak, İbrahim, *XVI. Asırda Maraş Kazâsı (1526–1563)* (Ankara: Akçağ Yayınları, 2004).

Stanziani, Alessandro, *Histoire de la qualité alimentaire (XIXᵉ–XXᵉ siècle)* (Paris: Seuil, 2005).

Stello, Annika, "La traite d'esclaves en mer Noire (première moitié du XVᵉ siècle)", in *Les esclavages en Méditerranée: espaces et dynamiques économiques*, ed. Fabienne Guillén and Salah Trabelsi (Madrid: Casa de Velázquez, 2012), pp. 171–9.

Taş, Kenan Ziya, "Tapu Tahrir Defterlerine Göre 16. Yüzyılda Bolu Sancağı", Unpublished Ph.D. Dissertation, Ankara Üniversitesi, 1993.

Tekin, Oğuz, "Mangır", *Türkiye Diyanet Vakfı İslâm Ansiklopedisi*, vol. 27 (2003), p. 568.

Tızlak, Fahrettin, "Osmanlı Devleti'nde Ham Bakır İşleme Merkezleri Olarak Tokat ve Diyarbakır", *Belleten*, 59/226 (1995), 643–59.

Tızlak, Fahrettin, "Osmanlı Toplumuna Şans Oyunlarının Girişi", *XV. Türk Tarih Kongresi. Kongreye Sunulan Bildiriler, 11–15 Eylül 2006*, 4. Cilt, 3. Kısım (Ankara: Türk Tarih Kurumu Basımevi, 2010), pp. 1877–99.

Toksöz, Meltem, *Nomads, Migrants and Cotton in the Eastern Mediterranean* (Leiden: Brill, 2011).

Toprak, Zafer, *İttihat Terakki ve Cihan Harbi: Savaş Ekonomisi ve Türkiye'de Devletçilik* (İstanbul: Kaynak Yayınları, 2016).

Tuchscherer, Michel, "Activités des Turcs dans le commerce de la mer Rouge au XVIIIᵉ siècle", in *Les villes dans l'empire ottoman: activités et sociétés*, two vols., ed. Daniel Panzac (Paris: Editions du Centre national de la recherche scientifique, 1991), vol. I, pp. 321–64.

Tunçay, Mete, *Türkiye'de Piyango Tarihi ve Millî Piyango İdaresi* (Ankara: Milli Piyango İdaresi Yayını, 1993).

Türkhan, Mehmet Sait, "18. Yüzyılın İkinci Yarısında İstanbul'un Et İaşesinin Temini: Hassa Kasabbaşılık Kurumu", Ph.D. Dissertation, Marmara Üniversitesi, 2006.

Türkoğlu, Sabahattin, *Tarih Boyunca Anadolu'da Takı ve Kuyumculuk Kültürü/Jewel and Jewellery Culture in Anatolia throughout History* (Istanbul: İstanbul Kuyumcuları Odası and Lidya, 2014).

Uğurluer, Murat, *Osmanlı Dönemi Gaziantep Bakırcılığı* (Gaziantep: MCG Kültür ve Sanat Yayınları, 2015).

Ülkütaşır, M.Ş., "Sinop'ta Selcukiler Zamanına Ait Tarihi Eserler", *Türk Tarih, Arkeologya ve Etnografya Dergisi*, 5 (1949), 112–151.

Ünal, Mehmet Ali, *XVI. Yüzyılda Harput Sancağı (1518–1566)* (Ankara: Türk Tarih Kurumu Basımevi, 1989).

Uzun, Ahmet, *İstanbul'un İaşesinde Devletin Rolü: Ondalık Ağnam Uygulaması (1783–1857)* (Ankara: Türk Tarih Kurumu Basımevi, 2006).

Uzunçarşılı, İsmail Hakkı, "Sadr-ı Âzâm Kâmil Paşa'nın Siyasî Hayatı İsimli Eser Dolayısile II Abdülhamid Döneminde Kâmil Paşa", *Belleten*, 19/74 (1955), 203–45.

Vasiliev, A.A., "The foundation of the Empire of Trebizond (1204–1222)", *Speculum*, 11/1 (1936), 3–37.

Veinstein, Gilles, "On the çiftlik debate", in *Landholding and Commercial Agriculture in the Middle East*, ed. Çağlar Keyder and Faruk Tabak (Albany, N.Y.: State University of New York Press, 1991), pp. 35–56.

Venzke, Margaret L., "Aleppo's mālikāne-dīvānī system", *Journal of the American Oriental Society*, 106/3 (1986), 451–69.

Venzke, Margaret L., "The Ottoman tahrir defterleri and agricultural productivity", *Osmanlı Araştırmaları – The Journal of Ottoman Studies*, 17 (1997), 1–61.

Warburg, Gabriel A. and Gad G. Gilbar (eds.), *Studies in Islamic Society: Contributions in Memory of Gabriel Baer* (Haifa: Haifa University Press, 1984).

Williams, Judith, *British Commercial Policy and Trade Expansion, 1750–1850* (Oxford: Clarendon Press, 1972).

Winfield, David, "The northern routes across Anatolia", *Anatolian Studies*, 27 (1977), 151–66.

Yakupoğlu, Cevdet, "Kastamonu'nun Doğal Zenginliklerinden Küre Madenlerinin Tarihî Arka Planı", *Kastamonu'nun Doğal Zenginlikleri Sempozyumu, 16–17 Ekim 2012* (n.p.: n.p.p., n.d.), pp. 36–45.

Yediyıldız, Bahaeddin, *Institution du Vaqf au XVIIIe siècle en Turquie: étude socio-historique* (Ankara: Ministère de la Culture, 1990).

Yediyıldız, Bahaeddin, *Ordu Kazası Sosyal Tarihi* (Ankara: Kültür ve Turizm Bakanlığı Yayınları, 1985).

Yıldız, Hakkı Dursun (ed.), *150. Yılında Tanzimat* (Ankara: Türk Tarih Kurumu Basımevi, 1992).

Yörük, Doğan, *XVI. Yüzyılda Aksaray Sancağı (1500–1584)* (Konya: Tablet Kitabevi, 2005).

Yücel, Yaşar, *Anadolu Beylikleri Hakkında Araştırmalar. XIII–XV Yüzyıllarda Kuzey-Batı Anadolu Tarihi. Çoban-oğulları Beyliği. Candar-oğulları Beyliği. I* (Ankara: Türk Tarih Kurumu Basımevi, 1988).

Yücel, Yaşar, "Candar-oğlu Çelebi İsfendiyar Bey 1392–1439", *Tarih Araştırmaları Dergisi,* 2/2–3 (1964), 157–74.

Yücel, Yaşar, "Candaroğulları", *Türkiye Diyanet Vakfı İslâm Ansiklopedisi,* vol. 7 (1993), pp. 146–9.

Yücel, M. Yaşar, "Kastamonu'nun İlk Fethine Kadar Osmanlı-Candar Münasebetleri (1361–1392)", *Tarih Araştırmaları Dergisi,* 1/1 (1963), 133–44.

Zachariadou, Elizabeth A., "Gazi Çelebi of Sinope", in *Oriente e occidente tra medioevo ed età moderna. Studi in onore di Geo Pistarino,* ed. Laura Balletto (Genoa: Glauco Brigati, 1997), vol. II, pp. 1271–5.

Zachariadou, Elizabeth A. (ed.), *The Ottoman Emirate (1300–1389)* (Rethymnon: Crete University Press, 1993).

Zilfi, Madeline, "Women and society in the Tulip Era, 1718–1730", in *Women, the Family, and Divorce Laws in Islamic History,* ed. Amira El Azhary Sonbol (New York: Syracuse University Press, 1996), pp. 290–303.

Online Sources

Ciolek, T. Matthew, *Georeferenced Data Set (Series 1 – Routes): Trade Routes in the Ottoman Empire 1300–1600 CE.* OWTRAD Dromographic Digital Data Archives (ODDDA). Old World Trade Routes (OWTRAD) Project (Canberra: Asia Pacific Research Online, www.ciolek.com/OWTRAD/DATA/tmcTRm1300.html, 2005).

Index

Printed in the United States
by Baker & Taylor Publisher Services